CC21427

DATE DUE

DEC 11 1995	
ILL 3-25-96	

*Wagnerism in
European Culture
and Politics*

Wagnerism in European Culture and Politics

Edited by

DAVID C. LARGE
and
WILLIAM WEBER

in collaboration with ANNE DZAMBA SESSA

Cornell University Press, Ithaca and London

Cornell paperbacks edition first published 1984 by Cornell University Press.
Second printing, 1985.

International Standard Book Number 0-8014-9283-1
Library of Congress Catalog Card Number 83-45936

Printed in the United States of America

Librarians: Library of Congress cataloging information appears on the last page of the book.

The paper in this book is acid-free and meets the guidelines for permanence and durability of the Committee on Production Guidelines for Book Longevity of the Council on Library Resources.

Contents

Preface

If one were asked to name the main cultural and intellectual movements of the nineteenth century, those that deeply affected the thoughts and attitudes of people throughout Europe and had an impact in a variety of fields, we would perhaps think first of Romanticism, positivism, socialism, and Darwinism. Wagnerism might well appear on this list, too. The music, texts, and ideas of Richard Wagner stimulated a cultural movement that attracted dedicated adherents throughout the world, especially in Europe and the United States. This movement was by no means confined to music lovers, though they, of course, constituted an important group among Wagner's supporters. The ideas and values that Wagner expressed—his attitudes about society, religion, romantic love and sexuality, politics, and art—proved to be a potent mixture that evoked a deep response from people with strikingly varied interests and from markedly differing constituencies: political radicals and monarchists, decadent poets and Victorian moralists, Darwinists and ministers of the cloth. Wagnerism influenced not only the world of music but other arts as well—painting, poetry, theater, dance, literature—and also left its mark on philosophy, religion, and social and political thought. The ability of Wagnerism to appeal to so many different groups is one of its most definitive—and intriguing—characteristics. Because of this unique role, the impact of Wagnerism was far more than that of a passing fad, a momentary cliché: this broad cultural movement interacted with some of the most

7

important currents in European culture and politics between the Revolutions of 1848 and the First World War.

It is not possible, of course, to treat all aspects of the Wagnerian movement in one volume; this book is necessarily selective, focusing on places and periods of special importance. Chapter 1 examines the role of the Wagnerian movement within the evolution of musical taste and values during the nineteenth century, focusing primarily on Germany and Austria. The succeeding chapters move from discussion of the Wagner circle in Bayreuth, where Wagner built the famous Festspielhaus (Festival Theater) for the performance of his music dramas, to analysis of the movement in France, Italy, Russia, England, and the United States, Wagnerism's first outpost in the New World. This organizational strategy inevitably calls attention to the significant national distinctions within Wagnerism, but it also provides a comparative framework within which we can begin to pull together the intellectual and cultural threads running through the movement as a whole. We hope the result will interest readers from a variety of related fields. All of the contributors are historians by profession, members of a discipline that often has fostered intellectual synthesis. All wrote their contributions especially for this volume.

The contributors are particularly grateful to Vernon Lidtke of the Johns Hopkins University for suggesting the idea of the book and for making several of us known to each other. David C. Large thanks Walter H. Lippincott, Jr., of Cornell University Press for his steadying encouragement and Felix Gilbert of the Institute for Advanced Study for his invaluable criticism of the manuscript. William Weber extends his thanks to Eric Hobsbawm of the University of London for his incisive comments on a paper given at his social history seminar; to Malcolm Cole of the University of California at Los Angeles for the stimulation of his Wagner seminar; and to California State University, Long Beach, for its support of the research for the book. Gerald D. Turbow thanks Richard Sogliuzzo for his help in preparing chapter 3. Bernice Glatzer Rosenthal thanks the National Endowment for the Humanities for the fellowship that made the research for her study possible; George Kalbouss, Malcolm Brown, and Susan Summer for bibliographical suggestions; and Marvin Perry, Charlotte Douglas, and Elaine Crane for helpful comments. Finally, Marion S. Miller offers her thanks to the staff of the Newberry Library and to Alexander

De Grand of Roosevelt University for criticism of her manuscript, and Anne Dzamba Sessa expresses her gratitude to the late Wagner scholar George C. Windell for the crucial assistance he lent her.

D.C.L., W.W., AND A.D.S.

Contributors

DAVID C. LARGE (Montana State University), author of *The Politics of Law and Order: A History of the Bavarian Einwohnerwehr*, has written on the Bayreuth Festival in the *Journal of the History of Ideas* and *Central European History* and has contributed an article on Richard von Kralik to the *Austrian History Yearbook*. He was awarded a Morse Junior Faculty Fellowship from Yale University for research on the rearmament of West Germany.

MARION S. MILLER (University of Illinois at Chicago) has written on mid–nineteenth-century Tuscan society in *The History Journal*, Italian Jacobinism in *Eighteenth Century Studies*, and the nationalism of Pasquale Mancini in the *Canadian Review of Studies of Nationalism*. A former Fulbright scholar, she is presently writing a book on agrarian Tuscany, 1830–1930.

BERNICE GLATZER ROSENTHAL (Fordham University) is author of *D. S. Merezhkovsky and the Silver Age: The Development of a Revolutionary Mentality* and has written on symbolism, religious thought, and the theater in Russia in the *Slavic Review* and other journals. The recipient of a fellowship and a conference grant from the National Endowment for the Humanities, she is presently editing a collaborative volume on Nietzsche's influence in Russia.

ANNE DZAMBA SESSA (West Chester State University) is author of *Richard Wagner and the English*, a history of the Wagnerians in England; her main research interest presently is in the history of women in late nine-teenth-century Europe.

GERALD D. TURBOW wrote his Ph.D. dissertation at the University of California at Los Angeles, entitled "Wagnerism in France, 1830–70: A Measure of a Social and Political Trend," has taught at William and Mary College and at UCLA, and is now writing a book on European émigrés in Hollywood, 1933–1963.

WILLIAM WEBER (California State University, Long Beach) is author of *Music and the Middle Class: Concert Life in London, Paris and Vienna, 1830–48,* and has written on musical taste in the eighteenth century in *Past and Present* and the *Proceedings of the Royal Musical Association.* He has been awarded a Rockefeller Foundation Humanities Fellowship for research on the rise of historically oriented musical taste during the eighteenth and nineteenth centuries.

*Wagnerism in
European Culture
and Politics*

Introduction

The name of a great artist may earn immortality, but such a name is not often adopted to form the title of a social movement. Much of what was extraordinary about the support for Richard Wagner can be seen most simply in the widespread use of the English terms *Wagnerism* and *Wagnerian,* the French *wagnérisme* and *wagnérien,* and the German *Wagnerismus* and *Wagnerianer,* to cite but three of the languages in which such words were coined. His name became affixed to magazines as well—*La revue wagnérienne* in Paris, *Cronaca wagneriana* in Bologna, and *The Meister* in London—and to organizations—the Wagner-Verein in many German and Austrian cities, the Wagner Society in London, and the Associazione Universale Ricardo Wagner in Bologna. Why did Wagner's name mean so much to so many people, and what is the significance of their enthusiasm for "the Master?"

Wagner did not stimulate admirers alone—he stimulated a cause. To some extent he *was* the cause. One can argue that in building his own theater in Bayreuth he took the Romantic idea of genius—of the artist as a culture hero—further than any other artist in the nineteenth century, and the advancement of his work therefore became a crusade for many people who believed in that idea. But Wagnerism ultimately departed from Wagner the man and became a movement in its own right—with principles, goals, and possibly doctrine often only loosely related to the original source of inspiration.

We cannot speak of Wagnerism as it evolved in various national contexts as a completely coherent system of thought or artistic styles. As is often the wont of disciples, Wagner's followers tended to emphasize the aspects of his thought that were of most concern to themselves. The composer's name was invoked for a large array of contradictory purposes and linked with a baffling variety of cultural fashions, political crusades, artistic controversies, and sweeping theories of human renewal. Whereas in America Wagnerism was used to underpin an upright type of transcendentalism, in France and Russia it contributed to quite amoral kinds of literary decadence. In England alone it was linked variously with eroticism, spiritualism, and social reform, while the most musical Wagnerians exhibited eminently Victorian moral tastes. Some Wagnerians all but said that they projected themselves upon Wagner. As the French poet Edouard Dujardin put it: "We found ourselves in Richard Wagner."[1] Oscar Wilde's Dorian Gray spoke likewise of his "listening in rapt pleasure to *Tannhäuser* and seeing in the prelude to that great work of art a presentation of the tragedy of his own soul."[2]

The political contrasts among Wagnerians were equally great. In Bayreuth the Master's heirs and closest disciples built an image of him consistent with the prevailing ideas of Wilhelmian conservatism and *völkisch* nationalism; in Russia, revolutionaries made his ideas an integral part of their theories of popular theater; and in France Jean Jaurès called Wagner's works "communist."[3]

Yet for all the varieties of Wagnerism, its representatives had one important characteristic in common. They shared deep reservations about aspects of their society and culture and were looking for a vital new alternative. That characterization applied as much to the nationalists in Bayreuth as to avant-garde poets in Paris. Admittedly, many of the people who went to Bayreuth were simply following musical fashion, as Wagner himself complained in his last years. But for others—those who journeyed there in order to "transcend" their previous existence—the experience in the Festspielhaus can be said to have been as all-consuming as the embrace of a utopian vision and to provide the answer to problems that deeply troubled nineteenth-century society.

Some historians have doubted the intellectual seriousness of Wagner's followers. It is true that some Wagnerians used the Master's ideas in ways that had so little intellectual substance and so little to do with Wagner's purpose that one wonders if the movement was just what one English critic dubbed it: the "Wagner Bubble."[4] Did "union of the arts" mean anything when voiced by a poet who had never heard a note of Wagner's music? Did the pamphleteering for Wagner amount only to literary puffery? In some cases "Wagnerism" was undoubtedly shallow and intellectually empty, but for many people it helped to meet vital cultural, social, and psychological needs.

Let us now look at the context in which Wagnerian ideas rose to popularity. One of its important aspects was the disillusionment with positivist thinking about social issues that developed in the last half of the nineteenth century.[5] Positivism itself had emerged as a response to the social, economic, and political dislocations of the early nineteenth century. As articulated by its most important theoretician, Auguste Comte, it amounted to an attempt to impose order and discipline on the chaotic human experience of the age; by reducing "quality to quantity in all realms of existence" and by confronting existential and epistemological anarchy by a vast systematizing of human knowledge, positivism offered "a form of intellectual countermagic, an attempt to triumph over fear."[6] Although capable by mid-century of attracting a wide and influential intellectual following (Wagner himself was said to be under its influence in the 1840s),[7] it by no means achieved that triumph over intellectual anarchy that was the principle goal of its exponents. This is hardly surprising, since positivism was not at all a uniform body of thought: Comte himself progressed through three distinct intellectual stages that led him through a revolt against the "tyranny" of reason over feeling to the elaboration of a bizarre "religion of humanity."[8] Moreover, the movement engendered a variety of competing and often mutually exclusive systems, all of them claiming a monopoly of insight into the human condition. But positivism's main failing had less to do with its internal heterogeneity than with its intellectual style. Despite Comte's latter-day injunction against the neglect of feeling, positivism increasingly stood for a highly mechanistic and deterministic view of the world, one that seemed all too arid in its hyper-rationalism and intellectually (as well as politically) stifling in its "scientific fatalism."[9] This last quality applied even to that apotheosis of nineteenth-century positivism—Marxism—for if this ideology had begun as a call to arms against the "alienation" inherent in industrial capitalism, it had become by the 1870s and 1880s a deterministic dogma that by stressing the inevitable demise of capitalism relieved the Marxists themselves of the duty of bringing this about.[10]

But whatever its guise, positivism proved ultimately incapable of satisfying the need for intellectual synthesis and order without at the same time neglecting or inhibiting the equally pressing demands of intuition, feeling, and creative activism.

The same can be said for the primary political dogma of the mid- and late nineteenth-century European bourgeoisie—liberalism. The European liberal parties of the 1860s and 1870s were able to enshrine rationalism and legalism as the main determinants of contemporary political culture, but in most countries this triumph turned out to be very short-lived. As the franchise expanded in the late nineteenth century, the liberals proved unable to win over voters from the lower middle and working classes for whom the values of parliamentary legalism and utilitarian rationalism had little appeal. Confronted with new mass political movements—Social Democratic, Christian Socialist, Labor, Pan-German and Pan-Slav—Europe's bourgeois liberals retreated into an ever more rationalistic and class-bound corner. Some of the younger liberals tried to arrest this trend, and proving unsuccessful sometimes abandoned liberalism altogether for the new mass parties of the Left or Right.[11] In doing so they were giving vent to a widely felt need for a politics that transcended the narrow confines of class interest and the allegedly sterile rituals of rationalistic debate. Carl Schorske has called this the "politics of the new key."[12] It might also be called the politics of Wagnerism.

Given the deficiencies in the positivist-liberal world view, it is not surprising that the majority of middle class Europeans, including a host of prominent and influential intellectuals, turned to the religion of their fathers for their emotional anchor in troubled times. Marx's judgment that religion was the "opium of the masses" was thus off the mark, for, as Peter Gay has recently noted, in the nineteenth century "religion remained, or rather became once again, the opium of the middle classes, particularly in Great Britain, the United States, and Germany."[13] But organized religion was often an inadequate defense against such corrosive and destabilizing forces as rapid industrialization and urbanization, not to mention the troubling advances in the natural sciences. There was a pervasive need for an emotional piety that was less vulnerable than orthodox religious observance to the desiccating effects of rapid social change, scientific progress, and higher biblical criticism. Thus even devout Christians sometimes found themselves searching for some kind of supplement, some added spiritual dimension, to their traditional religious beliefs. Fashionable new cults like Christian Science and theosophy catered to this need.[14] So, as we shall see, did Wagnerism.

If important groups within the nineteenth-century bourgeoisie were prepared to seek their spiritual fulfillment in rather more adventurous forms of religious expression, the same can be said for their attitude toward sexuality. The nineteenth-century bourgeoisie was by no means sexually anemic, or so caught up in the demands of making money that it had lost sight of the pleasures of making love.[15] Unquestionably, however, sexual love and the whole rich fantasy world that surrounded it were often confined by prevailing moral convention within tightly prescribed boundaries. These boundaries may have widened over the course of the nineteenth century, allowing the curious libido more room to roam, but the barriers remained formidable enough to insure that certain pressing libidinal needs could often find satisfaction only through sublimation. Various forms of cultural expression, both "high" and "low," have always served such a sublimating function.[16] The late nineteenth century, with its expanding and yet often still frustratingly narrow sexual horizons, allowed (and in fact demanded) forms of artistic expression that were more frank and open in their sensuality, yet still veiled in the comforting rhetoric of high idealism. Perhaps no late nineteenth-century art met these requirements more closely than the music dramas of Richard Wagner.

Wagner, then, was very much a man for his times. His art brilliantly exemplified what was new and exciting in late nineteenth-century culture and yet at the same time seemed to offer a refuge from the bewildering forces of social change. But of course Wagner offered his age more than a corpus of artistic works. He did not present himself merely as a composer, or even as a composer who dabbled in social theory, but as a cultural messiah. Speaking the language of the philosopher and gathering disciples like a prophet, he claimed a "holy gift" by which he would cleanse and heal the fallen world of not only the opera but society at large.

In seeking converts through his writings, Wagner's primary purpose was not to promote a literary or philosophical career. On the contrary, he used his writings to dramatize the theatrical reforms he thought essential to a truly meaningful experience of the opera and the salvation of society through art. His overriding desire was to see his music dramas staged and performed as closely in accordance with his ideals as possible, and he became antagonistic to some of his followers who moved off in intellectual directions not directly related to that goal. Nonetheless, in calling for reform of musical theater he raised a set of issues that on a far broader plane mattered greatly to the people of his time. When he called for opera to function not as entertainment but as the most serious form of art, he rallied the idealists from all the other arts. When he let loose polemics against the frivolous operagoing public, he awakened a widespread resentment against the urban upper classes. When he declared that his theater would reunite the *Volk* and revive the sense of its past, he offered a common meeting ground to diverse cultural and political groups searching for links with popular traditions. When he dwelt upon the psychological and religious themes of his music dramas, he opened up an exciting new direction to people then turning away from positivism and utilitarian rationalism. And when he inveighed against crass materialism and held up love—both spiritual and sensual—as the best antidote to mammon, he appealed not only to the professional bourgeoisie baiters among the intelligentsia, but also to those important elements among the middle classes given to ostentatious self-laceration and public declarations of their sins against culture.

We must not underemphasize the role that musical experience played in converting individuals to the Wagnerian faith. Even if few of the French Wagnerians seem to have heard much of his music before embracing his cause, in many other cases the first experience of his music was reported as overpowering and awakening, as an event that amounted to a kind of conversion. Thomas Mann was "transported" when he first heard *Lohengrin* as a young man;[17] Houston Stewart Chamberlain experienced "seraphic bliss" upon entering the Festspielhaus;[18] the young Romain Rolland fell into "a state of painful yet delicious torpor" at the opening notes of a Wagner concert in the big Cirque d'Hiver.[19] Yet others were repelled by his music with an equal force. Leo Tolstoy found *Siegfried* so "artificial and stupid" that he had "great difficulty sitting it out." Indeed, he fled the theater before the performance's conclusion, "with a feeling of disgust I have not yet forgotten."[20] John Ruskin said about *Die Meistersinger,* commenting on his first (and last) Wagnerian experience,

> Of all the bete, clumsy, blundering, boggling, baboon-blooded stuff I
> ever saw on the human stage, that thing last night beat—as far as the

story and acting went; and of all the affected, sapless, soulless, beginningless, endless, topless, bottomless, topsiturviest, tuneless, scrannelpipiest tongs and boniest doggerel of sounds I ever endured the deadliness of, that eternity of nothing was the deadliest, as far as the sound went. I was never so relieved . . . in my life, by the stopping of any sound—not excepting railway whistles—as I was by the cessation of the cobbler's bellowing; even the serenader's caricatured twangle was a rest after it. As for the great *Lied* I never made out where it began or where it ended—except by the fellow's coming off the horse block.[21]

Intellectual reactions to Wagner's essays were similarly strong. The German journalist and music historian Franz Brendel, for example, said that after first reading an essay by Wagner he knew he had found his true leader.[22] But the music critic for the *Saturday Review* complained that Wagner's prose works displayed a "complete absence of the sense of humour."[23] This same periodical's book critic thanked the author of a new volume on Wagner "for not having wearied us with the philosophical theories Wagner amused himself by spinning when he was not seriously occupied with composition."[24]

Moreover, the controversiality of Wagner's reputation augmented the sense that there was a movement behind him; attack stimulated ever more vigorous defense. The exoticism of much of Wagner's prose and enthusiasms had a great deal to do with this. He dealt not only with operatic reform and contemporary composers (often, ultimately, with venom) but also ventured into anti-vivisection, vegetarianism, the role of Jews in music, Schopenhauerian metaphysics, the perfidy of the French, the perfidy of the English, and the philosophical errors of Darwin. The same characteristic passed on to the movement. Wagner seems to have attracted people who thrived on controversy. Perhaps it would not be overstating the case to say that the typical Wagnerian was someone with a fight to pick.

Public confrontations between Wagnerians and their antagonists intensified the sense of cause. Performances of his works could easily degenerate into donnybrooks, as the ritualistic rivalries so common in literary and musical life took a physical turn. The most famous instance of this was the Parisian premiere of *Tannhäuser* in 1861, when young bucks from the Jockey Club rioted in protest against an event they considered a departure from hallowed convention (an opera without the traditional grand ballet) as well as politically suspect (thanks to Napoleon III's support of the performance). In another confrontation,

Thomas Mann's later father-in-law, a passionate Wagnerian, smashed his beer stein over the head of a fellow who dared malign the Master; for this act he proudly bore the title *Schoppenhauer* (stein masher).[25] George Bernard Shaw indulged in only mild hyperbole when he suggested that "the wars of religion were not more blood-thirsty than the discussions of the Wagnerians and Anti-Wagnerians."[26]

The breadth of Wagner's support arose partly from his idea of the union of the arts, or the *Gesamtkunstwerk* (total work of art). Drawing upon Hellenic parallels, he dramatized this notion in ways that had a magnetic appeal to literary and aesthetic figures. Then as now, the idea had a utopian quality to it when voiced breathlessly in intellectual journals; it is the ideal to which many an artist has since aspired. It was, of course, ultimately impracticable, and probably unrepresentative of Wagner's own approach to the music dramas. Since the concept involves an inextricable interweaving of the elements of all the arts in single works of art, it could not easily serve as a model for any one form of art. But no matter: the spirit of the idea carried enormous weight and was probably the leading aesthetic concept around which the Wagnerian movement formed.[27]

Creative artists indeed made up an extremely important group among the Wagnerians. As suggested earlier, the growth of the Romantic idea of genius may be said to have reached its peak in Wagner, or perhaps in his founding of his own artistic community, the Bayreuth Festival. The Wagnerian movement was unique in its time in endowing one artist with such stature and respect that a special institution was built to perform his art according to his wishes. Artists of all kinds looked in wonder at the festival, at the independence and power it afforded Wagner, as well as at the movement that had grown up around him by that time. Had any other artist—novelist, painter, or poet—achieved anything as extraordinary as this? His awed admirers certainly did not think so, and he became for them the model of how the artist might win the respect and stature he deserved.

Wagner and Wagnerian ideas became a rich source of allusion, often indeed of influence, among artists of different kinds. While we cannot trace in detail Wagner's impact on specific artistic disciplines, it is useful to note the number and variety of such figures. In the realm of painting they included the Frenchmen Charles Toché, Auguste Renoir, and Henri Fantin-Latour; the Germans Hans Thoma, Arnold Böcklin, Wilhelm Kaulbach, Walter Püttner, and Angelo Jank; the

Englishmen Marcus Simmons, Arthur Rackham, and Aubrey Beardsley; the American John Singer-Sargeant; and the Russians Aleksandr Benois and K. A. Somov.[28] In literature his impact was even more extensive, certainly deeper, as has been shown in numerous studies.[29] Among those well known to have been influenced by Wagner were Stéphane Mallarmé and his fellow symbolists Théodor de Wyzewa and Edouard Dujardin; the Italian novelist Gabriele D'Annunzio; the Russian poet Alexander Blok and the playwrights Vyacheslav Ivanov and Georgi Chulkov. In the world of dance his aesthetic ideas left echoes in both Serge Diaghilev's Ballets russes and the influential style of Isadora Duncan.[30] Wagner's influence extended as well to performing institutions, for the ideas behind Bayreuth were applied in many settings. Among them were not only the Munich Wagner Festival after the turn of the century but also the more broadly focused Wurms Festival, begun in 1889; the Glastonbury Festival, founded in 1914; and the Salzburg Festival, founded in 1920.[31]

If we now look more closely at the political aspect of the Wagnerian movement, we encounter probably the most potent myth about both Wagner and Wagnerism. Wagner's political legacy has often been equated with fascism, and Wagner himself is sometimes held up as one of the main "forefathers" of National Socialism.[32] Connections between Wagner's thinking and that of Hitler can certainly be traced, but the Master's world view differed significantly from the Führer's. Some of Wagner's followers, especially those who claimed to perpetuate his ideas in Bayreuth, did their best to promote intellectual and political ties between *Wagnerismus* and National Socialism, but what might be called the proto-fascist dimension of Wagnerism by no means dominated or shaped the movement as a whole. There were in fact an array of conflicting political tendencies in Wagnerism from its inception right up to the First World War.

As the art historian Timothy Clark has suggested in his works on Courbet, artists do not tend to look at the political situation of their time in anything like the same way the statesman does.[33] It is not advisable to try to pigeonhole Wagner politically; even the terms *revolutionary* and *nationalist* are too crude to mean much. If his participation in the Dresden uprising of 1849 should not be forgotten, we should also take care not to read too much into this example of revolutionary activism. Just why Wagner did what he did stemmed from a complicated set of political, philosophical, and artistic notions that is understandable in the context of the times (see chapter 1 for a brief discussion of this). He paid for his role in the Dresden uprising with an extended exile from Germany and quickly renounced it in his subsequent writings.[34]

Wagner's main characteristic as a political theorist was the ambivalence of his thinking vis-à-vis the Left and the Right. On the one hand, he shared the social posture of the radical Left in his broad critique of society and his demand for human equality, most of all in the theater. On the other hand, he was quite skeptical of parliamentary government and very suspicious of the principles of liberalism. His involvement in the study of German folk myth drew him into increasingly close association with the political Right, especially as the Bayreuth Circle came to the fore. The jumble of metaphysical and artistic notions in his writings confused any clear sense of political direction in his public role. That had its advantages for him, for he stressed whichever side of his political personality was useful at any given moment, and people believed what they wanted. After returning to Germany in 1864, he meddled in the affairs of Ludwig II's court in Munich, claiming to be a Bavarian patriot.[35] After 1866, sensing in which direction the political wind was blowing, he threw in his lot with the ascendant Prussian monarchy, subsequently trying to ingratiate himself with Bismarck. But when he failed to make any headway in that direction, he retreated from further political involvement and spent his last years grumbling about the ills of the new German Empire.

To what degree were Wagner's political aspirations expressed in the music dramas? George Windell has argued forcefully that the *Ring* cycle was originally conceived under the strong influence of the Revolution of 1848–1849 and the social thinking surrounding it.[36] While Wagner's later changes in the libretto and the score blurred these tendencies considerably, Windell sees the mark of social protest remaining indelibly upon the work. Carl Schorske, however, has argued differently in a penetrating essay on Wagner and William Morris. He makes the case that in the course of writing the *Ring* Wagner shifted to a viewpoint of philosophical despair and to a concern chiefly with the psychological dimensions of human life. To Schorske, *Tristan und Isolde* best defines Wagner's attitude after the mid-1850s. Politics thus disappeared in the music dramas, save for a brief reappearance in *Die*

Meistersinger, as Wagner immersed himself in what Schorske calls his "psychological metaphysics."[37]

But whatever we conclude regarding Wagner's politics, the chief source of politicization in the dissemination and reception of his influence resided more in the uses to which his work was put than in the work itself, or even in the various interpretations of that work. Both his adherents and opponents seemed bent on employing performances of his music dramas as occasions for political demonstrations and testimonials. Often these outbursts had little to do with what Wagner may have been trying to say through the medium of musical dramaturgy. By proclaiming oneself a Wagnerian—or proclaiming the opposite—one made a gesture weighted with political meaning, though exactly what political meaning varied from place to place and from time to time in a way that adds yet another dimension to the Wagnerian confusion. The injection of political passion into the already overcharged atmosphere of emergent Wagnerism had mainly to do with nationalist rivalries. The air was rife with varying claims of cultural/political superiority, denunciations of cultural/political imperialism, and appeals for the defense of cultural/political values and the moral fiber of the native youth. Italian opera enthusiasts, for example, eventually rejected Wagner not only because they objected to the contents or the style of his works but also because his burgeoning influence seemed to threaten the status of the national culture and thereby the nation itself.

To confuse matters even further, Wagnerism sometimes became embroiled in the tangled web of late–nineteenth-century European diplomacy. Both Bismarck and Napoleon III thought they saw diplomatic repercussions in their relationships to him and his equally controversial followers. Wagner naturally himself added fuel to these fires through his polemical prose writings on political topics and his quite impolitic statements about other countries' political and cultural deficiencies. (In this respect he had about as much tact as Kaiser Wilhelm II, with whom he was often to be compared by contemporaries.) But the Master (again like the Kaiser) never fully understood why and how he had such difficulties on the diplomatic front—why he was not universally loved. It is therefore not surprising that in his last years he waxed nostalgic about the essential simplicity and artistic purity of his original aspirations, and even fell to pondering whether it would not still be possible to throw it all over and emigrate to Minnesota.

While Wagnerism on an international scale had no integral history, and differences among separate countries complicate any periodization, five phases of the evolution of Wagnerism can be tentatively defined. The first period comprised 1849 to 1861—a time of intellectual preparation. Though Wagner was somewhat known before 1849, he had few active adherents of the kind who gathered around him later on. His essays published between 1849 and 1851, rather than his music, first made him widely known throughout European literary and musical life. Though living mostly in Switzerland, he attracted a strong band of supporters in Germany, primarily around Franz Liszt's residence in Weimar and the militantly Wagnerian *Neue Zeitschrift für Musik* in Leipzig. His widely reported trip to Paris in 1859–1861 climaxed this period that marked his arrival as the Bad Boy of European musical life.

The second period runs roughly from 1861 to 1872. During this time Wagner traveled through Europe conducting performances of his works and enlisting support for new productions. In 1864 he moved to Bavaria under the protection of the young King Ludwig II but was forced to flee that kingdom in 1866 after having made himself persona non grata with the local population. He spent the next six years in Triebschen—his house near Lucerne—where he received his first visits from Nietzsche and finally married Cosima von Bülow, his mistress of the past six years and the exwife of his former friend Hans von Bülow. Such events dramatically increased his notoriety, but his fame increasingly rested on the more solid foundation of his music dramas, which became much better known through more frequent productions and the wide dissemination of the operas in the form of librettos and scores. Though Wagner did not yet have any organized movement behind him, he had attracted a number of disciples in Germany and France who called themselves Wagnerians and who would subsequently play roles in the blossoming of Wagnerism.

The *Blütezeit* of the Wagnerian movement occurred between 1872— the year of Wagner's move to Bayreuth—and his death in 1883. With the foundation of the Festspielhaus and its opening in 1876, the movement acquired its Mother Church, and a full ecclesiastical bureaucracy in the form of the Richard Wagner Society. Organizations of that sort (generally independent of Bayreuth) appeared in many parts of Europe, from Vienna to Bologna to London, usually presenting concerts and literary meetings concerned with his music and ideas. The custom of making pilgrimages to Bayreuth began as Wagnerians went there for the productions of the *Ring* in 1876 and *Parsifal* in 1883. Most of the Wagnerian magazines first appeared during this period as well, as the Master became one of the most revered, if still no less controversial, figures in European culture.

For fifteen or so years after his death the movement maintained itself in varying states of cohesion. National differences are particularly marked in this phase. Little sense of a movement remained in Paris after 1890, since there it had been too deeply divided to persist, but in Italy and Germany Wagnerism flourished throughout the decade. In Vienna it would seem to have continued, though in less active form than during the 1880s. Finally, in the first two decades of the twentieth century it displayed a fascinating late bloom in Russia, where certain strands of Wagnerian thought maintained their potency as late as the early 1920s.

This brief introduction has, we hope, suggested some of the reasons why the contributors to this book believe that Wagnerism well deserves to rank as an "ism." Wagnerism was a movement—a cultural, social, and political movement—and not simply the love of Wagner's music. The latter phenomenon is perhaps more aptly described as *Tristanism,* a term coined by Elliott Zuckerman to denote the intensely private, transcendental experience that Wagner's music dramas evoked in many people and that became a literary tradition in its own right.[38] While that kind of experience played an important part in bringing individual admirers to Wagner, it was not a public movement. André Coeuroy has spoken of the various dimensions of Wagnerism in yet a different way: "When acting as a subject, Wagnerism was a system: truly a creation whose vitality radiated influence. When viewed as an object, Wagnerism was that influence itself and the infatuation that followed."[39]

In this volume we will be interested in both these aspects: in the infatuation that surrounded Wagner's legacy, and in the ways by which that infatuation developed a life of its own, as a distinctive approach to contemporary culture. Whether Wagnerism was a system, as Coeuroy claims, or simply a way of doing artistic battle is one of the main questions we will consider. That can best be done by looking separately into the movement in its different national centers and assessing what resulted from its work.

1. *Wagner, Wagnerism, and Musical Idealism*

WILLIAM WEBER

In the history of nineteenth-century music, Richard Wagner stands like a Napoleon Bonaparte, dominating our perspective so thoroughly that our attention has been diverted from the social and cultural context in which his music and his ideas emerged. We as yet know little about how opera houses were managed, what kind of works they produced, where public taste was moving, or even what the musical styles of many other composers were like. Thus, if we are to comprehend—indeed, weigh—Wagner's influence, we must first do some fundamental work on these and other matters.

Musicologists have made a good start at establishing the context in which Wagner worked by looking at the early influences upon his musical style. Robert Laudon, taking a long view, has shown in an excellent study how Wagner's style grew out of a creative exchange between the French and German musical traditions.[1] Others have shown that he borrowed freely from a host of seemingly unlikely composers.[2] Nonetheless, our knowledge of the social and institutional framework of concert and opera life remains extremely limited, in part because attention is generally focused on the lives of socially atypical composers (Frédéric Chopin, especially), rather than on the texture of musical life itself.

My purpose here is to examine Wagner and the Wagnerian movement with reference to a set of social and cultural tendencies that first became apparent at the turn of the nineteenth century and that I choose to call "musical idealism." The most striking of these tendencies was a shift in musical taste from a preference for contemporary music to a preference for works by dead masters. Related to this change was the rise of an austere new code that singled out the music itself for veneration and insisted that it not be trivialized by commercialism or by association with frivolous social activities. These changes were accompanied by a whole realm of new customs, practices, and institutions— the trappings of classical-music taste as we know it today. The ideals of musical experience that Wagner enunciated and tried to apply in Bayreuth grew out of this movement in musical life.

Just as musical idealism influenced Wagner profoundly, so too did it pave the way for Wagnerism and a larger current in taste—musical modernism. The followers of Wagner launched the first movement that saw itself as a musical avant-garde, an intellectual cadre supporting works that it claimed were progressive and, by definition, controversial. In so doing Wagnerism laid the intellectual and social groundwork for the rise of the self-contained cultural world of new music, which today devotes itself primarily to contemporary works. Contradictions within the principles of musical idealism are responsible for this development. As devotion to the classical masters became the dominant trend, new music was effectively squeezed out of the repertoire, and the new-music world went in its own direction. Since this change came about just before the blossoming of Wagnerism in the 1870s and 1880s, it is necessary to see the turnabout in musical taste if we are to fully understand the role of the Wagnerian movement.[3]

To show how this came about we will investigate three successive phases in the growth of musical idealism. First, we will investigate the rise of the principles of musical idealism at the turn of the nineteenth century; next we will examine how Wagner's writings grew out of these principles; finally, we will trace the evolution of Wagnerism as it developed into an early form of modernism. Our main agenda concerns attitudes and values, not the music itself, but in section III we will pause to inquire what relationships these ideas had with various aspects of the music dramas.

I

When we enter an opera house today, we feel that we must abide by certain social and cultural assumptions—specifically, a code of behavior that first emerged in nineteenth-century concert halls and did not invade the opera houses (except the Festspielhaus in Bayreuth) until the twentieth century. The etiquette at eighteenth-century musical events was not idealist, in the sense in which we have defined it. Well-born gentlemen and ladies went to the opera to socialize, to politick, to keep up with local gossip, or simply to escape the confines of their own fairly cramped and musty residences. It was a smaller world, one in which people had to lead their lives in closer proximity to one another than we do today. The world of opera was suffused with sexual overtones; men often attended with the object of courting members of the chorus or ballet corps or the leading divas, some of whom lived extraordinarily affluent lives as a result of these relationships. People took this situation very much for granted and felt it did not compromise serious musical activity.

Moreover, neither the concert nor the opera was thought of as primarily an individual internal experience to be valued for its *Innerlichkeit,* the feature that the Romantics would later stress. So much socializing went on within the halls that in the Paris Opéra there was a special booth where people could exchange their tickets for seats in other parts of the theater, presumably in order to be near someone particular.[4] At the opera, people felt free to talk during the recitative, and operas houses were always lighted throughout the performance, a practice that permitted patrons to converse in an intricate social language spoken by the hand, the eye, the fan, and the lorgnette. Fisticuffs were not unknown, particularly in the pit, where gentlemen touring the various pleasures of the evening might end up picking a fight in the close quarters down front.

We should not imagine these events anarchic in the manner of some contemporary rock concerts, however. Every hall had its police, and even aristocratic gentlemen might be arrested for trouble making. Moreover, the flourishing system of patronage tended to keep people's attention focused upon the proceedings: most of the better-off listeners employed opera singers or players in their own homes and thus had good reason to stop talking and listen. The old social order, though allowing behavior that may seem excessively free to us, was still controlled by its own etiquette and, in the eyes of the connoisseurs of music, it served the "progress" of the art. People whose musical needs differed sharply coexisted successfully enough. Some people listened and some socialized, but no one objected to their being together in one audience—as would not be the case today.

The connoisseurs exerted only a weak authority in musical life. Since no corpus of musical works had come down from ancient Greece and Rome, the only classical tradition in musical life was the written tradition of scientific and philosophical music theory, which had little to do with musical performance or taste. Lacking any source of ancient authority for music itself, the musical connoisseur did not exert as much influence over the general public in the molding of taste as did his colleague in painting or poetry.[5] The connoisseur, in fact, was frequently an object of ridicule; as a pamphleteer in the legendary Querelle des bouffons of 1752–1754 declared, "In the Opéra I sleep, since I am a connoisseur."[6] Once when Mozart wrote to his father about a new set of piano concertos he was composing, he said that he hoped they would strike "a happy medium between what is too easy and too difficult. . . . Here and there are things which connoisseurs can appreciate, but I have seen to it that those less knowledgeable can also be pleased without knowing why."[7] The naive ease with which he said this derived from the limited role of the connoisseurs in that age.

The final decades of the eighteenth century witnessed the beginning of a fundamental transformation in musical life. Just what took place, indeed why or even when it occurred, has been only hazily understood; study of the role of the publishing industry, in particular, is still in its infancy. Nevertheless, it is clear that a commercial revolution played a primary role in transforming not only the economic base of musical life but also the nature of musical taste. This revolution undermined the social structure that had enabled different musical purposes—those of the connoisseurs and the public—to live in relative harmony. Old musical values gradually decayed, and the modern dichotomy between "light" and "serious" music emerged in their place. Musical idealism was a powerful force in that process.

The new social reality of early nineteenth-century musical life originated in the family. Playing keyboard instruments and singing had long been common among the middle and upper classes, but by the late eighteenth century such activities became far more conventional, indeed, almost universal, among the most prosperous classes in the largest cities.[8] As early as 1778 an English commentator complained about the number of parents who were forcing their children to perform music in the family salon, and similar complaints were heard frequently in the nineteenth century.[9] Among the better-off classes, aristocratic as well as bourgeois, the salon was in effect the place where marriages were made and family fortunes disposed of, and musical performance was part of this setting. The ability to entertain guests with music was a genteel accomplishment that marked a family as possessing requisite social graces and gave children an advantage in the marriage market.[10]

These tendencies drastically expanded the number of people involved in some aspect of musical life. The growth in the affluence of the upper middle class contributed considerably to this process, but since the aristocracy remained powerful in setting tastes and not all members of the lower middle class prospered equivalently, the change cannot be attributed to the "rise" of a homogeneous middle class.[11] Instead, the growth of the music public is best understood as an expansion in the purposes music itself served within the higher social classes. We might compare it to the equally drastic expansion that rock music underwent in the 1950s and 1960s, as musical activities became increasingly important in the lives of young people. Technological breakthroughs played a central part in both instances, making possible new musical activities and expanding the size of the public. Just as the long-playing record and the electric guitar facilitated the burgeoning of rock music, so the invention of cheaper, easier ways to print sheet music helped the spread of family music making in the nineteenth century. With the invention of lithography, improved processes for engraving, and the mechanization of typesetting, music publishing took on a much more commercial character.

In the nineteenth century, music became a business and a "mass culture" phenomenon. In the eighteenth century, music, both manuscript and printed, had been distributed by musicians and their patrons in person, but from the early nineteenth century on distribution became an impersonal process conducted on a mass scale and manipulated through such devices as clever product design and advertising.[12] All areas of musical life were affected by the new commercialism. The sheet music intended for home consumption was most often an arrangement of melodies from new operas produced in the major cities. A leading virtuoso would write instrumental medleys of these tunes, perform them in concerts, and publish them in simpler form for amateurs to play on all kinds of instruments. The pianist Henri Herz led the way in Paris during the 1830s and 1840s; as a performer, composer, publisher, concert hall manager, and entrepreneur *extraordinaire,* he milked the new market like an international merchant or rising industrialist. Although composers who wrote primarily for the opera generally did not follow such a career, they too were expected to write with the home market in mind, since that is where financial return was the most lucrative. Let us look ahead to what Wagner wrote to Franz Liszt on this matter in 1853: "We all know that the so-called *morceaux detachés* are the chief source of profit in the case of operas; to publish such would in the case of *Lohengrin* be impossible on account of the peculiar character of the opera, in which there are no single vocal pieces that in a manner detach themselves from the context. . . . *Nine* such pieces, short, easy, and even popular, I gave you some time ago."[13]

Concerts themselves were really an appendage of the home music industry. During the late eighteenth century, far fewer aristocratic households maintained domestic ensembles, and many musicians found that they could make a better living as independents, primarily by teaching and performing for various wealthy families in a major city. By the first decades of the nineteenth century the most common kind of concert was an ad hoc affair sponsored by such a musician at which many of his or her colleagues performed gratis and for which all the sponsor's patrons were expected to buy tickets. The pieces consisted primarily of opera scenes and variations on famous tunes, which the amateurs could then go home and play themselves. By touring, musicians tried to make their names and thereby settle down with remunerative connections in one city.[14]

The rapid expansion of the music market led to many economic and musical abuses. Publishers felt even freer than before to put out pirated editions of scores; performers advertised falsely that famous virtuosos would appear at their concerts; and teachers made extravagant claims about how fast they could instruct children to learn to sing or to play the piano. Music was intensively—often deviously—entrepreneurial in its economic practices, probably as much so as any other consumer business. The popular music business of the 1960s and 1970s offers an intriguing parallel, since it shows the same cutthroat competition and a similar sense of giddy opportunism.

This musical commercialism stimulated a powerful countercurrent of musical idealism. Initially the trend manifested itself as a moral critique of the social and musical tendencies evident in the music busi-

ness, a warning against bad taste and the quest for gain. Appearing as
early as the 1770s, it became widespread in the new music journals of
the early nineteenth century, which were generally written and read by
the more serious musicians and amateurs. In time this moral critique
grew into a complete musical ethic, a new way of defining music's
purposes and controlling the manner in which it was performed. Music now became a "high" art, a pursuit much more lofty than simple
entertainment. These attitudes were closely linked to a reverence for
the music of Handel, Haydn, Mozart, and Beethoven, the "classical"
masters—the word came into use in this sense in musical life early in
the century—whose authority demanded a strict code of behavior and
taste.

   During the first half of the century the idealists were a distinct
minority within musical life, and their beliefs lay outside the mainstream of popular taste. Only during the middle of the century did the
classical repertory and the new musical ethic gain preeminence. Romanticism was of course a major factor in this process, and most
studies of the cult of Beethoven treat that cult as an aspect of Romantic
aesthetics and the influence of such ideas on musical taste.[15] But Romanticism was first and foremost a literary movement, and we distort
discussion of musical life if we try to understand it only in terms of the
influence of Romanticism. Here we are concerned neither with Romanticism nor with formal aesthetics but rather with the cultural and
social assumptions that guided musical idealism. The language of the
movement will interest us as much as its ideas, for this rhetoric proved
a powerful cultural weapon.

   The central theme in musical idealism was a suspicion of mode and
fashion—a suspicion that extended to both the manipulators and the
manipulated. Virtuosos sparked the most concern. We can see this
particularly clearly in the *Allgemeine musikalische Zeitung,* a Leipzig
journal founded in 1798 that was the most powerful exponent of the
new movement during the first part of the century. In 1802, Friedrich
Rochlitz, its editor, published an anonymous article that inveighed
bitterly against "traveling virtuosos": "The best artists find themselves
compelled to waste their time in deceitful practices of petty artistry and
charlatanism, because the little band of connoisseurs cannot pay for the
real art of which musicians are capable. The contortions and excres-
cences, which the crowd is accustomed to seeing as something sublime, are among the many unfortunate effects of virtuosos upon the

public."[16] The public worried Rochlitz as much as the virtuosos did. In his opinion these musicians played to the worst side of public taste, drawing the level of musical life down farther and farther. He frequently speaks of "the crowd" and even "the masses," indicating a suspicion of the general public that was rare in eighteenth-century writing. *Dilettante* and *virtuoso* soon became the idealists' most important code words for musicians who capitalized on bad taste, and forty-five years later, in 1847, the same journal quoted a recent book on the subject of *Virtuosentum* and *Dilettantismus:* "Two forces in musical life today, towering above the truest, are misguided musical principles, able to bring under their sway the majority of all enterprises: dilettantism and virtuosity." The article concluded by asserting that "the affected artistic sense and the blatant dogmatism of modern dilettantism are just as despicable as the empty husks of modern virtuosity, which—God help us—makes itself known more and more for its vanity and its baseness."[17]

These are strong words. A basic principle of the musical idealists was the conviction that performance must be entirely true to the music, regardless of the eminence (or glamor) of the performing artist. Such a notion was unabashed idealism in that day, for it was generally assumed that opera and other virtuoso genres were designed as vehicles to display the skill of the performers. The idealists were also hostile to ostentation on the part of the public, opposing self-display of any kind that might detract from the music. The social aspect of musical experience was now suspect unless it directly served the most serious musical purposes—a drastic switch from the moral neutrality and strongly social character of eighteenth-century musical taste. In 1846 the *Allgemeine musikalische Zeitung* turned its attention to the ostentation of women in the audience: "The worst enemy of musical performance in concert halls and theaters is fancy toilette. Because women want to be seen, indeed because they want to arrive at just the right time to be seen, they must come late to performances! From the sound of a squeaky door they are sure to get the attention of everyone, gaining either jealousy or awe. But what on earth does all this have to do with the music!"[18] The growing importance of applause in early nineteenth-century concert halls also provoked the idealists. In 1849 the *Neue Zeitschrift für Musik,* the journal Robert Schumann had established in 1834, decried the extremes of the custom: "The value of art in itself alone, that great and humble purpose, remains unrecognized; the public judges more the performance than the content of the performance. Undying masterpieces, which once brought the highest character of their time to expression, now have the meanest fate of being judged by applause, the most trivial of all modish things."[19] Note as well how crucial the authority of the classical repertoire—those "underlying masterpieces"—was to the idealists' moral code.

The idealists gradually developed their own distinctive and powerful rhetoric. *Fashion* and *mode* were the unkindest words in their vocabulary, but *gain* and *profit* came a near second. "Modish things by any standard," said the article just cited, nearly always predominated in musical life. "The artists in the mode, those who become the heroes of the day, are capable of saying nothing with charm, but rather use their fine sensitivity only to cater to the mood of the public. Gain comes through this means, and the greatest master and the ordinary composer stand on the same level for the general public."[20] Felix Mendelssohn's *Lieder ohne Wörte,* the author admitted, was a remarkable exception—a well-written piece that had become popular without any fashion mongering on the part of the composer.

The idealists' powerful moral revulsion against conventional musical taste reflects an attitude toward mass culture that has become commonplace in the modern world. In their own time, however, they defined a wholly new role for the most serious amateurs and musicians. In declaring their independence from public taste, the idealists established themselves as the first self-styled elite in musical life. There was now a group whose members felt that they could tell the public what to listen to. Rochlitz's remark in 1802 about *die Kenner*—that "little band of connoisseurs"—demonstrates this new sense of intellectual independence.

Music critics led the way. In the eighteenth century, critical commentary had operated under the guise of simple reporting and thus made no claims to authority; writers often introduced their opinions by saying that they were merely repeating what the connoisseurs had said. After the turn of the century, music reviews became a conventional genre of formal criticism. In 1823 an article in the *Allgemeine musikalische Zeitung* suggested that the new authority of the connoisseurs had removed the former unitary sense of public taste when it asked, "Can we believe . . . the connoisseurs, those who are now called such, and can one really designate them as a special class of people? From them we only get fault finding and caviling without end, so that there is hardly a true critic left, far less any common taste."[21] Thus had this "special class of people" destroyed the "common taste" in the old order of musical life.

Until now I have referred only to comments published in Leipzig, since that city's journal was central to the movement—and since Wagner grew up there. But musical idealism sprang up all across Europe, generally appearing in journals of the same kind. In 1819, for example, a Viennese writer voiced the familiar suspicion of popular taste when he wrote, concerning the rage for Rossini, that "people here related to his happy-go-lucky quality, to that quality by which the great mass of the city [die Menge] is accustomed to quench its thirst for music."[22] In 1848 another commentator lauded the supporters of the classical repertoire who wished to "build a dam against the flood of modern musical wares, . . . against the emptiness, superficiality, and thrill mongering of the modern style of composition."[23] In 1829 London's Harmonicon spoke derisively of certain kinds of music, "that insipid, mawkish kind, which the singers, together with a few tasteless people of influence, are at present forcing into the ears of such people that are passive." In 1833 the same journal went so far as to suggest "rules for composing fashionable music"—all modeled upon the arias of Rossini.[24]

Disillusioned with the commercialism of musical life, the idealists started looking back in time. A variety of factors contributed to the rise of the classical repertoire, but the search for firmer bases of musical taste was prominent among them. As early as the 1770s, a few commentators had begun to question the meaning of novelty as a principle of taste. John Hawkins made the most formidable case of all against novelty in his history of music, published in 1776, but only six years earlier he had declared bluntly that "nothing in music is estimable that is not new. No music [is] tolerable, which has been heard before."[25] In 1799 a contributor to the Allgemeine musikalische Zeitung asked why concert programs included so many scenes from the most recent operas: "In the musical as well as the theater world, the first cause is that ever-increasing stream of loathsome taste for new and only new—and always nothing but new pieces."[26] The first issue of the journal had printed a portrait of Johann Sebastian Bach, and its contributors proceeded to lay down the principles of a classical-music taste based upon the musical models first of Handel, Mozart, and Haydn, then of Beethoven and Weber, and eventually of Mendelssohn and Schumann.

Reverence for these composers was often accompanied by laments about the moral decay evident in contemporary culture. In 1799 Rochlitz mused about what he saw in musical life: "Peace and well-being have given way to a dedication to luxury and lazy pleasure; to a decline in independence and originality; and to feelings that are crassly self-serving, unnatural, and unsatisfying." More specifically, he found that "Gluck is scorned, Handel is no longer known, the Bachs extolled only out of duty but put well to rest; crowds of virtuosos; and the sinking of the finer German operetta."[27]

There was nothing new, of course, in deploring a decline in musical taste, but this time the protest led to the preservation and performance of old music in a systematic way. During the early decades of the nineteenth century, the idealists established the pantheon of great composers against whose music, they insisted, all new works had to be judged. In the process they claimed for themselves a new sort of authority as the interpreters and judges of this tradition. Another part of their program was the principle that knowledge of music was necessary for appreciating it. This precept, applicable to amateurs and professional musicians alike, became one of the most powerful aspects of the classical-music tradition, leading to the printing of often quite technical program notes for concert audiences from the 1850s on.

The idealist movement developed chiefly in the context of symphony orchestra concerts. The repertoire of the Leipzig Gewandhaus Orchestra illustrates the change best, for it was the only formal ensemble to survive from the eighteenth into the nineteenth century. Gradually the orchestra programmed more pieces by composers who were no longer living, the percentage of such works growing by about 10 percent each decade after the turn of the century. In 1781–1785, works by dead masters made up 13 percent of the repertoire; in 1820–1825, 23 percent; in 1828–1834, 39 percent; and in 1837–1847, 48 percent. The final consolidation of the classical repertoire for the Gewandhaus Orchestra came when the number of these works claimed 61 percent of the orchestra's program in 1850–1855 and 76 percent in 1865–1870.[28] In Vienna the Concert Spirituel had already taken the same path; at the time of Beethoven's death in 1827, 75 percent of its repertoire consisted of works by dead composers,[29] and the same was true of the London Philharmonic Society somewhat later.[30] By the 1870s the end product was the same in orchestras across Europe—a repertoire that focused on great works by dead masters. Nevertheless, the number of concerts of this kind remained small before the middle of the century, rarely accounting for more than one-quarter of a season's total offerings in any major city. Leipzig was an exception because of its small size and the central position held by its symphony orchestra, but even there the most popular concerts were the *Extraconcerte,* virtuoso programs presented by visiting performers with the orchestra's consent.[31]

Symphony orchestra concerts met idealist standards not only in repertoire but also in the new social etiquette they imposed. To show proper respect for the music, the audience was now expected to remain seated and silent during the performance, and orchestral concerts were soon characterized in religious terms. "One goes to the Conservatoire with religious devotion," said a French writer in 1846, "as the pious go to the temple of the Lord."[32] The orchestras institutionalized the emerging distinction between art and entertainment, according to which devotion to art was clearly a much higher taste than the desire to be entertained. In 1847 an article in the *Allgemeine musikalische Zeitung* echoed the new outlook when it said that "a scale, a spectrum of lighter and more serious goals, is natural to the affairs of musical activity." The scale was not entirely rigid: "Even in certain kinds of everyday amusement there can appear a glimmering of the *higher* light, and they can perhaps approach the kind of art which seeks the eternal."[33]

Though it was not obvious at the time, a gap was already opening between those with a taste for the classical repertoire and those who were interested in new music. From the start, both the public who attended symphony concerts and the musicians themselves had tended to be quite conservative, preferring to hear a limited number of classics rather than sample recent works by living composers. A kind of classically minded philistinism took root in this musical world, and it has proved stubbornly resistant to new styles ever since.

The problem went largely unnoticed, not only because the classical-music public was still quite small, but also because the most distinguished composers were among the most important advocates of the classical repertoire. Schumann, Berlioz, and Wagner all devoted themselves to this music and viewed it as a force that helped to foster good taste and thus supported their own creative endeavors. Only Wagner foresaw the difficulties the classical repertoire would eventually pose for their profession, but he did not go far in this direction. The dead masters held such formidable authority among their devotees that only the adherents of a militant and single-minded movement—the Wagnerians—dared oppose them.

II

By the time Wagner launched his career in the 1830s, musical idealism had firmly established itself as a small but highly vocal element in the musical world. Wagner's program for opera life, his vision of a purer musical community, emerged from the idealists' moral critique of musical life and the ethical code they propounded for the concert hall. Thus the social values he applied to musical life originated not in the opera house but in the symphony hall, a circumstance that explains why he always felt so alienated from the ways of the opera world. His values were those of the austere—most people would say puristic—advocates of the classical repertoire. The powerful influence of this idealist tradition is especially obvious in Wagner's writings.

It is not often remarked how novel a role Wagner had as a writer and a thinker. In the eighteenth century, few musicians wrote on the scientific and harmonic theory of music, on musical aesthetics, or even on day-to-day events in musical life; such writing was seen as a matter for educated amateurs. Moreover, many musicians had only marginal verbal literacy and evinced little interest in intellectual matters; they certainly did not write on subjects outside music itself. But from the turn of the nineteenth century on, a growing number of professional musicians became active in music theory, aesthetics, and history—among them Anton Reicha, Jean François Lesueur, the abbé Georg Vogler, François-Joseph Fétis, and Hector Berlioz. Wagner outdid them all, in a number of respects. Not only did he plunge headlong into discussions of political ideas, but he also pursued philosophical matters further than almost any other musician-writer of the nineteenth century. His philosophical writings were far below the level of an Arthur Schopenhauer or a Ludwig von Feuerbach—Wagner was first and foremost a theatrical entrepreneur, not a thinker—but his writings had considerably more to do with the initial spread of his reputation than did his music. He was a quick study; endowed with an extraordinary ability to write provocatively, he exploited the topics and ideas of the day in order to dramatize his musical goals.

The journalistic pieces that Wagner wrote from Paris between 1839 and 1842 vividly reveal his links to the idealist ethic. From the 1820s on, Paris was the power center of the music business and of fashion generally, and Wagner was instinctively suspicious of it. As something of a small-town boy—a Saxon who spoke French crudely—he was forced to come to grips with his most basic social values for music and, in so doing, drew richly upon the moral language of Rochlitz and E. T. A. Hoffmann. The nationalist theme so marked in his prose is often merely his way of voicing the young provincial's typical hostility to the values of the big city. In a piece entitled "German Music," Wagner played the German David against the commercial Goliath, Parisian commerce.

> One can take it then that in Germany music has branched out to the humblest, unlikeliest places—indeed that perhaps it has its roots there. For in this connection the higher, more brilliant society in Germany can be regarded merely as an extension of those humble, narrow circles. Let us assume then that it is among those quiet, unpretentious families that German music feels truly at home—and indeed among those families where music is regarded not as a medium for showing off, but as a spiritual refreshment German music really is at home.[34]

In "The Virtuoso and the Artist," he reiterated the belief that the performer must be the servant of the work of art:

> For what matters is that we should hear the work itself, ideally reproduced, and that our attention to it should in no wise be distracted by the special qualities of the performer. Unfortunately this legitimate demand is completely contradicted by the conditions under which music is performed in public today. All the public's interest and curiosity are directed in the first place to the performer's skill; it is only the pleasure in this which leads to consideration of the work performed. Not that one would dream of blaming the public, that tyrant whose favors we all seek![35]

Finding the worst abuses at the Paris Opéra, he warned his readers: "Very well, go to the Opéra and you will find that you haven't escaped from the concert and salon. Here too you will find a virtuoso with whom you will be compelled to come to terms. And this virtuoso, believe me, you will find the most dangerous of all, since opera is the sphere in which you can most easily be deceived."[36] Like any good idealist, he used the word *mode* (*Mode*) often in his rhetoric, as in this biting attack on Rossini's *Stabat Mater:* "Rossini is pious—all the world is pious, and the Parisian salons have been turned into praying-cells. It is extraordinary! So long as the man lives, he'll always be the mode, or makes it him? 'Tis a ticklish problem."[37]

Wagner quickly learned how to ridicule the philistine public. "What if already I have up my sleeve," he asked in one article, "compositions garnished with those horrible modernistic effects that go down with the superficial public and which even the most important artists haven't disdained in order to ingratiate themselves?"[38] He put into Beethoven's mouth words that damned applause: "There's nothing more to all that hand-clapping than mere vanity, you can take it from me: the people think it was their advice I was following when I made all those revisions. Now they want to repay me for my trouble, and so they cry 'bravo.'"[39] Another article described bitterly—and accurately—the difficulties artists faced in gaining high patrons and making themselves known in the world of commercial music: "But, my dear good friend, you grossly underestimate the difficulty of reaching the public. It is not a competition of talents that you have to face, but of reputations and of personal interests. If you have a reliable and influential patron, well and good; but without that, and with no money in your pocket the case is hopeless; you'll go under and no one will even notice."[40]

Wagner subscribed fully to the new principle that art was a higher realm than mere diversion. As he once put it in passing, "I write reports on the daily doings of the Parisian world of entertainment or art (call it what you will)."[41] In an account of an outdoor concert ("A Happy Evening"), he took the new idealism to its logical extreme. Though it was a lovely spring evening, he was concerned that visual aspects of the occasion seemed to distract listeners from the music: "We always pitied those unfortunates who at every concert, whether in gardens or in salons, felt themselves obliged, or indeed preferred, to sit right close to the orchestra. We found it impossible to understand how they could enjoy *looking* at the music instead of listening to it."[42] For him music was now an individual, indeed an internal experience. The change in social and aesthetic values in just one decade seems extraordinary; one cannot imagine Schubert or the *Schubertianer*—those who sang his music out in the Wienerwald—limiting musical experience thus.[43]

Wagner, too, swore himself to the musical trinity of Haydn,

Mozart, and Beethoven. His reports on the orchestra of the Paris Conservatoire—"that citadel of true and genuine music"[44]—show the power of the cause shared by the early exponents of the classical repertoire. Wagner was deeply awed by Anton Schindler, the amanuensis to Beethoven who had made a career touring Europe, retelling his experience.[45] "He has left his home," said Wagner, "driven by his master's voice to go out and preach to the heathens; for the light has not yet dawned in the world, we are still groping in the dark, ignorant of the master's mighty teachings." The religious theme suggests the passion of the new musical faith: "I must speak in priestlike tones, for the man to whom I refer is an anointed man—indeed he bears a striking resemblance to one of the apostles, whose appearance I cannot at the moment recall."[46] The same theme pervades "Death in Paris," the story of a poor, dying old man who talked his way into the back of the Conservatoire and gave his last will and testament to the narrator:

> "And now," the dying man resumed after a pause compelled by his growing weakness, "a last word regarding my faith. I believe in God, Mozart, and Beethoven, likewise in their disciples and apostles; I believe in the Holy Ghost and in the truth of the one and indivisible Art; . . . I believe in a Day of Judgement upon which all who dared to exploit this chaste and noble Art for the sake of profit, and all who in the baseness of their hearts dishonored and disgraced it for the sake of sensual pleasure will be fearfully punished; I believe that they will be condemned to listen to their own music for all eternity.[47]

Perhaps it was in this hall that Wagner first dreamed of Bayreuth; for the first time he had encountered a deep commitment to the highest musical principles—the commitment on which Bayreuth was to be founded.

The literary style of these pieces derived less from Hoffmann than from Berlioz, who was then the leading musical *feuilletoniste* in Paris. The Frenchman's tone may not have been as heavily moralistic as Wagner's, perhaps because his philosophical interests were not as wide, perhaps simply because he was not a North German Protestant. Yet their outlooks were quite the same in almost all other respects—hatred of commercial standardization ("Operas off the Assembly Line," as Jacques Barzun translates the title of a Berlioz piece)[48]; alienation from public taste; horror at the disrespect shown to music in performance; and devotion to the cult of the great masters. People outside the idealist clan seemed to enjoy reading Berlioz's high-minded pronouncements, even though they did not adhere to them in their own musical taste. Berlioz wrote for the *Journal des débats*, the leading organ of the *juste milieu*, and the popularity of his *feuilletons* fore-shadowed the general public's eventual acceptance of both musical idealism and Wagner's own ideas.

The most important common ground between Wagner and Berlioz was their distrust of the public. In a piece on the composer Gasparo Spontini, Berlioz wrote that "the stultification of the majority of the public, its lack of understanding in matters of imagination and the heart, its love of brilliant platitudes, the vulgarity of all its melodic and rhythmic instincts, have of necessity driven the performers along the road they now follow."[49] In an article entitled "Euphonia, or the Musical City: A Tale of the Future," he dreamed of a place where musicians would present their works to a public that shared their principles—a dream, as has often been noted, remarkably similar to Wagner's concept of Bayreuth. Berlioz envisaged Euphonia as "a great conservatory of music, since the exercise of this art is the sole purpose of its inhabitants' labors." Drawn from the most skilled and en-lightened musicians, its citizens would study how to communicate the composer's true musical intentions. Like Bayreuth, Euphonia was to have an artistic, not a political elite, since Berlioz saw the town not as a national center but simply as the place where the enlightened few would gather to pursue their special goals: "We Euphonians, it is true, preserve all those glories which art has firmly consecrated; but we are not 'the people' in the highest sense of the term. We represent, admit-tedly, a very small fragment of the people, lost amid the mass of civilized populations."[50]

The differences between their ideas are nonetheless instructive. Wagner gave Bayreuth a much broader, more philosophical rationale than Berlioz gave Euphonia, envisioning it as the means by which society could regenerate itself. Berlioz was interested in art alone, but in that respect he looked further into the future than Wagner did, conceiving Euphonia not just as a personal project but as a festival of new music run by composers for their common benefit. Wagner had little interest in helping his colleagues advance their work. Although he talked about playing music of Beethoven there, he conceived of Bayreuth as a center dedicated to the performance only of his own works and the education of performers to that end. Euphonia, in contrast, prefigured the activities of early Wagnerians and of Arnold Schoenberg. As such, Euphonia more than Bayreuth was to be dedicated to the composing profession as a whole—indeed, to the idea that new music needed supporting institutions of its own.

Still, Berlioz did not try to build Euphonia nor did he ever declare his full independence from the general public. Unlike Wagner at Bayreuth, he oriented his concerts toward a broad audience, presenting them in a horse palace (the Cirque Nationale) as something of an extravaganza. Since he wrote primarily for the symphony orchestra rather than the opera, he could give concerts of his own accord and suffer fewer of the interpretive indignities Wagner encountered in the complex process of mounting an opera. Wagner had much more reason to break with conventional institutions and build his own hall.

Between 1849 and 1851 Wagner put out a body of prose writings that were of primary significance in the development not only of his career but also of the early Wagnerian movement. The essays from *Art and Revolution* (1849) to *Opera and Drama* (1851) made his name all over Europe with a breadth and an intensity that his music had not effected. By the middle of the 1850s he was the bad boy, the troublemaker, and in some people's eyes the revolutionary of musical life. The character of his writing in this period contrasted greatly with that in the *Vormärz*. While earlier he styled himself as a *feuilletoniste*, as a musical and literary commentator, now he wrote as a polemicist and put forth what amounted to a social and cultural program for musical life. Through reform of the opera, and indeed all areas of musical institutions, he sought to bring about a regeneration of German society and a rebirth of the *Volk*. Though some of the themes in the essays remained after the 1850s (the idea of the *Volk,* especially), he abandoned the political ideas expressed in some of these essays after they had helped bring him such extraordinary prominence. While it can be argued that his political views shaped much of the original libretto of the *Ring* cycle, from the time of *Tristan,* in 1859, he was moving in a very different direction.[51]

The social and political issues raised in these essays were influenced by Wagner's experience in the Revolution of 1848, most important of all by his presence in Dresden during the uprising of the spring of 1849. Throughout the struggle his only important goal was to reform the theater of which he was head; at no time did he show an inclination to political leadership, as did his assistant August Röckel. But to gain what he wanted he entered so closely into revolutionary events—writing inflammatory newspaper articles and drawing up plans for the theater's governance—that he was eventually banished from the German states until he was granted amnesty in 1860.[52] Though he disavowed the revolution immediately after its repression, he continued to borrow from the kind of political language he had used in his pamphleteering. The idea of a social program for the opera grew out of his revolutionary experience, as did the critique of capitalism and class oppression that some interpreters find expressed in the libretto of the *Ring*. However much the revolution had failed, much of cultural life remained politicized on a broad plane. As he wrote to Liszt in June 1849, "Well, money have I not, but a tremendous desire to practice a little artistic terrorism."[53]

Principles of musical idealism had wider implications in these essays than in his earlier writings. In *The Art-Work of the Future* (1849) Wagner developed a broad philosophical scheme for the reshaping of musical life, mapping out the ways by which a true devotion to art could revivify the nation as well as musical institutions, forms, and performance practices. "The need of Fashion," he wrote, "is the diametrical antithesis of the need of Art; for the artistic need cannot possibly be present where Fashion is the lawgiver of life."[54] In *Art and Revolution* (1849) he put these ideas into a more explicitly political form, though remaining careful to characterize the work as a response to the ills brought by the revolution. The moral tone of the earlier rhetoric was now used to demand that the state assume responsibility for the arts—for programs that could end the abuses of musical commercialism. Free admission was the prerequisite for an artistically "free public":

> So long as money is indispensable for all the needs of life, so long as without pay there remains naught to man but air, and scarcely water: the measures to be taken can only provide that the actual stage-performances, to witness which the populace assembles, shall not take on the semblance of *work paid by the piece*—a mode of regarding them which confessedly leads to the most humiliating misconception of the character of art-productions—but it must be the duty of the State, or rather of the particular Community, to form a common purse from which to recompense the artists for their performance as a whole, and not in parts.[55]

Wagner spelled out his vision in greatest detail in his *Plan of Organi-*

zation of a German National Theater for the Kingdom of Saxony (1850). In this extraordinary product of revolutionary thinking he not only worked out a program for the reform of the Dresden opera house that he was directing but also cast his net over all musical institutions in the city and the court. Thus he brought aesthetic theory to bear upon the most practical details of management, programming, and the development of new works. The theater was no longer to be a "habit" or "a mere source of entertainment" (no music was to be played between the acts, for example) but would rather act as a force to reawaken national consciousness in Germany.[56] The director and the composers were to share authority in the manner that would best serve the composers' intentions.

Wagner delivered his most comprehensive attack upon the current state of the opera in *A Theater in Zürich* (1851). The city fathers of Zürich had offered him the directorship of the city's theater, convinced that he was the man who could revive it. Wagner ultimately refused their offer, deciding that he must not divert his energies into theatrical infighting, and instead conducted the concerts of the local music society. In his pamphlet, portions of which he reprinted in the Leipzig *Neue Zeitschrift für Musik,* he set forth his hopes and fears for the theater, in the process articulating ideas for what was to become the Bayreuth Festival. He depicted grand opera—"so-called," as he put it—as a frivolous extravagance devised for the ruling classes of the decadent French capital, that city he called "a mere husk without a kernel. . . . All the rich and notables, who settle in the monstrous world-metropolis for its out-of-the-way amusements and distractions, are driven by *ennui* and unsated cravings to the sumptuous chambers of this theater, there to get set before them the fullest draughts of entertainment."[57] Here again we see that powerful resentment that the less prosperous citizens of small cities felt toward the urban rich. It was moralistic through and through, the backlash of traditional local values against modern urban extravagance.

Wagner came back to the moral theme in 1861 in a pamphlet entitled *Zukunftsmusik* (*Music of the Future*), in which he tried to lay to rest the slogan that his opponents used to deride him. In sketching out the development of his principles and his career, he explained his refusal to undertake the directorship of a theater at this point in his life:

It would be a mad attempt, undoubtedly, to take an institute whose public function was almost exclusively directed to the distraction and amusement of people bored to death by pleasure—and further, to earning money to cover the cost of exhibitions reckoned for that end—and employ it for a diametrically opposite object, namely the snatching of a populace out from its vulgar interests of everyday, to attune it to a reverent reception of the highest and sincerest things the human mind can grasp.[58]

The moral quality of this passage is drawn from the idealist tradition, but it shows a more militant and more systematic social critique than his writing had before 1848 and reflects the powerful influence of his revolutionary experience.

The main values expressed in Wagner's program of reform came from outside the opera. They derived in part from nineteenth-century notions of the ancient Athenian theater, the loftiest and most idealistic intellectual authority he could point to. In antiquity, Wagner wrote, art did not have to worship "the golden calf of wholesale speculation."[59] But the most immediate model for his program was the symphony orchestras of his own time, or at least the ideals that these institutions espoused. Thus, though Wagner's concept owed much to the theater in theoretical terms, his program was essentially an effort to imbue the theater with the values and practices that had evolved outside it in the world of "absolute" music. He showed his hand in this regard in the plan for the Dresden opera, saying that "with tolerable certainty we may contend that those inspired by Beethoven's music have been more active and energetic citizens-of-state than those bewitched by Rossini, Bellini, and Donizetti, a class consisting for the most part of rich and lordly do-nothings."[60] That small German cities had the resources to support a symphony orchestra but not an opera house suggests the provincial roots of his moralism.

He was supported in this regard by trends in musical taste. During the 1840s an increasing number of amateurs seem to have become dissatisfied with the low musical taste and commercial hokum of virtuoso concerts, and the values of musical idealism began to attract a wider set of supporters. In 1845, for example, the London *Musical World* reported that "many musical enthusiasts are perpetually enquiring what remedy could be most serviceable in so dangerous a crisis" and suggested that concert programs be reformed by "a wholesale system of classification," to bring greater coherence to their fare.[61] A spirit of reform was in the air, a demand for higher and firmer musical standards.

A serious, indeed idealist mood took hold in musical life during the 1850s. A new generation of virtuosos—most prominently Henri Vieuxtemps, Joseph Joachim, and Anton Rubinstein—began to play the concertos and the chamber music of the classical masters along with their own works, gaining dignity by their association with these revered composers and seeing themselves as custodians of their tradition.[62] Conservatories, which were coming into their own just at this time, introduced a new academic curriculum based on the masterworks and sent a new generation of graduates trained in this repertoire out into musical life. Critics, now professionals, likewise established themselves as powerful figures in the music world, and men such as Eduard Hanslick in Vienna and James Davison in London came to be recognized as the interpreters of the classical works.[63]

By 1870, European musical taste was very different from what it had been fifty, indeed just twenty, years before. All but the most casual members of the musical world now venerated the classical masters. Symphony orchestras were no longer the isolated province of connoisseurs; they had become well-established civic institutions, many of the newer ones charging prices that even prosperous workers (artisans, especially) could afford. In the concert halls a strict social demeanor was replacing the more relaxed manners of earlier days, for the performances were now seen as rituals honoring high art. Moreover, opera houses no longer dominated musical life. A decline in the number of highly popular new works limited the attention that opera houses received. Rossini had long since retired; Bellini had died in 1835, Donizetti in 1848; and no new major work of Meyerbeer's was produced between 1849 and his death in 1864. Since Verdi did not elicit as passionate a response in northern Europe as his predecessors had, Italian opera did not hold the unchallenged position in musical fashion that it had held during the 1830s and 1840s.

Symphony orchestras had become virtual musical museums, for by 1850 most of them had accumulated repertoires that concentrated primarily upon the classical masterworks. The orchestra of the Paris Conservatoire went the furthest in this direction; by the late 1850s, about 90 percent of the works it performed were by dead composers, and in 1863 its directing board announced that it would consider new pieces from only the most famous composers, and only occasionally at that.[64] Even the opera repertoire had aged considerably, since the works of Rossini, Donizetti, and Bellini remained popular, along with a few by Mozart, Weber, and Cimarosa. If opera houses did not yet function as musical museums, neither did they play strictly to the present as they had in the earlier decades.[65]

The consolidation of the classical repertoire thus exposed the contradictions inherent in musical idealism. Reverence for the masterworks may initially have provided a standard of taste that supported such composers as Schumann and Wagner, but by the 1860s it was clear that this same taste was intolerant of much new music. A few critics began raising questions about the decreasing opportunities to hear the orchestras play new works. In 1847, for example, the Paris correspondent for the *Allgemeine musikalische Zeitung* said that at the Conservatoire "not much new music is offered in these so highly respected concerts these days; the public accustomed to attending is so used to Beethoven, Mozart, and Haydn that it is almost always cold to the unknown, and especially to the new.[66] This situation does not seem to have arisen from any disillusionment with new music in general, an attitude that appeared only at the turn of the twentieth century. Berlioz made a telling point when he observed that a new opera stood a much better chance of being accepted than a new orchestral work, simply because an opera was given more often. While opera houses had performances several nights a week for most of the year, sometimes offering long runs of a single work, few orchestras had more than a dozen annual concerts.[67]

While Wagner looked to the masterworks of Mozart and Beethoven as models for his own music—and wrote about them on numerous occasions—he had stronger fears about the growth of the classical repertory than did Berlioz. He was suspicious of the academicism involved in rediscovery of old music other than the acknowledged classics, thinking that it went against the emotional experience that he believed was so fundamental to music as an art. In 1840, for example, he saw little point in the presentation of Giovanni Pergolesi's *Stabat Mater* and regarded its sponsors as pedants. "The exclusive admirers of the ancient school have fallen into a vicious exaggeration, through attaching the same value to its imperfect canons as to the depth and thought revealed in its works." Evident in his remarks is the idea of musical progress, a notion that had been common since the early eighteenth century. "Grand and noble as are those thoughts," he said of the piece, "the details of material execution show inexperience and the gropings of a science in its infancy."[68]

Moreover, Wagner could not accept the intellectual elitism of the classical-music public, the insistence that musical learning was necessary to appreciate the masterworks. This precept went against his wish to democratize musical life, a theme that was particularly prominent in his thinking during the 1850s. In *The Art-Work of the Future,* for example, he challenged the authority of those who had set themselves up as the interpreters of the classical repertoire, claiming that they had usurped a role that was proper only to the performer:

> Art has become the private property of an artist-caste; its taste it offers to those alone who *understand* it; and for its understanding it demands a special study, aloof from actual life, the study of *art-learning.* This study, and the understanding to be attained thereby, each individual who has acquired the gold wherewith to pay [for] the proferred delicacies of art conceives today that he has made his own; if, however, we were to ask the Artist whether the great majority of art's amateurs are able to understand him in his best endeavors, he could only answer with a deep drawn sigh.[69]

Wagner's limited formal education made him especially sensitive to a musical intelligentsia that included such figures as François-Joseph Fétis (the head of the conservatory in Brussels) and Eduard Hanslick (professor of music history at the University of Vienna). Much of his intellectual bluster arose from his efforts to prove himself their equal.

Thus Wagner had a conflicted set of relationships to the idealist tradition. He was deeply influenced by its condemnation of virtuosity, embraced its lofty idea of art, and accepted the classical masterworks as musical models. Indeed, the general acceptance of the classical repertoire at mid-century greatly assisted his efforts; he was not a lone prophet. Yet Wagner disapproved of any interest in old music other then reverence for the acknowledged classics. From the 1850s on, he became increasingly independent of the idealist tradition and in some respects came into conflict with its spokesmen. For all the prestige of the symphony orchestras, their social model had not changed the moral tenor of opera life very much, and the musical theater remained the playground of the upper classes. Consequently Wagner left both the concert hall and the conventional opera to found his own musical utopia.

III

Having examined the social idealism of Wagner the essayist, we must now turn to the music itself and ask whether his music dramas can be regarded as "idealist" in any similar sense. Our attempt to answer this question is complicated by the fact that Wagner rarely wrote—or spoke—about his music in technical terms. In a letter to the young tenor Ludwig Köhler in 1853, he argued that "the *content* of an art-work is a matter for the individual [composer]" and that "one can talk about *that,* though naturally among artists alone: the laymen should never hear anything about it."[70] Though he wrote at some length on Beethoven's music, he abstained from doing the same for his own compositions.

Moreover, musicologists have found his theoretical writings about the dramas uninformative, if not downright misleading. In *Opera and Drama* (1851), for example, he insisted categorically that the poetry of an opera must dominate its music, but it is difficult to square this statement with the music dramas themselves. Though the vocal line may dominate the harmonic structure, acting as the most decisive component harmonically, this does not mean that the poetry proper controls the evolution of the music, except in a broad dramatic sense. It is particularly difficult to apply his ideas to the works after *Das Rheingold.*[71]

Wagner's contention that the poetry must be primary was, of course, very much an idealist attitude, since opera of the period provided many opportunities for the display of vocal virtuosity not closely tied to the text. So unpopular a viewpoint as Wagner's needed strong intellectual support. It is hard to escape the conclusion that Wagner exaggerated the role of the poetic element in his creative process in order to argue for a new, dramatically integrated kind of opera. While a case has been made that he was influenced to some degree by ancient Athenian models, that does not bring his music dramas any closer to his theory.[72] He tried to gain support for his operas by presenting his aesthetic views in an imposing philosophical manner and by claiming the most lofty precedents for the music dramas. But his rhetoric tended to outreach musical reality, and that has confused understanding of his works ever since.

Something of the same problem surrounds discussion of the structure of the dramas. In a time when an opera made money mostly through editions of individual numbers, Wagner took the idealist stance (though departing from it at times, as we have seen) that a music drama must have an organic structure. Many of his supporters have since portrayed the works as seamless webs of musical expression and have viewed their organicism as far superior to the adherence to set forms that was said to characterize the works of Rossini and Meyerbeer. The Wagnerian tradition has tended to fix this assumption about the music dramas, rejecting any critical perception of them that links them to either musical formalism or commercial exploitation.

The German theorist Konrad Lorenz was the first to oppose this way of perceiving Wagner's music. Dissecting the *Ring* in fine detail, he attempted to show that beneath the musical surface of what Wagner termed *unendliche Melodie* (unending melody) lay the standard forms of traditional German song and opera—the *Bar*, the *Bogen*, the strophe, and the rondo. To prove how strict a formalist Wagner had been, Lorenz tried to show not only that these forms pervaded his music but also that large-scale units followed them on a higher level.[13]

Lorenz now has few defenders, since it is recognized that he forced patterns, reductio ad absurdum, upon the music, with little sense of its dramatic meaning. But since the 1970s a new group of musicologists has turned to the subject without Lorenz's preconceptions and has taken quite a new approach to analysis of the operas. Robert Bailey led the way with an analysis of Act I of *Tristan und Isolde* and a theory about the overall musical plan of the *Ring*.[14] He showed that the most fundamental structure in Wagner's music is tonality, the manipulation of "families" of related keys that provide musical shape over long sections, a technique that can be traced back principally to the symphonies and operas of Mozart. Wagner laid down the scheme of keys while making sketches for the *Ring* between 1850 and 1853, and although his style underwent major changes after that time, that structure remained intact.

This new outlook on Wagner in part strengthens the case for a kind of musical idealism in his music—a focus on breadth of dramatic conception rather than on individual numbers. Wagner was not the first to take such a direction in opera, however. Robert Laudon has traced the evolution of such dramatic structure within the French and German operatic traditions, showing how composers such as Luigi Cherubini and Gasparo Spontini developed powerful new harmonies to use as integrating elements in opera. These techniques emerged in close relationship with new theories of harmony and form by such writers as Anton Reicha and François-Joseph Fétis.[75]

But at the same time, the new view of Wagner has revealed strong lines of symmetry in the music dramas that go against the idealist criterion of organic musical structure. Though these patterns do not amount to fixed forms in the sense in which Lorenz defined them, they do suggest that Wagner's musical thinking involved structure of a kind that the Wagnerian interpretive tradition has generally denied. In analyzing Act I of *Tristan,* for example, Bailey delineates ten "periods," each focused upon a single dramatic event and upon a single key (generally using both the major and minor modes in each period). Symmetries appear in the ordering of the periods according to the disposition of keys, repetitions, and the like; events in the first five periods have direct parallels in the last five. Bailey is the first to say that proof of the analysis must come in the listening, and his ideas must not be written off as mere intellectual theorizing.

Ultimately, however, these structures simply reveal Wagner's vast technical facility at applying his idealist principles. Once we clear away the ideas he advanced for tactical reasons—chiefly the notion of the absolute predominance of poetry in his operas—we can see a real coherence between his ideas and the works themselves. To a historian, that coherence is not essentially philosophical, as suggested by nineteenth-century (or even latter-day) Wagnerians; it is rather the result of long-range dramatic planning, in both its musical and its poetic aspects.

Musical and social aspects came together in the composition of his operas in another way. Just as the values he applied to musical life came directly from the symphonic tradition, so an important aspect of his musical technique was inspired by his deep knowledge of the classical symphony. His style exhibits the strong influence of the techniques used by Mozart and Beethoven in the development of motives—fragmenting them, extending them, building sequences around them, and making melody a dynamic, linear force.[76] Laudon has shown how some French and German composers—the Parisian Cherubini most prominent among them—had begun to do the same. The direction of the flow of musical influence between opera and instrumental music was thus now the reverse of what it had been in the classical period. In the eighteenth century, the symphony had emerged in large part out of the aria and the overture; now the classical symphony affected opera writing just as deeply. That is not to say, however, that the music dramas should be considered "absolute" music, or indeed symphonies put on stage, as has sometimes been argued. It can be shown that the musical functions of leitmotives in the *Ring* sometimes operate quite independently of their nomenclature, but that does not deny their dramatic purpose.[77] Though Wagner's personal experience of music and musical life was primarily in the symphonic tradition, he was first and foremost a man of the theater.

IV

We have seen how Wagner's ideas about musical life and about his operas grew out of musical idealism but took that tradition in something of a new direction. If we now turn to the early history of German Wagnerism in the 1850s and 1860s, we will see that the movement reoriented these values even more than the Master himself did. We can discern a layering of historical influences in the ideas and activities of Wagnerism. In its critique of commercialism and its demand that performance not overshadow the music, the movement maintained links to the idealist tradition. From Wagner it received a political thrust and a suspicion of musical historicism, born of conflict with the classical-music establishment. But the German Wagnerians themselves pressed the implications inherent in the emerging division between new music and the classical repertoire much farther. If Wagner was pragmatic in his main goals, aiming primarily at having his works performed in the way he wanted, his followers turned their ideals into a matter of party. From that came the conception of musical modernism.

The continuity between the stages of musical idealism can best be seen in the rhetoric of the Wagnerians. The language developed earlier by musical idealists to castigate shallow virtuosity proved useful in the battle against frivolous vocalism in the opera. Merciless in the use of pejorative vocabulary, Wagnerian writing kept the rich moral tone of early nineteenth-century idealism. The word *mode* remained every bit as powerful as before, even when put in neo–Hegelian terms. In 1884, for example, the beautifully designed *Bayreuther Festblätter im Wort und Bild,* a collection of articles published by the International Richard Wagner Society in Bayreuth, included a piece by Friedrich Haussegger called "Richard Wagner and Modism." After quoting the Master many times on the subject, Hausegger said that Wagner was intensely aware of the opposition between a spontaneous, creative drive and the external world, which contradicts its process of becoming with the power of convention, authority, and mode."[78]

The terms used by the idealists to criticize the quest for gain also remained central to Wagnerian writing. In the same book, Hans von Wolzogen, one of the key members of the Bayreuth circle, attacked the commercialism of opera life: "Before the Bayreuth Festival all one found was a strictly outward kind of popular excitement, which, as the ruling taste, was run as a business for worthless, ephemeral worldly goods, aimed toward financial gain and manipulation of the bad taste of the mass of the people."[79] Bayreuth thus engendered a devotion quite similar to that which the symphony orchestras had focused on Beethoven earlier in the century; indeed, what Wolzogen said about the Bayreuth Festival was remarkably similar to what the idealists had said about the orchestra of the Paris Conservatoire forty years earlier.

The Wagnerians whose chief concerns were musical generally remained more faithful to the idealist tradition than those who were drawn to the movement primarily by their literary interests. Writers such as Rochlitz, Fétis, and Schumann retained a stern moral perspective and did not flirt with such movements as Saint-Simonianism or other exotic cults; Franz Liszt was rather an exception in this regard. Even though Wagner introduced rich sexual themes and a touch of theosophy into his librettos and other writings, in his musical values he remained a conservative moralist throughout his life. The German Wagnerians discussed later in this chapter also tended to stay within this rather Victorian ethic, but the moralistic tendency weakened among literary figures who transplanted Wagnerian ideas into other intellectual areas. As Anne Dzamba Sessa has shown, some English Wagnerians associated his music with the revolt against moral prudery and drew it into movements for free love, theosophy, vegetarianism, and other radical causes.[80] After 1870, French Wagnerians showed similar tendencies as they gravitated toward a hermetic conception of poetic meaning. In Paris especially, the proponents of these ideas clashed with the less outlandish, more musical Wagnerians.

Early German Wagnerism arose less from the impact of Wagner's music than from that of his essays. While by 1850 his operas had been performed in only a few cities, his essays immediately made their way around Europe, either through publication or through reports in the music journals. Almost everywhere they raised a storm of criticism against their presumptuous author—a mere musician who claimed to have the secret for translating Greek tragedy into modern form—and against the categorical manner in which he dismissed the conventions of opera life. In the repressive mood of postrevolutionary Europe, he was seen as a dangerous man, someone who had attacked the very foundations of musical life and thereby the social order. The scale of the controversy has been rivaled on only a few other occasions in musical life. We might compare it to the legendary dispute over J.-J. Rousseau's *Lettre sur la musique française* in 1753, or to that over John Cage's *4' 33"*, the "silent" work of 1952 that implicitly attacked the classical-music concert as a moribund institution. All three iconoclasts raised issues that were to trouble musical life profoundly for decades thereafter.[81]

The shift of public taste toward the classics that occurred at mid-century was in part responsible for the severity of the controversy. Once the great masters had been established as the highest source of musical authority, the professionals who had taken on powerful positions as interpreters of the classics—critics, academics, and leading performers—viewed with alarm anyone who called for further reform of musical life. The conflict was not so much generational (young Eduard Hanslick, for example, was anti-Wagnerian fairly early on) as it was dialectical: the rise to power of a new group led to the reorientation of all the parties. Thus, for example, Fétis launched a full-scale attack on Wagner in 1852 in the *Revue et gazette musicale*, the Paris journal that had first championed the classical repertory during the 1830s. The innovator had now become the conservative.

Those who rushed to Wagner's defense then began a movement. In an article published in 1884, Richard Pohl, Wagnerism's first historian, suggested that the movement was born in 1852.[82] Pohl maintained that the production of *Lohengrin* in Weimar on August 28, 1850, which gathered together the composer's strongest supporters—Hans von Bülow, Carl Klindworth, Peter Cornelius, August Röckel, and their host Franz Liszt—was the most important event in the movement's prehistory. Nevertheless, Wagner's support was limited to a scattering of dedicated followers until January 1, 1852, when Franz Brendel, editor of the *Neue Zeitschrift für Musik* in Leipzig, announced that the magazine would dedicate itself to furthering the cause of Richard Wagner and his music. Henceforth Wagnerism was a self-conscious movement, and Brendel's journal was its official organ.

The journal's central role in the championing of Wagner shows how deeply the movement was rooted in the idealist tradition of musical life. Begun by Robert Schumann in 1834, the *Neue Zeitschrift für Musik* was one of the few music publications not sponsored by a major music publisher; its founders intended to avoid the compromises they thought characteristic of other journals, especially the influential *Allgemeine musikalische Zeitung*. However much the editors of the older magazine had inveighed against commercialism, they were subsidized by the publishing firm of Breitkopf & Härtel and were thus obliged to tread lightly when choosing reviewers for the works put out by the firm. Schumann coined the term *Davidsbündler* for his idealistic followers and for the articles in which they attacked the Goliath of the musical press. We should not, however, exaggerate the distinction between the two journals, for the older one had an honorable intellectual tradition, and the upstart sheet attacked partly out of personal spite.[83] Thus when Brendel took over as editor in 1843, he followed Eduard Rochlitz and Robert Schumann as the third generation of idealists in music journalism.

Brendel did not mince words in his 1852 announcement. After opening with a wide-ranging discussion of the ills of musical life, he said that the time had come to speak with complete frankness about what ought to be done: "More and more two parties are diverging from each other, so different from the calm old days; on the one hand there is thoughtlessness and indifference, and on the other energetic movement in progressive directions. The times demand that a clear position be taken by a music magazine, a specific party position." He related how, from his first awareness of Wagner, he had seen him as his leader: "As far as I am concerned, the arrival of Richard Wagner was of prime significance. I found in him more with which I could agree, I found in him a determination to act for the things I struggle for, and I found in him as well new things such as can be found only in a path-breaking, creative artist, new things which reveal for us a distinct ideal for the future." The "music of the future" had already become a derogatory catchword for Wagner, and Brendel began employing it in a positive sense. Even though Wagner objected to its use, his followers were to use it as their intellectual standard. Brendel made clear that he was just as serious about the word *Partei:* "Determined adherence to party is therefore the new principle for which I call, determined struggle against that which is not vital, opposition to that thoughtless routine which frustrates striving for the better."[84]

The political origins of Brendel's language are manifest. Such phrases as "determined adherence to party" and "energetic movement in progressive directions" were borrowed directly from the vocabulary of the liberals, among whom the Wagnerians undoubtedly intended to rally support. Again, as in Wagner's case, there is a distinct contrast between the journal's conduct before and after the *Vormärz,* since if it had been contentious before 1848, it was now factional and militant and acted in a rather mean-spirited way in its vendetta against musical conservatives. In 1853 a journal critical of the *Neue Zeitschrift* characterized the change in the journal's approach to issues: "If the earlier faction only showed itself in general ways—in a vague sense of fermentation—the new one presents itself with a crystal-clear program."[85] The word *program* carried strong political overtones; one could indeed describe the development of the liberal movement during the 1840s and 1850s in much the same terms. It is also interesting to find the word *progressive* used as a Wagnerian slogan, since it was usually associated with the more leftist liberals. Brendel in fact articulated leftist views, especially on social equality for women, servants, and workers in the craft trades, in another journal that he edited between 1856 and 1861.[86]

The militancy of the early Wagnerians may seem contradictory to the usual assumptions about the conservative politics of the 1850s. But as J. L. Snell has pointed out, even though the Revolution of 1848 must be accounted a failure in its main goals, it initiated many of the most important tendencies in the democratic movement for the rest of the century. The revolutionary experience politicized much of the population and opened up new kinds of political activity—organizing, program building, and propagandizing—that affected musical life in a vital way. While revolution as a means of protest was dead, the tools of dissident political activity were now far richer than previously, and it makes sense that they would be used again in a relatively safe artistic context. It may also seem odd to ascribe militancy to bourgeois liberals. Here again, even though they ultimately failed to gain control of German politics, we should not underrate their political vitality. These educated middle class men were using a politically weighted vocabulary during a highly repressive era, and, while such language was usually permitted when applied to artistic issues, they were still taking a risk in writing in such a manner.[87]

Wagner did not do much to lead the movement, however. Brendel's declaration of support for him came after the journal had published excerpts from Wagner's writings, introduced and annotated by young Theodore Uhlig. Uhlig, a violinist in the Dresden opera orchestra that Wagner had directed, was the most devoted disciple of all, a man who dropped his own composing to write about Wagner, to help him find opportunities for performance of his works in Germany, and in effect to act as amanuensis through the mail.[88] Brendel, by comparison, kept his distance from Wagner, devoting himself to the journal and pursuing his own ambitions as a historian of music. Indeed, the 1852 article seems to have come about in part because Wagner grumbled about a few critical comments concerning him that had slipped into the journal, leading him to threaten not to contribute to it in the future.[89] But a letter to Uhlig in early January showed a new attitude, evidently a response to the news of Brendel's announcement of support: "Brendel has written me; his letter and his latest explanations in specimen sheet have somewhat disposed me in his favor. His recent fervor, nay enthusiasm, rejoices me. Now I will again write a letter for his paper."[90]

Though Wagner could thus demand rigid partisanship among his followers, he had remarkably little to do with the day-to-day conduct of the movement. Prevented from returning to Germany until 1860, and still watched by the police wherever he went, he set his mind on a theatrical dream, not on musical politics. However much he welcomed support, he does not seem to have been greatly interested in generating an artistic movement. His central interest from this time on was the presentation of the *Ring* in as ideal a setting as possible, and Wagnerism concerned him only as much as it helped him to achieve that goal.[91] This is not to say that he was a complete pragmatist, since he never ceased to go off on wild intellectual tangents. But he did not take it upon himself to develop the Wagnerian movement for itself alone and indeed sometimes tried to impede its development.

The real leader of the movement was Liszt. Having become the most sought-after virtuoso of his time, a lion of salons all across Europe, he made a drastic shift in careers in the late 1840s when he began limiting his performances at the keyboard and took the position of Kapellmeister for the duke of Saxe-Coburg-Meiningen in Weimar in 1848. For a fashionable virtuoso he had always had unusually educated tastes; he periodically had played works by Beethoven and had kept in touch with leaders of the classical-music scene. After the late 1840s, his composing became increasingly symphonic rather than soloistic, focused on the tone poem and large-scale cantatas. Portraying himself as the most serious of composers, and leader of the avant-garde, he advocated such progressive techniques as chromaticism and tone painting, in the manner of a prophet. Liszt proceeded to become a musical politician par excellence, dominating the headlines even more frequently than Wagner. He drew upon his fame and fortune, and his connections in high places all over Europe, to gather about him all the musicians sympathetic to his ideas. This group, known as the Neuromantiker (New Romantics) or the Neue deutsche Schule (New German School) was soon regarded by everyone conversant with musical matters as constituting a cabal.[92]

From Liszt's standpoint, the movement gathering behind Wagner was an impetus to the development of the most progressive kinds of composition and the highest standards of taste. He was increasingly concerned about the hardening of the classical concert repertoire, which he saw as a threat to innovative composers, and he used Wagnerism to put pressure on the musical world to gain support for composers of his own school. Of course, he did not entirely agree with Wagner's theory of the music drama, and his own compositional interests did not include opera. But he felt comfortable enough with Wagner's main principles so that he threw himself behind the movement with all the forces he could muster.

Liszt orchestrated the struggle with political finesse. In 1850, for example, in writing to Wagner about plans for the upcoming production of Lohengrin, he specified that "the press will not be forgotten, and suitable and seriously-conceived articles will appear successively in several papers."[93] In 1853 he passed on the advice that "Brendel has grand schemes, which he will probably communicate to you," suggesting that they were thinking of establishing another journal which would be even more strongly partisan of Wagner.[94] The competing Leipzig Fliegende Blätter told the tale on all this that same year: "[Wagner's] advocates, partly under the aegis of Liszt, partly under the banner of the Neue Zeitschrift für Musik in Leipzig, have during the last few years made stirring shows of propaganda for the Master with enthusiasm in word and deed."[95]

Attitudes toward the classical repertoire were also divided along factional lines. In September 1848 the Neue Zeitschrift attacked the growing historicism of musical taste:

No rational person can say that the eternal significance of the Masters can be denied, any more than Homer, Sophocles, Raphael, etc. might be taken as unimportant. The conservative party must agree that all these great figures from the past have taken their intellectual stances from conditions which do not apply to the present. . . . The artist must not cut himself off from his time and attach his existence to the past; it is fundamentally false to set up the past against the present. Whoever exclusively praises the great Masters of the past and still claims to lead the present, such a person slanders and disdains his time, indeed should not complain when he is not respected in the present.[96]

Liszt suggested the same polarization of attitudes in a letter he wrote to Wagner in 1852. In discussing the publication of Wagner's works by Breitkopf & Härtel, he advised him that "the Härtels belong to the 'moderate party of progress,' and are influenced by several friends of the so-called historical school." The publishers had kept their distance from the new avant-garde but were eager to print Wagner's scores, thereby earning Liszt's description of them as belonging to the "moderate party of progress." Nonetheless, he admitted that "your and my friends Pohl, Ritter, Brendel, etc., are a little in their bad books."[97]

The movement was exceedingly clannish. Liszt and his colleagues tried to use the slogans of musical idealism to establish their leadership over both the composing profession and the music-loving public. If one did not follow their lead, they implied, one was part of the philistine pack. Another article in *Fliegende Blätter*—"Where Is the Talk about the Musical Future Coming from, and What Are Its Consequences?"— threw the old rhetoric back in the faces of the Wagnerians. The movement was characterized as an "epidemic" of "future telling": "Even if you do not accept the comparison with an epidemic, you will agree that it is a mode, and by the same interpretation let us see it as the propagation of empty future telling. The power of a mode shouldn't intimidate anybody, even if the most unreasonable modes sometimes get supporters."[98] The journal also tried to remind Liszt that he had once favored Berlioz, Schumann, Spohr, and other composers now in disfavor among many Wagnerians. "Liszt may now strive for the recognition of Wagner's works by word and deed, certainly a praiseworthy thing," it remarked, but "he cannot be a factionalist in matters of art, since he has not always been one-sided in his opinions."[99]

In the phrase "future telling" we are observing among these Wagnerians the first current of modernism in musical culture. As used here, the term *modernism* refers not to a trend involving the characteristics of works of art in themselves but rather to their perception and manipulation—that is, to the assertion by an avant-garde that such works establish the lines that taste must follow. Musical modernism emerged in a period when the classical repertoire was being systematized, a situation that imparted a special urgency to the new movement. The German Wagnerians made the first significant response to this reorientation in taste; they tried to reassert the primacy of new music by defining it as modern, indeed as controversial. Berlioz had made no such assertion, for he wrote before the classical repertoire became predominant, did not see Euphonia in partisan terms, and did not argue for his music on the grounds of its modernity. When the Wagnerians promulgated the notion of a "progressive" musical style, however, they made modernism a permanent part of our musical life. By associating forward-looking styles with the highest musical principles, they established the primary justification for contemporary avant-garde music. Yet for all its novelty, their idea derived from the most basic principle of musical idealism, from the demand that music be taken seriously, and that helped modernism to acquire a powerful public role.

In 1859 the Wagnerians set up an organization that had considerable significance not only in the history of their movement but also in the evolving social basis of new music. On June 1 the Tonkünstler-Versammlung (Musicians League) of Leipzig founded the Allgemeine deutsche Musikverein (General German Music Association), an organization intended to further Wagnerian ideals for reform of musical life on a national scale. The club, which drew most of its members from outlying areas of Saxony and a few from Prague, was composed primarily of musicians but also included a few schoolteachers and professionals, an industrialist, and a wealthy landowner from Oberlausnitz.[100] The leadership came primarily from those who had contributed to the *Neue Zeitschrift für Musik*. A description of the new society's principles, written by Pohl, greatly resembles the political style of Wagner's postrevolutionary essays in calling for "a principled, systematically constructed program raising the call for musical progress; . . . establishment of personal ties and closer relationships among common minds; the strengthening through these means of the sense of purpose among the musically active; finally the foundation of a General German Music Association."[101]

The society included among its goals the promotion of German music, support for the careers of professional musicians, and the unification of the nation's musical life. The appeal to German national unity came at the very time of the founding of the Nationalverein (National Association), the liberal political organization formed to advance German unification, and the leaders of the Musikverein may have hoped to obtain such liberals as members. The promise to work for the musicians' interests coincided with an idea being promoted by new organizations all across Europe—that of guaranteeing payment of performing fees and royalties. Behind the stated goals of the Musikverein lay a strong sense of faction. In an article about the founding of the organization, Brendel reaffirmed "music of the future" as his slogan, giving it blatantly political overtones by calling it "the slogan of the party of the opposition." He suggested that the organization was rooted in the idealist tradition: "The present-day situation of parties is a consequence of an older tendency which has since manifested itself in events themselves. Struggles between parties are necessary to bring clarity to contemporary opinion. . . . The annual meetings have the purpose of awakening a common spirit among artists, and of spreading the awareness of a common struggle."[102]

The main activity of the Musikverein was an annual music festival, generally held in Weimar, in the early years. Liszt was the godfather of it all; musicians—composers especially—went to pay their respects to the man whom they saw as the dominant figure in their profession.[103] The programs were focused upon new works by composers associated with Liszt's school of new music and works from the classical repertoire that were not often played in conventional concerts. The choice of new works came under heavy criticism for their sectarian bias, though Pohl, showing himself uneasy on this question, endeavored to point out that pieces by such non-Wagnerians as Ignaz Moscheles, Ferdinand David, Luigi Riccius, and Alfred Jaell had been included.[104]

The Musikverein set itself against the policy of the symphony orchestras, which, as we have seen, now mostly played works by the dead masters. An article about the 1864 festival listed the few recent works considered to be of any value that had been presented at the concerts of the Leipzig Gewandhaus Orchestra that season, suggesting, probably naively, that they were included to satisfy popular demand and to increase the profits of the orchestra's pension fund. Other than that, the chronicle argued, the orchestra had offered only trivial new concertos designed to bring "artificial triumphant processions of virtuosi."[105] The article also criticized the conservatism of musical taste in other places, lamenting particularly that "England, as far as the progressive movement is concerned, is increasingly bound only to the Masters."[106]

The Musikverein did not, however, achieve much beyond its annual festivals. In 1872 a writer in the *Neue Zeitschrift für Musik* called upon the organization to set up local concerts in the larger cities to serve as "salons" for presenting new works, much as was done in the art world. Each city, the author suggested, should have a committee to choose the pieces.[107] But the Musikverein was too much the creature of Liszt and Brendel to become a broadly based national organization. Little is known of its later history. The present opinion is, that while it lasted into the twentieth century, it receded in prominence after Brendel's death in 1868 and Liszt's withdrawal from the Weimar court, which was nearly complete by that time. We read of it upon occasion when the more militant local musicians' societies wanted to stress their links to the radical tradition of Wagner and Liszt.[108]

The most important accomplishment of the Musikverein lay in its very failure to unify German musical life. It was necessarily divisive to build a social and intellectual basis for concerts devoted to avant-garde music, as the organization did. As Karl Storck suggested in a probing study of German musical life published at the turn of the century, the Musikverein was not "general" at all, despite the prominence of the word in its title.[109] By then its public was made up overwhelmingly of music professionals—composers, performers, and critics—because most concertgoers did not care for its choice of music. As another commentator of that time put it, the organization chose to wage a futile battle against the classical repertoire, with the result that "today just as fifty years ago, we still hear 'that awful Wagner' or 'that awful Liszt.'"[110] Even though the music of both composers was performed often enough, the vast majority of the concertgoing public balked at the idea of listening to programs devoted primarily to new music written under their influence. Without intending it, the Musikverein had inaugurated a kind of concert that has been the basis of the new-music world ever since. Since symphony orchestras and chamber music ensembles—not to speak of fashionable singers—now generally resisted all but fairly conservative new works, composers needed places where they could present their music, if only to their colleagues and a few friends.

Thus even though the Musikverein did not become a major institution, the values it propounded persisted among socially and musically progressive musicians and amateurs. From the 1870s through the First

World War, a wide range of writings on the problems of musical life appeared that owed much to Wagner's social idealism—his critique of musical institutions, his call for regeneration through the *Volk,* and his vision of a musical culture based upon true artistic principles.[111] The current of musical modernism that first appeared under the leadership of Liszt grew in an unorganized but still quite distinctive and influential way. The musicians and amateurs who followed in this path had increasingly little to do with the Wagnerian establishment in Bayreuth, whose leaders were hostile to the idea of performing new works in the Festspielhaus.[112] Members of the avant-garde tended to be politically on the left, unlike the reactionary Bayreuth circle, though they were usually still nationalist in their own way; their idea of social regeneration included the democratization of musical life. We need to know a lot more about the activities of these radical Wagnerians on the local level, for they included many of the most vital figures in the reform and development of concerts and the opera.

The most important example of such activity by avant-garde Wagnerians occurred in Vienna. As William McGrath has pointed out in his superb study, during the 1870s and 1880s Wagnerian ideas exerted a powerful influence on a diverse group of young intellectuals at the university, among them the composer Gustav Mahler and the future socialist leader Victor Adler.[113] Growing up in the period when Austria was being industrialized, these young men were disturbed by the divisions that this process was creating in society and by the resistance to any political or social reforms among bourgeois liberal leaders. Wagner offered a rich vision of how society could be regenerated and reunited to its deepest traditions. He also touched their disillusionment with the narrow rationalism of positivist thought, offering new perspectives upon human emotions. Wagner's music dramas—especially when heard during a pilgrimage to Bayreuth—provided a focal point for the diverse ideas they had imbibed from Schopenhauer, Nietzsche, and such movements as vegetarianism and *völkisch* nationalism. While the various members of the group (dubbed the Pernerstorfer Circle) went their separate ways after the 1880s, McGrath depicts a unity of intellectual impulse, indeed a common idealism, which shaped their minds at a critical time in their lives.

The Akademische Wagner-Verein (Academic Wagner Society), founded in Vienna in 1872, attempted to put these ideas into practice. Supported primarily by university and conservatory students, it had a more strictly musical emphasis than the Wagner societies that sprang up elsewhere in Europe. Literary discussions, for example, generally took place in meetings of other groups such as the Pernerstorfer Circle, even though many of the same people belonged to both groups. In its early years, the Wagner Society performed an important role in helping to expand the tiny and cliquish Viennese concert world. Contrary to the legend of Musikstadt Wien, the city had remarkably few concerts by professional orchestras before the turn of the century—a mere twelve per year as opposed to a minimum of one hundred (and often almost twice that) in London and Paris. Since the seats for the concerts by the Philharmonic Orchestra and the Society of the Friends of Music were passed down as legacies through wills, few Viennese were able to hear the classical repertoire played by the city's famous orchestras.[114] (Students at the conservatory, however, were given special access, at least to standing room.) During the late 1870s and 1880s the Wagner Society put on concerts featuring excerpts from the music dramas, sometimes scheduling world-renowned performers. In 1887 Albert Gutmann, the city's leading concert manager and a considerable Wagnerian, proposed a series of low-priced orchestral concerts, but the project was reportedly killed by the two established orchestras.[115] In 1899, Wagnerians such as Felix Mottl and Joseph Schalk helped to establish the city's first orchestral series with low-priced tickets. It was performed by the Concert Orchestra, later renamed the Vienna Symphony Orchestra.[116]

But the Wagner Society also moved in a very different direction—toward the support of new music. Its attention was focused primarily upon Hugo Wolf, who had quickly been taken into the Wagnerian fold after arriving in Vienna in 1875. His music became the focus of the organization's concerts during the second half of the 1880s, bringing him a great deal of patronage in the process. For example, in 1883 he was given the use of a fine home by a wealthy leather merchant who was a devoted Wagnerian, and in 1890 a group within the Wagner Society pooled money to provide him with a stable income.[117] The role of a formal organization in marshaling people, funds, and performing opportunities for Wolf and other composers was a distinct innovation compared to the strictly personal assistance that friends had given Franz Schubert in the 1820s.

The Wagner Society became deeply divided over the importance of this focus to its activities. The society was no longer predominantly a student group, and many of the older and musically more conservative

members wanted to follow the Wagnerian leaders in Bayreuth in working to promote only the music of the Master. In 1898 the supporters of
Wolf set up the Hugo Wolf Society to continue their advocacy of this
composer's work and stimulated a similar organization in Berlin.[118]
Wolf attacked the leaders of the Wagner Society for presenting concerts
on an ever-larger scale with the very kind of commercialism that
Wagner had sought to escape. The conflict stemmed in part from the
increasing focus upon chamber music among the more radical composers, who had difficulty getting their orchestral works performed and
even at that feared that writing for the symphony orchestras would tie
them to a philistine public.[119]

The Viennese Wagnerian movement was thus torn between popu-
larization and artistic separatism. Some of the Viennese Wagnerians,
following their Master's philosophy, worked to expand the size of the
concert going public; others drifted away from the general public in
establishing programs designed to support the music the public did not
like. But at that very point in history the two goals were becoming less
and less compatible. During the 1890s there began a powerful tendency
for avant-garde musicians to radically reject public taste and to define a
separate role for themselves both socially and musically. The cult of
Hugo Wolf not only continued the defense of new music by Liszt's
Musikverein; it also led to the much more decisive declaration of
independence for composers made by Arnold Schoenberg after the turn
of the twentieth century. And in this way one strand of musical idealism
diverged into a radical form of modernism.

We can see the avant-garde's alienation from the general public
vividly expressed in the feud between the followers of Brahms and
Wagner. Though the episode had many dimensions, one important
factor was the identification of Brahms by his opponents with the small,
conservative public of the Vienna Philharmonic Orchestra—and thus
with the social elite that was so much hated by many members of the
younger generation. By the 1880s Brahms had acquired an eminent
status as dean of Viennese composers, and his works were often performed at the Philharmonic concerts.[120] The youthful Wagnerians saw
an enormous injustice in the contrast between his social position and
Wolf's, especially when they saw Brahms, so unapproachable in his
authority, sitting in a box at the Philharmonic concerts. As the critic
Max Graf later wrote, "Hugo Wolf belonged to us and we belonged to
him. There is a secret understanding among young men of the same

generation. So we stared at the pale man [i.e., Wolf] who stood in the standing-room section, just like ourselves, while Brahms sat in a box like God sitting on high."[121]

Wolf's savagely critical comments about the music of Brahms seem to reflect the depth of social alienation among these men and to augur the cultural revolution experienced by the following generation. He inveighed against "that blankness, shallowness, and cowardice" in the E Minor Symphony and the overly analytical "drive to artistic self-dissection" (kunstlerischen Selbstzerfleischungstrieb) he found in Brahms's style. Of this powerful man's influence he wrote, "The press orders: You must play Brahms, or we will not go to hear your concert."[122]

Yet the Wagnerian and Brahmsian factions were both branches of the idealist tradition. It was Brahms, after all, who wrote concertos of ultimate seriousness, works that shunned the technical display and sentimentality characteristic of the genre during the late nineteenth century. He refused to pander to the frivolous public, even though editions of his songs did earn him a decent income. His idealism limited his popularity among the music public, many of whom wanted to hear either classics or saccharin new concertos. As Peter Gay has shown in his probing discussion of the reception of Brahms in this period, many reviews pictured his music as difficult, overly intellectual, and unimaginative.[123] But let us not dwell too much on Brahms as "victim" of the public, or indeed of the Wagnerians, for that strain of musical thinking has, I think, a narrowing effect upon discussion of the role of new music in society. It is more to the point to see the Viennese dispute in a broader perspective and to view it as the fundamental transformation in musical taste that led to decreasing public interest in any kind of new music. If the Wagnerians were ungrateful to their master, it was because their profession was in a state of crisis, and that affected Brahms just as keenly as the modernists.

One might say that the history of Wagnerism in Vienna culminated in Arnold Schoenberg. Born in Vienna in 1874, Schoenberg became a student at the end of the most active period of the Wagner Society and did not identify himself with the movement. Brahms's musical influence on him was probably greater than Wagner's; the title of Schoenberg's essay "Brahms the Progressive" (1933/1947) illustrates how he applied the Wagnerian vocabulary to the movement's former rival.[124] But his social and cultural leadership among composers derived directly from Wagnerism, for he in effect summoned the members of his profession to declare their independence from the conventional musical world. If his music had a revolutionary impact upon composition, his social influence brought composers to the radical step of organizing their own institutions in order to bring their music to the small, enlightened public that would understand it. We should note, however, that he never rejected the models of the classical masterworks: he in fact demanded that his students have an intimate knowledge of those works before beginning composition, and he programmed lesser-known classics at his concerts.[125]

His organizations were the original prototype of the new-music concerts found around the world today. In 1903 he helped Alexander Zemlinsky set up a short-lived society of this sort, and in 1919 he began the Verein für Privat-Aufführungen (Society for Private Performances) in Vienna, through which his social philosophy for new music became widely known.[126] His exclusion of the press from these concerts demonstrates Schoenberg's militance and independence, and also that of his followers. He contributed as well to the founding of the International Society for Contemporary music in 1922, an organization still in existence today. Similar concerts have since appeared in almost every major city in Europe and America—among them the Donaueschingen Festival in Baden-Baden, the Domaine Musicale in Paris, the League of Composers in New York, and the Evenings on the Roof (now the Monday Evening Concerts) in Los Angeles.

V

By looking at the history of Wagnerism in the context of evolving musical taste, we have seen that the movement involved much more than reverence for a great composer and his music. Wagnerians used the ideas or the music of Wagner for a variety of purposes, just as much as he manipulated them. Moreover, Wagnerism was not simply an exotic set of aesthetic ideas, as some histories of the movement imply. In some instances it was a powerful and serious force in the shaping of musical taste. But perhaps most important of all, the Wagnerian movement blossomed at a time when new music—whether creative or not—had first come under the shadow of classical masterworks. That affected many aspects of how Wagner's music dramas and ideas were viewed, and we have seen how one strand of the movement in Germany and

Austria was principally concerned with the problems raised by this change.

We have followed a thread in this history, a sequence of ideas and movements concerned with the moral and artistic integrity of music in society. It has led us from the cult for Beethoven to Berlioz's dream of Euphonia; from there to Wagner's Bayreuth and Liszt's Musikverein; on to Wagnerian support of Wolf and to Schoenberg's private performing society; and finally to the independent world of new music today. The intellectual movement that began all this—music idealism—arose in the reorientation of musical values at the start of the nineteenth century. It established the first musical classicism and lofty new artistic principles for music but left contemporary music in an ambiguous and secondary position. Wagner took the idealist tradition in a fresh direction, and his followers took it in yet another. His notion of a community dedicated to pure artistry put musical idealism into actual practice in a way that intoxicated all around him, suggesting a new world of possibilities to the supporters of avant-garde music. Disillusionment with the social consequences of the classical tradition, though not with the music itself, brought the Wagnerians to take a path that Berlioz had dreamed of but Liszt was the first to blaze. The whole development came home to Vienna when a uniquely single-minded set of artistic radicals put these emerging notions of modernism into practice.

German Wagnerism thus played a special role in the evolution of Western musical taste. Its activities under Liszt and his Viennese successors provided the intellectual thrust and worldly acumen that established firm social bases for new music. Born in the aftermath of the Revolution of 1848, Wagnerism interjected an ideological tendency into musical life that is still powerful today. Since that time, factionally conscious schools of composition, defined by musical style and some kind of social ideology, have formed the principal structure of the composing profession. Arnold Schoenberg, Pierre Boulez, and John Cage have all followed in Liszt's path. The idea that music must be appreciated for itself alone, apart from virtuosity, fashion, or indeed any social aspect, thus moved in two opposing directions—to veneration of music from the past and to support of music written in the intensely controversial present.

2. Wagner's Bayreuth Disciples

DAVID C. LARGE

Friedrich Nietzsche often insisted that he wanted no disciples, but of course he attracted them, especially after his death. Richard Wagner never claimed not to want disciples, and he attracted them too, many during his lifetime and many more in the century since his death. In both instances the disciples have done considerable damage to their masters' legacies, damage that has only recently (and only partly) been undone.

Of course, there are disciples and there are disciples. With Wagner the damage was done not by the millions of devotees who simply enjoyed the spectacle of his music dramas, but by the much smaller contingent of zealous Wagnerites who accepted Wagner's claim to be a great social thinker as well as a great musician. Such zealots could be found throughout Europe (and even in America) during the late nineteenth and early twentieth centuries, but they were most numerous— and most influential—in central Europe. There, more than anywhere else in the Wagnerian orbit, *Wagnerismus* came to be taken seriously as a basis upon which to reform not only art but the entire social order.[1] Of course, this is not to say that the majority of German Wagnerians entertained such a notion; most of them had no more interest in using Wagner's ideas to bring about social reform than had ordinary Wagnerians in England, Italy, Russia, or France. But central Europe did spawn a number of small communities or movements dedicated to the exegesis and dissemination of Wagner's philosophy. Outposts of *Wag-*

nerismus cropped up in most of the leading universities, especially in Berlin, Leipzig, Munich, and Vienna. At these institutions Wagnerian students banded together in so-called academic Wagner societies, which went farther than the nonacademic Wagner clubs in committing themselves to furthering the Master's program of spiritual and social reform, rather than simply raising money for Bayreuth.[2]

Important as these groups were, however, the heart of the Wagnerian enterprise, the sanctum sanctorum, remained Bayreuth itself. It was here in this small Franconian town that first Richard, then his widow Cosima, his son Siegfried, and finally his daughter-in-law Winifred held court for the small coterie of fervent disciples that became known as the "Bayreuth Circle." This group's history between the first Bayreuth Festival (1876) and the triumph of Nazism is fascinating indeed, and it offers ample testimony to the wisdom of Nietzsche's reluctance to attract disciples.[3]

Small as this group was, its full dimensions cannot be encompassed in an essay of this scope. All we can attempt here is a brief look into the careers and intellectual contributions of a few of its leading lights. But this will, we hope, allow us to reach some tentative conclusions about the nature of German Wagnerism and about the role that the movement played in recent German history.

Before examining the Bayreuth discipleship, however, we must say something about the intellectual legacy that the disciples inherited from Wagner. It was not, to say the least, an unambiguous legacy. Wagner's mercurial temperament, his highly impressionable imagination, and above all his tendency to shape his political and philosophical views according to the demands of his art caused him to embrace a confusing variety of social-political causes, ideas, and potential allies.

In politics Wagner had been about as consistent as he was in love. Although he later denied it, he had been active in the Saxon revolutionary movement of 1848–1849, going so far as to deliver a rabble-rousing speech before the Fatherland Association, an organization dedicated to unifying the German states as a republic. His political engagement in this instance stemmed largely from a conviction that only political revolution could clear the way for the music of the future. (After all, were not the Saxon king's courtiers, especially Baron von Lüttichau, director of the Dresden Court Theater, allied in a conspiracy to retard the young conductor's progress?) The failure of the revolutions of 1848–1849 forced Wagner into exile in Switzerland, where he gradually shed the rather superficial revolutionary optimism that had animated his Dresden years. Now he stayed clear of political intrigue, had nothing to do with the radical exile community in Switzerland and France, and devoted himself to an art that was beginning to take on the weight of Schopenhauerian resignation.

In 1864, as is well known, Wagner was suddenly reprieved from his exile by the new king of Bavaria, Ludwig II, who brought him to Munich so that the two of them might work closely together on the realization of Wagner's artistic dreams. But this "collaboration"— which amounted primarily to Ludwig's putting up money and Wagner's spending it—floundered when the now middle-aged Master took the liberty of advising his young friend on political as well as artistic matters. The citizens of Bavaria, made aware of Wagner's role by the local press, did not welcome the news that their king was receiving political advice from the likes of Wagner. Denouncing him as "Lolotte"—an uncharitable reference to the mistress and "adviser" of Ludwig I, Lola Montez[4]—the Munich citizenry demanded that either Wagner or Ludwig go. For a moment Ludwig indeed contemplated abdication—free of kingly burdens, he might truly become Wagner's artistic and spiritual collaborator—but Wagner himself hastened to discourage this plan: A Ludwig without power and money would be useless to him.

Once again in exile, and now convinced that he could not realize his most ambitious artistic projects (in particular his plans for his own theater) in Ludwig's capital, he began casting about for new places in which to produce his work and for new princes who might pay the bills. His choice eventually settled on Bayreuth, not only because it was small and provincial and therefore conquerable, but also because, though part of Ludwig's Bavaria, it had strong historical ties to Prussia and to the Hohenzollerns. While living in Munich and "advising" Ludwig, Wagner had advertised himself as a Bavarian patriot and prussophobe; now, vaguely hoping that he might secure patronage from an ascendant Prussia as well as Bavaria, he contemplated "an expedient change to the side of power."[5]

That change in political coloration became clearer after Prussia took the lead in unifying the German states in a glorious new Reich. Wagner celebrated Prussia-Germany's victory over France in 1870–1871 by writing a tasteless paean to Germany's militaristic prowess (and to France's humiliation), entitled "Eine Kapitulation" (A Capitulation), and he dispatched a poem to Bismarck called "An das deutsche Heer vor Paris" (To the German army before Paris). Following up on this overture to Germany's new masters, he composed a "Kaiser March" that he hoped might become the national anthem. A rebuff in this matter from Berlin did not prevent him from paying personal court to Bismarck in April 1871. On this occasion he made clear his desire for imperial financial support of his Bayreuth venture: the new Reich, after all, needed an "artistic monument" to symbolize its grandeur. When Berlin (and in particular Bismarck) proved unwilling to take up Ludwig's Wagnerian burden, the Master lost his patience. In 1866 he had toasted Bismarck as Germany's greatest political hope; now he denounced him as a "demagogical pig" (*Sauhetzer*) and a coward.[6] As for his Bayreuth enterprise, that most ambitious of artistic ventures materialized only because Wagner's much abused previous patron, Ludwig II, stepped in at the last minute to save it. True, Kaiser Wilhelm I did make an appearance at the premiere of *Der Ring des Nibelungen,* but he left in the middle of the cycle to attend a military maneuver. Wagner's response was to denounce German militarism and to vow never to let his young son Siegfried enter the army.

In these waning years of his life Wagner became increasingly afflicted with anti-imperial sentiments and began to wonder if his earlier faith in his countrymen's purity of soul—a faith reflected in his essay *German Art and German Politics* (1868) was not misplaced. The German people, after all, were now allowing Bismarck, a Prussian *Junker,* to remake the nation in his own image, with the result that the new empire possessed great power (*Macht*) but no spirit (*Geist*). In his disillusionment with the Fatherland, Wagner even contemplated emigrating to Minnesota, whose German-American citizens he hoped to persuade to subsidize a new Festival Theater and music school. (Wagner, quite characteristically, sought to justify this brief temptation by claiming that the purest Germanic stock was now to be found in the American Middle West; the racial theorist Count Arthur de Gobineau eventually disabused him of this notion.)

If Wagner's erratic political views were shaped largely by the demands of his artistic career, his intellectual development betrayed the inconsistencies of the impressionable autodidact. He seems to have read voraciously but indiscriminately. He would take up a particular writer or thinker, proclaim himself a devotee (and often, if the writer was a contemporary, would send him fan letters and copies of his own work), then move on to another sometimes quite contradictory enthusiasm without entirely discarding the intellectual baggage of the previous mentors. His prose essays and music dramas alike reflect the chaotic quality of his "learning": they ride intellectual hobby horses of varying colors and breeds, and some of the most ambitious artistic works, like the *Ring* tetralogy, ride several horses at the same time.

Wagner began his career as aesthetic and social theorist as a follower of left Hegelianism. The influence of Feuerbach pervades *Art and Revolution* (1849), and there are elements of Hegel's system in the libretto to the *Ring,* the earliest sketches of which were written in the same period.

In *Art and Revolution* Wagner argued in essence that social-political revolution was a prerequisite for artistic and spiritual regeneration, since "true" art could prosper only in a society free of the alienation imposed by governmental and religious tyranny.[7] If the ancient Greeks had produced a pure and noble art (classical tragedy), this was because they lived in a free and self-confident society, one that took delight in nature and the gods. Since the days of Grecian glory, man had produced one despotic regime after another, and the result had been nothing but sham: Imperial Rome's gladiatorial combat and vulgar comedy; the decadent court culture of the absolutist princes; finally the "civilized" art of modern industrial capitalism. Western man could rediscover the wellsprings of genuine culture only by relearning how to be free.[8]

Later in this same year, in *The Art-Work of the Future,* Wagner sharpened the focus of his radical attack on contemporary industrial society. He berated this society in particular for its denial of what was truly "necessary" in the human condition—namely the expression of man's innate creativity and his harmony with nature—in favor of an artificial and unnatural pursuit of purely "utilitarian ends."[9] Necessity versus utility: this polarity lay at the heart of Wagner's world view and explains both his categorical rejection of nineteenth-century culture and his utopian vision of a "purely human" society based on "inner necessity" rather than external imposition. The "art of the future" would both guide and reflect the transition to such a culture simply by "being itself"—that is, by being what it truly was rather than what it was forced to be. The result would be perfect freedom: not freedom *from* nature but freedom *in* nature, for man could be truly free "only when joyfully conscious of his connection to nature," and art could be truly free "only when no longer ashamed of its connection to life."[10]

Wagner's first sketches of the *Ring* also reflected this left Hegelian world view. As George C. Windell has pointed out, change in the *Ring* occurs through a dialectical process. We find, for example, Alberich's original sexual love transformed by repudiation into a condemnation of all love and into a wish to seize the power represented by the gold in order to enslave all those who love. A passion, in other words, becomes its opposite. One sees in this not just the dialectic at work but also evidence of a hidden design. A step never has the hoped-for result, but it nevertheless produces the fated change: Wotan, to take another example, hopes that Brünnhilde will induce Siegfried to return the gold to the Rhine; he cannot foresee that because of her passion for Siegfried she will regard the gold as a lover's gift.[11]

Throughout his life Wagner never entirely discarded these early influences—bits and pieces of the left Hegelian perspective would crop up from time to time in his later work—but within a few short years of his cultivation of Feuerbach and his friendship with Bakunin, a new and quite different mentor would come to dominate his view of the world: Arthur Schopenhauer.

Wagner first read Schopenhauer in 1851, and the experience was—as it has been for so many impressionable minds—apocalyptic. Perhaps the effect was all the more potent in Wagner's case because it came at a time when his somewhat facile optimism was already giving way to doubts about the possibilities of establishing heaven on earth. In any event, Schopenhauer's philosophy of resignation and renunciation, as well as his theories about the relationship between dreams, the Will, and art, eventually found their way into some of Wagner's essays, such as "Beethoven" (1870), and into the middle and later music dramas. *Tristan,* for example, is awash in Schopenhauerian metaphysics, and rewritings of the *Ring* overlaid Schopenhauerian motifs on the original Hegelian substructure.[12] This does not mean that Wagner translated Schopenhauer's philosophy directly into his art; rather, he picked up certain Schopenhauerian themes, such as the ideal of achieving nirvana through nonwilling, and then modified them to suit his purposes. Still, he certainly thought of his work as an artistic monument to that philosopher's genius, and he sent Schopenhauer a copy of the *Tristan* poem as well as the libretto to the *Ring,* neither of which the latter even bothered to acknowledge.

If Schopenhauer would have nothing to do with Wagner, claiming that Wagner knew nothing of music, Friedrich Nietzsche became an enthusiastic Wagnerian at an early age and rejoiced at the prospect of meeting the Master in 1868. The complex relationship between Nietzsche and Wagner cannot be analyzed here,[13] but it should be noted that Nietzsche's enthusiasm for Wagner was requited in the Master's admiration for this passionate young disciple. And if Nietzsche could claim to find inspiration for his *Birth of Tragedy* in Wagner's concept of the "total work of art" (*Gesamtkunstwerk*), Wagner allowed that he had found intellectual nourishment in Nietzsche's interpretation of Greek tragedy and in his thoughts on the Apollonian-Dionysian polarity. Although Wagner was somewhat disappointed to discover that Nietzsche's *Birth of Tragedy* was not about *him,* he could write to its author that he had "never read anything more beautiful than your book. It is marvelous. . . . I told Cosima: after her, you are next."[14] Nietzsche, then, was clearly another Wagnerian enthusiast whose own rather unsystematic observations on art and life found their way into the Master's protean view of the world.

In breaking with Wagner, Nietzsche listed among other offenses the charge that Wagner had turned "Reichsdeutsch"—that he was toadying to Bismarck and the Kaiser in the most disgusting manner. In fact Wagner's imperial toadying, opportunistic as it was, proved very short-lived. As we noted above, he soon developed second thoughts about these Prussian heroes and the Reich they had created. The new regime's failure to make Bayreuth the "artistic sister of German unification" was primarily responsible for this, but such personal disillusionment was reinforced by the literary–philosophical models Wagner was embracing at this time.

One of the most important of these was the orientalist and cultural philosopher Paul de Lagarde.[15] It was Nietzsche, ironically enough, who first informed Wagner and Cosima about Lagarde's writings in 1873, and soon Lagarde's quixotic call for a "Germanic Christianity" to respiritualize the arid Bismarckian Reich was echoing through the halls of Wagner's home Wahnfried. Cosima could report in her diary that she and Richard found much to agree with in such Lagardian tracts as *On the Current State of the German Reich,*[16] which condemned the Reich for its lack of cultural vitality, its sterile statism, and above all for its "hostility toward the individual, who alone can bring it life and honor."[17] As he had with Schopenhauer, Wagner sent Lagarde copies of his work and tried to strike up a friendship. But Lagarde, again like Schopenhauer, proved unreceptive: the fact of the matter was that he simply could not stand Wagner's music. (After witnessing a performance of *Siegfried* he was moved to comment: "I was bored to extinction. Four hours of recitative is intolerable. . . . I am completely cured of Wagner; of my own accord I shall not again expose myself to such suffering.")[18] Wagner, however, was not put off by Lagarde's hostility and continued to regard the philosopher as a source of wisdom and inspiration. There can be little doubt that his last music drama, *Parsifal,* reflected certain Lagardian traits, especially in its celebration of a vague "Aryan Christianity." (We should add, however, that Wagner's ultimate faith in redemption for the race was considerably stronger than Lagarde's.)

Another important influence on Wagner's later career was Count Arthur de Gobineau, who eventually emerged as one of the nineteenth century's most prominent racial theorists.[19] Wagner met Gobineau in Rome in 1873, having already familiarized himself with the Frenchman's magnum opus, *Essai sur l'inégalité des races humaines (An Essay on the Inequality of Races).* It was Wagner, in fact, who made this previously unheralded work famous—a service that hardly stands to his credit. Wagner was attracted to Gobineau's work because he thought he found in it scientific corroboration of his own rather impressionistic notions about race. It is difficult to assess, however, the precise influence that Gobineau had on the Master. Certainly he supplied him with ethnographic and pseudoscientific ammunition for his racism, but he did not succeed in making Wagner's perspective more "scientific" or systematic. And although there are certainly Gobineauist motifs in *Parsifal,* it is an exaggeration to assert, as does Robert Gutman, that Gobineau's ideas provided that work's primary "validating spirit."[20]

Mention of radical rightist or *völkisch* writers such as Gobineau and Lagarde requires a somewhat more prolonged excursion into the boggy terrain of Wagner's racism. Our purpose here will not be to fully survey this issue, but only to suggest that it—like the entire corpus of Wagner's thought—reflects a kind of personal imperiousness and disregard for consistency. (We do *not* suggest that such traits make it any less repellent.)

The origins of Wagner's anti-Semitism have exercised a number of his biographers, some of whom have sought to find them in an alleged fear on the part of the Master that his own blood was perhaps "tainted."[21] Such an explanation is not only doubtful—it is unnecessary. Wagner grew up in an era when anti-Semitism was very much "in the air," not the least among the left-wing intellectuals whom he admired.

Added to such cultural influences in his early years were certain personal experiences during the formative stage of his career that apparently reinforced the young composer's prejudices. One thinks in particular of his dealings with Meyerbeer and Mendelssohn, both of whom he attempted to court in hopes of winning their support and both of whom he believed deliberately thwarted him. Believing himself victimized by these two Jews, he then went on, in characteristic paranoid fashion, to see all Jews as the enemies of his art.[22]

Later on, however, his collaboration with men like Joseph Rubinstein, Hermann Levi, and Angelo Neumann obliged him to conclude that *certain* Jews might indeed be friends of his art. Toward these "friends" he could be both brutally cruel and strategically supportive; he could bait them for belonging to an "inferior" race and praise their artistic instincts.[23] When criticized by other anti-Semites for this collaboration with the enemy, he would invoke the higher claims of art. (He reminds us here a little of the anti-Semitic mayor of Vienna, Karl Lueger, who responded to similar criticism with the famous quip: "I'll decide who's a Jew.")

As for Wagner's writings on the subject of race, they were if anything more repellent and obtuse than his actions, but even they were not without their ambiguities. His most famous anti-Semitic essay, *Judaism in Music,* spoke of a "natural abhorrence" of Germans for Jews, of a "repulsive otherness in the Jewish character,"[24] and seemed at one point to propose something like physical self-annihilation as the Jews' only redemption from their "curse."[25] And yet in this same essay Wagner could urge the Jews "to stop being Jews" and cite the case of Ludwig Börne as proof that they were capable of "joining us in becoming truly human."[26] (Hardly an edifying sentiment, this, but we should remember that Wagner shared it not only with many Christian anti-Semites of his day but also with certain "enlightened" Jewish assimilationists. Again, an Austrian parallel comes to mind: in assessing Wagner's racism we might do well to recall that the eventual founder of Zionism, Theodore Herzl, once entertained the bizarre notion of combating anti-Semitism by leading Vienna's Jews through a mass conversion to Catholicism in St. Stephen's Cathedral.)[27]

This assimilationist ideal, however, did not continue to guide the Master's thinking on race throughout his life. When he returned to this subject in a series of essays for the *Bayreuther Blätter* shortly before he died, he showed how powerfully he had fallen under the influence of *völkisch* theorists, especially Gobineau. These unfortunate pieces were littered with the count's biological phraseology and echoed his warnings of racial degeneration through miscegenation. Now Wagner saw no real hope that Germans and Jews might save themselves together; only the former might find salvation (and in this he departed from Gobineau's apocalyptic vision of irreversible decay for the entire white race) through a combination of purified German art, Aryan Christianity, and cleansed German blood.[28]

Having discussed some of the inconsistencies and ambiguities in Wagner's social and political thought, we must caution against drawing the conclusion that there was no coherence to his ideology whatsoever. G. B. Shaw was certainly correct when he insisted that Wagner could be "quoted against himself almost without limit,"[29] but it is also correct to suggest that Wagner's world view displayed a certain "integrating unity."[30] That unity manifested itself above all in the concept of the "purely human," an admittedly vague reformist ideal to which the Master returned repeatedly over the course of his life. This ideal involved at once a set of positive values and an indictment of contemporary society. Its goals of inner freedom, selflessness, creativity-for-its-own-sake, and communal harmony could be achieved only by purging the social order of materialism, utilitarianism, and mindless hedonism.

When Wagner contemplated the possible actualization of his reformist vision he tended to single out the Germans as the people most likely to achieve this social transformation. He did so because he saw the ancient German *Volk* as the archetypal representative of the "purely human" ideal.[31] Even his eventual despair over the historical evolution of the German nation under Bismarck did not completely extinguish his belief in the regenerative potential of this people.[32] Wagner's faith in the inherent superiority of the German *Volk* could at times lead him to a nationalistic posture characterized by the narrowest chauvinism and xenophobia. For example, his "Eine Kapitulation" both exulted in Germany's military victory over France and chastized his countrymen for continuing to accept cultural tutelage from Paris, a city the Germans could have (and perhaps even should have) destroyed.[33] And yet Wagner's original conception of the German mission was not narrowly nationalistic but quite cosmopolitan: in "healing" themselves, the Germans would heal the world. In articulating this vision of the Germans as the most "universal" of peoples, Wagner was restating one of the central tenets of German idealist thought.[34]

Whether or not one places much stock in the cosmopolitan dimension of this German mission, Wagner's followers throughout Europe and America were generally quite capable of finding a message in his work that transcended its Germanic inspiration. As we point out in this volume, this message differed considerably from place to place and from time to time, but it almost always derived from a deep dissatisfaction with nineteenth-century culture and society, especially with its alleged aridity and lack of "soul." Wagner's communication of this perception to his cosmopolitan following was inhibited neither by his nationalism nor by the many ambiguities or outright contradictions inherent in his thought.

Richard Wagner himself was not unaware of the inconsistencies in his world view and for most of his life was not even troubled by them. Only in his waning years did he begin to worry about tidying up his intellectual bequest to posterity. It was then that he became aware of a need to organize and discipline the "friends" of his art, and accordingly he began to gather around him disciples who would not merely assist him with the development of his Festival Theater but who would also assume responsibility for the dissemination of his philosophical and political views. Earlier experiences with such supporters as Eduard Röckel, Gottfried Semper, Georg Herwegh, Hans von Bülow, and above all Ludwig II and Nietzsche, had taught him that originality and unquestioning loyalty do not always mix (he might have learned this even more quickly by studying his own example), and in the Bayreuth period he often chose disciples who combined mediocrity with sycophancy. These attributes do not characterize all the Bayreuth disciples—some of them, as we shall see, had minds of their own—but they were prevalent enough to give Wagner's circle the atmosphere of a tyrant's court. The problem with this was that Wagner was no genuine tyrant—he was capable at times of laughing at his own pretensions—and it must have been no small burden for him to be constantly surrounded by such dull-witted piety. He said as much himself on several occasions, and yet he never openly repudiated these devoted lackeys the way he repudiated Nietzsche. They were, after all, the "truest of the true."

II

Perhaps the truest of them all was Hans von Wolzogen.[35] Now almost entirely forgotten, he was, in the period between the first Bayreuth Festival and his death in 1938, one of the dominant figures in German Wagnerism. He achieved this distinction through his unflagging devotion to Wagner's work—not so much to his artistic work as to his ideas. He was, in short, the perfect Bayreuth disciple, a status that the Master himself was not hesitant to recognize: "I have finally found in Hans von Wolzogen the one man who fully comprehends the ideal meaning of my work and who will devote his life completely to furthering that ideal. He perfectly represents the aesthetic and social side of my art; when it comes to maintaining the purity of my ideas, I can count on him to function as my alter ego."[36]

For Wagner's alter ego, the arrival in Bayreuth came as the fulfillment of a spiritual quest. At age nineteen he had declared that he would dedicate his life to an artistic "reformation," to a "new form of theater, built on the true foundations of art, . . . unified and not fragmented, serious and not escapist or entertaining: a 'Temple' and not a 'Luxus.'"[37] Lacking significant creative talents of his own, he could realize his dream only by becoming an apostle of others. He began typically enough as a Goethe-Schiller enthusiast, then lost himself for a time in Schopenhauerian metaphysics, and finally experienced his epiphany while witnessing a *Tännhauser* performance in 1866. From that moment on he knew where his calling must take him: he would hasten to the side of the Master, wherever that might be. He began showering Wagner with effusive fan letters and managed to secure an audience in 1875. Then, like Nietzsche before him, he became a regular houseguest *chez* Wagner (but, unlike Nietzsche, never contradicting his host nor daring to play Brahms on the piano) before permanently settling in at Bayreuth in 1877.

One year later Wagner entrusted him with the editorship of the *Bayreuther Blätter,* a monthly journal he founded to spread his aesthetic and social philosophy throughout the German-speaking world. This journal, however, was always more Wolzogen's project than Wagner's; the Master would have preferred to perpetuate his legacy through a school for young musicians, and only when this failed to materialize did he allow the *Blätter* to be born. He turned the operation over to Wolzogen not only because he was impressed by his "deep and earnest character" but also because he felt a need to recompense this man for his doglike devotion. As Cosima Wagner put it in her diary, "The presence here of H. v. Wolzogen, who is otherwise of much value to us, obliges R. to find some activity for him. And so the periodical!"[38] Somewhat later Wagner confessed to Cosima that he was sick of Bayreuth: he would love to burn his theater to the ground and just be done with it all, but he could not do this because that would leave poor Hans in the lurch. Wolzogen had "based his existence on the future of the *idea,* and this put [Richard] under an obligation to him."[39]

Thus Hans von Wolzogen soldiered loyally on as editor of the *Blätter,* which he rapidly turned into the official organ of German Wagnerism. It contained news of the various Wagner societies (*Vereine*), announcements of concerts and lectures, and, above all, long essays on aesthetic, social, and political themes. These essays tended to be written by the same small group of contributors, number after number. Wolzogen himself wrote dozens of them, and he maintained a sharp editorial vigilance over the entire enterprise. His greatest editorial coup was in persuading the Master himself to write for the journal: Wagner contributed several essays, though not always enthusiastically or without certain ironic condescension. He once told Cosima with a laugh: "I am now writing for Wolzogen, like Kant for Lampe."[40]

Despite the inclusion of Wagner Society news, the *Bayreuther Blätter* never found much of an audience among the broad masses of ordinary Wagnerians, nor was it meant to. It was designed by Wolzogen to provide a forum for the inner circle of Bayreuth disciples, and its heavy diet of social-philosophical commentary, served up in barely digestible prose, guaranteed a highly restricted readership. Of course Wagner himself read it, but perhaps more out of duty than inclination, and he often complained that it was "poorly written," "sloppy," and "unclear in style."

But Wolzogen was hardly troubled by the *Blätter's* opaque style and attendant inaccessibility. If his journal, like so many of those esoteric "little magazines" of the nineteenth century, was read primarily by the people who produced it, so much the better. After all, the "true friends" of Bayreuth could be found only among those who took "German art seriously," who sought in it "not vulgar amusement but a true cultural experience, the highest and noblest efflorescence of the national spirit."[41] Wolzogen did not even expect to convert the heathen; he saw Bayreuth as a haven or refuge for the already saved—or, to change the metaphor slightly, as "an out-of-the-way island, where on the altar of the Sublime [we conduct] a holy service of noble joy."[42]

As may be gleaned from the above passages, Wolzogen was not a man attuned to the mundane realities of life. Indeed, he liked to call himself "unworldly" (*weltfremd*),[43] and everything he ever did or wrote suggests that this was an accurate self-appraisal.

And yet Wolzogen was not so unworldly or isolated as to be completely out of touch with the intellectual and social concerns of his day, especially as those concerns impinged upon what he took to be the Wagnerian mission. He read widely in the contemporary literature of *völkisch* conservatism, and he balanced his *Blätter* essays on the narrower Bayreuth scene with commentaries on the broader social and political world outside. He turned his attention, understandably enough, chiefly to those waves of change that he believed threatened to swamp his little "island."

Marxism was one of these, and Wolzogen did his best to demolish it intellectually by pointing out that it was a foreign ideology, the product of a "Jewish social theorist living in England." None of Marx's theories applied to Germany because they were "extracted exclusively from the conditions of English factory life." Marx's analysis of class conflict was especially inappropriate for Germany, because that country did not have serious class discord; its people were not and never would be working-class types in the English sense, and its leading capitalists, with the exception of a few "un-German" (read Jewish) speculators, could never become genuine oppressors.[44] If this alien doctrine was nevertheless making converts in Germany and thus threatening to become a real danger to the nation's stability, this was because all too many Germans had lost touch with their own social-political heritage: with the "bravery, loyalty, discipline, and order" inherent in the Prussian-German military tradition.[45]

Another contemporary scourge was the stock market.[46] If for Wagner man's chief corrupter was gold, for Hans von Wolzogen it was paper—stocks and bonds. He detected an unwholesome shift away from an economy based on real goods, such as land and craft products, to an economy based on speculative exchange, and this, too, he blamed on "un-German" elements—those Jews who allegedly controlled the stock market.

Next to the stock market, the most corrupting institution in contemporary life was the parliament. Its philosophical justification was a conception of freedom that had less in common with true freedom than with *Frechheit* (insolence).[47] For what, asked Wolzogen, was all this clamor for political freedom but a presumptuous attempt to dethrone God and to deify man, to overthrow the natural hierarchical social organism in favor of an atomized society based on individual greed? True freedom was something entirely different; it involved the striving to be free of all that was base and impure and ignoble and to be in harmony with all that was Good and Moral—a goal that was realizable, however, only in the next world. "Yes," concluded Wolzogen, "the true freedom is in the deepest sense a matter of religion."[48]

For Wolzogen, indeed, everything he encountered somehow became a matter of religion. This was especially true of art: he claimed that his "tragic baptism in Wagner's art had inspired a deeply Christian response in his still childlike spirit,"[49] and he went on to perceive all great art as an expression of the religious sensibility. As religion's most valued ally, art's chief function was to assist in the spiritual struggle against the corrosive influence of reason: "In those cramped chambers of time, where the bacillus of reason poisons all that is spiritual and holy, art throws open a window to the Eternal and readmits the light of true intellectual freedom, thereby allowing the otherworldly power of Belief to reconsecrate those very chambers of time as the temples of the Eternal."[50]

Such effusions sound ecumenical enough, but by the time he wrote this last passage (1895) Wolzogen had embraced orthodox Lutheranism as the only true expression of "Germanic Christianity."[51] In taking this tack he was emulating the Master's widow, but not the Master himself.[52] Although Wagner was certainly given on occasion to pious posturing and became in his declining years a proponent of a vague "Aryan" Christianity, he was never a religious sectarian. Moreover, he had little use for Wolzogen's eternal coupling of art and Christianity. When the latter interpreted Goethe's *Faust* as a Christian parable, Wagner could only shake his head in wonder at his pious disciple.[53]

Wolzogen, like many Christian zealots of his day, was an anti-Semite, but not simply a religious anti-Semite. His case against the Jews derived more from the pseudoscientific arguments of Count Gobineau, whose *Essay on the Inequality of Races* he summarized for the German Wagnerians in the *Bayreuther Blätter*.[54] The point he stressed in this explication of Gobineau was that all men were first and foremost members of a particular race (*Racenmenschen*), a condition that determined the salient features of their behavior.[55] Although he recognized historical conditioning as an influence on racial behavior and was by no means a strict biological determinist, Wolzogen can be said to have had a hand in advancing the spread of a more systematic and "scientifically based" racism among his fellow Wagnerians.

In addition to his long tenure as editor of the *Blätter*, Wolzogen also served the Wagnerian cause by helping organize and promote the so-called Society of Patrons (Patronatsverein). The Master himself saw this Society, which spawned branch associations all over the world, chiefly as a fund-raising organization for Bayreuth, and when it proved inadequate in this capacity he rapidly lost interest in it.[56] (Indeed, he eventually did his best to undercut it by opening the 1882 festival to the general public rather than reserving admittance to "patrons.") Wolzogen, on the other hand, always regarded the society as a potential carrier of the Wagnerian idea, not simply as a fund-raising device.[57] The problem with this ambition was that most members of the local branches (with the notable exception of the students in the academic societies) were not overly interested in the Master's philosophical views; they simply wanted to see his music dramas—or perhaps *be seen* at his music dramas in Bayreuth—and they could not be bothered with spreading the Word.

This attitude was especially characteristic of the Wagner Society in the new imperial capital of Berlin. Dominated by the aristocratic haut monde (so much so, indeed, that it was ironically labeled by some the Richard von Wagner Society), this group was more a prestigious social club than an arm of Wagnerian ideology. Wagner himself had little use for it, and Wolzogen would eventually complain that the Berlin Society had done "absolutely nothing" for the Wagnerian movement.[58]

This, of course, was an exaggeration, for one of its members, Countess Marie von Schleinitz, had been instrumental in persuading Kaiser Wilhelm I to attend the 1876 premiere of the *Ring* in Bayreuth. Another member, the Jewish publicist Georg Davidsohn, employed his *Berliner Börsenkurier* as an important voice speaking on Wagner's behalf, despite the Master's notorious anti-Semitism. Whatever the contributions of Wagner's Berlin friends, however, it must be admitted that the imperial capital was somewhat slow to accept the music of the future.[59] No doubt this had something to do with lingering opposition from the city's Brahms enthusiasts, who were led by the influential violinist Joseph Joachim. The Royal Berlin Orchestra did not begin performing Wagner regularly until the mid-1870s, and the new Berlin Philharmonic Orchestra (founded in 1882) was resistant until Hans von Bülow took up its directorship in the late 1880s. By this time Wagner had also found a champion in the new emperor, Kaiser Wilhelm II, who occasionally visited Bayreuth and who became an honorary member of the Berlin Wagner Society.

The movement of Wagner societies as a whole reached its peak in the last decade of the nineteenth century, then began rapidly to decline. Ironically enough, Bayreuth's commercial success was partly responsible for this decline. The societies could justify their existence as long as Bayreuth floundered financially and therefore needed all the support it could muster, but when the festival became a profitable enterprise, as it did in the 1890s, one of the original motivations for the patron movement evaporated. Not surprisingly, then, membership declined in the first decade of the new century, and declined even more dramatically during the First World War.[60] By the war's end the whole enterprise seemed on the verge of extinction, and most Wagnerians seemed content to let it die in peace.

But not Hans von Wolzogen. For him the cascading evils of the hour—"cowardice, disorder, treason, dissolution"—demanded more than ever that the Wagner Society make its influence felt on the national scene.[61] Wagnerism, he reminded his *Bayreuther Blätter* readers in 1919, was more than just a love of brilliant music and theater; it was an "ideology," a view of the world based on a deep consciousness of the German spirit and culture.[62] The task of the Wagner Society, therefore, was to employ that Wagnerian consciousness in the cause of *völkisch* revival: "This reconstruction on a solid *völkisch* foundation must constitute the essential mission of the Wagner Society; it hardly needs to be said just how important such an endeavor is for the German national spirit at this time."[63] Wolzogen did not spell out exactly how the Wagnerians should accomplish this mission, and he certainly did not prescribe which political parties the movement should support. On the contrary, he urged that the society remind Germans once again of the essential difference between "political" and "*völkisch*." "One must not," he insisted, "misunderstand our intervention for the German people as a commitment to any political party."[64]

Of course such protestations were part and parcel of an "idealist" world view that had quite definite political implications, especially during the Weimar period.[65] This was certainly the case with Wolzogen, whose idealistic and unworldly proclivities led him eventually to that eminently "unpolitical" movement of National Socialism. There is no evidence that he actually joined the Party, but he openly embraced the Nazi cause as truly representative of Wagnerian ideology. Indeed, he became so enthusiastic about the Nazis that one of his colleagues in the Bayreuth Circle called him a "true HJ [Hitler Jugend, Hitler Youth] man."[66] When he died in 1938 the Führer himself placed a wreath on his grave, and the *Völkischer Beobachter* ran a short obituary honoring this "loyal Eckart" (recalling thereby Tannhäuser's trusted armor-bearer).[67]

This is not to argue that Wolzogen was genuinely committed to all that the Nazis came to represent—he abhorred violence, vulgarity, and unprincipled *Realpolitik*— and his attachment to the cause no doubt reflected a certain naive guillibility—the consequence, perhaps, of his vaunted unworldliness. The Nazis, for their part, privately sneered at this pious enthusiast. The same Hitler who placed a wreath on his grave could also call him a "flat-head" for interpreting *Parsifal* as an expression of Schopenhauerian-Christian philosophical piety.[68] No doubt there is something tragicomic (as Winfried Schüler has suggested) in this relationship between a gullible ideologue and a cynical opportunist.[69] And yet the element of tragedy certainly predominates. Wolzogen's faith in Nazism was, after all, terribly emblematic of the delusion that afflicted that whole generation of German "idealistic" enthusiasts who saw in Hitler a kind of Lohengrin figure come to redeem a fallen world.

III

"We have no doubt about whom we must thank first—that is, after Wagner's wife—when we pay tribute to those who in the Bayreuth of the previous century created a cultural work of the highest importance: [we think] of Freiherr Hans von Wolzogen."[70] This statement by a Bayreuth commentator in 1913 correctly assessed Wolzogen's importance in the Wagnerian movement: he was the most significant figure *after* Cosima. Cosima Wagner, who exerted such a powerful influence on Wagner's life, would eventually emerge as the true claimant to the departed Master's throne: the "Mistress of Bayreuth."[71]

Yet if it is true that Cosima became the mistress of Bayreuth, this is one of the odder facts of recent European cultural history. Cosima, the illegitimate daughter of Franz Liszt and the Countess Marie d'Agoult, had grown up in a sophisticated ambience; she was well traveled and well educated; early on she had shown talent as a translator and political commentator for the *Revue germanique;* she had learned to play the piano and possessed a natural affinity for music. Moreover, she had played an important role in the realization of her husband's Bayreuth dreams, advising him on everything from costumes and stage design to music, and above all buoying up his spirits when they threatened to sink under the manifold burdens of his genius. Yet it must be remembered that this was still the nineteenth century, an era in which a woman, whatever her talents, would not have been expected to command an artistic-cum-business enterprise as ambitious as Bayreuth. Wagner had certainly never groomed her for this role, and she had given no indication of such lofty ambitions while her husband was alive. On the contrary, her view of herself, as recorded in her recently published diaries, was that she was happy to remain in "R.'s" shadow. She was forever contrasting her own nothingness to Richard's greatness, expressing her infinite gratitude for the opportunity to serve him in the humblest of ways. "My life is pedestrian," she wrote at one point, "I care for the children, but R.'s life is defined by the godly gift of genuis."[72]

But was Cosima really so humble and self-deprecating? Was she really so content to remain in Richard's shadow? George Marek points out in his recent biography of Cosima that it was she, not Richard, who took the lead in the early stages of their relationship: "She was more the wooer than the wooed."[73] At one point in her diary Cosima recorded approvingly Richard's observation that she possessed the "Apollonian element," he the "Dionysian."[74] This is a revealing moment, for it would seem that from the outset of their relationship, Cosima, sensing Richard's vulnerability and insecurity, decided that she must act as the shaper of his unruly genius, the ordering force in his life. Thus she stood guard at the shrine, doing her best to screen him from what she took to be unwholesome influences. And although she never openly commanded him, she subtly nudged him in directions she thought best for him and best for his art. It was chiefly Cosima, for example, who encouraged those mystical-Christian tendencies that are evident in his latest work—a service for which her erstwhile friend Nietzsche was never to forgive her. And while Cosima by no means "made" Richard a racist or German nationalist—indeed, it was probably he who turned her into a francophobe and German chauvinist—she proved the perfect sounding board for his prejudices and ultimately reinforced whatever proclivities he had in these directions.

Still, Cosima's full capacity for the ordering of her husband's Dionysian legacy did not emerge until after Richard's death. Wagner himself had not named a successor at Bayreuth; like Bismarck he could not be bothered with training a replacement, indeed could not imagine having a replacement at all. Shortly before his death, he wrote the impresario

Angelo Neumann: "My Bayreuth creation will surely perish with my death, for I cannot conceive of a person capable of carrying it on according to my ideals."[75] With Wagner's demise, then, it seemed more than possible that the festival might simply collapse, or that if it survived its direction would most likely pass to representatives of the Society of Patrons, who since 1876 had been clamoring for a role in the administration of the festival.[76] If neither of these things in fact happened, this was because Cosima Wagner soon made certain that she would ensure the "salvation" of Bayreuth.

She did not do this immediately upon Wagner's death, and she did not do it without help. The passing of the man to whom she had devoted herself unreservedly for twenty years stunned her into uncharacteristic apathy. She suddenly ceased making entries in her diary and when urged to press on with arrangements for the 1883 performances of *Parsifal,* she answered: "Leave me to the grave and my sorrow; our friends can carry on with [my husband's] work."[77] But this apathy proved amazingly short-lived: within that same year Cosima was busy drawing up plans for the festivals from 1884 through 1889, and with the indispensible aid of her business adviser Adolf von Gross she prepared a series of legal documents that transferred trusteeship of the festival to herself and her son Siegfried, who was at the same time declared Wagner's sole legal heir.[78] All this was done in such a way as to endow the transfer with the posthumous blessing of Wagner.

When Cosima began her moving "self-sacrifice" to Wagner's genius, she was a restless, high-spirited young woman, prepared first to attempt a life of deception and then, when the deception failed, to defy moral orthodoxy for the sake of the man who was her first true love.[79] Her betrayal of her first husband, Hans von Bülow, caused her considerable pain and guilt, however, and this guilt expanded like a canker in her soul as she grew older. Her diary provides ample documentation of this growing guilt: in April 1871, having finally mended fences with her father, who had strongly disapproved of her liaison with Wagner, she lamented, "Oh, would it were possible that a fourth [Bülow] might be won over, but that is denied me by Fate, and with a cry of self-lacerating remorse I must forever shut myself off from true happiness and exaltation."[80] In her guilt and morbid self-pity Cosima sought the solace of religion and the reassuring sympathy of an increasingly narrow circle of friends. Once a voracious and eclectic reader, she began to brag that she could put all the books she now admired on a single shelf.[81] Spiritual, intellectual, and social parochialism became her haven, her defense against the world and against herself. By the early 1870s, when her husband was busy touring Europe in pursuit of backing for Bayreuth, Cosima was counseling the comforts of Schopenhauerian resignation and Christian piety. When the two of them departed for the new national capital in 1871, she could not help worrying that Richard might be murdered "by a Berlin Jew."[82]

Given this trend in her life toward increasing rigidity and conservatism, it is not surprising that her administration of the Bayreuth Festival was marked by "intolerance and narrowness," by an obsession with "maintaining the status quo."[83] In fact, however, one might legitimately ask whether she did not in some ways inaugurate a regime that departed significantly from her husband's intentions.

Wagner's Bayreuth, we should remember, was nothing if not a bold artistic experiment, bristling with innovations of every sort. There is no reason to doubt that the Master would have continued as long as he lived to explore innovative techniques in the production of his music dramas. There is even reason to believe that he might have staged works by other composers. (Only his advanced age, he told Friedrich von Schön in 1880, prevented him from mounting productions of *Die Zauberflöte, Der Freischütz,* and *Fidelio.*)[84] Cosima, on the other hand, was dedicated to so-called model productions of her husband's work: although she was certainly capable of making changes in the music dramas (such as, for example, her elimination of the cymbal crash from the end of the first act of *Tristan*), her approach was to impose a particular interpretation on the material and then to repeat it summer after summer. It was as if the Bayreuth stage had become a kind of artistic assembly line, or better yet an altar: the music of the future was becoming liturgical. As for the works of other composers, there was certainly no chance that they would be allowed to distract festival visitors. Cosima had once waxed indignant over the Berlin Wagner Society's "ridiculous intention of serving not only Wagnerian art, but art in general."[85] Certainly Cosima harbored no such foolish ambitions, and once in control at Bayreuth she made sure that the Festspielhaus remained an exclusively Wagnerian shrine.

Cosima not only decreed the order in which Wagner's works would be mounted; she also intervened directly in the minutiae of production. From her special enclosure in the wings of the theater, hidden from the performers by a black screen, she would pass notes down to the stage dictating how a particular scene was to be played.[86] One wonders why the performers did not rebel en masse against this high-handed widow who ordered them about as if she herself were an artist.

The first and most obvious answer is that Cosima was something like the moon; she did not need her own light to shine. The daughter of Liszt and the wife of Wagner: how much closer to Genuis could one come? Cosima understood this relationship and exploited it for all it was worth. She was especially adept at shrouding herself in her dead husband's aura: whenever challenged she could always assert: "I speak for Him!"

Yet it would be unfair to deny that Cosima possessed a certain charisma all her own. Although by no means beautiful in the classic sense—her face was too thin, her nose too long—she was physically captivating: a kind of pale, ethereal presence, elegant and poised. She was also acutely intelligent, strong-willed, and genuinely responsive to that world of high culture in which she had been steeped since childhood. Moreover, as she grew older, she increasingly assumed an air of frosty dignity, a quality that had a way of making everyone (even Albert Schweitzer!) feel somehow morally inferior.[87] How curious it was then: this woman who had openly defied convention ended up becoming a legend in her own time of bourgeois respectability.

Another change occurred as Cosima gradually consolidated her rule at Bayreuth. Increasingly she regarded what transpired there as *her* work, *her* artistic accomplishment. True, she claimed to be carrying on Richard's "ideals," but now when she said, "We know the tradition," she was using the royal "we."[88]

Cosima Wagner was thus a formidable figure indeed, and she commanded considerable respect not just in Bayreuth but around the world. This does not mean that she was invariably able to impose her will or that there was not occasional sharp criticism of her reign. She was not able to retain (how brazen of her even to have tried!) her former husband Hans von Bülow as conductor at Bayreuth in 1883 or to prevent Gustav Mahler from becoming opera director at Vienna in 1897.[89] In 1883–1884 she had to fight off a major challenge from the Wagner societies of Munich and Leipzig, which were the primary backers of a new International Richard Wagner Foundation designed to wrest control of the festival administration from the Villa Wahnfried.[90] This attempt failed, but it shows that Cosima's seizure of power was by no means unanimously applauded among the German Wagnerians.

Cosima's artistic staff in Bayreuth also engaged in occasional lese majesty. Members of the orchestra made it clear to Albert Schweitzer that they "were not unanimous in their opinion that it was a real advantage to have a woman of such an imperious will as Madame Cosima directing the performances."[91] Felix Weingartner, whom Cosima had hired as her musical assistant in 1886, questioned her reverence for both Liszt and Wagner and thereby effected his own permanent banishment from Bayreuth.[92] Lilli Lehmann, the great prima donna, once had the temerity to question some of Cosima's artistic interpretations, but as usual the latter threw up an impregnable defense. Turning to her son, she said: "That was the way the Master did it, don't you remember, Siegfried?"[93]

Even the Bayreuth disciples were sometimes less than reverent. Wolzogen, one of her closest supporters, lamented privately that she invariably viewed the world "through little spy holes covered with her own specially frosted glass."[94] The Austrian Wagnerite, Friedrich von Hausegger, gave vent to an objection that must have bothered many of his male colleagues: "It is impossible that a woman, even if she were extremely talented . . . , were energetic, and were ready to make sacrifices (and these qualities are certainly in evidence)—could embrace the wide range of a man like Wagner."[95] Of course Cosima was not just a woman, but a "foreign woman" and thus doubly suspect as the interpreter of Wagner's "Germanic" genuis. Martin Plüddemann, another Wagnerian ideologue, warned Ludwig Schemann that Cosima's "foreign spirit" was violating her husband's national legacy. "[Her] pure French character is dangerous," he wrote, "in that it has brought about a Bayreuth internationalism. At any rate, she is un-German from head to toe, and this will bring about the ruin of Bayreuth."[96]

This last charge is curious, for in the end Cosima's alleged "internationalism" hardly amounted to more than an avoidance of public slurs against the foreign visitors upon whose pocketbooks the Bayreuth Festival depended. In private Cosima was as xenophobic—even francophobic—as any *völkisch* zealot in the new German Empire. Her Parisian upbringing and her "pure French character" did not prevent her, in 1871, from rejoicing in the German bombardment of Paris or from denouncing alleged misbehavior of the French soldiers. "It disgusts me," she fumed in her diary, "that such creatures have dared to fight against our noble Germans."[97] The Germans: they were for Cosima the only people capable of genuine greatness. She insisted that with the possible exception of Shakespeare and Cromwell, all the "great men" (she had been reading Carlyle) of recent centuries had been German.[98] German culture, too, was the only truly serious, profound culture in the world: the French were superficial, the English commercial, the Russians barbaric, and as for the Americans, well, America proved that it took more than railroads and wide open spaces to produce a culture.[99] These views, to be sure, were confined to the privacy of her diary, while in her public capacity as mistress of Bayreuth she welcomed guests from around the world with remarkable energy and grace. Whatever her talents in this regard, however, they did not make her a genuine cosmopolitan, only something of a hypocrite.

She could be hypocritical, too, when it came to the question of race.[100] She well understood that Bayreuth could not afford to alienate the international Jewish community that played a surprisingly important role in the Wagnerian movement.[101] Indeed, she once expressed the hope that Bayreuth's financial future might be secured by "some rich Jew, anxious to atone for the sins of his race."[102] She knew, too, that Jews were important to Bayreuth's artistic viability, and when the *Parsifal* conductor Hermann Levi tried to resign in 1892, Cosima insisted he stay on. (After all, Levi believed not only in Wagner the musician but in Wagner the "thinker.") At the same time, however, she did her best to make Levi's life miserable, for she could not forgive him for being a Jew, and a talented one at that.[103] So she was constantly reminding him (as had her husband before her) that he harbored a "tragic flaw" that he might redeem only through baptism. (She felt obliged to add, however, that while a Jew might become a Christian, he could never receive the blessing of Teutonism.)[104] Like Richard, then, Cosima was much distressed that circumstances forced her to cooperate with Levi, just as she was distressed to discover on a visit to Frankfurt that the city of Goethe and Schopenhauer had allowed its culture to become "dominated by Jews."[105] Hans Mayer is thus surely wrong when he embraces the "suspicion"—initially harbored by Cosima's Bayreuth rivals—that she was "secretly un-German and cosmopolitan."[106] Her only secret was the depth of her growing parochialism.

Another measure of Cosima's parochialism was her insistence that Wagner's legacy in all its dimensions belonged only to Bayreuth, indeed only to the Villa Wahnfried. Soon after her husband's death she attempted to recall some of the letters he had written, and even destroyed some of the correspondence he had received.[107] In addition, she gave

Adolf von Gross instructions to obstruct all biographical publications that did not receive the official or semiofficial blessing of Wahnfried.[108] In this way she clearly hoped to shape the world's perception of Wagner's life and work, much as Elizabeth Förster-Nietzsche sought to manipulate the reputation of her brother.[109]

Cosima also fought long and hard to control, limit, or in some cases prevent the production of Wagner's music dramas outside Bayreuth. Here too, as in the area of Wagner biography, Wahnfried sought conformity to a Bayreuth "ideal," and when this was not forthcoming it tried to scuttle the offending production by withholding rights or personnel.[110] But even productions that successfully emulated the Bayreuth model were not exempt from criticism; on the contrary, these were perceived by Cosima as the most threatening of all, for they compromised Bayreuth's monopoly of the "true" Wagnerian heritage. Vienna and Munich were the major offenders in this regard, since both these cities had first-rate orchestras and opera companies, many of whose singers had already performed at Bayreuth. The Munich Court Theater, moreover, owned the rights to the *Ring* and *Parsifal* because the Master had signed them over to Ludwig II in exchange for desperately needed financial support. And although Adolf von Gross managed to retrieve these rights for Bayreuth after Ludwig's death, the director of the Court Theater, Ernst von Possart, regularly began mounting productions of Wagner's works in 1893, a development about which Cosima complained indignantly but in vain. ("Munich," she fumed to Richard Strauss, "sits on everything, from *Der fliegende Holländer* to the swans and the dragon.")[111] In 1901 Munich intensified this invasion of Bayreuth's territory when its new Prince Regent's Theater, built in accordance with Ludwig Semper's original designs for a Munich Festspielhaus, inaugurated its own Wagner festival. Cosima and von Gross tried to obstruct this by going to court and claiming that only the Court Theater—not the new Prince Regent's Theater—had a legal right to stage Wagner's works.[112] The court did not accept this argument, but Cosima and von Gross did manage to secure an agreement that Munich would not mount the same works as Bayreuth in any given year. Bayreuth would also receive a percentage of the new theater's profits. These concessions helped to smooth Cosima's feathers considerably, for in buttressing the festival's financial position they were almost as useful as a "rich Jew eager to atone for the sins of his race."[113]

Nevertheless, Cosima continued to view the production of her husband's work outside Bayreuth as a kind of sacrilege, as a "betrayal" of

Richard's memory. In general her piety on this score was misplaced, for Wagner had not hesitated to let his works be mounted elsewhere when this stood to earn him a profit. He allowed the impressario Angelo Neumann to produce the *Ring* in Leipzig in 1878, and in Berlin in 1881. He even contemplated giving Neumann permission to tour *Parsifal,* the one work that he had vowed would never leave the Festspielhaus.[114] But Cosima wished to take no chances with competition, even if it might eventually have benefited Bayreuth by introducing more people to Wagner's work. So when the new Metropolitan Opera Company of New York announced its intention of mounting *Parsifal* in 1903, Cosima again took to the courts. This time she had the support of the entire Wagnerian movement in Germany, as well as that country's nationalist press. All howled in unison over New York's "robbery of the Grail."[115] Cosima helped lower the tone of the campaign by focusing on the Jewish origins of the Metropolitan's director, Heinrich Conried, and by threatening banishment from Bayreuth for all those artists who participated in the New York production.[116] None of this availed: America had not subscribed to the international copyright agreement that protected *Parsifal,* and the singers would not or could not break their contracts with Conried. So *Parsifal* made its New World premiere in 1903, ten years before it became available to the European nations that were obliged to honor the thirty-year copyright protection. This time Bayreuth received no royalties, and Cosima had to content herself with making good on her threat to banish offending performers: the singers of Parsifal and Gurnemanz (Alois Burgstaller and Anton van Rooy) were never allowed to return to Bayreuth while Cosima guarded the shrine.[117] New York's "Grail robbery," however, had one advantage for Wahnfried: it brought Bayreuth's and Germany's racist-chauvanists together in a common struggle, thereby solidifying an alliance that would continue through the Third Reich.

Munich's, Berlin's, and even New York's successful productions of the *Ring* and *Parsifal* not only challenged Wahnfried's monopolistic pretentions; they suggested that the great urban opera houses—not Bayreuth's "Green Hill"—might soon become the most active promoters of Wagner's work. Indeed, the 1890s saw just such a trend, with the large European houses, especially London's Covent Garden, mounting so much Wagner that the once revolutionary music dramas quickly assumed the status of repertory staples. In 1895 the music critic for the *Saturday Review* could observe: "We are all Wagnerians now."[118]

This did not mean that people stopped making the Bayreuth pilgrimage; on the contrary, they came in droves to the 1888 and 1889 productions of *Die Meistersinger,* as they had not done to the four *Parsifal* series or to the *Tristan* production of 1886.[119] The box office success of *Die Meistersinger* allowed Cosima to pay off her debts and even to begin accruing a surplus that kept increasing until the inflationary collapse of the postwar period. Still, the artistic center of gravity had shifted away from Bayreuth, where Cosima's heavy hand eventually alienated some of Europe's most talented performers as well as some of its more discerning opera aficionados. (Included among the latter were Thomas Mann, who complained of Cosima's "unsavory influence;"[120] and George Bernard Shaw, who after witnessing the Bayreuth productions of 1894 noted that their poetic exposition resembled a "good Budget speech" and that they had about as much "charm of voice and style" as a "conference of the National Liberal Confederation.")[121]

Not surprisingly, the younger generation led the revolt against Cosima's rule. In 1892 the directress tried to establish a music school for young performers (*Stilbildungsschule*),[122] but only seventeen enrolled, of whom the majority soon dropped out. By 1898 only five students remained, and Cosima was obliged to close the school. One of the graduates, ironically enough, was Alois Burgstaller, whom Cosima was later to banish for performing in the 1903 New York *Parsifal*.[123]

After suffering a partially incapacitating stroke in 1906, Cosima retired from active direction of the Bayreuth Festival. Her son Siegfried, then thirty-seven years old, assumed her duties. Before examining Siegfried's tenure, however, it is necessary briefly to discuss some of the other disciples who helped shape the German Wagnerian movement during the late nineteenth and early twentieth centuries. After all, Cosima may have been queen of Bayreuth, but she was surrounded by powerful courtiers.

· IV

One of the least known but most influential among them was a young academic named Heinrich von Stein.[124] Born in 1857, Stein studied theology and eventually philosophy at Heidelberg, Halle, and Berlin. His most influential mentor was Eugen Dühring, whose materialist teachings Stein tried to reconcile with the heritage of German idealism. While at Berlin he began reading Schopenhauer, an experience that proved decisive in the evolution of his world view. Although he continued to see himself as a synthesizer of Christian theology, materialism, and Kantian idealism, he increasingly operated on the Schopenhauerian premise that art, in particular music, was the key to the regeneration of society. He was thus naturally drawn toward Wagner, and when the Master (on the recommendation of Malwida von Meysenbug[125]) offered him a position tutoring Siegfried, he accepted with alacrity.

Stein arrived at Wahnfried in October 1879. He described his first meeting with Wagner as "a convulsion of the soul."[126] The Wagners, for their part, were equally impressed. They had hardly dared hope to find a tutor who might educate little Siegfried "according to our own ideas, [who could] lead him on a pious, safely un-Jewish, path toward Holy Communion." Although shocked to discover that their "young friend" was (in Cosima's words) "a Dühringianer and therefore an enemy of Christianity," they soon forgave him this fault. After all, noted Cosima, he was "a young, blond, sturdy fellow, every inch the German," and she could not help but believe that "with him all will work out smoothly, but also nobly." Richard agreed. "Stein is our pride," he said of his newest disciple.[127]

It is not surprising, then, that Stein rapidly became a confidant of the Wagners, actively participating in their evening discussions of books, people, and politics. Stein contributed his share to the conversations, but he was especially valued as a listener, as a reaffirmer of Genius. The Wagners were therefore much saddened when their young friend, on orders from his father, decided to leave Wahnfried and pursue his academic studies at the University of Halle.[128]

Stein's academic ambitions eventually led him to a university teaching position in Berlin, where he lectured on aesthetics. It was here in Berlin that he produced his more important scholarly work, most notably *The Origins of Modern Aesthetics*. This erudite study of the aesthetic tradition from the French classicists to Winckelmann won praise from the philosopher and historian Wilhelm Dilthey, whose historicist method it emulated. Stein demonstrated in this work that he was much more than Wagner's favorite sounding board; he was a considerable talent in his own right, a young man to be reckoned with in the demanding world of German scholarship.

Stein's migration to Berlin, while disturbing to the Wagners, by no means meant a severing of his ties with Bayreuth. On the contrary, Stein kept in constant contact with the Wagners, especially with Cosima, who admired him more than any of the other disciples.[129] He also continued to contribute regularly to the *Bayreuther Blätter,* concentrating mainly on literary and philosophical topics. The writers and thinkers he focused on—Shakespeare, Rousseau, Goethe, Gobineau, Schopenhauer—all belonged to Bayreuth's special pantheon: they were part of a "tradition of Genius" that, according to Stein, culminated in Wagner.[130] (Wagner himself claimed that it made him "feel peculiar" to be compared to Shakespeare, but he did not reject the comparison.[131]) Stein also took up such favorite Bayreuth topics as antivivisectionism and Eastern mysticism. In each of these efforts he mingled an ostentatious display of learning with a penchant for the most convoluted forms of expression. The result was a literary style that must have been heavy sailing even for Wagnerians: the Master himself confessed to having trouble with one of Stein's pieces, which he found "sketchy and bombastic."[132]

Almost a part of the Wagner family, Stein was naturally devastated when Richard died. Like Cosima, he wondered at first whether he would be able to go on at all. But then, again like Cosima, he suddenly realized his work had just begun. In the words of his biographer: "He saw that he had the great duty to further Wagner's work at a time when [it] was threatened by the Master's death."[133]

Stein's pursuit of this mission resulted in a number of important contributions to the Wagnerian movement. The most significant of these were his editorship (along with Karl Friedrich Glasenapp) of the so-called *Wagner-Lexikon*[134] and his inauguration of the first university course on the works of Richard Wagner. Both of these enterprises were curious, and yet typical. The *Wagner-Lexikon* was a kind of encyclopedia of Wagnerian wisdom; organized alphabetically, it contained excerpts from Wagner's writings on every imaginable subject, from atoms and architecture to blood, vegetarianism, and the soul. Like Cosima's diary, another repository of the Master's wisdom, it presumed that Wagner was equally profound on all subjects, that he was truly a great thinker whose every observation merited preservation for posterity. Stein's Wagner lectures at the University of Berlin also focused on Wagner the thinker. The university officials at first refused to allow such a course (perhaps they were not convinced of

Wagner's stature as a philosopher), and Stein was unable to begin the course until 1887, the year of his untimely death.[135]

At the time of his death (he lived only to age thirty) Stein had written very little specifically on Wagner. He had published a short introduction to the *Lexikon* and an essay entitled "Die Darstellung der Natur in den Werken Richard Wagners" (The depiction of nature in the work of Richard Wagner).[136] Nevertheless, he left his mark on German Wagnerism. He did this above all through his personality, which in its own way was quite charismatic.[137] Cosima, who appears almost to have worshipped him, declared: "His was a character which showed us what was possible in the realm of nobility, purity, fire, and enthusiasm."[138] Houston Stewart Chamberlain confessed to "a kind of sacred awe for the nobility of his character" and feared that it was beyond his powers to do justice to Stein's "angelic pure nature."[139] Eventually Stein's students at Berlin caught the fire of his enthusiasm as well, and his lectures, at first poorly attended, became popular forums for the discussion of his highly idiosyncratic philosophy. At his death in 1887 Stein had clearly emerged as one of the most influential of the Bayreuth group. Wolzogen was correct to eulogize him as "our most promising and noblest comrade."[140]

Stein, then, became a kind of myth figure for the German Wagnerians. He was enshrined in their pantheon as the most noble representative (after the Master, of course) of disinterested idealism, high-minded seriousness, and the willingness to sacrifice health and happiness for the high cause of art.

But the Bayreuth Wagnerians were not the only ones to be beguiled by this promising young aesthete. Friedrich Nietzsche, too, admired Stein's precocious talents—indeed, admired them enough to ignore his own advice against acquiring disciples and to court young Stein as a potential follower.[141] After Stein had paid him a brief visit at Sils-Maria in 1884, Nietzsche could rhapsodize: "At last, at last a new man who belongs to me and instinctively respects me! To be sure, for the time-being still *trop wagnerisé,* yet quite prepared for me through the rational discipline he received in the proximity of Dühring. In his company I felt very sharply what practical task my life's work includes once I have enough young people of a very certain quality."[142] But Nietzsche's enthusiasm began to fade when he found he could not inculcate in Stein the full meaning of Zarathustra's mission. For this he blamed the continuing influence of Wagner, the arch-deceiver: "The youth becomes mooncalf—an *idealist*. He is beyond science, hereby attaining the level of his master. Instead, he acts the philosopher."[143]

As Nietzsche's comment suggests, Stein's short career as Wagnerian missionary was marred not only by its untimely end. His legacy was more complex than a hallowed memory of personal nobility, enthusiasm, and dedication. For if he indeed embodied that spiritual purity that Cosima and others took to be the essence of Wagnerism, he also embodied that neurasthenia, that hypersensitive vulnerability, that likewise often accompanied the Wagnerian infatuation. Stein was also an intellectual dogmatist of the first order, intolerant of any who did not see art as he did: as an instrument for the moral regeneration of humanity. In taking this line he saw himself as furthering the cause not just of Wagnerism but of the German idealist tradition generally. He was, indeed, the consumate German Idealist. He shared in that tradition's worship of the Idea and in its belief in the primacy of art and religion. Unlike later *Vulgäridealisten,*[144] he did not employ this intellectual stance as a justification for specific political and social policies; he did not place idealism in the service of reaction. And yet he was not without some responsibility for the gradual corruption of this tradition. His idealistic vision was ultimately quite parochial, embracing elements of anti-Semitism and German cultural chauvinism. For him, as for so many latter-day *völkisch* writers, the Germans alone were genuine "idealists," capable of inward ennoblement and spiritual transcendence, while other "races," especially the Jews, were consigned to the worship of Mammon. The historian Richard Stackelberg is thus surely correct when he interprets Stein's legacy as a step, however tentative, toward the "debasement of idealism into messianic nationalism."[145]

V

If Heinrich von Stein wrote relatively little about Wagner, his co-editor in the *Wagner-Lexikon,* Karl Friedrich Glasenapp,[146] wrote little that did not deal with Wagner. Born in Riga in 1847, Glasenapp lived a life that was unremarkable except for its single-minded devotion to the Master. He had no special gifts, no originality. ("I lack ideas of my own," he once admitted, "and therefore I am not cut out to be a creative writer.") What Glasenapp did have, in addition to his fanatical loyalty to Wagner, was plodding tenacity, and this enabled him to churn out a mammoth six-volume Wagner biography,[147] a Wagner "encyclopedia" (subtitled: "The greatest Moments in Art as Illuminated by the Thought of Richard Wagner")[148] and a number of essays and reviews—almost all of them devoted either to Wagner or to his son Siegfried.

Glasenapp's most important work, his Wagner biography, was anything but a critical dissection of the Master's work and life; although packed with important (and still very useful) information, it was essentially a hagiography. True to Cosima's idealization of her husband, it downplayed or ignored the Master's shortcomings as man and artist. In doing so, it also fulfilled the rather selective image that Wagner in his later years had been trying to create for posterity. Thus, although Wagner liked on occasion to make fun of Glasenapp's doglike devotion,[149] he encouraged his loyal biographer by allowing him access to his private correspondence and to his as yet unpublished autobiography. Cosima, too, took Glasenapp into her confidence and provided him with material for his great work. Glasenapp's study, then, can be termed the first "authorized" Wagner biography, and as such it was endowed with a kind of gospel status among the German Wagnerians.

This biography, however, was not designed simply to reinforce the devotion of the believers. As we suggested above, it was also calculated to "revise" the public's perception of Wagner as amoral or hedonistic, as a corrupter or a dandy. In Glasenapp's portrait the Master emerged as a kind of Victorian pater familias, albeit given on occasion to the harmless eccentricities one had to expect and forgive in an artistic genius. Richard Wagner as pious, patriotic, bourgeois gentleman, lover of children and dogs, personal life essentially as morally edifying as his great art: this portrait required some very fancy brushwork and a highly selective use of the palette. Glasenapp proved up to the task; carefully screening the mass of material at his disposal, sometimes distorting documents and perhaps even destroying a few of the most problematical,[150] he achieved a result that even the ever-vigilant Cosima could applaud. He also set a precedent for Wahnfried hagiography that later disciples might emulate. Count Richard Du Moulin-Eckart did so in his "official" biography of Cosima;[151] Houston Stewart Chamberlin followed suit in his own biography of the Master,[152] which also made creative use of historical fact in achieving a "higher verity." In this Chamberlain was, of course, emulating not only Glasenapp but Wagner himself, whose autobiography *Mein Leben* was not overly scrupulous when it came to nit-picking detail. Again we see how one of Wagner's foibles was made into a kind of article of faith by his followers: "Higher Truth" at the expense of lower fact clearly became an essential component in the ongoing mythologization of the Master and in the evolution of *Wagnerismus*.

As Wagner's "official" biographer, Glasenapp enjoyed a privileged position at the court of Wahnfried. Although he continued to reside in Riga, he visited Bayreuth often, and every time he did so he found ready access to the Wagner household. There he would participate actively in the evening conversations, go for long walks with the Master, all the while taking mental notes for his biography. Both Richard and Cosima professed admiration for this loyal scribe, whom Cosima at one point considered appointing Siegfried's tutor.[153] This is not to say, however, that the Wagners were entirely unaware of Glasenapp's limitations. They knew he was incapable of originality, and Richard in particular could be condescending toward his uncritical devotion (while nevertheless demanding it). Once, when toasting Glasenapp's health, he could not help adding maliciously: "[He] brings the dead to life, and kills off the living with his biography."[154]

Glasenapp's fanatical devotion to Wagner could occasion mild derision even among the other Bayreuth disciples, themselves for the most part hardly above the charge of blind loyalty. Ludwig Schemann (of whom more below) saw Glasenapp as that quintessential "Wagnerianer" described by the anti-Wagner press: a man for whom the world "began and ended" with the Master and who unfailingly divided all humanity into Wagnerians and non-Wagnerians, as if "the one were the ewes and the other the rams."[155] Schemann was surely correct in this appraisal: when the non-Wagnerian (or rather, the unorthodox Wagnerian) Josef Kürschner asked Glasenapp for permission to photograph a Wagner portrait that the latter had commissioned for the Riga Wagner Society and that was shown only to the elect, Glasenapp refused. Kürschner denounced this example of "Phariseeism" on the part of one of Wagner's "allegedly most loyal followers" but to no avail.[156]

Glasenapp, in short, was a man of such transparent mediocrity that no one, not even Glasenapp himself, could fail to recognize it. And yet three of his colleagues in the Bayreuth disciplehood, Hans von Wolzogen, Henry Thode, and Siegfried Wagner, took the strange step of nominating him for the Nobel Prize for literature in 1902. Nothing much came of this quixotic gesture, for even devoted Wagnerians, let alone the uninitiated, refused to associate themselves with it.[157] Still, the very fact that it was made at all is significant, for it shows how self-satisfied and myopic the Bayreuth inner circle could be. These crusaders must have viewed their cause as so noble that even one of its least distinguished proponents was worthy of the world's recognition.

VI

Among the prominent disciples who refused to have any part in the pathetic Glasenapp promotion was Ludwig Schemann.[158] Born in 1852 in Cologne, Schemann had studied classical philology and history in Heidelberg and Berlin before settling in Göttingen as a librarian at the local university. Interestingly enough, he could have become a professor of classics, but he regarded a specialized academic career as incompatible with his need for "universality."[159] He later wrote that the influence of Wagner and Schopenhauer was decisive in his rejection of academia: "I was almost prepared to throw myself into a specialized academic discipline, and thereby sacrifice my essential universality, when [my encounter with] Wagner and Schopenhauer inspired me to make myself more fully at home with the arts and philosophy."[160] Schemann had hoped that his position as librarian would leave him ample time for his philosophizing, but—as with Nietzsche—the combined pressures of holding an official post and pursuing a private career as artist-philosopher proved too much for him. Eventually released from his librarian's duties and supported by a small pension and contributions from friends, he spent the rest of his life as a "private scholar" in Kassel and Freiburg.[161]

Bayreuth, however, not Kassel or Freiburg, was always his "spiritual home." He had attended the first festival there in 1876 and was thenceforth committed to the Wagnerian cause. By the late 1870s he was a prominent fixture in the Bayreuth discipleship, giving lectures on Wagner's art, helping organize the Society of Patrons and contributing regularly to the *Bayreuther Blätter*. The reward for all these services was personal contact with the Master himself—the chance to join the inner circle at Wahnfried and learn at first hand what the great man had to say about everything from Voltaire to vivisection. Schemann,

however, did not just passively listen; he held forth himself, sometimes at great length, and this caused Wagner to lament to Cosima
about how "*young* and immature his friends were."[162] Nevertheless,
Wagner admired his young friend enough to invite him to settle permanently in Bayreuth, just as he had done with Wolzogen. Although
highly flattered by this offer, Schemann ultimately decided against
accepting it, thereby displaying a strain of independence from Wahnfried that was to increase over the years.

Indeed, what is striking about Schemann's relationship to Wagnerism (and what helps to explain his eventual refusal to take part in
the Glasenapp promotion) was his ability to combine reverence for the
Master with a certain willful independence of mind. Cosima had noted
this early and become uneasy about it; here was a young man who had
"curious ideas" about the relationship between master and disciple.[163]
Curious indeed—for it became increasingly clear that Schemann had
nothing but contempt for the knee-jerk Wagner adoration of Glasenapp and Wolzogen. He above all rejected the latter's tendency to accept
uncritically everything the Master said, including his dismissive pronouncements on other musicians. An admirer of Schumann, he fumed
when the *Bayreuther Blätter*, ever loyal to Wagner, parroted the Master's attacks against this composer. This kind of automatic dogmatism
was enough to make him reassess his entire relationship to Bayreuth, or
at least to its house journal; he warned Wolzogen that if the attack on
Schumann were to be the first of many such "indecencies on behalf of
Wagner" then he must sadly step aside and declare: "The way of the
Bayreuther Blätter is no longer my way."[164] Indeed, somewhat later
(1887) Schemann did announce his determination to sever his ties with
Bayreuth, and after 1889 he no longer attended the festival.

In fact, however, Schemann never entirely cut himself off from the
Wagner circle. He continued to correspond with Wolzogen, and he
even wrote articles for the *Blätter*. More important, he took it upon
himself to promote alliances between the somewhat incestuous little
world of Bayreuth and the gathering forces of right-wing radicalism
and organized anti-Semitism. He thus helped make Bayreuth an
important bastion of what Fritz Stern has called "the politics of cultural despair."[165]

Schemann's first such contact was with Count Gobineau, whose
Essay on the Inequality of Races he translated and about whom he wrote a
massive two-volume biography.[166] This biography not only lauded
Gobineau's racist theories; it also took special pains to point up the

connections between Gobineau's and Wagner's legacies. According to Schemann, Gobineau was a great admirer of Wagner; indeed, Gobineau regarded his friendship with the Master as "the natural culmination of his development toward Germanism." In Wagner's work he found "the most complete embodiment of his own theories on race, heroes, gods, survival, and disintegration." Wagner in turn, noted Schemann, saw Gobineau as a trusted ally; he sent him an edition of his collected works with the inscription: "Das wäre ein Bund / Norman und Sachse: / Was da noch gesund, / Dass das blühe und wachse!" (T'were that they were bound / Norman and Sax' / What between them's still sound, / Let that blossom and wax).[167]

Schemann's celebration of Gobineau did not end with this hagiography; he also took a leading role in the so-called "Gobineau Society" (Gobineau Vereinigung), which was dedicated to the promotion of the Frenchman's theories in Germany. This enterprise was launched in Bayreuth with the full blessing of Cosima, although she was later to complain that Schemann overestimated the importance of Gobineau's ideas.[168] Cosima's objection notwithstanding, Schemann saw his promotion of Gobineau as a natural extension of his Wagnerism; the "naturalization" (Einbürgerung) of Gobineau, he said, was in fact "an accomplishment for Bayreuth."[169]

Schemann believed the same of his championship of Paul de Lagarde, the reclusive *völkisch* guru whom Wagner had tried unsuccessfully to cultivate. Schemann had more luck with the querulous Lagarde: a devoted admirer of his works, he was the first to systematically explicate them and thus make Lagarde's "Germanic Christianity" more accessible to the forces of *völkisch* radicalism in the new German Empire. In the process he managed to strike up a lasting friendship with the orientalist, who tended to alienate everyone, especially his academic colleagues. It was therefore something of a personal tragedy for Schemann when he proved unable, despite repeated efforts, to win Lagarde over to the Wagnerian movement. The latter, as we noted above, simply could not abide the "music of the future." Lagarde's distaste for Wagner's music, however, did not prevent Schemann from insisting on the essential compatibility of their respective philosophies. Lagarde may have remained strangely unmoved by "the earth-shaking power of Wagnerian art," but he nevertheless followed the Master in his efforts to "completely regenerate Germany"—an effort that he, too, coupled with an elimination of Jewish influences.[170] "Not since Schopenhauer and Wagner," wrote Schemann in an obituary for Lagarde, "has a German thinker so consistently repudiated this alien race, which defiles our holy places, poisons our people, and attempts to rob us of our land so as to completely oppress us."[171]

If, as Schemann insisted, Lagarde's achievements were insufficiently appreciated by his fellow Germans,[172] the same was true of another of Schemann's eccentric friends, Moeller van den Bruck. Schemann prided himself on having recruited Moeller to the *völkisch* cause and on recognizing just how useful this young cultural critic might be to the "regenerative" efforts of the Wagnerians.[173] And for his part, Moeller, who tended to see himself as a lonely crusader against the "liberalism" of official Germany, credited Schemann as "the only German who had understood his books."[174]

Schemann was also close to the anti-Semitic publicists whose articles appeared in Theodore Fritsch's journal, *Antisemitische Correspondenz*. Prominent among these were the Förster brothers, Bernard and Paul. Bernard, the brother-in-law of Nietzsche and one of imperial Germany's most rabid anti-Semites, achieved notoriety chiefly through his founding of an (ultimately abortive) "Aryan" colony in the jungles of Paraguay. He promoted this quixotic venture in the *Bayreuther Blätter*, maintaining that it was something the Master would have heartily endorsed.[175] Bernard's brother Paul rode a different hobby horse, that of antivivisectionism.[176] He, too, invoked the Master's blessing, and with solid justification, since Wagner had made it known that he was as opposed to dissecting living animals as he was to eating dead ones.[177] Both Försters were friends of Schemann and through him of Bayreuth; they were never, however, part of the inner circle, for as devoted as they were to Wagner's art and philosophy, they did not make the Master's legacy the center of their lives.

Nevertheless, their affiliation with Bayreuth through Schemann expanded the ties between *Wagnerismus* and the *völkisch* Right in Imperial Germany. Such contacts ensured that if Bayreuth's festival, under Cosima, slipped to the status of a cultural backwater, Bayreuth's politics pointed very much to the future.

Schemann himself lived to see that future, or at least a part of it, for he died five years after Hitler's seizure of power. Like his friend Moeller van den Bruck, however, he did not entirely like what he saw. Shortly before his death in 1938 he wrote that he regarded "Germany's recent development with the greatest trepidation."[178] Winfried Schüler explains this by citing Schemann's "good measure of human-

istic scholarship and conservative consciousness."[179] No doubt he possessed these traits: his writings displayed great erudition as well as a
pronounced Christian piety. Like many neoconservative intellectuals
he must have been deeply troubled by the Nazis' combination of vulgarity, mindlessness, and crude social Darwinism. And there is also no
doubt that his sense of trepidation embraced his beloved Bayreuth as
well: he expressed his "sadness" at "recent developments" there, too,
a reference to the fateful intimacy between Bayreuth and the Nazi
regime.[180]

One could argue, however, that genuine as Schemann's despair over
this intimacy might have been, his own career as Wagner missionary
helped make it possible. As we have seen, he did much to promote
extensive ties between the Bayreuth discipleship and various factions
in the *völkisch* Right. No wonder, then, that the Nazis themselves
ultimately saw the pious "Dr. Schemann" as a kindred spirit, as a
valuable "early fighter" for their cause. In recognition of Schemann's
"services" to *völkisch* science Hitler awarded him the Goethe Medal for
Art and Science on his eighty-fifth birthday.[181] Walter Frank, the
Nazis' official historian, wrote an obituary for him in the *Historische
Zeitschrift* which quoted a eulogy from another Nazi scholar, Hans
Bogner: "He [Schemann] was an intellectual model for us as a servant
of rigidly objective scholarship; an ideological model as a tireless pros-
elytizer of racial thought, who did much to ensure the penetration of
the sciences, especially historical science, by racial ideas; a model finally as a political fighter, who committed his entire existence to the
triumph of his people and who as a result of his true German thinking
suffered considerable persecution."[182]

VII

Ludwig Schemann was too independent-minded to be entirely comfortable within the confines of the Bayreuth Circle, however essentially compatible that group's politics and philosophy may have been.
Cosima, it would seem, was never quite able to educate him regarding
the proper relationship between disciple and master, or between disciple and mistress. One might have thought she would have had an
easier time with her two sons-in-law, Henry Thode and Houston
Stewart Chamberlain. Both these men, like Schemann, were part of

Bayreuth's inner circle, and yet both showed themselves capable of a certain rebelliousness.

If Ludwig Schemann shunned the academic world, Henry Thode[183] sought to embrace it. Trained in Vienna as an art historian, he eventually found a teaching post at the University of Bonn, where he lectured on the art of the Italian Renaissance. His interpretation of Renaissance culture[184] evolved from his conviction that all great artistic periods drew their inspiration not from contemporary social, political, and religious conditions but from the values prevailing in the immediately preceding era. This meant that the civilization of the Renaissance, which Burckhardt identified with a renewal of classical humanist ideals, was for Thode a transmutation of the profound religiosity that had animated the Middle Ages and reached its apogee in the preaching of Saint Francis, about whom Thode wrote one of his most famous works. Thode further argued that a period such as the Renaissance, in which religious energies were absorbed in artistic and political achievement, would inevitably give way to another epoch of more simple religious feeling, when men would turn away from individualistic artistic and political enterprises in favor of a profound communal spirituality. He thought he saw the beginnings of just such a transition in his own era: an age of egocentric and "decadent" artistic production was slowly yielding to a new "religious yearning," a new "passion for community."[185]

Thode's somewhat rigid and dogmatic "system" for interpreting the history of culture by no means convinced the majority of his professional peers,[186] but he gradually won a large popular audience for his books and lectures. He also achieved considerable popular success with his university and public lectures on another topic: the art of Richard Wagner.[187] He interpreted Wagner's work in terms of that transition to a new religious community that he found dawning in his own era. Wagner's art, he believed, was spiritually akin to the art of the Middle Ages: anti-individualistic, full of reverence and piety, essentially otherworldly. In an essay on the importance of Wagner's work for German academic youth,[188] Thode argued that an immersion in Wagnerian art would inevitably inspire a revival of old-Germanic mystical spirituality: Wagner, in short, was the spiritual heir of Albrecht Dürer. Since this interpretation of Wagner's legacy harmonized closely with Cosima's, Wahnfried and Thode soon struck up an alliance. Indeed, Cosima even helped further Thode's academic career by facilitating his move from Bonn to the University of Berlin, where he taught until his retirement in 1911.[189]

Wahnfried meant more to Thode than a source of patronage. In the same year that he began his highly successful teaching career (1886), he married Cosima's eldest daughter, Daniela von Bülow. This alliance could not help but make him proud. He had been a passionate Wagnerian since his youth; he attended the first Bayreuth Festival in 1876, the *Parsifal* premiere in 1882, and met the Wagner family in Venice in the same year. Wagner, he believed, was "the greatest genius the world had ever produced." In his work "all great artistic and philosophical strivings reached their culmination."[190] No wonder he regarded his affiliation with the Master's family as "the greatest piece of fortune that could ever befall a man."[191]

But marriage to Daniela (and hence to Bayreuth) proved ultimately to be a severe trial for Thode. Much as he admired Wagner, he had very limited respect for the disciples around his widow. He once noted that he maintained his loyalty to Wagner despite all the "nonsense" perpetrated in his name by his closest followers.[192] (A strange revelation, one might note, coming from a man who would eventually conominate Karl Friedrich Glasenapp for the Nobel Prize.) Although he still wrote on occasion for the *Bayreuther Blätter,* Thode increasingly kept his distance from Bayreuth itself and from the circle of disciples that he had once hungered to join. His relationship with Daniela, too, suffered over time. She was subject to severe melancholia, which in turn plunged Thode into depression. He finally divorced her in 1914 and remarried in the same year.

This ended Thode's personal relationship with Wahnfried but not his enthusiasm for Wagner. He continued to see himself as a proponent of the "Bayreuth intellectual world" and as a kind of disciple in exile until his death in 1920.[193]

Thode's lifelong commitment to Wagner had a definite impact on his work as an art historian. Indeed, he once insisted that all his ideas in the field of intellectual history, especially in the history of art, were based on the views of the Master and that his deepest insights were rooted in revelations from Bayreuth.[194] He was, he believed, following the views of the Master not only in his interpretation of the Renaissance but also in his perspective on the art of his own day. Like Wagner, he saw much that appalled him in what passed for contemporary "culture." Particularly appalling was the sudden vogue at the turn of the century for French Impressionism. By 1905 Thode had become alarmed enough by modern artistic trends to deliver and subsequently publish a series of lectures that spelled out his views on the contemporary cultural scene. He displayed his colors prominently in the very first lecture when he expressed his baffled outrage at the "fanatical admirers of modern French Impressionism . . . , who go so far as to declare Manet a genius comparable to the greatest [painters] of all time, who find in him and in others like Renoir, Monet, Degas, Seurat, Signac a new artistic movement of the highest importance, to which we owe new aesthetic insights." Thode was especially exasperated by the fact that some of these admirers of Impressionism were German critics who defamed the best of their own nation's recent art (the work, for example, of the traditionalist painters Böcklin and Thoma) in favor of the foreign imports. What consequences, he asked, might this have for German culture?[195]

One of them, clearly, was that a whole generation of young Germans was in danger of losing its ability to distinguish foreign "trash" (Manet et al.) from "the truly great and eternal" (Böcklin and Thoma). Another was that German artists themselves would start emulating the French passion for pure "technical virtuosity"—all that *plain air*—at the expense of edifying content. Indeed, German painters like Max Liebermann, president of the "Berlin Secession," were already afflicted with the foreign bacillus. According to Thode, none of Liebermann's work was truly original, despite its "slickness of technique and finesse with light." Liebermann did, however, show himself to be a genuine "impressionist," for in the end this term meant nothing more than "sensationalist."[196]

Thode, as we noted, insisted that he conducted his crusade against the "decadence" of his time in the name of Richard Wagner. This is highly significant, for it meant an identification of Wagner's art with the antimodernist element in German culture. Just as Germany was beginning to open itself to new artistic influences from abroad—for example, to the glories of French Impressionism[197]—the disciples of Germany's most celebrated composer of the era were waging a war against that new culture and holding up their Master's work as an example of healthy native art. No wonder *Wagnerismus* now found an ally in that most hidebound of fin-de-siècle "art experts," Kaiser Wilhelm II. Wilhelm had no real understanding of music (or any other art, for that matter), but he accepted Thode's judgment that Wagner's work was safely conservative and wholesomely Germanic. He had written Cosima as early as 1887 of his "enthusiasm" for her husband's work and of his "joy in furthering [that work's] proper recognition."[198] Actually, Wilhelm's support would hardly prove necessary, for, as we have seen, the Berlin aristocracy had already "discovered" Wagner in the mid-1870s. By the end of the century, he would seem quite acceptable in comparison with such "ultramodern and therefore unenjoyable" composers as Richard Strauss.[199]

The negative side of this development was that Germany's more progressive intelligentsia increasingly found Wagner unacceptable. In Heinrich Mann's *Der Untertan* (The Subject), for example, Wagner's music is closely identified with the chauvinistic, militaristic, and reactionary ideals that pervaded the Second Empire. For Mann, Wagner had become to music what the Siegesallee was to sculpture.

Heinrich Mann had some justification for this coupling of Wagner— or rather, the official Bayreuth image of Wagner—with German militarism. In 1876 Wagner had not succeeded in making his festival the artistic sister of German unity, but by 1914, when invading German troops paused to celebrate their recent victories at the Cathedral of St. Quentin in Lille, they listened to "Die Weihe des Grals" (The consecration of the grail) from *Parsifal*. The military reporter rhapsodized, "Here the tones of the glorification of the pure fool, out there [in the field of battle] the deeds of the pure sword of the Germans."[200] Of course, Wagner himself was partly responsible for all this. He had railed against unhealthy foreign influences in German life and culture, and he had offered his own art as an antidote to such alien corruption and as a source of Germanic political-cultural revival.

On the other hand, Wagner was never, strictly speaking, a cultural atavist. He may have employed ancient legends or myths in his work, but his artistic rendering of them was strikingly modern. Thode and his conservative admirers had no appreciation whatsoever for the fundamental radicalism of Wagner's art, and so they cheerfully invoked the Wagnerian legacy in their ongoing war against the most innovative trends in European culture. This, like so much of the Bayreuth interpretive canon, was less true to Wagner than to *Wagnerismus*.

VIII

Wagner's other son-in-law, Houston Stewart Chamberlain, was perhaps the most troublesome and complex of all the disciples who interpreted the Master's legacy.[201] On the one hand, he was capable of an almost childish devotion to Wagner, whom he never knew but only worshipped from a distance, yet he was equally capable on occasion of questioning the Master's abilities as a cultural philosopher and social theorist. He ultimately became a stout defender of Cosima and Bayreuth orthodoxy, yet at the same time could be even more critical of knee-jerk *Wagnerismus* than Schemann or Thode. In addition, perhaps more than any other prominent Wagnerian, he insisted on Wagner's essential "Germanness," a quality that allegedly made the profoundest secrets of the Master's art impenetrable to foreigners. And yet of course Chamberlain was himself a foreigner—a born Englishman who lived the first ten years of his life in France, attended schools in England, and took his university studies in Switzerland. Although he had developed an early fascination for things German, his loyalties and identity remained severly confused until he managed to put himself through a Germanic conversion that left him feeling *plus royalist que le roi*. Born again as a "German" and a Wagnerian, Chamberlain eventually became so confident of his ability to penetrate the Master's subtleties that he could risk putting some intellectual distance between himself and the rest of the Bayreuth inner circle.[202] Ultimately he could risk something yet more daring: he could claim to have transcended the Master's influence and to have substantially improved upon his philosophy of social-cultural reform. He made these claims in rebutting Henry Thode's charge that he had plagiarized from Wagner in his magnum opus, *Die Grundlagen des neunzehnten Jahrhunderts (The Foundations of the Nineteenth Century)*. Whatever the merits of Thode's accusation or of Chamberlain's defense (of which more below), this so-called Foundations Conflict (*Grundlagen Konflikt*) has contributed to the sense of ambiguity surrounding Chamberlain's relationship to his father-in-law's legacy. What, then, was the essence of this relationship, and how are we to define Chamberlain's position within the Wagnerian movement?

Chamberlain himself wrote fairly extensively about what Wagner meant to him in a memoir he published in 1917.[203] This piece is extremely interesting, for it shows how Chamberlain tried to walk the fine line between his loyalty to Wagner and his claims to originality.

Chamberlain did not depict his road to Bayreuth as having been straight and smooth, as it was for Wolzogen or Glasenapp, but rather circuitous and somewhat rocky. It began, he reminisced, when as a child he happened to pass by Wagner's Swiss refuge, Triebschen, and to hear the name of its famous occupant. The name meant nothing to him then, and yet it somehow penetrated his subconscious "like the secret promise of some future blessing."[204]

The blessing took time to materialize. Chamberlain's interests were protean and included music, but eventually he found himself focusing his studies not on music or literature but on natural science, especially plant physiology. He was a gifted researcher, and he might have lost himself forever in his laboratory had it not been for his chronic ill health. He was forced periodically to suspend his studies and regain his strength at various continental watering places. At one such spa (Interlaken), he met a Viennese Jew named Blumenfeld who initiated him into some of the more rudimentary Wagnerian mysteries.[205] Blumenfeld informed him, for example, that the Festspielhaus lay not in Beirut, Syria, as the *London Times* had reported, but in Bayreuth in the heart of Germany. More important, Blumenfeld introduced Chamberlain to the text of the *Ring* operas, in whose poetic cadences and symbolic profundities he began to realize the promise of Triebschen. But only partly to realize it. Chamberlain now knew that he had to see the *Ring* performed on stage, indeed had to go see it performed at this magical Bayreuth and in the presence of the Master himself.[206]

But Chamberlain, like so many young Wagner admirers, was impecunious, and so "with beating heart" he dispatched a letter to Wagner in which he declared his undying devotion, explained his straitened circumstances, and requested free admission to one of the *Ring* cycles. (After all, had not Wagner himself promised to set aside a certain number of free seats for needy students?) Alas, his request must never have reached the Master (or so, at least, Chamberlain was obliged to conclude), for he received only a form letter from the festival administration notifying him that there were still seats available for the second and third cycles at a price of one hundred talers each (p. 195).

Yet even this rebuff did not cool Chamberlain's ardor. Unable to witness the *Ring* premiere in Bayreuth, he contented himself for the time being with attendance at Wagnerian concerts presented by the resort band at Interlaken. Then in 1878 he saw a production of *Tannhäuser* in a German provincial town that turned out to be a "crushing disappointment" (p. 208). Shortly thereafter, however, he attended Munich's first complete *Ring* cycle, and despite the fact that his seat allowed him virtually no view of the stage he was reconfirmed in the faith by this oceanic experience (pp. 210–11).

Indeed, the Munich *Ring* so transported him, had so "elevated his spirit," that he sat down immediately to compose his first appreciation of Wagner's genius. He then sent this piece, again with "beating heart," to Wolzogen at the *Bayreuther Blätter*. Chamberlain admitted that this step was "rather bold," for he was but an unknown young Englishman, and his essay combined a celebration of Wagner with an attack against the periodical to which it was submitted. In particular, it railed against "the clear tendency of the *Bayreuther Blätter* to force the members of the new Society of Patrons to adopt specific philosophical, religious, and political beliefs." Wolzogen and his colleagues allegedly demanded that their contributors "regress to the mental style of Buddhism and cleanse their limbs of science in the waters of the holy Ganges." This all came about, insisted Chamberlain, from the "totally false and reprehensible procedure of extracting elaborate philosophical positions from works of art" (p. 219).

Needless to say, Wolzogen rejected Chamberlain's piece. He also observed in the very next issue that foreigners could never truly understand Wagner, and he offered as evidence for this observation the inanities of a recent submission by a young English enthusiast (p. 218).

Chamberlain was momentarily crushed: "These words pierced a heart full of love, enthusiasm, and the desire to serve; I felt as if I had been cast out of an enterprise which was sacred to me" (p. 218). Again, however, he recovered quickly, and soon he was making plans to attend the next Bayreuth Festival, the premiere of *Parsifal* scheduled for 1882. This time he would let nothing deter him, neither limited resources nor the pressures of work. A true pilgrimage, after all, demanded sacrifice, and Chamberlain was now prepared to sacrifice anything—even his precious laboratory water cultures—in order to join the faithful at Bayreuth (p. 233).

The rail journey from Geneva, where Chamberlain was then living, lasted thirty hours. At a stop in Nuremberg he encountered other pilgrims, veterans of the 1876 festival, greeting each other with "stormy embraces." As a stranger and neophyte he at first felt out of place, but it was not long before his traveling companions, sensing his discomfort, put him completely at east with their friendly attention. By the end of the trip he realized that these Wagnerians, though maligned by all the world, were in fact "spiritually and morally far superior to their detractors" (p. 234).

Once in Bayreuth, the young man emulated his new friends in the rituals of fan worship. He thought of nothing but Wagner and lived for the moment when he might see him in the flesh, perhaps even hear his voice. That moment arrived when Wagner appeared at the Festspiel- haus restaurant on the eve of opening night. Chamberlain had been waiting in the restaurant for hours: "At last . . . he entered the room. . . . My heart skipped a beat, and I remember having to hold fast to a railing to keep from swooning." Despite his intoxicated state (and his nearsightedness), Chamberlain was able to discern the "ex- traordinary nobility" of Wagner's presence. He sensed that the Mas- ter's whole demeanor projected "a superiority of spirit and a strength of will" unmatched by any other person he had ever seen—unmatched even by Bismarck, who had conveyed an impression of "great peace" but also of "ineffable sadness," while Wagner resembled nothing so much as "a great proud ship, all sails unfurled, making resolutely for port, the waves and the weather be damned" (p. 237). After drinking a few toasts, Wagner made the rounds of the restaurant, going from table to table, even climbing up to the balcony where the less priv- ileged disciples were assembled. This afforded Chamberlain his one and only opportunity to see the Master up close and to record forever in his mind the features of that remarkable countenance. "I will say only this: around the sharp, willful features floated an expression of unutterable Goodness; eyes and mouth had something childlike, yea, almost divine, about them" (p. 239).

After such a moment, the actual performance of *Parsifal* must have been anticlimactic; at least Chamberlain says little about it in his memoir, save that his initial entry into the Festspielhaus inspired a never-to-be-repeated "seraphic bliss" (p. 241). More important than the details of the performance was the general impression left by this pilgrimage on the consciousness of the young man. Suddenly he had a place in life: "From then on my wandering soul had a home. I did not merely live from festival to festival, I put down my spiritual roots in that place where I found, as nowhere else in the world, a practical realization through clear-sighted genius of completely selfless, com- pletely idealistic goals" (p. 243).

Of course Chamberlain found not only a home in Bayreuth but also a family. He met Cosima in 1888, having been brought to her attention through the publication of his first Wagner essays in Dujardin's *Revue wagnérienne*. Cosima was quite taken with the young man, so much so that she immediately entrusted him with one of the more delicate maneuvers in her ongoing monopolization of her dead husband's legacy: the recovery of Wagner's correspondence with Theodore Uhlig, which she wished to "edit."[207] Chamberlain performed his duty well, and a long and generally warm-spirited relationship developed between him and Cosima. They were close enough, indeed, for Cosima to give her eventual blessing to Chamberlain's marriage to her daughter Eva, a step that brought this now not-so-young disciple literally "into the family."[208]

And yet Chamberlain's place in that family, or more precisely, in the extended Bayreuth family, became somewhat problematical well before it was finally secured through the marriage to Eva in 1908. His very first essays in the *Revue wagnérienne* adumbrated the problem, for they betrayed the most damning characteristic in a budding acolyte: a critical and independent spirit.[209] While full of praise for Wagner's art and aesthetic theories, they were—as his first submission to Wolzogen had been—highly heretical in their condemnation of those Wagnerians who sought specific philosophical or religious dogmas in the Master's work. For the young Chamberlain, true art soared above political, philosophical, or even religious concerns; it affected man directly, more through the heart than through the brain. Elaborating on this theme, he could argue that there was nothing really Schopenhauerian about *Tristan;* that there was no more Christianity in *Parsifal* than paganism in the *Ring* cycle.[210]

Chamberlain's irreverent rejection of the Bayreuth dogma in these matters is surprising, considering his later emergence as a zealous proponent of "Aryan Christianity" and a distinctly *völkisch* interpretation of Wagner's art. But it must be remembered that Chamberlain always prided himself on his independence from received dogma, whatever its origin. He could thus criticize his fellow Wagnerians not only for their tendentious interpretations of the Master's art but also for the opposite failing: for their tendency to treat the entire Wagnerian legacy as if it were Holy Scripture, sacrosanct from critical analysis. Disciples like Stein and Wolzogen had no critical acumen of their own; they were simply "mirrors . . . reflecting a light which radiated from the great man."[211] Chamberlain, on the other hand, came to see himself as an original and creative spirit, a man who could stand close to Wagner's genius without being overwhelmed by it. (After all, as he recalled in his memoirs, had not another genius—Goethe—written: "Mit Kleinen tut man kleinen Taten/ Mit Grossen wird der Kleine gross"? ["With little people one achieves little results; with the great the little man also becomes great"].[212]

Chamberlain's ambitions as a cultural commentator, nurtured through very wide reading and foreshadowed in his early writings on Wagner, blossomed fully only with the publication of his magnum opus, *The Foundations of the Nineteenth Century,* in 1899.[213] This long, complex work cannot be analyzed in detail here.[214] What needs to be discussed is the book's place in the history of Wagnerism, for that place is appropriately controversial.

The first question concerns the originality of the central argument of the book. In 1900, one year after its publication, Henry Thode published a review in which he stated that Chamberlain's entire approach was based on Wagner's prose publications, especially *Religion and Art,* and that one might therefore "wonder why this [debt] is acknowledged neither in the preface nor in the text of the book."[215] Chamberlain did not publicly respond to this charge until 1901, when, in the preface to the third edition of his *Foundations* he insisted that the ideas he had allegedly stolen from Wagner were not the latter's "private property" but part of the "common cultural heritage of European humanity."[216] He concluded his defense by acknowledging the genius of the Master.

Thode's attack, and Chamberlain's defense, were the public manifestations of a dispute about Chamberlain's book that had long been brewing in private and that involved Cosima as well as her present and future sons-in-law. Chamberlain had shown Cosima a draft of his manuscript in 1896, and she had been much distressed by its inadequate acknowledgment of Richard's influence. She no doubt communicated this disenchantment to Thode, for he would probably not have launched his public attack without the belief that Cosima would support him.[217] As it turned out, however, Cosima played less a supporting role for either party than a mediating one; she hated to see Bayreuth's dirty laundry aired in public. Eventually she was able to impose a kind of peace on the troubled family, without, however, getting Chamberlain to modify his claims. On the contrary, he hardly altered the acknowledgments in the various editions of his book, and in a letter to his antagonist Thode he protested yet again (in 1901) the originality of his work. "I do not demand," he declared, "that people find my child pretty, but I demand that they recognize it as *my child, free and nobly born.*"[218]

Just how legitimate were Chamberlain's claims in this regard? A recapitulation of the central themes of the book reveals some striking parallels to the arguments set forth in such Wagnerian tracts as *Religion*

and Art and *German Art and German Politics*. Chamberlain argued, as
had Wagner, that all that was positive and healthy in modern European
society could be traced back to the influence of the "Germanic peoples." All that was corrupt and debilitating, on the other hand,
stemmed from the undiminished potency of Germany's ancient and
modern nemeses: Roman imperialism (in both its secular and clerical
manifestations), international Jewry, atheistic materialism, and liberal-
capitalist utilitarianism. And Chamberlain, like Wagner, viewed the
suppression of this constellation of evils as the greatest challenge facing
the German people.

The parallels, then, are clear enough, and they suggest that Wagner's
English disciple might indeed have been well advised to acknowledge
his intellectual debts more openly. On the other hand, Chamberlain
was undeniably correct when he insisted that Wagner had no unique
claim to these ideas. They were, in fact, essentially the ideas of those
thinkers from whom Wagner himself had borrowed so heavily (and so
unsystematically) in the elaboration of his protean "philosophy of regeneration." But these were not, it should be recalled, the same thinkers who had inspired Wagner's revolutionary activism of 1848: not
Hegel and Feuerbach, but first Schopenhauer, then Lagarde, and finally Gobineau dominated his middle and later prose writings, thus leading him (to Nietzsche's disgust) away from the essentially neo-
humanist position of his Dresden period. Chamberlain, too, borrowed
from these latter thinkers, and from a host of others as well. His tutors
ranged from Kant and Goethe, whom he passionately admired but
only imperfectly understood, to *völkisch* thinkers like Lagarde and
Julius Langbehn, whom he understood all too well. Darwin, too, was
an important influence, although Chamberlain's attempt to apply Darwin's principles to human affairs represented a particularly crude example of social Darwinism.[219] (Nevertheless, Chamberlain insisted in
the preface to the third edition of *Foundations of the Nineteenth Century*
that he owed his views on race primarily to scientists like Darwin and
Blumenbach. Wagner, significantly enough, was specifically rejected
as a racial mentor; his views on race were too "unscientific" to be of
much practical value.)[220] Quite clearly, then, Chamberlain did not
need the Master's guidance to discover the "true" foundations of the
nineteenth century.

Chamberlain's assertion of intellectual independence from Wagner's
philosophical legacy did not end with his protestations regarding the

originality of the *Foundations*. Although in general he avoided any public criticism of the Master's attempts at philosophical theorizing, on one occasion, in a speech on "Richard Wagner's Philosophy" before the Philosophical Society of Vienna in 1898, he clearly distanced himself from what he (quite correctly) described as the "inconsistencies" in the Master's thought. Alone among the inner circle of disciples, Chamberlain perceived that Feuerbach and Schopenhauer were hardly compatible influences in Wagner's philosophy and that the Master may not have thoroughly understood the thinkers from whom he so liberally borrowed.[221] There it was then: Wagner may have been the world's greatest artist, but he was not much of a philosopher. Although the latter charge might justifiably be leveled at Chamberlain as well, the point to emphasize here is that the disciple perceived shortcomings in the Master's thought that he believed made that thought somewhat doubtful as a blueprint for reform. More "science" (*Wissenschaft*) was clearly needed, and Chamberlain held himself up as the man to supply it.

Cosima Wagner was understandably horrified when she read Chamberlain's Philosophical Society speech. She immediately took him to task for his views, which she saw as both ill founded and subversive: "You are in error regarding the facts," she huffed. "The relationship [of Wagner] to philosophy and his study of philosophers was quite different from what you have described. . . . The noble spirits in your lecture hall—so I fear—have been sadly disturbed; the others, arrogant and superficial, will have returned home regarding the *Gesammelte Schriften* condescendingly as philosophical bungling."[222]

Cosima was justified in her anxiety regarding Chamberlain—he *was* hard to keep safely within the fold—and yet in the larger sense his goals were really the same as hers: he, too, sought to create an image of Wagner that was compatible with Wilhelmian conservatism in all its dimensions. In his biography of Wagner he had skirted such delicate issues as the Master's marital misbehavior and his exploitation of Ludwig II. Wagner's political career, too, was tricky terrain, and here Chamberlain relied less on circumlocution than on creative reinterpretation. Put most simply, he took it upon himself to overturn the prevailing view that Wagner had once been a revolutionary.[223] The Master, insisted Chamberlain, had played no part whatsoever in the Dresden uprising of May 1849. The entire extent of his political activity in the years 1848–1849 had been the delivery of the speech before the Fatherland Association, a speech in which he not only did not foment revolution but urged the retention of law and order. If Wagner was critical of prevailing political conditions, said Chamberlain, it was of creeping constitutionalism rather than of monarchical absolutism. Indeed, what the "genuine" Wagner "really" wanted in 1848–1849 was a return to the "ancient Germanic order" that combined "absolute loyalty to the king with an indestructible pride in freedom."[224] In other words, Wagner had always been solidly on the Right, had always been a firm believer in kingly authority grounded in *völkisch* freedom. Any arguments to the contrary were the fruit of misunderstanding, if not pure fancy.

Certainly there was considerable misunderstanding and fantasy in the public perception of Wagner's political career, and specifically his behavior in 1848–1849. Wagner himself had contributed to this by later denying his radical past, and it was this denial that Chamberlain focused on in his apologia. Perhaps he was not entirely unjustified in casting doubt upon his hero's revolutionary credentials: Wagner's commitment to political change stemmed at least partly from artistic considerations, and his instinctive preference was probably always for some kind of authoritarianism, however vaguely defined.[225] Chamberlain's interpretation, however, contained no such nuance, no hint of the Master's political inconsistencies or confusions. In denying Wagner's revolutionary past tout court it simply ran roughshod over the facts, thereby setting an example for the historians and biographers of the next generation.

Chamberlain's writings, unlike the theoretical outpourings of most of the Bayreuth disciples, enjoyed tremendous success. His *Foundations of the Nineteenth Century,* in particular, reached thousands of readers through some thirty editions and translations in several languages. Its influence at the turn of the century has been justifiably compared to that of Spengler's *Decline of the West* after World War I.[226]

Whatever his reservations regarding Bayreuth's other disciples, Chamberlain did not hesitate to call his seminal work "a product of Bayreuth."[227] There can be no doubt that with its publication he emerged as Bayreuth's chief philosophical emissary and that his missionary efforts were crucial to the dissemination of what had come to be known as the "Bayreuth Idea." He was thus instrumental in promoting Bayreuth's importance as a center of *völkisch* ideology, at precisely the moment when it was fading as a center of artistic creativity.

Of course, for most people "Bayreuth" still meant music, but the emphasis among the Wahnfried disciples was less on music per se than on political and cultural redemption—redemption, however, not so much for all mankind as for the Germans as the ascendant nation in Europe.

Chamberlain was a pivotal figure in this development, for if he (rightly) denied the exclusively Wagnerian provenance of his ideas, he at the same time heralded the Master's work as the inspiration for his "conversion to Germanism."[228] While, like Cosima, he welcomed foreigners to Bayreuth, he also—again like Cosima—wished that more Germans would attend so that the festival would not be dependent on outsiders. He harbored this wish because he was convinced that Wagner's work was too quintessentially German for anyone but a Teuton to understand. The fitness of even non-German Europeans (let alone Americans) to appreciate Wagner's art was questionable. Contemplating Bayreuth's international audience, he could write: "A very large proportion of the dwellers of Europe is made up of . . . savages wearing the dress of civilization, and that is why I think that the far-reaching thought which inspired Wagner's entire work like a life-giving atmosphere will continue to be 'an enigma or an abomination' to many."[229]

Chamberlain's own work continues to be an enigma or an abomination to many of those who still read it, but one suspects that this readership is not large. In the early twentieth century, on the other hand, Chamberlain was not only read by thousands; he was lionized as the new sage of Bayreuth, the thinker best able to interpret the Wagnerian heritage in terms of the cultural and political climate of the day. Indeed, so secure was his status that he was invited by a popular American magazine, the *Ladies' Home Journal,* to interpret the Master's work for American women.[230] Closer to home, the new Kaiser Wilhelm II became one of his great admirers and handed out copies of Chamberlain's book to court visitors.[231] None of this is surprising: Wagnerism, after all, was now completely acceptable in good society, thanks at least partly to the influence of this earnest English disciple.

It is perhaps also not surprising that when the First World War broke out Chamberlain became one of Germany's most vituperative propagandists against England (converts, we know, often despise most what they have cast aside).[232] But Chamberlain's anglophobia went beyond what might have been expected even from an apostate. In a piece on England in his *Kriegsaufsätze* (War essays)[233] he condemned every aspect of English life and character: set foot on that cursed island, he shrieked, and one would encounter nothing but "hatred, money, noise, pomp, percentages, vulgarity, arrogance, distrust, and envy."[234] On and on he went in this vein, outdoing native anglophobes from Lissauer to Sombart—outdoing even the Master himself, who during a trip to London in 1855 had complained about English philistinism and artistic insensitivity.[235] War fever, however, made Chamberlain's hysteria seem sane, and his essays on the war further solidified his position on the German Right.[236]

They also, needless to say, made him persona non grata in his erstwhile homeland. The British government retaliated against Chamberlain by publishing its own version of the war essays; entitled *The Ravings of a Renegade,* it was offered as evidence of what prolonged contact with German culture could do to a man of uncertain loyalties. (Chamberlain, it should be noted, retained his British citizenship until 1916.) Wagner, of course, was regarded as a chief agent in Chamberlain's corruption, indeed, as a potential corrupter of sounder English spirits as well, and his music suddenly disappeared from English symphonic and operatic repertories.[237]

During the war, Chamberlain gradually jettisoned his commitment to the Hohenzollern monarchy in favor of a more populist politics. By 1917 he was looking to Hindenburg and Ludendorff, rather than to the discredited Kaiser, as Germany's saviors. When the generals failed in turn, Chamberlain, in desperation, sought even more radical solutions to the country's ills. In the immediate postwar period he was, like so many so-called new conservatives[238], ready for anything. He was, that is, ready for Hitler.

Chamberlain's flirtation with Nazism began in the early 1920s. He met Hitler for the first time in 1923 and offered the following observations in a letter to the future Führer:

> You are not at all, as people have maintained, a fanatic: on the contrary, you are just the opposite. A fanatic overheats the head; you warm the heart. . . . You have violent tasks to accomplish, and yet despite your strong will I do not see you as a man of destruction. You understand Goethe's distinction between the different forms of violence. There is a violence which emerges from chaos and leads back to chaos, and there is a violence whose essence is to shape the cos-

mos. . . . It is such a cosmos-shaping violence I have in mind when I put you in the category of violent men.[239]

One can never know how Chamberlain might have reacted to the manifold horrors of the Third Reich, for he died in 1927, six years before Hitler came to power.[240] All we know is that until his last days he gave the Nazis his full support and that while it is always difficult to calculate the significance of ideas in politics—especially Nazi politics—this support was hardly negligible. Chamberlain, as Geoffrey Field points out, was "the first person of national and even international reputation as a writer to align himself with the Nazi movement."[241] Hitler recognized the value of the Chamberlain alliance: he published Chamberlain's letter of support, thereby suggesting to all the world that Bayreuth was firmly in his camp.

IX

In contemplating the career of Louis Napoleon, Karl Marx was moved to amend Hegel's famous dictum that all facts and personages of great importance in world history occur twice: "They occur," he declared, "the first time as tragedy, the second as farce."[242] It would not be entirely appropriate to apply this adage to Richard Wagner's son Siegfried.[243] In the first place, he was not a personage of great importance in world history, or even in operatic history; and second, he was less a figure of farce than of domestic melodrama. Nevertheless, there was something reminiscent of the second Napoleon in Siegfried's life: like Louis, he made it his mission to carry on a great legacy, a great name; and like Louis, he proved not quite up to the task. And if Siegfried was no match for his ancestry he was also, again like Louis, no match for the women who dominated his life. He emerges finally as a mildly pathetic figure, anything but a Siegfried, except for the fact that he died on the eve of Bayreuth's (and Germany's) Götterdämmerung.

An enemy of Cosima's (Annette Kolb) insisted that Richard Wagner, after assessing his son's capabilities, determined that Siegfried should become an architect, because this was an art that embraced many humble offices.[244] In fact, though he often despaired over the

child's lack of musical aptitude ("He hasn't the trace of a musical ear!")
Wagner sometimes allowed himself to hope that his son might yet
carry on his great work.[245] And Siegfried, though by no means forced
into musical studies, imbibed enough of the atmosphere of the Festspielhaus to dream of one day conducting there.

This day would not be long in coming. For a time, however, Siegfried did indeed contemplate becoming an architect, and he studied this
discipline briefly at the Polytechnic in Karlsruhe. But the musical
dream persisted, and eventually, after studying composition with Engelbert Humperdinck in Berlin and listening to Felix Mottl conduct his
father's works in Karlsruhe, he made up his mind: he would become a
musician.[246]

He pursued his goal with great resolution, and by 1907, when Cosima's failing health allowed him to finally take over direction of the
Bayreuth Festival, he had gained considerable experience as a pro-
ducer, conductor, and even composer. (He had conducted the *Ring*
cycle in 1896, produced Bayreuth's first *Fliegende Holländer* in 1901,
and written several operas, four of which had been performed in German opera houses.) This was a substantial apprenticeship indeed, and
through it Siegfried had developed sound technical skills and a thorough grounding in the Bayreuth tradition. He had also developed a
very tentative rebelliousness, a sense that once *he* gained control of the
festival he would make it truly Wagnerian by making it truly creative.[247]

In this he did not succeed. The "old Bayreuth" of Cosima lingered
on through the war and postwar period, lingered on indeed until
mother and son died within months of each other in 1930.[248] Why did
Siegfried fail to create something new? The problem was partly that he
could never follow Nietzsche's advice and flee the influence of women.
The women in Siegfried's life—his ailing though still manipulative
mother, his assertive sisters—kept pressuring him to "remain faithful"
to the old ways, to keep using, for example, the very sets that had
"once brought tears to the eyes of the Master."[249] But if Siegfried in
general succumbed to such pressures, risking only the most cautious
innovations,[250] he did so because he himself harbored deep-seated
conservative tendencies and an active contempt for the latest trends in
musical dramaturgy. He once declared that "Bayreuth is not there for
any sort of hyper-modern vogues. This would contradict the style of

works which after all were not written and composed as cubist, expressionist, or dadaist."[251]

The style of the festivals under Siegfried, then, was for the most part an anachronistic style, one that made Bayreuth synonymous with artistic reaction. This was especially true during the time of the Weimar republic, which was so closely identified with cultural modernism. Siegfried and Bayreuth could have shared in the Weimar spirit by employing the talents of such innovative conductors as Bruno Walter, Erich Kleiber, Otto Klemperer, or Leo Blech. These men, however, were all Jewish, and although Siegfried often protested that Bayreuth was open to all, he did not mean quite all. So instead of Klemperer or Walter he hired Karl Muck, Michael Balling, Karl Elmendorff, and Franz von Hoesslin. True, he brought in the brilliant young Fritz Busch to conduct *Die Meistersinger* in 1924, but Busch did not relish his curitorial duties and pleaded illness the next time he was asked. Another departure from the norm of mediocrity was the appointment of Arturo Toscanini to conduct a new *Tannhäuser* production in 1930. This *Tannhäuser* indeed represented a genuine shift toward more contemporary tastes, and its conception suggested that Siegfried might at last have been willing to move Bayreuth into the modern era.[252] Alas, he did not live to see its premiere, for he suffered a fatal heart attack during its rehearsals.

Siegfried's interpretation of his father's works suffered from a kind of workmanlike piety, but he was unable to render them boring or banal. It was otherwise with his own compositions. He wrote some thirteen operas over the course of his life, and here, much more than in his conducting or producing, he displayed the severe limitations of his talent. This is not the place for a critical review of Siegfried's operas:[253] suffice it to note that in this domain Siegfried truly substantiated Marx's dictum. The first Wagner turned myths into music drama; the second turned fairy tales into operettas. These works enjoyed some success in the provinces, where conservative audiences applauded their political soundness and kitschy effects, but they never were performed in the big opera houses in Munich or Berlin, where the directors were staging brilliant new productions of the *Ring* but would not touch *Herzog Wildfang*. The generally good-natured Siegfried became embittered over this reception of his creations. He railed especially against the cultural arbiters in Berlin, where he suspected the local Semites of plotting against him.[254] In this, at least, he was like his father.[255]

He was not like his father when it came to money. Richard had affected a disdain for financial considerations, though in reality he spent a good deal of time worrying about how to make ends meet. Siegfried, on the other hand, never pretended to be above such mundane matters as paying the bills, and in fact he found his true calling in the art of making money. It was fortunate that he possessed this gift, for the absence of festivals between 1918 and 1924 and the great inflation of the early 1920s wiped out the Festival Fund so painstakingly built up by Cosima and Alfred von Gross. In order to reopen in 1924 Siegfried needed a sudden influx of capital, a requirement he was unlikely to fulfill in exhausted Europe. Thus Richard Wagner's son did what the father once considered but ultimately rejected: he went on tour in America.

This was logical enough. America was about to help Germany meet her financial obligations through the Dawes Plan; certainly she might do the same for Bayreuth. Siegfried was shrewd enough to see the advantages of courting America and democratic enough in his sensibilities to do so with gusto. The people whom his mother had dismissed as barbarians were to Siegfried valued allies, "special friends" who by flocking to prewar Bayreuth had proved that they understood "the importance of the festivals to the entire world of culture."[256] Thus Siegfried spent much of his time during the America tour cultivating these special friends in their native habitats: New York, Baltimore, St. Louis, Detroit. He met brew masters and ball-bearing manufacturers. He made a special visit to Dearborn, Mich., where, as the local paper reported, he "spent several exciting hours with Mr. and Mrs. Ford."[257] From Ludwig II to Henry Ford: this, too, was perhaps a substantiation of Marx's dictum.

Ironically enough, Siegfried's American tour proved more an artistic than a financial success. It garnered some eight thousand dollars for the Festival Fund, which was certainly better than Richard had done on his fund-raising trip to England in 1877, but Siegfried was not satisfied. "The financial result is soso lala," he wrote as he prepared to sail home to Germany.[258] What was not soso lala was the local reception of the concerts he conducted, and even of the special productions of his own operas. The American critics loved these performances, or claimed they did, and Siegfried loved the Americans in return. When he got back to Germany, he could not help but look back with nostalgia on his reception in the United States:

> I truly enjoyed myself in America, and I'm having trouble readjusting to the small-minded atmosphere in Germany. Hatred, envy, discontent! No generosity! Even the press over there treated me a lot better than it does here. [Those Americans] simply have better manners and more respect for creative accomplishment. I'm fed up with Germany! If I didn't have Wahnfried and the Festspielhaus to worry about, I'd get out of here. Oh well, I guess one has to hang on and do what one can to save the German spirit from complete collapse.[259]

When Siegfried spoke of the collapse of the German spirit, he was not referring merely to the cultural disintegration evidenced in the rejection of his operas. He was also making a political statement—indeed, a political statement typical of Bayreuth, where, as Michael Karbaum has noted, the tendency was always "to speak about art when one meant politics."[260]

Siegfried rarely spoke openly about politics. He had enough sophistication to realize that partisan politics could be bad for business, especially if that business depended on attracting an international clientele. Nevertheless, his entire approach to art and culture was informed by nostalgia for an idealized past and by contempt for the new order. He identified artistic modernism with political modernism, labeling such works as *Salome* and *Der Rosenkavalier* as "cultural Bolshevism."[261] He saw his own operas as antidotes against a mentality that could "mock the strategy of Hindenburg and Ludendorff."[262] His adherence to inherited canons in the administration of the festival could serve as a model for what a "healthier" state government might do in the realm of politics. There was some irony in this: Weimar culture may have involved a modernist "revolt of the sons" against the conservatism of their fathers,[263] but here was a conservative son resisting the forces of change in the name of his modernist father.

Of course, in one sense Siegfried was a revolutionary. His political views placed him more or less within the camp of the so-called conservative revolution. And indeed Siegfried's Bayreuth was one of those places in postwar Germany where conservative revolutionaries could feel quite at home. When the festival reopened in 1924, opponents of the Weimar government gathered there to call for the destruction of the new regime. At the end of *Die Meistersinger* a group of war veterans in the audience rose and sang *Deutschland über Alles*. This, however, was too much for Siegfried: it could not help but unsettle the foreigners. He therefore felt obliged to appear on the stage and remind his countrymen that art was above politics. "This is a place for art!" ("Hier gilt's der Kunst!") he admonished.[264]

X

Of course this was never quite the case at Bayreuth—and it was certainly not true of the Bayreuth of Siegfried Wagner. Between the November Revolution of 1918 and Hitler's seizure of power in 1933, the Wagner circle in Bayreuth went through a process of political radicalization that left most of its members outspoken champions of the Nazi movement.[265] We have already mentioned the contributions of Houston Stewart Chamberlain, whose work was recognized even then as instrumental to the Nazi cause. Josef Goebbels, after meeting Chamberlain in 1926, gushed in his diary: "Father of our spirit, we greet you! Pathbreaker! Pioneer! You will stay us from doubt and despair!"[266] The *Bayreuther Blätter,* during the 1920s, was filled with political commentary of a more or less Nazi character. In 1924, the year the festival reopened, the *Blätter*'s first number began with a quotation from Hitler: "The inner struggle must precede the outer struggle."[267] The aging Wolzogen documented his faith in the national revolution with a collection of chauvinistic jingles entitled *Deutsche Sprüchen* (German proverbs).[268] One of the journal's book review editors, Hermann Seelinger, contributed a piece that celebrated the racist theories of Hans F. K. Günther.[269] And finally, the year 1925 saw the founding of the "Bayreuth Union of German Youth" (Bayreuther Bund der deutschen Jugend), a group that emphasized in its official program "the deep interrelationship between the great German . . . cultural ideas of Adolf Hitler and the work of Bayreuth.[270]

As for the Wagner family itself, it first became acquainted with National Socialism in 1919, when M. G. Conrad, the Wagnerian who led Bayreuth's campaign against New York's "Grail robbery" in 1913, came to Wahnfried with news of a new party and a man called Adolf Hitler.[271] Two years later this fledgling party had a local branch in Bayreuth, and in 1923 Hitler himself visited the town and spoke at the Riding Hall. He took advantage of this opportunity to visit Wahnfried and pay his respects to Siegfried and his young wife Winifred, whom he had previously met in Munich.[272]

This was the beginning of a fateful relationship in the history of German culture—an unholy alliance between politicized art and "artistic politics" that was to last until Wagner's Bayreuth, and indeed much of Germany, were reduced to rubble.[273] For a considerable time, however, both sides found this partnership highly satisfactory.

It was clearly so from Hitler's point of view. Through the sponsorship of the Wagners he gained entrée into the fashionable Wagnerian circles of Munich and Berlin, an inroad that proved of considerable value to his still embryonic cause. Wealthy socialites like the Bechsteins and the Bruckmanns came forth with modest financial contributions for the Party, but more important they taught Hitler how to move more gracefully in high society. Frau Bechstein and Frau Bruckmann, who both took a motherly interest in the awkward young man, encouraged him to exchange his old army rags for snappy blue suits and patent leather shoes. Frau Bruckmann taught him how to eat an artichoke. Thus transformed by his new social mentors, Hitler was able to hobnob confidently with rich reactionaries and attract a whole new type of upper-class follower.[274]

The Wagners, for their part, seem to have seen in this intense young Austrian, this mezmerizing creature who could cite from memory long passages from the Master's operas, a new hero come to slay the evil dragons that terrorized their land. As early as 1923 Siegfried Wagner described Hitler as a "magnificant man," with a "genuine folk-soul." Hitler would "make something happen," he proclaimed.[275] This was on the eve of the Beer Hall Putsch, whose failure embittered Siegfried. He wrote afterwards that the prosecution of Hitler and his cohorts was akin to the Spanish Inquisition. "The breaking of oaths and treason are proclaimed as holy acts, and Jews and Jesuits go arm in arm to destroy Germany." But was the great cause now dead? Siegfried could not be sure, but he did know one thing: "My wife is fighting like a lioness for Hitler."[276]

Indeed she was. Winifred and Siegfried just happened to be in Munich on that fateful November 9 when the Putsch was attempted. Afterwards Winifred published an open letter in which she documented what she later (at her postwar de-Nazification hearing) characterized as her "purely idealistic sense of Hitler's personality."[277] One wonders what it was about Hitler's personality that inspired such devotion from English ladies like Winifred Wagner and Unity Mitford. Whatever it was, it held its spell over Winifred throughout the Third Reich and even beyond.[278]

Hitler responded nobly to Wahnfried's loyalty. He promised that as soon as he came to power he would ensure that *Parsifal* was performed only in Bayreuth.[279] In 1924 he wrote Siegfried from his Landesberg prison cell expressing his sorrow that he had not been able to visit Wahnfried again in November 1923, since Bayreuth "lay on the march route to Berlin." But the news was not all bad: the Nazis had done well in the April elections in Bayreuth, a result for which he knew he had Siegfried and his wife to thank. And he added: "Great pride filled me when I saw the *völkisch* victory in precisely that city wherein first the Master and then Chamberlain forged the spiritual sword we now wield."[280]

Anxious as he was to have Wahnfried in his camp, Hitler was careful not to demand too much of his allies. Understanding Siegfried's sensitive position as director of the Bayreuth Festival, he never pressured him to join the Nazi Party. Moreover, he was careful during his visits to Bayreuth (he returned in 1925, then regularly after 1933 until the war) to appear "not as a political agitator but as a devoted admirer of the German genius of Richard Wagner."[281] With Winifred, however, he had no need to be so diplomatic; she, after all, was his "lioness," and when he discovered in 1926 that she had not renewed her Party membership (she had first joined in 1920 or 1921), he asked her to do so.[282] Winifred happily acquiesced, and why not? By now her pro-Nazi activities, which included supplying the paper upon which Hitler wrote the first volume of his *Mein Kampf,* had become well known.[283]

Michael Karbaum has argued that Richard Wagner's dream of making Bayreuth into a "true German theater" found its full realization only in the Third Reich.[284] There is much to be said for this point. Before 1933 Bayreuth never received financial support from the central German government; after 1933 Hitler made Bayreuth his "court theater" and kept it going even through the war years with generous subventions from the Reich treasury.[285] Foreigners were hardly in evidence now at the Festspielhaus; instead the theater was filled with Nazi Party bosses, "Strength through Joy" workers, and, eventually, with wounded soldiers transported there for rest and recreation.

But was this really the fulfillment of Wagner's dream? I think not. It is hard to believe that he would have seen those sleeping party bosses at

Winifred's festivals as "special friends" of his art.[286] It is hard to believe he would have welcomed the narrow provincialism and attendant
artistic mediocrity that now prevailed.[287] More important, it is hard to
believe that he would have mistaken the Third Reich for his ideal of the
"purely human" society, for what the Nazis had created was considerably more crass, materialistic, and dehumanizing than the "soulless"
Bismarckian Reich he had rejected so vehemently.

    This conclusion should not be interpreted as a denial that there were
any parallels whatsoever between Wagner's ideas and those of the
National Socialists. Some of his writings required little or no creative
editing to be useful to Hitler and his cohorts. Taken as a whole,
however, the exploitation of Wagner's legacy during the Third Reich
amounted to an intellectual abuse. It was an abuse made possible partly
by Wagner's penchant for vague and open ended formulations, partly
(and we would argue more importantly) by the abuse he had already
suffered at the hands of his Bayreuth disciples. No doubt there may be
a certain poetic justice in this: Wagner had made a habit of exploiting
and misusing some of his closest admirers; it is perhaps only fitting
that they should have eventually returned the compliment. In any case,
they did so with a vengeance. George C. Windell has argued that
Wagner's music dramas were not "proto-fascist."[288] The Bayreuth
disciples, however, focused less on Wagner's music dramas than on his
prose works. This was itself an injustice, for it neglected what was
truly great in the Wagnerian legacy for what was often bombastic,
mean-spirited, and ugly. The disciples took these ideas and made them
into the central components of what came to be known as "the Bayreuth Idea." This, too, was an abuse, for what it really amounted to
was a selective mining of Wagner's jumbled philosophy for its most
"valuable" deposits. The miners melted all this down into an ideological alloy of considerable rigidity. This, then, was the stuff of which
Hitler's "spiritual sword" was ultimately made, and for its usefulness
he had less Richard Wagner himself to thank than the industrious
dwarfs of Bayreuth.

3. Art and Politics: Wagnerism in France

GERALD D. TURBOW

The controversy that Richard Wagner's work engendered in France reached its height during the 1880s. Wagner did not live to see that day, but, ironically, his death in 1883 helped nurture a final flowering of French Wagnerism: the *Revue wagnérienne* and the symbolist poets hailed him as "god"; the leading intellectuals and composers made pilgrimages to Bayreuth; the Lamoureux and Colonne orchestras performed his music; and the Paris Opéra staged his music dramas. The triumphal return of *Tannhäuser* to the Opéra in 1895 pointed up the difference between this period of Wagnerian idolatry and that of a third of a century earlier, when Wagner had waged an unsuccessful campaign to conquer the city many called "the capital of the world." After the failure of the riotous French premiere of *Tannhäuser* in 1861, he had stayed away from France (save for a few brief visits), and the French had stayed away from him: they had staged but one minor production of his work in almost three decades.

Yet even as Wagner left Paris in apparent defeat in 1861, a Wagnerian movement began to emerge in France. To understand the nature of this highly complex and varied movement, we must examine its entire history, not just its acrimonious climax in the 1880s. It is also necessary to go beyond the two great literary personalities with whom Wagner is usually identified in France—Charles Baudelaire and Stéphane Mallarmé—and to see the movement within the broader context of French cultural and political history. Such a perspective will show that France developed a strong, self-conscious Wagnerian movement over a decade before any other country except Germany. The lionization of Wagner immediately following his death grew from one strand in this history and in some respects was not particularly representative of it.

We will thus be examining here not so much the aesthetics of French Wagnerism as its social, cultural, and, above all, political framework. My purpose is to trace the evolution of the movement in order to show how its different components related to one another. As was true of Wagnerism everywhere, the disciplehood in France was quite heterogeneous, and the various followers used Wagner's music and ideas to suit their own purposes.

The political framework within which French Wagnerism emerged deserves our special attention. While there have been numerous studies of Wagner's role in French aesthetic thinking, there has not been much inquiry into the political controversies that influenced the acceptance or failure of his works and affected the rise of Wagnerism in France. The movement emerged as part of the evolution of the Second Empire; many of French Wagnerism's early leaders, and much of their motivation, sprang from political causes. There was nothing new, of course, in close relations of this kind between music and politics, since the national opera house had been an instrument of state ever since the founding of the Académie Royale de Musique in 1661.[1] Musical theater was still the meeting ground of the ruling classes, a place where people went to find both power and pleasure and where artistic trends functioned as an important social lubricant.

Yet at the same time Wagnerism also drew its support from members of the artistic avant-garde of Paris. From the 1850s on, Wagnerian ideas acted as a major influence on artists and commentators on the arts who were exploring new aesthetic terrain. To be Wagnerian in thinking meant to be in some manner "progressive" in artistic taste. This dimension of the movement gradually grew in significance, until in the 1880s it virtually eclipsed the political aspect of French Wagnerism.

I

Wagner first came to Paris in September 1839. He went unnoticed by the local press until March 22, 1840, when the *Revue et gazette musicale de Paris* reported that François Habeneck had rehearsed the Conservatoire orchestra in "an overture by a young German composer with a very remarkable talent, M. Wagner[,] . . . to unanimous applause."[2] The members of the orchestra, however, were not so enthusiastic: they judged Wagner's *Christophe Colomb* overture "a long enigma" and decided not to perform it publicly.[3]

Despite this setback, Wagner's connection with the *Revue et gazette musicale de Paris* continued in a significant way. Between July 1840 and May 1842 twenty issues of the periodical, the leading musical journal of Paris, carried his articles, ranging from discussions of the *Christophe Colomb* overture through analyses of new works to novelas verging on autobiography.[4] Because of this association, the editorial staff of the journal organized a concert performance of the *Christophe Colomb* overture on February 4, 1841. Wagner's music was praised by the reviewer of the *Gazette musicale,* Henri Blanchard. But Blanchard's delight with the music was secondary to his interest in Wagner's thoughts on music. He compared the structure of Wagner's music to the composer's theory of overtures, recently expounded in the *Revue.*[5]

Indeed, it was as a writer and intellectual rather than as a composer that Wagner drew his earliest adherents. Hector Berlioz, music critic of the *Journal des débats,* the most influential newspaper in Paris, also called attention to Wagner's writings.[6] George Sand, charmed by the nationalism Wagner expressed in his two essays on Weber's *Der Freischütz,* alluded to him in her tale "Mouny Robin" (June 1841).[7] Fortified by such attention, Wagner left Paris in April 1842 and returned to Germany.

Here he immediately achieved more solid successes. His *Rienzi* was performed in Dresden on October 20, 1842, and two months later Wagner became *Kapellmeister* to King Frederick Augustus II of Saxony. News of these triumphs was reported to the readers of the *Revue et gazette musicale* by the enormously determined Wagner.[8] Hector Berlioz, touring Germany, arrived in Dresden just as Wagner was to be invested with his new office. Berlioz sent back his comments to the *Journal des débats,* and Wagner's latest opera, *Der fliegende Holländer* (January 2, 1843), enjoyed a favorable reception by the French composer.[9] Wagner continued to keep readers of the *Revue et gazette musicale* informed of his activities in Dresden, including his supervision of the world premiere of *Tannhäuser* on October 19, 1845.

Four years later, on May 18, 1849, Berlioz turned his column over to his friend Franz Liszt, who devoted an article to *Tannhäuser,* which he had recently conducted in Weimar. Significantly, Liszt did not limit himself to musical arguments in pleading his case for *Tannhäuser.* Instead he associated its young composer with the developing movement of realism, arguing that what was true for drawing and painting applied equally to music. "Just as we . . . want more realistic drawing, coloring, and perspective in art," he said, "we want more dramatic qualities and more firmly constructed libretti in opera."[10]

In that same year, 1849, Wagner participated in the Dresden revolution, joining Bakunin in the struggle against the Kingdom of Saxony; subsequently Wagner was banned from Germany until 1860. Thus Liszt's "realist" was identified also as a revolutionary, a correlation that would later gain him supporters and opponents both artistically and politically. But since the Revolution of 1848–1849 had so wide a spectrum of participants, some of whom later took very different political directions, the word *revolutionary* was ambiguous and could be interpreted in many ways.

It is perhaps most accurate to say that Wagner drew support from those in the arts who were attempting to break with tradition. A key example was Gérard de Nerval, who had been a leader of the Bohemians—the *Jeunes-Frances*—of the 1830s. When the world premiere of *Lohengrin* was produced by Liszt at Weimar on August 28, 1850, Nerval, a Germanophile, wrote an account published in the widely circulated *La presse.*[11] He was enraptured by the opera's music, though (as seems to have been typical of the French) he managed to make a chaos of the plot. His article began a current of strong literary interest in Wagner that was to continue through the 1880s. Backed by men of the stamp of Nerval and Liszt, Wagner was now able to have his music performed again in Paris. The period of the Second Republic provided the requisite liberal political climate for the progressive programs of François Seghers's Sainte-Cécile concerts. On November 24, 1850, Seghers conducted the *Tannhäuser* overture, a performance that made Wagner much more widely known and also helped interject him into the literary dispute over realism.

His following in France at this point was limited but promising. We are told by Henri Blanchard, critic of the *Revue et gazette musicale,* that a small group of *amateurs du nouveau* awaited the *Tannhäuser* overture with great impatience.[12] Though most critics proved hostile to it, Théophile Gautier responded quite positively in *La presse.*[13] By then a distinguished literary figure, Gautier showed his openness to new artistic tendencies by praising the learning and profundity of Wagner's music. Compliments from this member of the literary establishment suggest one side—if an atypical one—of the varied components that would come to make up French Wagnerism. The composer's supporters had little unity as yet as a group, however, and they certainly did not yet constitute a "movement." Liszt, Gautier, and Nerval were moving in considerably different directions in their careers and were not to join forces to help Wagner. Their one mutual effort in this area failed, for the *Revue des deux mondes* declined Nerval's request that it publish an article on Wagner by Liszt.[14]

Though Wagner's music was not to be performed again in Paris until 1858, his writings between 1849 and 1851 were analyzed in the French press, and this served above all to make him a figure of controversy. His theories of music and drama and the *Gesamtkunstwerk* (total work of art), elaborated in *Opera and Drama* (1851) and subsequently explained in his long foreword to the published collection of his three poems, *Der fliegende Holländer, Tannhäuser,* and *Lohengrin,* drew fire for their claim to establish an all-encompassing artistic theory.[15] The critic and musicologist François-Joseph Fétis, director of the Brussels Conservatoire, was the most important objector; he drew up what Baudelaire called an "indictment" of Wagner.[16] Seven issues of the *Revue et gazette musicale,* from June 6 to August 8, 1852, carried Fétis's articles on Wagner's life, his ideas for reforming opera, his works as poet and as musician, his cause in Germany, and the value of his ideas. One week later, Pietro Scudo, one of the most influential music critics in France, presented his case against Wagner in the *Revue des deux mondes* (August 15, 1852).[17] He and Fétis were incensed by Wagner's books and by the attention his music was gaining in Germany: "Northern Germany is preoccupied by Wagner," wrote Fétis.[18] These critics hoped to prevent a comparable reception in France. Wagner's association with the musical avant-garde, the ambitious claims advanced in his writings, and his purported "realism" were taken as a challenge to the existing order.

More specifically, Fétis and Scudo minimized Wagner's claim to be an innovator by noting that his desire to subordinate music to the poetry of the drama was as old as opera itself. Moreover, they declared that great composers of the past had had no need for involved theories: their music spoke for itself. Most of all, they criticized Wagner himself, branding him an egotist, a prideful opportunist, who substituted verbiage for music, doctrine for talent. "Unable to cultivate art in its ideal domain, he disdains it," said Fétis, "belittles it with guile, and pretends to see only puerile convention in order to prove the necessity of positive arts."[19]

The two critics further expressed their disapproval by adopting a well-worn epithet taken from the great artistic imbroglio of the day: they labeled Wagner the "Courbet of music."[20] It was a good polemic. Gustave Courbet's *The Stone Breakers* and *Burial at Ornans,* exhibited at the Salon of 1850–1851, had shocked, outraged, and even frightened the public.[21] Now Wagner was being linked with Courbet in an artistic movement—realism—that in its assault on traditional aesthetic rules and standards seemed to threaten the moral basis of civilization itself.[22] Courbet's name was also associated in Paris with that of Pierre Proudhon, the author of the frightening doctrine that "property is theft," and therefore regarded by the bourgeoisie as the embodiment of revolution. And now Wagner was again tarred with the same brush: in the very month that Proudhon was released from prison after serving a three-year sentence on charges growing out of the Revolution of 1848, Wagner was accused by Fétis of being an adherent of the socialist "school of M. Proudhon."[23]

We cannot take up here the knotty question of whether Wagner's operas did or did not manifest realism; suffice it to note that many people (Liszt above all) thought that they did. Champfleury, himself called the "Courbet of literature,"[24] thrust himself to the forefront of the French Wagnerians, and his engagement helped ensure that the dispute over realism would frame the debate over Wagner from then on.

The controversy around Wagner did not quickly die down. Three years after Fétis's and Scudo's articles, in 1855, Blanchard shook his head at the battles between Wagner's "flatterers and detractors"; he was one of the few writers who stayed relatively neutral in the controversy as to whether Wagner was "sublime or detestable."[25] Even at this early date there was little middle ground; the polarization had begun in earnest. The fact that there were no concert performances of Wagner's music until 1858 did not in any way pacify his detractors nor dampen the loyalty of his followers. Clearly, the Wagner battle was not fought over the music itself.

The controversy also earned a label. In 1849 a German journalist, Professor Ludwig Bischoff of Cologne—called by Champfleury the

"German Fétis"[26]—had concocted the phrase "Music of the Future" from the title of Wagner's book *The Art-Work of the Future*. Even though the composer refused to accept this label for his music, his critics used it endlessly to ridicule him. For example, in 1855 it was alleged that Wagner's concert engagements in London had shown the city to be "sunk in the impenetrable shadow of the present and deaf to the prophetic voice of the future."[27]

But in France many were proving susceptible to Wagner's art, however it was defined. Wagner continued to gain supporters, indeed converts, for in some cases adherence came with all the ardor of religious conversion. Thus the Countess Agénor de Gasparin, writing an open letter to *L'illustration* in 1857, described the "strange sovereign power" to which she had become subject since hearing Wagner performed in Prussia by a regimental band. She had been "invaded" and "overwhelmed" by the music. "The savage perfume" lingered long after the last notes had sounded. She predicted that the day would come when Wagner would "reign sovereign over Germany and France."[28] Dr. Auguste de Gasperini, a thirty-four-year-old physician of independent means who dabbled in literature and the arts, lived his moment of truth in Baden-Baden in 1857 when the salon orchestra at the fashionable spa struck up a piece from *Lohengrin*. He experienced a feeling of "sudden sympathy"; he was "dazzled . . . subjugated"; he felt as if "a new world had suddenly opened up" before him. All night long he thought of the "boldness of the rhythm, the harmony, the new melodic form, the warm instrumental color, the quasisavage vigor." Gasperini was now a Wagnerian. He dashed off to Karlsruhe the next day to see one of the operas.[29]

While there is no reason to suspect the genuineness of the emotions expressed by those who fell victim to Wagner, fashion and the power of suggestion may be presumed to have played their part in this process: it was becoming modish in advanced circles to "succumb" to Wagner. Moreover, the intensity of criticism leveled against him sometimes worked to his advantage. "A man who [has] been so much abused," declared one observer, "must have something in him."[30]

II

Changes in the French political situation in 1859 brought Wagner back to Paris. Napoleon III, in connection with his decision to help the

Piedmontese prime minister Cavour drive the Austrians out of northern Italy, embarked on a policy of domestic liberalization and began to
court the Left. To this end, on August 15, 1859, he issued a decree of
clemency to the revolutionaries of 1848.[31] France suddenly became
"possible" again for men with radical backgrounds. Here was an opportunity that Wagner, long desirous of conquering Paris, decided he
could not afford to pass up.

He opened his new assault by producing and conducting three concerts (January 25, February 1 and 8, 1860) at the Théâtre-Italien. The
first concert attracted such musical luminaries as Meyerbeer, Gounod,
Auber, Halévy, Thomas, and Berlioz.[32] One member of the audience
suggested the political overtones of the event when he noted that the
controversies at the Tower of Babel or the meetings of the National
Convention were as nothing compared with the feverish agitation
surrounding Wagner; Wagner, he said, was the new Marat.[33] After the
first concert, arguments raged along corridors and stairways and in
vestibules; some claimed that there was a riot just outside the theater,
in the Passage Choiseul. One critic reminisced that he felt himself
transported back to the golden days of the *Hernani* and *Lucrèce Borgia*
riots.[34]

Wagner quickly discovered a wide range of supporters little known
to him before. In Strasbourg in 1858 he had already come upon a
performance of the *Tannhäuser* overture preceding a production of
Amcet Bourgeois's play *Le fou par amour*. Recognized by the ket-
tledrummer, Wagner was given an ovation by the orchestra and audience. In Paris in 1859 he had more chance meetings with individuals
who knew and loved his music, most of them not professional musicians. In his autobiography, for example, Wagner told how at the Paris
Customs Bureau he encountered a supporter in an official named Edmond Roche. At Flaxland's Music Shop he found another partisan in
one Frédéric Villot, curator of the Imperial Museums. Early in the
visit, he got to know as well Count Foucher de Careil, who had
become acquainted with Wagner's operas in Germany, and Emile Perrin, former director of the Opéra-Comique.[35] Such recognition
spurred him on; fashion was going his way.

During Wagner's stay in Paris in 1859–1861, the political dimension
of his reception became especially marked. Politically, Wagner was a
complex and even contradictory figure. As we have seen, he was
regarded by many as a revolutionary: neither his participation in the

revolution in Dresden in 1849 nor his boldness in publishing a book called *Art and Revolution* could easily be forgotten. At the same time, however, Wagner admired authoritarian rule and the myths and symbols of romantic monarchism. He declared his aversion to parliamentary liberalism and laissez-faire capitalism. But after 1849, discouraged by the prospects of translating revolutionary art into revolutionary politics, Wagner had withdrawn from direct participation in the political arena. This, along with an instinctive opportunism that enabled him to adjust his politics to fit the occasion, allowed people to interpret him politically as they wished.

The fluidity of the situation in France upon his arrival in 1859 made such contradictions particularly advantageous. Napoleon III's opening overtures to the Left succeeded mainly in confusing the position of the republicans and liberals, many of whom were unsure whether to swear loyalty to the Empire or even whether to participate in the Assembly. The combination of forcefulness and political ambiguity in Wagner's reputation made him a useful rallying point for figures from a variety of groups. Though most of his supporters were from the Left, legitimists were among them as well, and, as we shall see, the emperor himself would eventually join the ranks of his supporters.

We can see the eclecticism of Wagner's support in the variety of salons he attended. On an evening shortly before the first concert, he went to a soirée given by the Count and Countess de Charnacé, leading members of the legitimists.[36] Their salon, however, was also attended by many republicans, a tendency that was not unusual, since leftist and rightist opponents of the regime often cooperated. The count and countess had been enthralled by Wagner's music upon first hearing it in Germany and welcomed the opportunity to present him at their salon. He was introduced there as a "victim of Saxon tyranny, a democrat and a revolutionary" by the eminent pianist Hans von Bülow, Liszt's disciple and Wagner's selfless friend.[37] The phrase "a democrat and a revolutionary" captured the quality of radical chic that Wagner now enjoyed and that so appealed to certain highly placed opponents of the regime.

The most prominent republican salon that Wagner frequented at this time was that of the Countess Marie d'Agoult, the mother of the Countess de Charnacé. She had forsaken her husband for the love of Franz Liszt, bearing him three children, including among them the future second wife of Richard Wagner; she had also become a leading literary figure under the nom de plume Daniel Stern. As hostess in her *Maison rose* off the Champs-Elysées, she was second to none in her ability to attract "*tout Paris* of the opposition to the Empire."[38] In the 1850s, however, she was leaning away from republicanism and displaying considerable breadth in her selection of guests.[39] They included, in addition to Wagner, the cautious liberal Emile de Girardin, publisher of *La presse;* his wife, the writer Delphine Gay; his colleague Auguste Nefftzer, later founder of the liberal *Le temps;* the republican activist Hippolyte Carnot; Jules Grévy, later prime minister under the Third Republic; the republican though antiparliamentary theorist Emile Littré; and the rightward-leaning scholar Ernest Renan.

It is thus an exaggeration to insist, as has Maxime Leroy, that Wagner associated mostly with republicans at this time.[40] Far better to suggest that he appealed to political dissidents of many shadings. He did not, however, endear himself personally to many of these people, for as one of them put it, he was "too infatuated with himself for Parisian taste."[41] This proud bearing may have stemmed in part from his innate suspicion of the high-and-mighty metropolis and its equally self-infatuated upper classes.

The most important supporters Wagner attracted in Paris were Blandine Liszt (illegitimate daughter of the Countess d'Agoult and Franz Liszt) and her husband, the eminent liberal statesman and eventual prime minister Emile Ollivier. Married in October 1857, the couple had a particularly strong interest in the arts; they were visited often by Blandine's father and by Hector Berlioz, and their guests included many other prominent musicians. After Liszt introduced them to Wagner, Ollivier undertook to manage the composer's copyrights in France, to arrange for translations of his libretti, and to propound widely the merits of his works.[42] Ollivier was no radical. Though he had participated in the Second Republic and continued to lean toward republicanism, he took the oath to the Empire and entered Napoleon III's parliament. As Stuart L. Campbell put it, he was "above all a man of '48—sentimental, overly optimistic, given to posturing, democratic, a little confused, and confident that Frenchmen could resolve their differences."[43] He—or perhaps Blandine—brought Jules Ferry, another future prime minister, into the Wagnerian clan. Again, Wagner was not overly friendly to Ollivier, finding the statesman "dry and superficial."[44] Though Wagner cultivated supporters, he refused to toady and could even prove standoffish. The fact that such behavior did not deter his greatest admirers is a testament to the intensity of their devotion to him.

Wagner was adopted by some noted republicans, at least temporarily. Most significantly, Juliette Adam, a dedicated republican and close friend of the Comtesse d'Agoult, claimed that she had sold many tickets for Wagner's January 25, 1860, concert. She had done so not because she cared about Wagner's music but because a show of support for Wagner was "expected" of those in her milieu. She confessed in her memoirs that she found the brass too loud but did not dare to say so.[45] Nevertheless, she and her fellow republicans smiled through every bar of music that evening; Wagner was one of their own.

Another group that showed its support for Wagner at the 1860 concerts consisted of artists, students, and bohemians. Though they had not previously been exposed to Wagner's music, they were nevertheless naturally predisposed in his favor. One of the concerts seems to have brought out more than the usual number of them, because "long hair, disheveled beards, and exotic dress" predominated in the audience. "The coiffures and dress of the future?" wondered one critic.[46]

Charles Baudelaire and Champfleury (Jules Fleury-Husson) were among the prominent converts Wagner made that evening. They had led the avant-garde of Paris throughout the 1850s and had earned the respect of the self-styled "new generation." As one observer said in 1859, the two authors were regarded as "the most remarkable artists that the new generation had produced."[47] Baudelaire had gone to the concert fearing that he might be duped yet again by a "charlatan with grand pretensions"; instead he had what he described as "the most joyous musical experience" of his life.[48] Indeed, he had been so transported by the experience that he attempted to force his new enthusiasm on his friends, but here he seems to have met with only limited success. "I do not dare speak of Wagner any more," he wrote to Poulet-Malassis on February 16, 1860, because "[my friends] are making too much fun of me."[49]

Thwarted in his efforts to make fellow converts of his friends, he decided to share his enthusiasm with Wagner himself. In a famous letter written to Wagner on February 17, 1860, Baudelaire called his experience at the recent concert "indescribable." He nevertheless proceeded to describe himself as having been swept away by the music's *grandeur,* carried to a state of "religious ecstasy," overwhelmed with sensations of *volupté* that made him feel as if he were ascending into the air or tossing about on the ocean. He suggested that during the *Tristan* prelude he had seen a vast expanse of dark red gradually become the incandescence of a furnace. A final explosion of white had seemed to him the cry of a soul risen to a paroxysm.[50]

To Wagner, Baudelaire's letter suggested that a man "of most extraordinary understanding" had followed "to their ultimate consequences" the impressions he had gained while listening to the music.[51] For the time being, Baudelaire's praise of Wagner remained a private matter, but a year later he would publish a treatise on the composer.

Champfleury, on the other hand, lost no time. "Impatient to cry the truth" about Wagner as widely as he could, he dashed from the concert hall to his writing desk, pushing aside even his most pressing work. Two days later his essay "Richard Wagner" was ready for the publisher A. Bourdilliat.[52] Wagner was understandably pleased by the book; nevertheless, he pointed out in *Mein Leben* that Champfleury's brochure seemed to be a string of "hastily written superficial aphorisms."[53] Airy or not, the brochure was of the first importance, owing to Champfleury's position in the literary and artistic world of Paris in 1860. As the 1867 *Larousse* put it, his "reputation as a man of original talent was founded on so much success that it could no longer be contested."[54]

Wagner was anxious to take advantage of his newly achieved status in Paris and have *Tannhäuser* produced. He admitted that in order to bring this about he was ready to "cultivate [influential] acquaintances" and to cut an appropriately eminent figure.[55] He therefore announced his intention at the time of the concerts of being "at home" every Wednesday evening, "entirely according to the fashion." (As he admitted, he had been told by his older Parisian friends that this was "the right thing to do in Paris"; it was what the Princess Mathilde did on Sundays, what Pauline Viardot, the prima donna, did on Thursdays, and what Rossini and Offenbach did on Saturdays and Fridays.)[56]

But Wagner had more in mind than a conventional salon. He wanted to provide a focus for a movement, a place where his disciples could come together and sit at his feet. He therefore welcomed a diverse group of followers, sponsored performances of his music by some of the greatest pianists of Europe, spoke in detail of his aesthetic theories and his plans, and thereby inspired the local Wagnerians to carry on with his cause after he left Paris.

As we can see from his guest lists, Wagner's contacts in his own salon were quite extensive. Among the nucleus of his salon were Ollivier and Blandine; Ollivier's rising political colleague, Jules Ferry; Baudelaire and Champfleury; Emile Perrin, former director of the Opéra-Comique and future director of the Opéra; Edmond Roche, the customs officer who had a portrait of Wagner over his desk; and Frédéric Villot of the Louvre, who knew all Wagner's scores. Two other regulars were Charles Cabrol, a music critic and journalist, and Gustave Doré, one of the first draftsmen of the time, and also one of the greatest social lions of Paris.[57] Finally, there were two more men of letters, Léon Leroy and Dr. Gasperini, each of whom had been a Wagnerian enthusiast for some time. Both were tremendously excited at the news of Wagner's arrival in Paris and had immediately put themselves at his disposal.[58] Not only did they publish articles to urge others to join their cause; they also used their connections to bring Wagner into contact with rising young journalists, politicians, and artists. Wagner was to be well served by Leroy and Gasperini in the ensuing decade; Leroy, in particular, fostered Wagner's connection with liberals as a writer for *La Liberté*.

Several others who came to Wagner's salon, though not "regulars," also deserve attention. Paul Challemel-Lacour, future foreign minister and ambassador to England, attended with his mistress, Eugénie Fétis, daughter-in-law of Wagner's nemesis. Malwida von Meysenbug, foster mother of Alexander Herzen's daughter Olga, represented the international society of exiles of 1848 that had its principal seat in London. The beautiful Mme. Marie Kalergis, the high-born friend of poets, composers, and royalty, arrived in Paris too late for the 1860 concerts but in time to bring an aura of the highest international society to many of Wagner's Wednesdays (and in time to make up Wagner's concert deficit).[59]

Other guests included the composers Gounod and Saint-Saëns; Gustave-Alexandre Flaxland, music publisher and proprietor of the most fashionable music store in Paris; the piano virtuosi Hans von Bülow, Alfred Jaell, Fräulein Ingeborg Starck, Joseph Wieniawski, and Karl Klindworth; and finally "the most Parisian of the Parisians," the acknowledged king of the *boulevardiers,* Nestor Roqueplan.[60]

Wagner had created his salon and played the social game in order to secure a *Tannhäuser* production in Paris. Influence had its uses, even for what appeared to be a difficult goal. He wrote despondently on March

3, 1860, that "every step toward [my goal] remains unblessed," and he lamented that "the obstacles that block my way to the opera house" could "be beaten back only by a despot's command." But this, he feared, he did not have the "zeal to procure."[61]

His fears on this score proved unfounded. On March 12, 1860, Napoleon III issued an order to the Imperial Opera to perform *Tannhäuser*. He did this partly in response to a request by the wife of the Austrian ambassador, Princess Pauline von Metternich, who was a fervent supporter of Wagner. The decree was part of the emperor's attempt to court Austria's favor, a step he believed he needed to take because he had recently alienated the Austrians through his military support of Italian nationalist aspirations against the Habsburgs. Paradoxically, however, Napoleon's *Tannhäuser* decree was also part and parcel of his ongoing courtship of the Left in domestic affairs. Wagner, it must be remembered, was the darling of the progressives, and by sponsoring *Tannhäuser* the emperor could effectively woo that liberal-leftist faction upon which he believed he must now rely in the Assembly.

The emperor's command had spectacular effect. In most quarters of the Tuileries, where heretofore the name Wagner had meant the empress's elderly confidant the Countess de Pons de Wagner, now "the domestics, the employees . . . everyone became Wagnerians."[62] Wagner became "the man *à la mode*," as Gasperini put it, even though few of the people involved in his lionization had heard a note of his music.[63] But this mattered little at the court of Napoleon III, composed, according to the Princess Pauline Metternich, of the "least musical group of people who ever lived."[64] The minions of the emperor and the slaves to fashion who followed the princess were now supporting Wagner. Indeed, the entire facilities of the Opéra were turned over to him, and he was given an unlimited expense account.[65]

Then he suddenly ran into trouble. In November 1860 the Librairie nouvelle brought out the four poems of *Der fliegende Holländer, Tannhäuser, Lohengrin,* and *Tristan und Isolde* translated into French prose by Paul Challemel-Lacour. Wagner prefaced the poems with a "Letter on Music" addressed to Frédéric Villot, in which he expounded for the first time his theories of music drama. Wagner described his musical development as he advanced his theory of the *Gesamtkunstwerk,* according to which music as well as all the arts should subserve the ends of the poet and should be utilized to convey the drama.

In writing this letter Wagner managed to revive the controversy that had earlier surrounded his name in France. By offering his theories to the French, he gave them a new chance to compare his words and deeds, as Fétis and Scudo had done in 1852. During the course of the letter Wagner tried to answer some of the charges leveled against him in the early 1850s. He denied that he wrote music without melody, and he also denied that he composed his operas in order to prove his theories. Such protestations only served to get him into more trouble. Even his supporter Gasperini was obliged to admit that he put his ideas in "clumsy and laborious language, studded with parentheses, reservations, vague and fleeting formulas."[66] A less sympathetic observer declared that "he presented himself as the musical dictator of the future, admitting none of the geniuses of modern or ancient art as equals and still less as masters."[67] This critic did insufficient justice to Wagner's reverence for the great composers when he went on to insist that Wagner announced himself as a "musical prophet of whom Gluck, Mozart, and Beethoven were only pale precursors."[68] In any case, to many Frenchmen Wagner's basic theory of the intimate union of words and music in opera seemed to be merely a restatement of Gluck's ideas in his famous 1769 preface to *Alceste*. What all these charges meant was that Wagner, having enjoyed a brief respite from newspaper attacks as a result of the emperor's decree, was now again a prime target for criticism. Because of his unfortunate letter, the "music of the future" and his aesthetic theories had again become subjects of derision.

Wagner's newly forged political connection also opened him to attack. He lost support among some of his republican partisans because they now associated him with Napoleon III, with whom they remained unreconciled despite the emperor's shift to the Left. The connection with Princess Metternich only reinforced their hostility, since they had little use for her in particular or for the Habsburg monarchy in general. While it is not clear how many republicans who had initially backed Wagner now became alienated from him, several prominent figures in this camp—chiefly Juliette Adam and Paul Challemel-Lacour—viewed Wagner's new alignment as an act of betrayal: it represented, Adam fumed, a "desertion of the Countess d'Agoult's salon for that of the Princess Metternich."[69] Needless to say, this hardly boded well for Wagner and for the premiere of his *Tannhäuser*.

"Stay away from the Opéra," warned the editor of the republican *Le siècle;* "trouble is brewing."[70]

Trouble was brewing not only among the republicans but also among the legitimists—specifically among the members of the infamous Jockey Club. The club was made up primarily of aristocratic young gallants who had very definite ideas about both politics and the theater. With respect to the latter, they generally preferred lighter fare: comedy, Italian opera, and above all the ballet. (Indeed, it seems that they attended the Opéra largely to admire the dancers.) Thus when they learned that M. Wagner planned to subject them to a long and apparently quite heavy evening without a single flash of the female leg, they were quick to voice their objection. Within two weeks of the emperor's *Tannhäuser* order, reported an equally indignant Wagner, the Jockeys had demanded "a grand ballet for the second act."[71] This was not a trivial matter, since ballet was central to the Opéra by tradition, and the issue dragged on for the entire year that elapsed between the command (March 12, 1860) and the first performance (March 13, 1861). No compromise appeared possible, since the Jockey Club wanted their ballet and Wagner would not bend: the Opéra, he insisted, was to perform his work as written or not to perform it at all. Finally, however, the composer relented by adding a short ballet to a revised Venusberg scene in Act I, a compromise pleasing to no one.

Minister of State Walewski and Napoleon III himself both sought to head off disturbances by the Jockey Club. They knew that the club had disrupted performances often enough in the past. Disappointment over the small part given one of their favorite actresses, for example, had once induced them to riot; the invasion of their theatrical domain by the emperor provided an equally good excuse.[72] And there was also a political dimension to their protest. As we noted above, the club's members had a predominantly legitimist orientation, which would turn any action they might take against *Tannhäuser* into a clear demonstration by the legitimist Right against the emperor.[73]

As it turned out, of course, no one, not even the emperor and empress, was able to prevent the Jockeys from having their day when Wagner's *Tannhäuser* finally premiered at the Opéra in March 1861. The Jockeys' disturbances, which involved a liberal use of dog whistles and escalated in intensity over the meager three-performance run, have been described so often that they require no detailed recounting here.

What needs to be stressed, however, is that much of their opposition to *Tannhäuser* was not to the music itself. We are told that one of the aristocratic demonstrators, an unnamed count, entered Princess Metternich's box during a performance and explained to her: "It's superb, this *Tannhäuser*, but what can I do? I whistle, for I am of the conspiracy."[74] Wagner himself enjoyed repeating this anecdote.

It was thus thanks to Napoleon III that Wagner had his opera performed in Paris at all, but it was also because of the emperor's authoritarian policies that the enemies of his regime had to resort to opera riots to express their convictions. Wagner, the recipient of imperial largesse, became Napoleon's stalking-horse. The "failure" of *Tannhäuser* was not, then, Wagner's. Public interest was no doubt sufficiently great to have drawn full houses for months to come if Wagner had not insisted on withdrawing his work after the rioting. True, it would be years until another opera by Wagner would be performed in Paris. But there would continue to be regular concert performances of his music, and he would continue to attract devoted followers. He had clearly left a permanent imprint on Paris.

As we have seen, the *Tannhäuser* affair had produced strange bedfellows both in support of and in opposition to Wagner's cause. As for the opposition, the alliance of republicans and legitimists against the production of *Tannhäuser* could hardly survive the event that brought it about. Indeed, five days after the third and final performance this "alliance" collapsed. On March 30, 1861, Auguste Vacquerie's play *Les funérailles de l'honneur* received a tumultuous premiere at the Porte St. Martin Theater. Because Vacquerie's brother had married Victor Hugo's daughter, the republicans demonstrated in favor of the play, thus revealing their support for the exiled Hugo and opposition to the emperor. They nevertheless lost out to imperialist rowdies, who successfully disrupted the play. "*Tannhäuser* was an imperialist defeat; *Funérailles de l'honneur* was a republican defeat," recalled Juliette Adam, conjoining the two events in her memoirs just as contemporaries did at the time.[75] For the poets, artists, and students of the avant-garde, notably Baudelaire, *Funérailles* represented a second defeat. In fact, coming so close together, the two defeats seemed as one to many observers.

A banquet was arranged in the Latin Quarter to honor Vacquerie and, in effect, to honor Wagner as well. Wagner tells us in *Mein Leben* that after the dinner he enjoyed such success playing selections from

Tannhäuser at the piano that soon Vacquerie was forgotten and the banquet was transformed into a tribute for him alone.[76] The questionable accuracy of Wagner's account is unimportant. The banquet was significant because it signaled the end of the factionalism among Wagner's supporters caused by the emperor's action. Wagner's more progressive advocates no longer had to weigh in the balance their political beliefs and their convictions in art.

Tannhäuser and the banquet were to shift the leadership of the Wagnerian movement away from genteel politicians to progressive artists. The death of Blandine Liszt Ollivier in 1862 was a loss to the movement; though Ollivier continued his support of Wagner, his salon no longer acted as a center for Wagner's backers. The banquet clearly identified Wagner's future supporters. They had already been singled out at the *Tannhäuser* performances by Pietro Scudo as the "Wagner partisans" and unkindly described as "mediocre writers, painters, suspect democrats and republicans, *esprits faux,* women without taste, and idle dreamers of nothingness."[77] A dress called *le manteau Tannhäuser* remained in vogue in Paris, but artists increasingly set the tone of Wagnerism.[78]

An argument could be made that Wagnerism was launched in France on April 1, 1861, when Charles Baudelaire's article "Richard Wagner" appeared in the *Revue européenne.* Under the title *Richard Wagner et "Tannhäuser" à Paris,* Dentu published the essay as a pamphlet in May, with an additional section, "Encore quelques mots." Here Baudelaire rebutted much of the common criticism leveled at Wagner, sought to explain the failure of *Tannhäuser,* and described his personal reactions to Wagner's music. He sounded the call for "*littérateurs,* artists, and even *gens du monde*" who were "well-bred, endowed with justice, and open-minded" to encourage the composer "to persist in his destiny." "At last the idea is launched," he concluded; "the breach is made, and that is the important thing."[79]

The office of the *Revue fantaisiste,* an avant-garde publication, acted as a leading center of Wagnerism in Paris during the journal's brief but significant history (February to August, 1861). Baudelaire, Gasperini, and Champfleury mingled there with newer and younger converts to the cause. Baudelaire was not surprised that "men of letters in particular should prove themselves to be sympathetic to a musician who would glorify being a poet and a dramatist."[80] Catulle Mendès, the nineteen-year-old editor of the *Revue,* sought Wagner out and induced him to lend his name to the masthead of the journal as a contributing editor. Mendès proved even more important than Baudelaire in attracting to Wagnerism the young artists who gave it a new character.[81] Throughout the decade, the rising young poets around Mendès, the so-called Parnassians, provided a key source of Wagner worship in Paris. One of Mendès's colleagues, Villiers de l'Isle-Adam—who declared that Wagner was "a genius such as appears on earth once every thousand years"[82]— later said that his fellow Parnassians regarded themselves as "the first *wagnéristes.*"[83]

Another circle of young *wagnéristes* consisted primarily of painters. This group of artists and art critics, influenced in many ways by Baudelaire, met regularly in the 1860s at the Café Guerbois and in the 1870s became known as Impressionists.[84] Zola's 1886 novel, *L'oeuvre,* based largely on the days when he was part of this youthful camaraderie, recaptured the flavor of their conversations about art theory, politics, and Wagner.[85]

Some of the artists, of course, were more interested in music than others. Frédéric Bazille, an ardent Wagnerian, played Wagner evening after evening with his friend and fellow pianist Edmond Maître, and he often went with Renoir to hear Wagner performed at concerts.[86] Suzanne Manet, wife of the artist, was a pianist who enjoyed playing Wagner's music for their many guests.[87] Some works of art were inspired by Wagner's music dramas. Fantin-Latour was so incensed at the adverse reception of *Tannhäuser* that he painted the dance scene, *Venusberg,* showing it in the Salon of 1864.[88] Cézanne, supposedly a hater of music, was affected deeply enough by Wagner to paint the *Ouverture du "Tannhäuser,"* an early version of *Jeune fille au piano.*[89]

The political dimension of Wagnerism, however, continued to animate some of the writers in the movement. Whereas Baudelaire, comparatively apolitical since the debacle of 1848, was content to admire the "popular" implications of Wagner's art and ideas and indeed dismissed his revolutionary opinions as "error," other followers took quite a different position.[90] One of those was the poet and dramatist Théodore de Banville.[91] He saw Wagner as a "democrat, a new man, wanting to create for all the people . . . a harmonious ensemble where all the arts, poetry, music, painting, and sculpture . . . could combine to produce a drama that would enchain the soul of the spectator."[92] Yet Banville also anticipated the symbolists in approaching poetry like music. He gave the idea of union of the arts a dual political and artistic meaning when he declared that the work of Wagner was a "*revolution-ary symphony*" that would soon achieve its aim—unity of impression.[93]

Gasperini and Léon Leroy wrote of democratic art as well. They voiced this ideal in their short-lived journal *L'esprit nouveau* (January 16–June 13, 1867). Though they did not cite Wagner in their theoretical articles, his influence is unmistakable. Whereas Baudelaire had concentrated on the "popular" and Banville on the "democratic," side of Wagner's aesthetics, Gasperini and Léon Leroy developed to the full the political implications of Wagner's revolutionary sympathies. Gasperini and Leroy dreamed of a "free, sincere, and vigorous art that would be accessible to all the people."[94] Good democrats that they were, they felt that art must belong to the people and that the people could truly understand it: "The rapid opening of the world of art to the appreciation of the masses: that is the aim; that is the dream!"[95] The political implications of these aesthetic discussions seem to have been appreciated in certain circles, for the minister of interior withdrew the journal's licence in June 1867. This brought to an abrupt end what was France's "first Wagnerian revue," but its brief history points up the persistence of a union between political and artistic interests in the Wagnerism of the 1860s.[96]

The "republicans in art" of the 1860s, as Maxime Leroy calls them,[97] drew some specific parallels between events in the political world and Wagner's operas. For example, Gasperini, writing shortly after the Geneva Treaty on War, the establishment of the Red Cross, and the organization of the First International, found the principle of world unity and peace in Wagner's operas. In characteristic utopian terms he maintained that just as Wagner had eliminated the barriers that existed between set numbers in the formal operas and just as the old boundaries between cities were vanishing, so now would they disappear between countries as well. Gasperini was much encouraged to find Wagner's operatic principles spreading to France and Italy, since Gounod and Verdi were, he thought, following Wagner's lead in taking new operatic freedoms.[98] Likewise, in *L'oeuvre*, Zola looked back on the 1860s and had the *wagnériste* Gagnière eloquently explain his fascination with Wagner: the "massacre of conventions, of inept formulas," he said, would produce a "revolutionary freedom." Wagner's music was the "sublime hallelujah of the new century."[99]

One of the main factors affecting Wagner's reception after *Tannhäuser* were the performances of his music at the Concerts Populaires, the orchestral series that Léon Pasdeloup began in October 1861 in the five thousand–seat Cirque Napoléon. Pasdeloup drew a completely new mass audience to symphonic concerts and thereby at least partially realized Wagner's ideal of music for the people. But he did not achieve this without encountering opposition from those who preferred the classical repertoire to the "music of the future." Since these people did not hesitate to make their objections known, the Concerts populaires were marred by battles between the conservatives and the Wagnerians, the two sides exchanging cheers and whistles, shouts and catcalls.[100] One witness to these Wagner battles at the Cirque Napoléon was the young Paul Verlaine; in a poem called "Epigrammes XX," written when he was fifty, he fondly recalled his youthful partisanship for Wagner on those occasions: "I struck a blow for Wagner to my utmost."[101] Battles and blows notwithstanding, Pasdeloup made notable progress in his campaign to popularize the Master's work. His strategy here was apparent to one critic of the *Revue et gazette musicale:* like Mithridates, who immunized himself against poisons by gradually increasing the dosage, Pasdeloup would immunize the Parisians by spoon-feeding them Wagner.[102]

Pasdeloup's proselytizing for Wagner reached its climax on April 6, 1869, when he presented at the Théâtre-Lyrique a production of *Rienzi.* The work drew mixed reactions, but enthusiasts outnumbered opponents.[103] Those critical of the work pointed out that *Rienzi* broke nearly every rule Wagner had been setting forth for his music, but his supporters insisted that *Rienzi* had been composed before the theories had been established—it was "the youthful work of a genius."[104] Twenty-six performances of the opera were given during the balance of the season.[105]

By the spring of 1870, Pasdeloup had performed his charge so well and the public response had been so positive that it seemed only a matter of time until Wagner's other operas would be produced in Paris and he himself would gain his full measure of appreciation by the Parisian public. Indeed even Wagner, always his own worst enemy, could not reverse this trend. In December 1867 the *Guide musical* had published Wagner's *German Art and German Politics*—a blast at the French and a paeon of praise for Prussia.[106] The appearance of *Judaism in Music,* in which Wagner paraded his anti-Semitism, was likewise noted in Paris in 1869.[107] And at least one critic, Charles Bannelier of the *Revue et gazette musicale,* pointed out that Wagner's new opera, *Die*

Meistersinger (1868), ended with a speech by Hans Sachs on the mission of German art now *"perverted by the Gallic taste."*[108] But before the Franco-Prussian war, these matters did not hurt Wagner much. His writings, though quite nationalistic, were consistent with a prominent strain in contemporary French artistic criticism that evinced an unmistakable tone of respect for the Germans—sometimes even at the expense of the French.[109]

Wagnerism gained as well from the growing prominence of certain members of the movement. In 1869, Édouard Schuré described the *wagnéristes* as the "elite of the authors, the critics, and the public."[110] Just as Wagner gained respectable support, so had some of his earlier advocates risen in general esteem. Gasperini, for example, who died in 1868, had won a reputation as a leading critic and savant.[111] Moreover, the success of Banville's *Gringoire* (June 23, 1866) at the Théâtre-français and later of Coppée's *Le Passant* (January 14, 1869), at the Odeon with Sarah Bernhardt, rebounded favorably on all the members of the Parnassian group.[112]

Indeed, by 1870 Wagnerism was far more prominent and respectable than it had been ten years earlier. In 1869 a popular satirist displayed a distinct admiration for the Wagnerian cause—something rare a decade before—in saying of Léon Leroy that "one could not pronounce the name of M. Richard Wagner without Léon Leroy's throwing himself into the discussion with a remarkable animation."[113] Bizet wrote to a colleague in that same year that "the bourgeois and the man about town know that [with Wagner] they are dealing with quite somebody, and it leaves them floundering. . . . Few people have the courage to persist in their hatred of Wagner."[114]

III

But all this suddenly changed with the outbreak of the Franco-Prussian war in 1870. Whereas previously Wagner's strident German nationalism had not been a major obstacle to his conquest of France, now, with Germans and Frenchmen locked in bloody battle, his German chauvinism could hardly be overlooked. It could be overlooked all the less because Wagner chose this painful moment to rub salt in Gallic wounds. In 1870 he wrote what he called a "harmless satire," the farce "A Capitulation," in which he mocked France's suffering during the German siege of Paris. There were apologists who pointed out that the work actually portrayed "a capitulation" of the Germans to the Parisian manner of life; they claimed that Wagner had merely written a parody of French frivolity.[115] Nonetheless, many Frenchmen could forgive Wagner neither for his tasteless portrayal of Victor Hugo rising out of the sewers of Paris nor for his jeering at the French loss of Alsace-Lorraine. The Parisians found it particularly hard to appreciate Wagner's jests about their starvation during the siege and their need to kill their pets for food.

Just as Germany was now viewed as the robber of French territory, so Wagner became infamous as "the insulter of France." Once again, attitudes toward Wagner would be based more on extrinsic political events than on the intrinsic merits of his music. Even Catulle Mendès had to say that though he would continue to applaud Wagner's music, he would no longer be his friend.[116]

The Pasdeloup concerts naturally became the battleground for this confrontation. The orchestra refused to accept Pasdeloup's request that they perform the *Rienzi* overture in October of 1872.[117] Wagner was performed again the following year but "not without stirring up tumult, rows, and public demonstrations of feelings."[118] The performance of October 29, 1876, typified the Wagner battles in the postwar decade. To fuel the anti-Wagner forces, copies of a supplement to the journal *L'eclipse,* containing Wagner's "A Capitulation" in French translation, were put on sale outside the concert hall. A demonstration started in the hall before the first chords of Siegfried's Funeral March from *Die Götterdämmerung* were sounded. Once the piece ended, a deafening uproar broke out; Pasdeloup's demand for a little deference to the artists could not be heard. The audience hissed the next selection, the overture to Weber's *Der Freischütz,* in the belief that the despised *Götterdämmerung* was being repeated.[119]

Clearly, then, Wagner's fortunes in France suffered a setback in the 1870s. And yet by the beginning of the next decade his cause was again on the rise. Two new concert orchestras joined Pasdeloup in programing Wagner. One of them, led by Edouard Colonne, began to perform his music in 1880 because public favor seemed clear; the other, conducted by Charles Lamoureux, presented his music with particularly high performance standards. Indeed, in the fall of 1882 all three orchestras played the prelude to *Parsifal* on the same Sunday. By the end of the 1880s Wagner's music was an integral part of the orchestral repertory.

Production of his operas was another matter, however, not only because of the special expense involved but also because of the larger intellectual and political issues that these works raised. In 1882 an attempt to perform *Lohengrin* at the national Opéra was killed in large part by the rising nationalist movement. In 1887 a production of the same opera was mounted but canceled after one performance, in part because of political attacks. The riots that threatened to bring General Georges Boulanger to power that year may have helped end the production, but they did not pose a serious obstacle to the establishment of Wagner in the repertoire or in public taste.[120] By the 1880s and 1890s, at least, sentiment for *revanche* did not seriously impede the French public's acceptance of Wagner's art, and productions of his works recurred fairly frequently from 1891 on. Even though the Boulanger affair possibly played a role in the withdrawal of *Lohengrin,* nationalistic attacks functioned largely to cloak more concrete objections to the performance of Wagner's music—the fears of performers and publishers that they would open themselves up to German competition. "Behind this campaign," said the *Guide musical,* "is a question of protectionism."[121] A few old liberals such as Juliette Adam joined in the affair as well, trying to revenge themselves upon Wagner for his "betrayal" of them in 1860.[122] Significantly, the nationalist leader Paul Déroulède took no stand on the issue, remarking that he rather liked what music of Wagner he had heard.[123]

Nevertheless, French nationalism probably inhibited the growth of democratic ideas or indeed of any kind of left-wing politics in the Wagnerian movement. After 1870, French Wagnerians stayed away from political issues of all kinds, except for some abstract social observations, since any such discussion led them into dangerous territory. And even aside from the problem of nationalism, the Third Republic was too new and too poorly defined for it to be an attractive target to any political critique from the Wagnerians. Wagnerism was by definition idealistic and antagonistic to convention; the new regime had as yet no clear-cut "establishment" against which a protest movement could be marshalled. The political dimension in French Wagnerism accordingly began to atrophy.

Still, certain strains in Wagner's social philosophy, especially his critique of liberalism, continued to attract a few adherents after 1870. Most important among these followers was Edouard Schuré, a musician and writer who knew Wagner and who was regarded by him as his chief French supporter. In 1876 he published *Le drame musical,* a study of Wagner and his works that quickly became the most important book of its kind in France. Here Schuré echoed much of Wagner's critique of materialism and profit-seeking theater managers. Like Wagner, he saw industrial civilization blinding men to all creativity in the arts. But these notions did not lead Schuré to any revolutionary fantasies or indeed to any concept of political engagement; rather he advocated a hermetic, individualistic artistic experience.[124] Other Wagnerians, especially the symbolist poets, voiced the idea of hermeticism in a way that was actually antagonistic to democratic social values. They spoke with awe of the now dying aristocratic tradition, especially in reference to their colleague Villiers de l'Isle-Adam's supposedly aristocratic background.[125] They thus brought out the rightward-leaning strand of Wagnerism we encountered before.

After 1870, French Wagnerism came increasingly under the sway of professional writers who joined the movement with career interests in mind. Compared with the 1850s and 1860s, the movement was now influenced much less by genteel amateurs like Ollivier or Gasperini than by men who were at least trying to sustain themselves through their writing. Social changes in cultural life may have had something to do with this, since after the war intellectually oriented salons enjoyed considerably less prominence than before, and cultural life in general became much more consistently professionalized and focused upon the printed word. The young writers who came to the fore as Wagnerians took full advantage of the movement to make their names known. Moreover, professionals from the arts other than literature now had rather less to do with Wagnerism than during the 1860s. Musicians who specialized in performing Wagner's works—above all Charles Lamoureux and Ernest Reyer—were identified with the movement but came into severe conflict with the most strong-minded writers. A few painters contributed illustrations to the *Revue wagnérienne* but had less to do with Wagnerism than had their predecessors.

The writers who now dominated the Wagnerian movement by no means agreed on the fundamentals of Wagnerism, and they soon split into two contending factions. On one side were those who owed principal allegiance to Stéphane Mallarmé and the cause of symbolist poetry. On the other side were writers who generally had musical as well as literary interests and who resisted the imposition of symbolist techniques upon Wagnerian writing. The latter group was older, more numerous, and more respectable but exerted rather less dynamic leadership during the critical years 1885–1887. While some of them had intellectual roots in Baudelaire's Wagnerism, they did not follow that tendency nearly so far as the symbolists.

The landmark work in the symbolist faction of Wagnerism was Joris Karl Huysmans's novel *A rebours (Against the Grain)*. Published in 1884, a year after Wagner's death, it linked the composer with the new artistic movement of decadence. As Huysmans himself noted, his book "fell like a meteorite into the literary fair ground." The novel stunned a generation of young malcontents who could identify with Huysmans's central character, duke Jean des Esseintes.[126] A frail, highly strung young man of thirty, des Esseintes is the last representative of a once great house. Overwhelmed by the mediocrity and ugliness of a world wrought by the bourgeoisie, des Esseintes determines to shut himself off from this world and indulge his senses. "Decadence" became the descriptive term for this new attitude and for the works of those who inspired des Esseintes—Redon, Moreau, Baudelaire, Verlaine, Tristan Corbière, Villiers de l'Isle-Adam, Mallarmé—and Wagner.[127] For the first time artists and writers who had been striving individually to find refuge in worlds of their own were now united in the preferences enjoyed by des Esseintes, lovingly described in the novel.

Some of these artists had begun as naturalists in the manner of Zola, but now, like Huysmans, they sought a greater truth that went beyond the precise recreation of objective experience to what they regarded as a deeper and more profound reality. This they thought could be found in the powers of the imagination and in the enlivening of the senses, which they sometimes regarded as ends in themselves, sources of unlimited self-gratification. In addition to this hedonistic delight in the senses, they also sought a spiritual fulfillment in mysticism. Predictably, they found in Wagner the consummate union of such sensory and spiritual quests. He assumed even greater significance in death than in life: the spiritual and creative force of a new age in the arts.

Wagner's impact on this age was crystalized by the creation of a new journal, the *Revue wagnérienne*. Conceived to disseminate Wagner's poetic and philosophical ideas, the *Revue* was founded by three ardent young Wagnerians: the former music student, Edouard Dujardin; the Polish-born musician and philosopher, Téodor de Wyzewa; and the renegade Englishman, Houston Stewart Chamberlain.[128] They shared a reverence for Wagner and the belief that his ideas were consistent with the new stirrings in thought and the arts.

The *Revue wagnérienne* began monthly publication in February 1885 and continued from July 1887 to December 1887 on a bimonthly basis, with one final issue in July 1888. As a kind of newsletter, it published monthly listings of Wagnerian concert performances and opera productions throughout France and abroad, reviews of new books on Wagner, reports from other cities on relevant activities, and discussions of current issues in the "Wagnerian movement."[129] As both an educational tool and a platform for Wagnerian propaganda,[130] the journal also carried translations of Wagner's writings, reprints of "classic" pieces of Wagneriana by such authors as Gérard de Nerval and Liszt, and sober analyses of Wagnerian music dramas. As a journal of record, the *Revue* covered in extensive detail the battles waged in the Parisian press on the controversies surrounding attempts to mount productions of Wagner in the opera house.

At the outset the journal had a diverse group of backers. Though conceived by Dujardin, Wyzewa, and Chamberlain at the *Ring* festival in Munich in 1884, it was supported financially by a Doubs industrialist, Alfred Bovet; a Geneva multimillionaire, Agénor Boissier; and a jurist named Arnold Lascoux.[131] Prominent among its regular contributors were the journalists Edouard Schuré, Camille Benoit, Louis Fourcaud, Charles and Pierre Bonnier, and the old Wagnerians Léon Leroy and Catulle Mendès. Primarily concerned with Wagner's music, these writers were not part of the poetic circle grouped around Mallarmé.

Nevertheless, Mallarmé's circle came to dominate the journal, and indeed the controversy over French Wagnerism. Most of these young poets were in their early twenties and had only recently come to Paris; none of them, except Mallarmé, had established himself very prominently before the journal was founded. Téodor de Wyzewa had left a position at a provincial *collège* to enter Paris with no reputation and little income; Edouard Dujardin had failed at the Ecole Normale Superieur, first in literature and then in music.[132] Wagnerism thus functioned for them as a way to make their names known. The editors of the *Revue wagnérienne* were open-minded enough to print a letter which argued that love of Wagner "has become an occupation, a profession; failures [*les fruits secs*], of whom there are so many in the arts, as in politics, want to make him theirs in order to draw to themselves a little of the attention the Master commands and deny any understanding of him to others. They close themselves in their closet, declaring that if one does not beg them to explain how precisely to appreciate Wagner, then one has no right even to open his scores."[133]

These young men took Wagnerism as a vehicle for a critique not of musical life but of the literary world. Proclaiming that Wagnerism pointed the new direction in which poetry had to move, they set themselves up as judges of this creed. The editors of the journal said as much in 1887: "*La Revue wagnérienne,* operating on the principles which we see as those of true Wagnerism, will judge, with the absolute independence which its special situation demands and which is incompatible with the conditions existing in most other publications, the Wagnerian concerns of the year 1887."[134] These young men certainly were not lacking in daring. Though having little knowledge of Wagner's music, the avant-garde *wagnéristes* were typical of the movement in general simply by virtue of their extreme idealism. As one observer put it, they exhibited "an almost unquenchable appetite for idealism" in calling upon others to subscribe to their high principles.[135] Having come into the Wagnerian movement with little influence in the literary world, they managed to make themselves and their ideas surprisingly au courant, if only for a short period.

The most important role of the *Revue wagnérienne* in literary history was its fostering of symbolism, the movement of French poetry that grew out of its predecessor, decadence. Stéphane Mallarmé acted as master to the young writers; he was the high priest of both symbolism and Wagnerism. Dujardin and Wyzewa argued the entire compatibility of these two philosophies. The two men regularly attended Mallarmé's Tuesdays (*les mardis,* as devotees called them) during which he talked about poetry in an almost religious atmosphere. Musicians as well as poets, Dujardin and Wyzewa found it impossible to explain the Wagnerian conception without recognizing its affinity with the "primordial elements of the new poetic doctrine." They insisted that Wagner's "conception of art, his philosophy, his very formula, were at the origin of symbolism."[136]

Much of the *Revue wagnérienne* was devoted to developing this link.

Numerous articles discussed Mallarmé and Wagner together. Two issues offered seventeen sonnets by as many symbolist poets paying homage to Wagner and to his works. An article by Wyzewa on Wagnerism and contemporary poetry in the issue of June 1886 formulated the basic tenets of early symbolism. Wyzewa hailed Mallarmé as "symphonist and Wagnerian poet" and claimed that Mallarmé was the first true French poet because he knew how to marry poetry to music.[137]

Mallarmé contributed one essay and one poem to the *Revue*. The article, "Richard Wagner: Reverie of a French Poet," scandalized many readers with what seemed to them unintelligible language. But as one observer noted, an even greater scandal would have occurred "if the Wagnerians had understood how emphatically the great poet separated his cause from the great musician's."[138] Mallarmé implied that Wagner's temple was only "halfway up the Holy Mountain," while his own goal was the "peak of the absolute."[139]

Mallarmé's poem, "Hommage," appeared in the January 1886 issue.[140] In implying that realism and naturalism would be replaced by the deeper truth of symbolism as revealed by "the god Richard Wagner," the poem displayed its author's characteristic intellectual arrogance. It also displayed another quality typical of the symbolist school: impenetrability. Indeed, the poem was so infuriatingly obscure that it provoked a demonstration of outrage at a banquet of writers.

The *Revue's* affinity for symbolism had deep historical origins in the work of Baudelaire. Twenty-five years earlier, Baudelaire's *Richard Wagner et "Tannhäuser" à Paris* had emphasized his kinship with Wagner based on their mutual objectives in the world of art. Baudelaire found a similarity between Wagner's attempt to create a synthesis of the arts and his own idea, stated in his poem "Correspondances," that our senses respond to forms in nature's language that are symbols of truths inherent in the world of the spirit. Baudelaire quoted part of his poem in discussing Wagner's prelude to *Lohengrin*. Inevitably, "Correspondances" became the symbolists' manifesto as well.

Baudelaire felt an affinity with Wagner's music and aesthetic theories but misunderstood the concept of the *Gesamtkunstwerk*. His errors were repeated throughout the life span of the *Revue wagnérienne*, which then propagated its own misconceptions. The result was symbolism in the guise of Wagner. As Lucy Beckett has said, "Baudelaire positively and Mallarmé negatively had exposed some of the central critical issues, but *wagnérisme* on the whole was a literary craze compounded of the sensational and the pseudo-mystical that produced neither good new art nor competent criticism of *Tristan* and *Parsifal.*"[141]

This kind of Wagnerism did not harmonize well with the more conventional—the more "musical"—branches of the movement. In Baudelaire's time the amateur and professional musicians among the Wagnerians had gotten along fairly well with avant-garde literary artists, especially the Parnassians. But the ideas and the language used by the followers of decadence and symbolism alienated many lovers of Wagner's music, as well as a number of Wagnerian writers, who found certain pieces in the journal offensively bizarre and outrageous. Huysmans, whose *A rebours* was called "the breviary of decadence," provoked such a reaction with his highly colored verbal paraphrase of the *Tannhäuser* overture, which featured pictures of Venus Luxuria and Sodomita Libido evocative of opium- or hashish-like visions. Dujardin drew similar criticism for his decadent "Amfortas," as did he and Chamberlain for their overly opulent translation of the first scene of *Das Rheingold.*[142]

The *Revue* also offered philosophical articles that traced the connections among the strands of pessimism, mysticism, and idealism that underlay both the decadent movement and the thinking of Wagner. Wyzewa, for example, wrote "The Pessimism of Richard Wagner," while Emile Hennequin discussed "The Esthetic of Wagner and the Spencerian Doctrine."[143] Once again, articles such as these were considered by many Wagnerians to be irrelevant to understanding or enjoying the music dramas.

Those opposed to the "symbolization" of Wagner complained that he had been taken over by a fanatical cult, the "Knights of the Wagnerian Grail."[144] The charge of cultism was not unwarranted. The symbolists associated with the *Revue wagnérienne* had deliberately isolated themselves through their arrogant impenetrability, a stance that stemmed naturally from their contempt for the bourgeoisie. After all, their revered des Esseintes had alienated himself from bourgeois society in order to gratify his senses and particular aesthetic sensibilities. The self-appointed propagators of the Wagnerian faith actually resented the increasing popularity of Wagner in musical life, as orchestral performances of his music became more frequent throughout the decade.

The French Wagnerian movement began to split apart as a result of these internal tensions and divisions. In November 1886 Lamoureux attacked the *Revue wagnérienne* for the decadence of its style and for the problems that it caused him in planning his production of *Lohengrin*. The journal accordingly took a dim view of his production. When Lamoureux eventually withdrew it, Dujardin accused him of trying to usurp control of the Wagnerian movement from the *Revue* by acting as though he were the greatest martyr for Wagner.[145] Competition for French translations of the libretti further complicated the situation, for the symbolist Alfred Ernst managed to beat out the more traditional writer Victor Wilder in gaining the Wagner family's approval to do the translations.[146] As a result of these squabbles, all but one of the financial contributors to the journal (Lascoux) ended their support, and no more issues were published after July 1888.

The opponents of the journal hoped to reawaken the Wagnerian cause purged of decadent or symbolist overtones. But after the controversies had abated, the excitement and esprit that had initially animated the Wagnerian movement also faded away. As Alfred Ernst put it so sharply in 1888: "From the point of view of Wagnerian art, the 'heroic' period is over, and to admire Wagner has become banal."[147] Intimately connected with this loss of avant-garde elan and radical chic was the growing popularity of the Master's music with the general public. Wagner's name had now become something of a household word, especially in the houses of the French establishment. In Proust's great novel *A la recherche du temps perdu,* we find the aristocratic Guermantes and their titled guests dropping the names Tristan and Lohengrin right and left at the dinner table; even the quite unmusical Odette Swann makes her way to Bayreuth. The musically far more serious Marcel, however, finds solace at the piano playing Wagner's music; the depiction of his reading through *Tristan* in a reverie on a Sunday afternoon echoes the symbolists' idea of hermeticism.[148] But public interest in Wagner's music still had little to do with symbolist thinking: from 1886 on attendance of Frenchmen at Bayreuth increased significantly;[149] in 1891 *Lohengrin* permanently entered the repertory of the Paris Opéra, and *Tannhäuser* returned with great success in 1895.

IV

Having surveyed the evolution of French Wagnerism, we can see that it showed considerable strength over an extended period—well-nigh forty years, one might argue. While Paris never had a formal organization, a Wagner society, the influence of Wagnerism there began earlier than in any other major city outside Germany. The French movement had its origins in the dispute over Wagner's writings in 1852, grew steadily after that, evolved a self-conscious sense of identity during Wagner's visit of 1859–1861, and survived the *Tannhäuser* fiasco to become the rage of the artistic avant-garde in the 1860s. Though the Franco-Prussian War set it back significantly, its influence soon revived, and it assumed a spectacular, if ultimately divisive, role in French cultural life during the 1880s. We have seen that its subsequent demise as an avant-garde cultural movement stemmed not only from its own internal divisions but also from the very success that the Master's music finally achieved with the French public.

In France, as elsewhere, Wagnerism functioned as an extraordinarily powerful vehicle for a great variety of artistic, social, and political currents. That this meant Wagner's ideas were misunderstood, and sometimes completely distorted, goes without saying, but the very variety of their uses and abuses suggests their potency. We certainly need to keep in view the intellectual and artistic inadequacies that Wagnerism displayed throughout Europe, not least in France,[150] but we must also recognize that no cultural movement had such a vital and varied impact as did Wagnerism.

The same holds true for the political role of Wagnerism in France. The movement owed much of its initial success to political circumstances, some of which had little to do with Wagner's works. On the other hand, Wagner would never have achieved such stature had his art not been so compelling. And, of course, he ultimately beguiled not only the radicals and the avant-garde bohemians, but *juste-milieu* liberals and even legitimists. We have underscored the crucial role of the Left partly because many historians assume that Wagner consistently drew his support from the Right. The fact of the matter is that his political following is best described by employing the Third Republic phrase "party of movement," as opposed to "party of the established order." Wagner's disciples may have differed significantly in political persuasion, but few can be said to have been defenders of the status quo.

We can see a similar quality when we turn to the artistic dimension of French Wagnerism. No matter how much French artists used Wagner's music and ideas to suit their own purposes, they maintained a consistent commitment to "progressive" taste. To say that all of them belonged to the artistic avant-garde would be an exaggeration, since that implies rather more self-conscious modernism than many of them (Ollivier or Schuré, for example) were willing to admit. But from Nerval and Ollivier to Mendès and Baudelaire and finally to Dujardin and Mallarmé, French Wagnerians were committed to furthering the cause of forward-looking trends in French culture. The movement indeed played a central role as a catalyst for the concept of the avant-garde in France, first among the Parnassians and then among the symbolists. Wagner need not have objected to the derisive label "music of the future," since in that appellation lay one of his most powerful contributions to nineteenth-century French culture.

4. Wagnerism, Wagnerians, and Italian Identity

MARION S. MILLER

The opening of *Lohengrin* in Bologna on November 1, 1871, launched the Wagnerian "invasion" of Italian opera houses and brought controversial Wagnerian theories to a volatile intellectual scene. Coming in the aftermath of the final stages of political unification—a process that left Italy deeply fragmented—the impact of Wagnerism between 1870 and 1914 may have had less to do with Wagner's ideas and music than with the problems of a divided Italian nation. The enthusiasm of a generation of Italian Wagnerians may have served to cloak a widespread disillusionment with unified Italy rather than to express a wholehearted acceptance of Wagner's ideas and the "music of the future." Thus the various debates on Richard Wagner's operas, theories, and influence that exploded in books, journals, and newspaper columns, in the halls of the opera houses and music conservatories, indeed in the chambers of the Italian parliament, tell us more, perhaps, about the preoccupation of Italians with their own character and destiny than about Wagnerism.

Clearly Wagner's innovations responded to a felt need for reform in Italian opera, and the growing acceptance of the music on its own terms is beyond dispute. But Wagnerism stood for something more; it became a cult and an ideology, ill defined and changing in content. To its advocates it could represent freedom and a program for growth, especially in the early decades; to its opponents it appeared to offer Italian musicians a foreign and therefore sterile model. And their differences were intensified by irrelevancies, by press exploitation, communal and commercial rivalries, and by xenophobia. But in time a more precise definition of aspirations and values could turn individuals against Wagnerism or toward reformulation of its content. Contradictory popular and elitist implications were apparent from the beginning.

The gradual but apparent decline of Wagnerism in Italy from the 1890s to the first World War may offer equally significant perspectives on Italian society. This change was at least partly precipitated by the shift after 1890 of Italian social and aesthetic values away from the abstract idealism Wagner was said to represent to a new emphasis on social realism—the so-called *verismo* movement. Moreover, the exchanges among journalists and musicologists on the character of Wagnerism suggest changing perceptions of both Wagner and Italian society, including an increased emphasis upon elitism in both. The fullest literary expression of elitism in the Wagnerian cult—that in the works of Gabriele D'Annunzio—reveals that the essential elements of the cult were undergoing rapid evolution far beyond the limits of Wagnerism. The Wagnerian fever had passed its peak even as D'Annunzio exploited it, but its decline was a deceptive phenomenon. The nonmusical and nondramatic values associated with the composer's work were not passing but were finding fuller development through other channels. Discontent with liberal Italy was crystalizing into new forms of aspiration, and Wagnerism had served as one of the catalysts in the emergence of new nationalist ideals.

I

As early as 1836 the Italian revolutionary Giuseppe Mazzini expressed in his *Filosofia della musica* (Philosophy of music) a set of ideas that foreshadowed some of Wagner's, a point that did not escape several critics during the debate on Wagner in later decades.[1] Mazzini's was a curiously prophetic essay, and most of his suggestions and predictions concerning music, and especially opera, were fulfilled in the following decades, though in an Italian rather than a German style. His views on music were a product of the same high idealism that inspired his advocacy of Italian political unity: Italy's Risorgimento was not to be merely social and political but also cultural and spiritual in character. But while Mazzini's message came in years of hope and aspiration, Wagner's came at a time when many Italians were disillusioned with the achievement of unity. Political unification had not brought about the hoped-for regeneration of social and cultural life.

For Mazzini, opera was not merely a medium of entertainment but an art form whose present degraded state was the direct reflection of a society itself in need of reform. Italian opera, he asserted, had lost its social mission, become materialistic, and been reduced to mere formula. Devoid of any unifying concept, it was a mosaic of unrelated parts, "a clash of diverse thoughts."[2] To this philosopher of an integral society, fragmentation was the ultimate indictment. He believed that exaggerated development of melody in Italian opera expressed an egoistic individualism, just as overemphasis on harmony in German opera revealed an excessive sense of community. And composition by formula prevented the shaping of the music in accordance with a controlling dramatic idea. Those familiar with Wagner's writings will recognize the indictment as well as the prescription for reform.

Believing that Italy stood on the threshold of a new age, Mazzini proceeded to suggest the techniques by which the dramatic unity that would revolutionize Italian opera might be attained: first, by the integration of all the arts, especially poetry, with music; second, by the characterization of persons through musical themes, that is, through employment of what would become known as the leitmotiv; third, by the active use of the chorus as an independent character, both in the story and in the structure of the music; and fourth, by the development of recitative as an additional means of exploring the emotional range of the characters.[3]

Mazzini dedicated his *Filosofia della musica* to that "unknown" future musician who would accomplish this aesthetic and social mission. Giuseppe Verdi's gigantic role over the next sixty-five years led some writers to suggest that he must be regarded as the fulfillment of the prophecy, just as Italian Wagnerians were to claim this honor for Wagner.[4] Mazzini himself refused to make a commitment to either. Equally unresolved was the question of whether Wagner had been influenced by Mazzinian ideas, for in none of his letters or prose writings did he acknowledge or make reference to the *Filosofia della musica*.[5]

II

The first Italians to display an interest in Wagner were more concerned with his theories on operatic reform than with his music, of which they had as yet heard little. One of the earliest articles on Wagner in an Italian periodical appeared anonymously in the Florentine journal *L'arte* on March 10, 1855; it displayed knowledge of Wagner's writings of the 1849–1851 period, especially *Oper und Drama*, which was not translated into Italian until 1894. Within a year, in February and March 1856, three more articles on Wagner's ideas for operatic reform were to appear in another Florentine journal, *L'armonia*, and a brief correspondence ensued between the author—Abramo Basevi, a local musician and doctor—and the German composer. Basevi nominated Wagner for membership in the Accademia dell'istituto musicale, and Wagner referred the Florentine to the first part of *Oper und Drama* for his analysis of the sickness of contemporary opera.[6]

It was a contact in Zurich, however, with the literary figure Francesco de Sanctis that led Wagner to seek an Italian publisher for his work. He wrote Verdi's music publisher and friend, Giulio Ricordi, in November 1861 (following the *Tannhäuser* debacle in Paris) and offered him the publishing rights to both *Tannhäuser* and *Rienzi*, confessing that "it will propagate my music in Italy, and it will help me at a difficult moment."[7] But Ricordi did not seize this opportunity, and in 1868 Wagner's works in Italy became the property (until 1894) of the publishing house owned by Giovannina Lucca and her husband. Signora Lucca became not only Wagner's ardent promoter but a devoted admirer.

Well before the appearance of the Lucca publications, the circulation in Italy of piano scores of Wagner's music, together with journalistic discussion of his ideas, stirred debate about the meaning of his work. In this a significant role was played by those of musical orientation among the bohemian writers and artists known as the *scapigliati* (literally, the "tousled" or "disheveled" ones). The *scapigliati,* many of whom were Mazzinian republicans, declared their disillusionment with unification and their contempt for the staid new Italy. Through a diverse range of publications and activities,[8] they expressed a rejection of the heroic rhetoric of the Risorgimento and a reaction against the philistinism of bourgeois society. Expounding a melange of contradictory complaints—political, social, and artistic—they mocked middle class conventions (though most, of course, were themselves of the middle class) and proclaimed a serious concern with social questions and the future of art. They attacked the various manifestations of lingering Romanticism, while themselves embodying the very essence of Romanticism. Two of the *scapigliati,* Arrigo Boito and Franco Faccio, aspiring composers both, had attended the highly prestigious Royal Conservatory of Music in Milan, but they registered their dissatisfaction in a succession of antiestablishment journals such as the *Gazzetino rosa.* The accusations of "Wagnerism" leveled in the 1860s against them missed the fact that the roots of their discontent was in their own society.

At times reflecting Mazzinian ideals in seeking a higher idealism, the musical *scapigliati,* especially Boito, demanded a new musical and dramatic expression in opera and the casting out of old formulas.[9] Boito's major effort as both librettist and composer, his opera *Mefistofele,* based on part 2 of Goethe's *Faust,* best exemplifies the *scapigliatura* phase of the opera scene. The riotous rejection of *Mefistofele* by the Milanese audience in 1868 was surpassed only by the similar reception accorded Wagner's *Lohengrin* there five years later.[10] The drama, the poetry, the leitmotivs (especially the use of a leitmotif for Mefistofele), and other techniques advocated by Mazzini were all there, and so were the social and political commentary reflecting a deeply felt anticlericalism and sense of political disillusionment. Not surprisingly, Giulio Ricordi thought he perceived Wagnerian influences, and his analysis of the opera discussed the good and bad aspects of the "music of the future."[11]

In the musical climate of the period, disparagement of the existing state of Italian opera tended to throw these young malcontents into an anti-Verdian stance, while their attempts at reform were quickly associated with Wagner. Indeed, the *scapigliati* were branded "Wagnerians" by their critics. Yet this polarization was more apparent than real, and the charge of Wagnerism was not entirely merited. Arrigo Boito had expressed enthusiasm for Wagner as early as 1862, but he wrote the words for Verdi's *Inno delle nazioni* (Hymn of the nations) in the same year and two years later acknowledged that his view of Wagner as the man "destined to fulfill the innovative mission" of opera reform had proved false.[12] Neither Boito nor Franco Faccio ever became a disciple of the German composer; and although they retained their appreciation for him, both subsequently became closer associates of Verdi. Boito, whose revised *Mefistofele* won a better reception in 1876 in Bologna, later served as librettist of Verdi's *Otello* and *Falstaff* and as translator of several of Wagner's operas.[13] Faccio left composing for conducting, leading performances of both Verdi and Wagner until his early death in 1891. The activities of these *scapigliati* testify less to Wagnerism than to ferment and growth in Italian musical drama, and this energy could easily turn in other directions. Other *scapigliati* would contribute to *verismo* opera at the turn of the century.

III

Fruitful discussion of the virtues and vices of Wagnerism could not develop on the basis of the piano scores that were the primary available source of Wagner's music in the 1860s, when orchestral renditions were not yet a feature of popular concerts and none of the operas had yet been performed in Italy. A full debate on Wagner was inaugurated by the Bologna presentation of *Lohengrin* in November 1871, the first Italian production of any Wagnerian opera and one that was followed by regular productions in the subsequent decades. This first presentation, of which there were eighteen performances,[14] resulted at least partly from Bologna's attempt to upstage Milan as a cultural center. The *Lohengrin* production was thus a phase in a centuries-old communal rivalry that the new political unity of Italy had been powerless to diminish. The interest of Wagner's publishers, the Luccas of Bologna, also played a part in the first production, as did their rivalry with the Milanese house of Ricordi.

Preparation for the Bologna event was as carefully orchestrated as the production itself and included (at the communal government's expense) a trip to preview the opera in Munich by the mayor and Wagnerian convert, Camillo Casarini.[15] Bolognese critics took advantage of the *appendice,* a newspaper feature of the time that was used to preview coming cultural events and was often placed on the front page. One such *appendice,* signed "XX" and entitled "Pensieri di un parziale," urged the Bolognese to avoid the "false and pretentious" supporters of national honor, to dismiss prejudices at the door along with their cloaks, and to approach the performance with objectivity.[16] Sangiorgi, music critic for the weekly *L'arpa,* who regarded Wagner as a genius, not only wrote comparisons of the two revolutionaries, Wagner and Mazzini, but also supplied his readers with a philosophical article on *Oper und Drama* and, perhaps more usefully, with a detailed analysis of the libretto.[17]

In the heady nationalist atmosphere generated by the transference of the Italian capital to Rome, the communal government of Bologna sought to endow their city with a cosmopolitan image by scheduling *Lohengrin* to coincide with an international prehistory conference attended by foreign scientists of reknown. As Sangiorgi wryly put it, "For a prehistory conference, music of the future is best."[18] Increased ticket prices restricted opera attendance to the more affluent, but no seat was vacant, and favorable comparisons with rowdy Parisian audiences were frequent, for the Bolognese took pride in maintaining decorum. A review in the *Gazzetta dell'Emilia* on November 3 compared the production to a Dürer painting, proclaimed the work a masterpiece, and piously concluded that to whistle at a work of Wagner's would be a sacrilege.[19] On the other hand, Sangiorgi, inspired by the presence in the city of the French positivist Ernest Renan, now asserted that Wagner was a scientist and his opera a product of positivism.[20] When Verdi slipped into Bologna on November 19 and sought to attend a performance unobserved, he was recognized and greeted by tumultuous applause as word spread through the theater of his presence.[21] Boito was so moved by the opera that he wrote an enthusiastic letter to Wagner; this evoked the latter's oft-quoted reply in which he hoped for an artistic marriage of Italian genius and German genius—an unintended echo of Mazzini's belief that Italian melody and German harmony might merge in a new European style.[22] Of course Wagner's comment was only a graceful acknowledgment, not a program, but the composer undoubtedly felt the contrast between the warmth of his Italian reception and the coolness he had encountered elsewhere. A year later, in writing his thanks for an award of honorary Bolognese citizenship, he may have contributed to the cosmopolitan self-esteem of the city by his remark that "a success such as my *Lohengrin* had at Bologna could never be imagined in any French city."[23] (He would receive his citizenship in person in December 1876 when he came to Bologna for a performance of *Rienzi*.)

Thus the first Italian production of an opera by Wagner was a triumph. The second, a production of *Tannhäuser* in Bologna a year later, was quite a different matter, but the real anti-Wagnerian storm would break in March of 1873 when *Lohengrin* opened in Milan.

The *Tannhäuser* premiere, despite cuts by Maestro Angelo Mariani, stirred shouts of "Viva Rossini!" and "Death to Wagner!" at the end of the first act. Sangiorgi's review qualified the revolutionary nature of Wagner, as he argued the line of musical continuity from Weber and Schumann to Wagner; moreover, he now conceded mere brilliance to Wagner rather than genius. Despite the catcalls from the audience, a Milanese critic commented on the "tolerant spirit" of the Bolognese.[24]

By the time *Lohengrin* opened at La Scala in 1873, however, Bologna's challenge to Milan's supremacy had begun to stir a faint element of xenophobia in the latter city. In the *Gazzetta musicale di Milano,* Isadore Licurgo, who had witnessed the *Lohengrin* triumph in Bologna, now described the Italian public as overly "impressionable" and "susceptible to delicate emotions," and he warned that every critic had the patriotic duty to combat this foreign influence.[25] Thus the old passions of xenophobia and cultural pride were employed to reprove a rival commune in the name of a new patriotism.

Well before *Lohengrin*'s swanboat glided onto La Scala's stage on March 20, 1873, the battle lines had been carefully drawn as preliminary salvos were fired through the columns and *appendici* of Italian newspapers. Like the smoke of battle, the activity of the press in exciting and conditioning opinion clouded the reality of the event itself. Some critics, like Filippo Filippi of the liberal journal *La perseveranza,* were already convinced Wagnerians. Filippi had been one of Italy's first pilgrims to the Wagner productions in Weimar, and his 1870 reports of his pilgrimage, with accounts of performances of *Lohengrin, Tannhäuser, Der fliegende Holländer,* and *Die Meistersinger,* were now reprinted.[26] Ricordi's *Gazzetta musicale di Milano,* on the other hand, was firmly in the anti-Wagnerian camp, both through loyalty to Verdi and through a deeply felt and often vehemently expressed *italianità,* an avowed nationalism both cultural and political. (Ricordi, as one critic was to remark on the publisher's death in 1912, had been a "nationalist before nationalism.")[27]

On the night of the performance pandemonium broke out, not only within La Scala itself but also on the piazza and streets outside. Despite the presence of Prince Jerome Napoleon and Princess Clothilde, the daughter of King Victor Emmanuel II, whistles, the sound of shuffling feet, and "vivas" to Italian composers, especially Verdi, disturbed the performance. Subsequent performances suffered even greater disruptions, and these led to cuts, suddenly lowered curtains, and interposed ballets (like the one by Ponchielli that followed Act I on March 23). Even the presentation of Verdi's *Un ballo in Maschera* between the second and third performances of Wagner's *Lohengrin* did not placate the audience. No doubt one of the main reasons for the continuing disturbances at the theater was the polarizing effect of the press reviews. Italy's journalists had kept the atmosphere electrified with their daily celebrations or denunciations of Wagner's music, and the usual division of the opera house along class lines was less significant than that according to the positions of the various gazettes and journals.[28] The literary civil war that had preceded the opening for two months was to continue long after the final curtain.

Generally, the democratic press (such as *Il pungolo*, the *Gazzettino rosa*, and *Il secolo*) indulged in anti-Wagnerian cartoons and satire expressing a veiled nationalism. Cartoons showing Wagner in a Prussian spiked helmet awaiting a summons from La Scala to receive ovations or as a dying swan inside a chianti bottle rivaled the wit of satirical poems. Filippo Filippi was drawn pointing to the *appendici* in which he predicted that *Lohengrin* would be regarded as a masterpiece in twenty years, while the caption observed that at least one's ears could count on a rest. In the *Gazzettino rosa*, vehicle of the *scapigliati* in the 1860s and now an important democratic organ, a column by "Fortunio" compared the public's boredom with *Lohengrin* to that engendered by the long speeches of a leading politician. "Oh Wagner! Wagner! Why do you persecute me? What have I done to you?" pleaded Fortunio. He concluded in a more serious tone that the Wagnerian school had "no past, no future, and no present."[29]

While the more liberal press such as *La perseveranza* (Filippi's journal) was ardently pro-Wagner, the conservative publications, with the exception of Ricordi's *Gazzetta musicale di Milano*, were generally content to argue the virtues of tolerance. Torelli-Viollier in the *Corriere di Milano* objected to any *cordon sanitaire* against the admission of French and German music and speculated on whether Mazzini's dream of fusion of German and Italian musical styles could receive a hearing in the present climate of opinion.[30] In contrast, S. Farina of the *Gazzetta musicale di Milano* discovered two reasons to rejoice over the experience of the thousands who had now heard and disapproved of *Lohengrin*: Wagner had taught them "to hold more dear, and to see greatness in, the great ones at home," and he had eliminated any danger that young Italian musicians might emulate him in an attempt to achieve popular acclaim.[31]

Given such an opening reception it is not surprising that La Scala produced no more Wagner until 1888, when it mounted another *Lohengrin.* This time Filippi's optimistic prediction of its reception was at least partly fulfilled as the press begged for tolerance and one veteran critic implied that an audience that disapproved of Wagner would bring greater discredit upon itself than upon the composer.[32]

IV

A cult of Wagnerism evolved despite admonitions from the anti-Wagnerian press and the scorn of defenders of Italian national traditions. Bologna and Turin, in particular, were the key centers of the promotion and organization of the movement. Journalists attempted to define the Wagnerian practitioner, often in terms of abuse: "To be Wagnerian," proclaimed *La nazione* as late as 1913, "one cherishes novelty and calls imitation originality."[33] In 1883, Francesco d'Arcais, critic for *Nuova antologia,* identified Wagnerians by types, delineating composers, critics, and pilgrims as the three main groups.[34] Indeed, many recorded pilgrimages had occurred since the end of the 1860s. Here we find evidence of the really serious devotees. Perhaps the most famous pilgrimage had taken place in 1876 when Giovannina Lucca, now a patroness at Bayreuth, had presented Wagner with a silver laurel wreath at the opening of the season. Filippo Filippi (whose first visit to Weimar has already been mentioned) came to love the isolation of Bayreuth and upon returning recorded what (and whom) he had seen in his "Secondo viaggio nelle regione dell'avvenire" (Second voyage into the future). Letters of 1876 to Cosima Wagner from Angelo De Gubernatis, a Florentine professor of Sanskrit and publisher, inform us of her assistance in getting him tickets and housing.[35] There were also contingents from Turin, which by 1876 boasted a hard core of Wagnerians including Giuseppe Depanis, the impresario, and Carlo Rossaro, a musician and an ardent Mazzinian. As the Wagnerian cult developed, then, pilgrimages became important religious occasions and embraced many degrees of commitment.

The activities of local Wagnerian organizations serve as an effective measure of the movement's strength when their records survive. By 1901, the year of Verdi's death, the group in Turin was strong enough to embolden Depanis to announce plans for a staging of the entire *Ring* cycle in the Turin opera house. This ambitious plan was not realized only because Giulio Ricordi of Milan, Verdi's great defender, intervened against the production with the mayor of Turin. Ricordi suggested that while the impulse to create an Italian Bayreuth was an "elevated artistic concept," surely the recent death of Verdi argued for a postponement of the *Ring*. To insure that his suggestion would be carried out, Ricordi then doubled the price of production rights for the *Ring,* which his firm had acquired in 1894 through a merger with the Luccas. (The Torinese, we might add, were to remain frustrated in their aspirations to mount the *Ring.* They tried again in 1911 but again failed because their plan conflicted with another national occasion, the fiftieth anniversary of the founding of the kingdom of Italy.[36])

Bologna's Wagnerians formed a local chapter of the Associazione universale Riccardo Wagner in 1893. Between June 1893 and April 1895, the Bologna group published the *Cronaca wagneriana,* with the announced purpose of following and recording all manifestations of the Wagnerian movement in Italy. Comprised at its peak of a select set of twenty-six members, not all of them resident in Bologna, this small coterie of Wagnerian disciples clearly enlivened the Bolognese musical scene. Their intransigency and eccentricities (one member wore a miniature of Wagner on his tie) were duly recorded by another member, Luigi Federzoni, one of the later leaders of the Nationalist Party, who had been converted as a young man to Wagnerism through a trip to Bayreuth.[37] Bologna continued to be the city where the premieres of most of the operas took place, including *Der fliegende Holländer* in November 1877, *Tristan und Isolde* in January 1888, and *Parsifal* in January 1914.

If *Lohengrin* initiated the rivalry between Milan and Bologna, *Parsifal* concluded it. While much of the controversy over Wagner had subsided by the eve of 1914 (except for a brief moment when Italy entered the war in 1915), the communal rivalry continued. Because of Wagner's wish that *Parsifal* be performed only at Bayreuth, its production in Italy had been delayed until 1914 (a year after the expiration of the copyright), even though the work had been inspired by Wagner's Italian sojourns in Naples and Siena.[38] Milan's 1914 production of *Parsifal* was only a week later than Bologna's, so that reviewers could immediately compare performances of an opera that many regarded as simply an illustration of intellectual decadence. Eugenio Giovannetti, music critic of the Bolognese paper *Il resto del Carlino,* perceived the Milanese production as "catholic and latin" while the one at home was "christian and universal," but he also sought to merge the two interpretations into an Italian unity, observing that the "Italian *Parsifal* made of sentiment and color [was] the most enchanting *Parsifal* of this world."[39]

v

In analyzing the importance of Wagner in an Italian context, one must note that the first phase of the journalistic debate had precious little to do with music per se, and this tends to confirm the suggestion that participants were discussing Wagner less than themselves and Italy. That a few attempted to consider music in purely technical terms (as when Sangiorgi related Wagner to Weber and Schumann in the Bolognese *L'arpa*) will hold significance for the musicologist but little for the social historian seeking to explain the impact of Wagnerism. When Italian audiences resisted Wagner's music, as of course some of them did, this resistance was immediately exploited by those who saw in this Teutonic import a threat to Italian cultural identity. What was regarded as an essentially Italian art form was not to be "reformed" by a foreigner. To this mentality even the Italian pilgrimages to Bayreuth were distasteful. Around the nationalist appeal other arguments soon clustered. Was not Wagnerism a corrupting influence upon Italian youth, separating it from its cultural heritage? Were not Italy's musical conservatories in danger of subversion, to the detriment of the training of young musicians in the Italian musical tradition? Did not the ongoing Wagnerian vogue represent a threat to the prestige of Italy's own Giuseppe Verdi, just as had the alleged Wagnerism of the *scapigliati* a generation before? In the 1880s the arrival of the *Ring* in Italy provided new fuel for controversy as journalists seized the opportunity to assess the implications for Latin culture of Nordic mythology.

There was reason for the nativists to be concerned. The diaries and memoir literature of the post-1870 generation documented an increasing adulation of Wagner among Italian youth. For example, the diary kept from 1887 to 1901 by Enrico Thovez, poet and critic, was filled with youthful alternation between the moral heights of pure love and the agonies of sensual longing, which the young man experienced along with such Wagnerian heroes as Tristan and Parsifal. "If one could hear Wagner in the country, I would no longer go back to the city," Thovez remarked at one point; elsewhere he recorded the fact that his brother had moved Wagner in his scale of values ahead of his love for Greek statuary and poetry.[40] Examples of the Wagnerian fever could be multiplied, but its significance was not always clear. The romantic stance of the aesthetically sensitive young artist was certainly not restricted to Wagnerians. Francesco d'Arcais suggested in 1883 that Wagnerism had become a substitute religion, not only in adopting the style of religion in its approach to art but in responding to the need for something spiritually new.[41] That later apostle of Italian futurism, Giovanni Papini, boasted of having been a Wagnerian "martyr" when he and several others were taken off to jail for expressing their "ecstasy" a little too enthusiastically at a concert featuring Wagner.[42] Like the *scapigliati* of a previous decade, Papini and his friends were apparently making a protest against bourgeois complacency, a theme they later stressed in their futurist manifestos.

Whatever the exact nature of the Wagnerian threat, those who feared that it could only subvert the integrity of Italy's young musicians could point to what became known as the "Gobatti case." Stefano Gobatti, a young composer whose opera *I goti* (the Goths) was rejected in Milan, brought the work to Bologna, where it appeared at the Teatro Comunale in December 1873. Hailed as an Italian apostle of Wagner, Gobatti was given fifty-one curtain calls and honored with numerous sonnets affixed to Bolognese city walls. Though his subsequent career was a failure and he soon faded into oblivion, for this brief moment he had proved to Bolognese Wagnerians that Italy could produce its own creators of the "music of the future," while to the anti-Wagnerians he and his Goths confirmed their forebodings about the future of Italian music.[43]

In the winter of 1873 the debate over Wagner even reached the floor of the Chamber of Deputies, newly established in Montecitorio in Rome. Amid discussions on matters of administrative unity, transformation of Rome into Italy's capital, the lingering problems of southern Italy, and projections of Italian foreign policy, the deputies debated the Wagnerian impact on Italian conservatories. Arguing how deplorable it would be if Italian political unity brought in its wake the decay of its artistic heritage, Augusto Righi spoke in favor of strict government regulation of Italy's musical academies to protect against moral corruption by foreign artistic invasion and to defend the national integrity. Righi drew support from the chamber's isolationists, but Camillo Casarini (no longer Bologna's mayor) rose to defend the ideal of an artistically and intellectually open society. In a Periclean speech on February 6, 1873, Casarini asserted that true decadence would result if future Italian musicians were cut off from foreign influence. Pointing out that both Rossini and Verdi had appeared at one time to be "dangerous innovators," Casarini protested: "For God's sake, we do not want to put a Chinese wall around our temples of art; if we do, we run the danger of destroying them." Finally, asking Righi what he meant by "foreign music" and whether this included the symphonies of Beethoven, Haydn's oratorios, and Mozart's *Don Giovanni,* Casarini concluded that Italian musicians should assimilate what was good from foreign schools of music, lest a vision of the future be lost.[44]

The apprehensions of the Italianists, however, continued. Verdi repeated his in 1889 in a letter to Franco Faccio when he called it a "musical national crime" for a descendant of Palestrina to imitate Wagner. And Giulio Ricordi renewed his vow that year to fight the "idolatry" of young Italian musicians in the conservatories—though he also went off to preview *Die Meistersinger* in Bayreuth before putting it on at La Scala.[45] Eventually this nativist component in the Wagner debate began to abate as journalists and musicologists sought to differentiate more objectively between the Italian and German musical traditions. Nevertheless some commentators continued to approach the issue simply by juxtaposing Wagner and Verdi, thereby renewing that old polarization that had done so much in the past to inflame Italian defensiveness.

Verdi himself continued to express occasional despair at imitators while strongly supporting the national character and traditions of Italian music. To him, imitation of a foreign idiom prevented the finding of one's own voice. He must therefore have found it particularly galling to find himself accused of imitating Wagner in his work after *Aida*. But he was never opposed to Wagner per se. In 1870, as he entered the final stages of his own career, he expressed interest in reading Wagner's prose works and even sent to Paris for copies, and in 1871, as we have seen, he attended one of the *Lohengrin* performances at Bologna. Interviewed by a reporter of the *Berliner Tagesblatt* in 1899, just two years before his death, Verdi expressed admiration for Wagner while pointing out that as an Italian he was ignorant of Wagner's pagan world of giants and dwarfs and regretted that he did not know more about Germany. When pressed to reveal what work of Wagner he liked best, Verdi replied: "The work which always arouses my greatest admiration is *Tristan!* Before this gigantic work, I stand in wonder and terror."[46]

Verdi's reference to Wagner's German themes came a decade and a half after the world of German myth had first been revealed to Italian audiences by a German production of the *Ring,* which had toured Venice, Bologna, and Rome on the occasion of Wagner's death in 1883. Probably most interested Italians would have associated themselves with Verdi's profession of ignorance. Wagner's religious world was one thing, but the mythical universe of the Nordic gods was another, a vast unknown. The critic of the *Gazzetta di Venezia,* while asking for patience and perseverance, prepared the audience with lengthy articles that themselves betrayed confusion regarding the race of the Nibelungs.[47] And Francesco d'Arcais, reviewing the performances in Rome for *Nuova antologia,* summed up the pervasive feeling of bafflement when he wrote:

> Germany cherishes [such] traditions still lively in popular fantasies, [but] the people of the Latin race find it hard to take seriously a supernatural world which cloaks itself in forms so different not only from the real world but also from that of Greek and Latin myth . . . [This world] of Wagner . . . is an art which does not respond to the spirit of the time.

This could be taken as implying that although Greek and Latin myths were no closer to the "real world" than were the German, familiarity rendered them acceptable, while the learning of a new mythology was not worth the effort. For d'Arcais both art and letters in some way had to be a "faithful mirror" of historical reality, since otherwise "we will have only an archaeological art or a new Arcadia" in the nineteenth century.[48] Serious attention to the "real world" would be a basic tenet of the *verismo* movement that d'Arcais would hail in the 1890s.

VI

In some ways *verismo* was a rejection of Wagnerism. Francesco de Sanctis, in 1871, had ended his history of Italian literature by encouraging a new Italian generation to seek the "elements of the real" in Italian life in order to create its own culture. Concrete elements of experience would be the content of that culture, and it would be shaped by observations of customs, ideas, and prejudices.[49] De Sanctis, who saw Wagner as a "corrupter of music,"[50] influenced many of the post-Risorgimento generation by his literary work and as minister of education.

The recommendation by de Sanctis was a protest against what he saw as an Italian intellectual tradition of engaging in idealist abstractions divorced from reality, and he was not alone in his reaction. Thus while Italian *verismo* was part of a wider European, and especially French, literary phenomenon, it was essentially a direct response to conditions within Italy. As the philosopher and historian Benedetto Croce defined it, *verismo* was the stripping away of the veil that hid the social sores and the initiation of a rebellion against injustice.[51] Industrial growth in northern Italy was sharpening the contrast with southern Italian poverty, and the "social question" of the south provoked radicalization of social and political issues by both republicans and socialists. Strikes and peasant uprisings became common occurrences. Italy was not only a country geographically divided against itself but also a divided society, and socialism contributed to the already existing divisions within the social structure. Artistic *verismo* accompanied political *verismo* as the fissures and stresses of society intensified. Those *scapigliati* whose Mazzinian republicanism had fostered social and political criticism could find no outlet in pure aestheticism or in literary decadence, and they helped to shape the *verismo* movement. Rather than exploring "states of mind," they wished to explore social realities—the natural instincts and typical behavior of all social classes, but especially the lower classes.

That Wagnerian theories and Mazzini's *Filosofia della musica* agreed concerning the unity of poetry, drama, and music, the use of leitmotivs, and the use of choruses seemed obvious to those who saw Mazzini as a precursor to Wagner. Yet Mazzini's insistence on a social mission for music that reflected the historical character of an epoch separated him from Wagner. Thus as *verismo* replaced "states of mind" with historical realities, it brought to the Italian opera stage a vogue for peasants, artisans, and seamstresses instead of Wagner's dwarfs, dragons, and epic heroes.

Pietro Mascagni's *Cavalleria Rusticana,* which burst upon the musical world in 1890, placed the world of the Sicilian peasantry in a musical context and began a new era in Italian opera. Francesco d'Arcais, reviewing the new work for *Nuova antologia,* praised the young composer for directing opera away from Wagnerian influences and back into an Italian tradition, although with a new realistic direction.[52]

Other composers also rejected the Wagnerian model, even though most had matured in a Wagnerian atmosphere. Giacomo Puccini, who had been to Bayreuth to hear *Parsifal* and enjoyed it,[53] ended by exclaiming: "Enough of this music! We may be mandolinists, dilettantes," he said in reference to Wagner's remarks about Italian musicians, but "woe to us if we let ourselves get caught! This terrible music destroys us and ends in nothing."[54] Ruggiero Leoncavallo's music was said to embody the concept of Wagner "dressed in Italian colors," but he found Wagnerians who imitated Wagner's so-called infinite melody "insupportable." And Umberto Giordano admitted to one of his librettists, Luigi Illica, that he had heard "too much Wagner."[55]

But it was Pietro Mascagni himself who clearly saw his work as a reaction against Wagner, for although he had once claimed to "esteem Vagner [sic] as Pope of all *maestri,*"[56] he believed Italian composers must shun this seductive influence. In a conference on the melodrama of the future, held in Milan in 1903, he warned: "It is necessary to begin to occupy oneself in earnest if one wishes to save the musical art of the nation from a real danger." Commenting further upon the Italian Wagnerians, he roundly condemned their activities:

> When Richard Wagner announced himself, preceded by his books and his formulas, these antimusicalists, these supercilious enemies of opera . . . became owners of such books, read them, postulated them, commented upon them, dissected them. They were ready to swear on the authenticity of the new word, on its validity and greatness. . . . They formed special societies with the purpose of developing in Italy the inclination for Wagnerian music; they published articles and volumes in order to divulge the new theories, they translated all the books of Wagner into the mother tongue. . . ; they organized expeditions to go first to Bayreuth and later to Munich for the German productions, [and] sought to inspire in the Italians a special religion and an absolute devotion for Wagner's music. . . . These fervent and determined propagandists left nothing untried . . . in order to enlarge the ranks of the initiates and neophytes. They finally even printed and distributed certain libretti containing a clear and detailed arithmetic exposition of the Wagnerian system through his operas. [This was done so] that any layman could learn, for example, that such a leitmotiv might be found

in a certain scene on such and such a page of *Siegfried* or in such and such a scene of *Götterdämmerung*. [This amounted to] a kind of railway schedule with stations, arrivals, and departures; with intermediate stops and above all with all the necessary connections.[57]

In an essay entitled "L'incorreggibile" (1903), Enrico Thovez recorded an interview with Mascagni, who continued lashing out at Wagner and defending Italian art. That the *veristi* themselves, in defining a new direction to Italian melodrama based on the realities of everyday life, were provoking their own debate with the critics is seen in Thovez's dry conclusion that Italian melodrama now consisted of sequences of Neapolitan songs and violin music.[58]

And of course, not all the Italian intellectual world applauded what the *veristi* had to offer. There were those who asserted that *verismo* denigrated Italian society by exposing only its seamier sides and also that it further commercialized the musical world by catering to vulgar tastes. To the extent that the themes of *verismo* meant a turning away from Wagnerism, they sharpened differences of opinion over the social content and role of music. *Verismo* thus added significant dimensions to the discussions on the future of Italian culture.

VII

If political ideas accompanied artistic *verismo,* as witnessed in the growth of socialism and mass democracy, political theories on elitism also complemented the volatile discussions of the late 1880s and 1890s on the aristocratic element in art. Here Wagnerism was drawn upon to sharpen previous perceptions and to project future ones concerning national music traditions, the elitist or popular purposes of music, and the roles of mythologies. Of particular importance in setting the context of such exchanges were the political writings of Gaetano Mosca for these, echoed later by the sociologist Vilfredo Pareto and others, exposed the "myth" of the democratic system. Mosca's *Teorica dei governi* (Theory of governments, 1884) and his *Elementi di scienza politica* (Elements of political science, 1896) denounced the representative system and the extension of democracy on the grounds that politics were always in the control of ruling elites who manipulated the system.

Such an intellectual context encouraged and focused, but did not create, elitist interpretations of Wagnerism, for they had been present from the very start of Wagner's influence in Italy. The elitist sympathies of one of the earliest of his supporters, Filippo Filippi, were always evident; throughout the 1870s he always claimed that Wagner could only be understood by an educated elite. In a dualism that distinguished between music for the public and music for intellectuals, he visualized a pyramid with the populace at the base and the elite at the top. With Wagner in mind, he also saw that prejudices of both "municipalism" and "nationalism" did great damage to any rapport between the two social groups. For Filippi a bridge was necessary, though he never attempted to find it as would other Wagnerian *literati* at the turn of the century.[59]

It was precisely this elitism, however, that other critics—such as Antonio Tari, the Neapolitan philosopher of aesthetics—criticized in favor of the more broadly based social element in Italian music. In "Avvenire ed avveniristi in musica" (The future and futurists in music, 1884, republished in 1911), Tari insisted that disastrous social consequences would emanate from Wagnerian drama because it was exclusively mythical rather than historical, excessively orchestral rather than vocal and melodic, and academic rather than popular.[60]

Indeed, the social and political implications of Wagner were a theme no musicologist could ignore. In 1887 the musicologist Gino Monaldi, in contrasting the social roles of Verdi and Wagner, perceived Verdi's liberalism as inspired by the liberalism of Risorgimento society. In responding to the tastes of that society, Verdi was slave to no theory but possessed a freedom that Wagner did not have. In this sense, Verdi was a *maestro* of the nineteenth-century Italian revolution in both a political and social sense; his art embodied a kind of Rousseauian expression of the will of the people. Monaldi in no way saw this form of popularism as a denigration of music. He believed that Wagner, however, rationalized and philosophized his art, forcing his public to join him in this esoteric enterprise. As a composer, in short, Wagner was a slave to his *idée fixe*.[61]

In view of Wagner's indictment of Italian opera nearly forty years earlier, Monaldi's evaluation is interesting. Wagner had argued that Italian opera was not an art form but an entertainment industry in which the composer simply supplied set pieces for exploitation by the performers. This was a criticism that Mazzini had also levied in 1836 and that Italian critics were now hurling at *verismo*, attacking it as a commercialization of art for a tasteless bourgeois audience. But Wagner might have claimed for himself the advantage that Monaldi gave to Verdi, since he described his own music as popular in nature, inspired by the deeper values and character of the German nation, and not merely entertainment for the prosperous.

The discussion of aristocratic art as opposed to popular art in its various definitions was conducted in the pages of the musical journals, especially in the *Rivista musicale italiana*. This journal was edited by the musicologist Luighi Torchi, whose comprehensive study of Wagner (1890) promoted an understanding of the composer's musical evolution while providing additional fuel for argument. In 1894 the *Rivista musicale italiana* embarked on a long career as a leading national musical journal, whose purpose as defined by Torchi was to elevate the level of music criticism. As one of its first editors (1894–1904), Torchi urged the scientific and historical method, rather than reliance upon subjective impressions, on those contributing biographical articles. He also encouraged articles on technical subjects, aesthetics, psychology of music, and acoustics.[62] But however objective its stance, the journal could not help but become a conduit for controversies, among which that concerning Wagner was prominent.

In 1896 Romualdo Giani contributed to the *Rivista* a series of articles on aristocratic as opposed to popular art in which he criticized Torchi for having denied the incomprehensibility of Wagnerian drama. Torchi thought that comprehension simply depended on familiarity with German society and tradition, and he responded to Giani by quoting a statement of Wagner's at Bayreuth thanking the German nation for their cooperation in the creation of German art. Giani countered by questioning whether the German people could appreciate what they could not understand, and he in turn quoted a letter in which Wagner complained to Franz Liszt that his public was limited to a few individuals.[63]

Torchi's position was supported by Vincenzo Tommasini in 1902 when the latter, writing in the same journal, took up the nationalist and popular arguments and implicitly rejected the aristocratic view. Arguing that no art was more truly universal than that which was "intimately national," he then declared: "No poetry is more hellenic than that of Homer . . . , none more Italian than that of Dante, none more Germanic than that of Richard Wagner," and all of this art came from the people. Tommasini cautioned against imitation as he encouraged Italians to work toward "a true art of a free people."[64]

Torchi's meticulous 1890 study of Wagner was a product of positivist methodology and was published when the influence of positivism in Italy was giving way to a new idealism. Through years of examining Wagner's prose writings and scores and through extensive travels and study in Germany, Torchi had sought to understand the social, political, and cultural environment that had produced a Richard Wagner. He found the essential element in the post-1849 era, when Wagner, disillusioned by the failure of the revolution, plunged from distressing historical reality into a mythological world. Torchi did not avoid the usual contrasts with Italian society, but his chief purpose was to explain the Germany of Wagner to Italians so that they might better understand Wagner. True understanding of the man's art, after all, demanded an appreciation of the spirit of German culture in contrast to that of the Latin. Torchi thus used his exhaustive scholarship to challenge those who were responding to Wagner on an intuitive and personal level, and his work tended to buttress that evolving musicological perspective that distinguished two quite distinct national traditions.[65]

And yet much as Torchi tried to make Wagner accessible to the Italians by elucidating the composer's "objective" environment, he did not want that accessibility to lead to emulation by Italian composers: "If Italy will yet have an art," he wrote, "this cannot be the result of assimilation of foreign tendencies and tastes, an error into which our new Italian *maestri* have fallen because of their lack of nationality."[66] This was an admonition but also a defense of an Italian tradition. The preface to his translation of Wagner's work on the music of the future (*Musica dell'avvenire*, 1893) sounds elitist rather than popular: he wished for "an elevated and energetic conscience which frees us from mediocrity and from the ordinary, from conventions and from the egoistic meanness of the daily commercial and bourgeois intuition, and which sees art as an extension of reality." This was a criticism of *verismo*, which he saw as a "distortion of Wagner."[67]

In 1902 Carlo Arner gave a curious twist to this debate in an article he published in Ricordi's *Gazzetta musicale di Milano* entitled "L'arte lirica e gli scioperi" (Lyric art and the strikes). Arner labeled Wagner a "socialist" because the composer saw art as a means of social regeneration and sought by his individualism to reflect as well as instruct his society with his music. The purpose of the article was to contrast Wagner's "socialism" favorably with the "socialism of the piazza," which was manifesting itself in strikes and demonstrations throughout Italy in that year. Composers who sought to encourage this kind of socialism, Arner asserted, lowered music to the level of the masses, and he warned that the politicization and socialization of art would mean forcing it to conform to Marxian principles, leading eventually to a requirement of state approval for all libretti. Seeing socialist agitation as neither "democratic" nor "aristocratic" but as a form of tyranny, Arner warned strenuously that it must be fought lest the destruction of creativity in music and art be total.[68]

VIII

At the turn of the century, some of Italy's leading *literati* were deeply engaged in attempts to transform the prevailing image of Italian culture from one essentially passive to one intensely active and vital; from one basically republican and democratic to one ideally elitist and imperial; from one explicitly realistic to one infinitely spiritual and mythical. Accompanying this emerging new image was the reshaping of an earlier humanitarian nationalism into a new "integral" variety in which all the old symbols—not the least, that of Rome—would be refurbished and new ones created. Wagnerism had its place in this transfiguration both directly and indirectly, but its role was to vary according to the idiosyncracies of its various intellectual promoters. Among the nationalist literati the novelist and poet of "decadence," Gabriele D'Annunzio, gave Wagnerism its fullest and most positive treatment, while the futurist Giovanni Papini relegated it to his youth and to the past. Most of the new "integral" nationalists, however, chose in general to ignore it.

Gabriele D'Annunzio's literary career was identified initially with a group of writers around the poet Giosuè Carducci and the *Cronaca bizantina,* an esoteric little journal that lasted but a few years (1881–1885). This group's essential character was expressed in the name of its journal: Italy had asked for virile Rome but instead received effeminate "Byzantium."[69] Here again we find expression of that disillusionment with the Risorgimento and contempt for the compromises and weaknesses of united Italy that so afflicted the postunification generations. Just as it had for the *scapigliati* twenty years earlier, this disillusionment with the results of unity fostered an urge to create something dynamic and revolutionary in its place. For the members of this new group, who in a kind of self-irony called themselves *bizantini,* the goal was a renewal of the virile grandeur that had once been Rome. Understandably, then, many of them turned up later in nationalist organizations and associations. But what primarily distinguished D'Annunzio was his extraordinary "heroic" personality and his subsequent career as the chief Italian exponent of decadence.

D'Annunzio first involved himself in the journalistic controversies surrounding Richard Wagner in three articles he wrote for *La tribuna* in 1893. He interpreted Friedrich Nietzsche's various assaults on Wagner as attacks against his own literary and political ideals, as attacks against the cultivation of the individual ego (the "I"), the aristocratic, and the heroic in music. This was, we hasten to add, a rather idiosyncratic reading of Nietzsche, and the same can be said for D'Annunzio's defense of Wagner. In response to Nietzsche's charge that Wagner had reduced music to theatrical rhetoric, the Italian poet wrote that Wagner's music had a "high and pure artistic value, independent of the tiring theatrical machinations and the superimposed symbolic significance." So much for the unity of music, drama, and poetry. As for his own attraction to Wagner, D'Annunzio paradoxically ascribed this not only to what he saw as a comradeship in heroic egoism but also to a common appreciation of art as a direct reflection of the people's will. Citing Hippolyte Taine, he claimed that art could not resist "the pressure of the public spirit." It was the old melody played by the shepherd in the final scene of *Tristan,* he concluded, that had revealed to him the essence of his (D'Annunzio's) soul and destiny.[70]

For D'Annunzio, as for Wagner and for Mazzini before him, the kind of musical regeneration offered by Wagner implied an accompanying social regeneration, and such was his absorption in Wagnerism in the 1890s that a Wagnerian "presence" became a crucial element in his novels of those years. It was a presence so effective as to lead one writer to observe that the enormous popularity of D'Annunzio's novels may have helped Wagner to be accepted.[71] While there is some truth to this, the Wagnerian furor was reaching its height by 1900, and D'Annunzio's exploitation of it for his own ends is more significant. Throughout his life he adapted the dominant intellectual trends of the moment to his own literary purposes, and his Wagnerian books both expressed and reshaped contemporary reactions to the German composer.

A crucial element in D'Annunzio's interpretation concerns the role of the artist in society. The familiar figure of the alienated artist or intellectual in the early decadent literature of nineteenth-century Europe usually represented a psychological withdrawal from a commercialized, materialistic society; whatever his personal courage or heroism, this figure saw himself as a victim of the modern bourgeois world, which had no place for him. D'Annunzio's Wagnerian novels both exploited this image and shifted away from it, all the while drawing upon associations with the operas to create appropriate emotional ambience.

Wagner's *Tristan und Isolde* was an obvious influence on one of D'Annunzio's early novels, *Trionfo della morte* (*The triumph of death,* 1894). The hero, Giorgio Aurispa, is an aristocratic, Tristan-like figure whose lover, Ippolita Sanzio, is of lower-class origin and the element of insanity and self-destruction are reminiscent of Nietzsche. In one of the final chapters Giorgio plays the Tristan music as a prelude to the novel's climactic suicide-murder. The novel also suggests Schopenhauer's theory of music, as Giorgio feels the unlimited power of music urging him to discover the inner universe of the soul and the real essence of existence. Much has been written about the work as an "operatic novel," and the Tristan chapter has been described as a "fine orchestral statement of the novel's themes."[72]

But D'Annunzio's reference point here was not only Wagner but also contemporary Italy. The freely chosen death in the novel was meant to suggest the victory of self-affirmation over accommodation to modern society; the novelist was reflecting and reinforcing a similar appeal among the nationalist intelligentsia for a more "heroic" exercise of will. Of course most intellectuals did not look to the ignorant masses or the complacent middle classes for leadership in this transformation; that would be the task of the intellectual elite—namely, themselves. D'Annunzio in particular was soon expounding the artist-intellectual as leader and shaper of society, abandoning the traditional image of the alienated victim. His stress in *Le vergine della rocce* (The virgin of the rocks, 1895) upon the need for intellectuals and artists to lead the politically dominant bourgeoisie to a revival of aristocratic spiritual values sounded like a parroting of Mosca's elitist theories. In fact D'Annunzio did not have to borrow directly from Mosca, for the latter's concept, while not universally accepted, was already a commonplace in the intellectual climate in which D'Annunzio worked.[73]

For the role of poet-leader (in which he naturally cast himself) D'Annunzio found a prototype in Richard Wagner. This amalgamation of Wagner, D'Annunzio, and the ideal of the artist-hero can be seen most vividly in *Il Fuoco* (The flame of life), which D'Annunzio completed in 1898. The novel is set in Venice and is dominated by the presence of Wagner, both alive and dead (the final scene depicts his coffin in a gondola heading for the railway station). The novel's protagonist, the poet-hero Stelio Effrena (in effect D'Annunzio himself), never exchanges a word with Wagner even though he and his friends come to the old man's aid when he has a heart attack and later serve as pallbearers at his funeral.[74] Yet the association in the mind of the reader is so close that Stelio's attitudes are linked to Wagner but not explicitly attributed to him. Thus the ostensible burden of the tale is Stelio's love affair with his actress mistress, whose dominant motive is a desire to serve him. She sacrifices her happiness by leaving him so that he can follow his bent and experience life to the full—that is, experience another woman. Nothing is said of Wagner's personal life (though he is attended by a solicitous Cosima), but Stelio remembers the words of Siegfried: "To follow the impulse of my own heart, to obey my own instinct, to listen to the voice of nature within me· let this be my only supreme law."[75] Stelio is a man of firm will, in control of a life that he embraces with joy (no victim, he), and he disagrees with those poets who complain of being born into a vulgar age, for "every man of intellect can, today as always, create in life his own beautiful fable."[76]

A good deal of the novel consists of conversation about Wagner among Stelio's aristocratic and artistic friends. Their discussions regarding the composer's visit to Venice echo the debates on him in the journals of the day. The views of Stelio's friend Baldassare Stampa, for example, seem to derive directly from that contemporary critical school that urged the Greek origins of Wagnerian theory.[77] But for Stelio himself, as for Torchi, Wagner's work is German in essence, the product of a "northern barbarian" (for all non-Latins are barbarian) sensibility.

Despite such backhanded compliments, the novel is steeped in reverence for Wagner, though Stelio expects to surpass him in Italy when his own works, in a new art form combining music, poetry, and dance, appear in the theater then rising on the Janiculum in Rome. This edifice, too, will outshine Wagner's achievement, for instead of the mere "brick and wood" of provincial Bayreuth it will be "a marble theater on our Roman hill."[78]

In addition to harboring such grandiose artistic ambitions, Stelio, it turns out, is also a man of politics, for politics is the true role of the poet. And, as one might expect of the politics of a poet, Stelio believed that the masses would be led to revolution by a charismatic heroic leader (some would say, demagogue). Thus we find Stelio expressing a preference for stirring the masses to action in the piazza over addressing an audience of affluent bourgeois in the doge's palace: "The words we address directly to a crowd should have no other end but action, even violent action. . . . Only on this condition can a spirit that is a trifle proud communicate by seductive voice and gesture with the crowd without lowering itself."[79] Otherwise, he adds, one would be a mere entertainer. Nevertheless, he manages to stir the middle class audience to whom he gives an ex tempore speech on the artistic glories of Venice, and recognizes that he has potential followers among them. Later his capacity for rapport with workmen on the basis of mutual respect for their artistic capacities is suggested in a brief encounter with a skilled craftsman in a glassworks at Murano.

Like so many of the principal themes in this novel, D'Annunzio's vision of the poet-politician as national liberator was intimately connected with his Wagnerism. Note the following meditations by Stelio on the ways in which Wagner foresaw and furthered German national aspirations:

> He had evoked the magnificent figure of Henry the Fowler rising up and standing under the ancient oak. . . . "Let the soldiers rise up from every German land!" At Sadowa and Sedan the soldiers had won. With the same impulse . . . the people and the artist had accomplished their glorious aim. The same victory had crowned the work of the sword and the word of the lyre. The poet as much as the hero had accomplished a liberating act. His musical figures had contributed as much as the will of the chancellor, as much as the blood of the soldiers, to the work of exalting and perpetuating the soul of his race.[80]

That the deepest dimension of the book is political is apparent in Stelio's catalogue of his own feelings:

The pride, the intoxication of his hard, persistent labor; his limitless, uncurbed ambition that had been forced into a field too narrow for it; his bitter intolerance of mediocrity in life; his claim to princely privileges; the dissembled craving for action by which he was propelled towards the masses as the preferred prey; the vision of great and imperious art that should be at the same time a signal of light in his hands and a weapon of subjection; all his strangely imperial dreams; his insatiable need of predominance, of glory, of pleasure.[81]

There was something strangely prophetic in this autobiographical novel, for D'Annunzio was eventually to transform Stelio's political ambition into reality when he stormed Fiume in 1919. In the 1890s, however, he provided the clearest example of how Wagnerism was appropriated for the expression of passions far beyond the original character of the cult. Instead of creating his own literary world, D'Annunzio exploited Wagner's "presence" and the emotional ambience of his music in shaping a positive imperial image of Italian society. With all due allowance for D'Annunzian excesses, *Il fuoco* demonstrated the intimate connection between Wagnerism and the new integral nationalism then developing in Italy. Antiegalitarian and authoritarian, it stressed strong leadership, heroic action, and its own mythology in rejection of the alleged mediocrity and materialism of the liberal past.

Not all the Italian *literati* viewed Wagnerism as positively as D'Annunzio did. To Alfredo Oriani, who had also been associated with that eclectic group of *bizantini* but whose nationalist rhetoric became even more pronounced, Wagner was an invader whose influence was increasingly undermining the native Italian genius. Catholic writers like Antonio Fogazzaro, whose novels such as *Malombra* (1881) and *Piccolo mondo antico* (The little world of the past, 1895) were imbued with a Christian mysticism, feared the "hypnotic" power of Wagnerian music, which carried "false" metaphysical philosophy in its wake.[82]

The proliferation in Florence of new literary journals during the decade before 1914—*Leonardo, Hermes, Lacerba, La voce,* and *Il regno,* among others—signaled a new renaissance in Italian letters, and several of them became the vehicles for the formulation and propagation of a new Italian cultural and political image. In heralding a revitalized nationalism, the contributors to these journals expected that the accompanying cultural revival would raise the spiritual level of Italian life. At the time there was wide agreement with Gian Falco's comment of 1903 in *Leonardo* pointing up the lack of aesthetic and intellectual development of the middle and lower classes: "A middle bourgeois and a worker . . . have this in common: they understand neither a symphony of Wagner nor a paradox of Nietzsche.[83]

The Futurist writer Giovanni Papini, who had been one of Wagner's earliest "martyrs," projected in his autobiography, *Un uomo finito* (*The failure*) a fantasy image that recalled that of D'Annunzio's Stelio Effrena in *Il fuoco:* "I dreamed of presenting [my drama] on a stage as big as a desert, with real mountains for scenery, and the words were to have the tremendous force of Dante's . . . , the music would be more divine than that of Wagner."[84] Absent here was D'Annunzio's marble theater (marble, to the Futurists, was a symbol of decadence and of Italy's dead past); present, however, was the sense of the infinity of desert and sea, as well as the ideal of creating an art grander and holier than Wagner's music.

In "Un programma nazionalista" (A nationalist program, 1904), Papini urged the now familiar ideal of fostering an aristocratic spirit among the middle class that he hoped would promote imperial expansion and the development of a higher culture. *Verismo,* for Papini, did not embody high culture but vulgarity. He observed caustically that the "mawkishness of the little romances of seamstresses" and "the realism of lower class life, poor and sad," had been nourished by the literature, theater, and music of recent times.[85] But young Futurists like Papini, once martyrs for Wagner, believed themselves to be pursuing a quite different form of literary activism, tossing their violent manifestos from lofty bell towers down to the crowded piazzas below, demanding the social revitalization of Italy and an amputation of the archaic past.

Of course, not all Italians were anxious to follow this provocative lead or even to acknowledge its self-proclaimed originality. Some saw it for something quite different: a bizarre recasting of D'Annunzio's already quite bizarre recasting of Wagner. "They do not realize," observed a writer in *La voce* in 1910, "that [their] D'Annunzian fantasies of reforming our drama, producing a Bayreuthian theater without Wagner, are [simply] the twin sister of their renovating Italian poetry by means of manifestos and buffoonish theatrical representations"—an obvious comment on the unstructured "happenings" of Futurist theater.[86]

The Futurists believed they were burying Wagner, Wagnerism, and their own Wagnerian past. Papini saw the 1914 *Parsifal* as five hours of boredom and monotony and one of the most "impotent of aborted masterpieces."[87] His fellow Futurist, F. T. Marinetti, who in earlier writings had spoken of a deep love for Wagner, now (in 1914) replaced Wagner with Stravinsky as he shouted, "Down with Wagner; long live Stravinsky!" and "Down with the tango and *Parsifal!*"[88]

Ricordi's new magazine *Ars et labor,* so characteristic of the merging of cultural and political interests in this period, recorded the meeting of prominent nationalist politicians and *literati* in Florence in 1908, two years before their Nationalist Association came into existence. Ricordi's nationalism was rooted in the older generation's distrust of foreign influence, and this attitude had found new adherents. The Nationalists, formally organized in 1910, were too busy with their new image to be concerned with Wagnerism. But World War I naturally heightened xenophobic tendencies in general, and therefore made the production of Wagner's work in Italy all the more controversial. Arturo Toscanini's announcement in November 1916 that he intended to conduct some Wagner (including the funeral music from *Götterdämmerung*) followed hard on the heels of an Austrian air raid against Padua, a coincidence that resulted in a pamphlet protest and a boycott of Wagner's music.[89]

Yet despite the wartime hysteria, Wagnerian influence was undeniably present in 1919 when D'Annunzio established his "Republic of Canaro" at Fiume. The hand of Wagner–Stelio Effrena guided D'Annunzio's pen as he inserted in that republic's most poetic of constitutions a special provision (article 64) that firmly established music as a "social and religious institution," one of the "corporations" of the new political creation. "Does it not seem," asked the sacred document, "that great music announces . . . to an anxious and intent crowd the kingdom of the spirit?"[90] What Wagner had failed to achieve in 1848 for Germany, D'Annunzio now hoped that he was achieving in a grander style for Italy—a political, social, and cultural revolution. Alas, it was short-lived. In 1919 the musicologist Giannotto Bastianelli worried about the blind exaltation of Italian musical values that appeared to be inseparably linked to melodrama and to D'Annunzian rhetoric and activism. Art and music were in danger of becoming the handmaidens of a strident new "integral" nationalism. There were reasons, it would seem, to harbor forebodings about the future.[91]

IX

In many ways Wagnerism in Italy had served as a cult for the dissident young who had not yet found the opportunity and means to
channel their energies into more constructive and concrete programs.
To identify with a Tristan or a Siegfried, to assert the primacy of the
aesthetic experience, to idealize a foreign theory and program with
semireligious devotion was to deny what liberal Italy appeared to stand
for. Wagnerism as a cult, in short, was a vehicle of protest but one
whose content was deceiving, for it had little to do with the real
dissatisfactions of Italian youth. Looking back to the 1890s from the
perspective of 1911, the critic Alberto Gasco remembered that "to be a
Wagnerian then meant to be contemptuous of national operatic productions: to cheer Brünnhilde was almost to offend the illustrious
memory of Norma, of Violetta, or of the younger Santuzza."[92] Such a
reference to the Santuzza of Mascagni's *Cavalleria Rusticana* might suggest that *verismo* was still no substitute, in 1890, for Wagner.

The cult really started when the music critics seized and exploited an
opportunity for a journalistic debate and aroused a nationalistic storm
about foreign music and theories and their relevance to Italian art. That
many youths promptly identified with Wagnerism only heightened
the hysteria, for this naturally stirred alarm for the integrity of the
established musical tradition. The Italian journalists, many of them
young protesters themselves, kept the Wagnerian controversy before
the public for three decades, as a whole generation grew to maturity.
These journalistic debates were terribly repetitive, but this did not
make them boring to their various participants, each of whom thought
he was shedding new light on what Wagner might mean to Italy.

The debate, though redundant, raised some intriguing questions
about liberal Italy. Was the earlier xenophobic reaction to a foreign
influence the product of the struggle for unity? The aggressive defense
of the new unity in terms of an established musical tradition seemed to
show more concern for the unity than for the tradition. The continuing growth of chauvinism carried disquieting portents for the future.
For the moment, however, the moderate reaction seemed much the
strongest. The defense of an open society willing to welcome foreign
influences suggested the value of dealing with social and historical
realities. But Wagner (to borrow the words of Alfredo Galletti) had
"excommunicated history as unaesthetic and antimusical."[93] The

composer found history to be inconveniently factual, while he could shape mythology to his own purposes, and so he took his Italian audiences to a mythical world that had no meaning for them. In reaction to this, Enrico Thovez proposed as an alternative the operatic exploitation of the Mediterranean world. Thovez, despite his early enthusiasm for Wagner's music, did not embrace its Germanic context, and some years later he championed the universality of Greek mythology in an essay on "Il tesoro mediterraneo" (The Mediterranean treasure). Why not substitute, he suggested, the Mediterranean for the Rhine, the home of Circe for that of the Rhinemaidens, and Achilles for Siegfried? In 1918 he expressed concern that Wagnerian influence would return after the war, and he hoped for the emergence of an Italian genius who would find gold in Mediterranean poetry.[94]

In effect, Wagnerism helped Italian culture define itself. Some of the young tried it on like a cloak, wore it for a while, and, eventually finding it did not serve their purposes, embraced other vogues like *verismo*. Others, perhaps more profoundly affected, adapted the composer's philosophy to aspirations of quite a different type. It is significant that D'Annunzio, who provided the clearest example of this, took care to stress the Germanic character of Wagner's creation. Admiration for a foreigner was no longer a weapon to shock one's elders and arouse their naive xenophobia; the aim was now to develop the unique character of the Latin genius, which would ultimately produce a national revival surpassing anything accomplished in Germany. In its later phase, then, Wagnerism served as a catalyst in the emergence of Italy's new "integral" nationalism and in the formulation of its generally illiberal character. The relationship was close and symbiotic and, paradoxically, most effective as Wagnerism appeared to decline. The new nationalism, to the extent that it succeeded in penetrating Italian awareness, acknowledged only its own roots and the Mediterranean world. And so on the eve of the First World War, Wagnerism—as social philosophy, not as music drama—was coming finally to represent the outmoded past—and not only to Futurists.

5. Wagner and Wagnerian Ideas in Russia

BERNICE GLATZER ROSENTHAL

Between 1890 and 1917 an explosion of creative activity transformed much of Russia's culture. Daring innovations, bold challenges to existing orthodoxies, permeated every area of art and thought, as artists and writers sought new means of aesthetic expression, new personal and social ideals. In this cultural ferment, known as the Silver Age, Wagner and Wagnerian ideas played major roles. Wagner's influence began in the 1890s, peaked between 1906 and 1914, revived in 1917, and remained important in the 1920s. The *Gesamtkunstwerk* was the single most important ideological influence on Sergei Diaghilev's famed dance company, the Ballets russes, and also motivated many other theatrical experiments. Wagner's operas so dominated the 1913–1914 season of the St. Petersburg imperial theaters that nationalists requested justification of the repertory selected and called for a Russian Bayreuth, a showcase for Russian composers. The popularity of Wagner's music stimulated interest in his philosophical and sociological writings as well. Symbolists, especially, hailed Wagner as a mystic and a prophet, progenitor of a revived Christianity or of a new cult. After 1905, some symbolists, as well as some Marxists, found inspiration in Wagner's radicalism of the 1840s, especially in *Art and Revolution* (1849).

The reception of Wagner and Wagnerian ideas in Russia cannot be fully treated in a single essay. I shall therefore confine myself to the influence of Wagner's ideas on the artists and writers who popularized them between 1890 and 1917—the high tide of Wagner's impact on

Russian culture. Eschewing a musicological analysis, I shall concentrate on three distinct but frequently overlapping elements of Wagner's appeal and influence: the aesthetic-cultural, the mystical-religious, and the revolutionary. The impact of these elements was felt in that order, though not necessarily with equal force, by the same individuals. For the aesthetes of the Ballets russes, Wagner's appeal was almost entirely aesthetic and cultural, while symbolist poets, entranced by his music, also responded to the mystical and religious dimensions of his art and thought; after 1905, however, some symbolists responded to the revolutionary elements as well. As I discuss each element, I shall focus on the person or persons who best exemplified it: Sergei Diaghilev and Aleksandr Benois for the aesthetic-cultural, the symbolist Vyacheslav Ivanov for the mystical-religious, and the symbolist Aleksandr Blok and the Marxist Anatoli Lunacharsky for the revolutionary.

Russian Wagnerians did not blindly imitate Wagner but selected those features of his thought that they found most relevant to their own concerns. They adapted and transformed his ideas to fit their own situation, grafting his theories onto Russian roots, often in combination with other ideas, both Russian and Western, that were in vogue during the Silver Age. Some Western sources of the Silver Age, such as Friedrich Nietzsche, the French symbolist poets, and avant-garde theatrical directors, were themselves influenced by Wagner.

BACKGROUND

Wagner's ideas, closely connected with Nietzsche's, took hold in the revolt of artists and writers of the Silver Age against the positivist-utilitarian world view. Best expressed in the nihilist Dmitri Pisarev's oft-quoted dictum, "Boots are higher than Shakespeare," this world view had dominated Russian artistic and intellectual life since the 1860s. Rationalism, worship of science, militant atheism, and dogmatic materialism combined with populist insistence that art advocate social justice and be comprehensible to the people to make realism the dominant style in literature, painting, and music. While such giants as Leo Tolstoy and Fedor Dostoevsky successfully defied what has been called "the censorship of the Left," "civic literature"—literature that preached a social message—dominated the "thick journals," the medium of the intelligentsia. Such personal and existential themes as love, the meaning of life, and the riddle of death were slighted; self-expression was considered a luxury, and imagination and fantasy were disdained. Poetry was almost moribund. The mainstream of painting depicted the suffering of the poor and the brutality of the ruling classes.

In music, the didactic spirit of the 1860s infused the realism, populism, and nationalism of the Five: Modest Mussorgsky (1839–1881), Nikolai Rimsky-Korsakov (1844–1908), Aleksandr Borodin (1834–1887), César Cui (1835–1918), and Mili Balakirev (1837–1910). Although the Five were not a monolithic group, all were hostile to Wagner, for they shared a determination to avoid Western influence and to create an authentically Russian musical style that drew on Russian folk songs, melodies, legends, and history for inspiration and subject matter. Hoping to clear the way for the leadership of the Russian school, which they represented, they attacked the "decrepitude" of German opera, as represented by Wagner, exalted the operas of Mikhail Glinka (1803–1857) and Aleksandr Dargomyzhsky (1813–1869), and systematically underrated Wagner's music and the music of his Russian disciple Aleksandr Serov.[1] Their champion, the leading positivist critic V. V. Stasov (1824–1906), attacked Wagner's "preoccupation with gods and goddesses . . . as the nineteenth century's most retrograde tendencies inflated to the point of decadence."[2] "What sort of feelings," Stasov asked, "what thoughts, can arise from Wagner's endless absurdities . . . fish women, whom fauns drag from the water in nets . . . the senseless secrets of the Medieval Grail and a hundred more such stupidities."[3] Tolstoy, who shared the populist view that art must preach, devoted a chapter and an appendix of *What Is Art?* (1896) to the *Ring,* which he called a "model work of counterfeit art."[4] Pretending naiveté, he ridiculed the music and the plot. He complained that "the music runs over something strange, like beginnings which are not continued and do not get finished" (i.e., the leitmotiv), and summarized "the contents of the Nibelungen Ring" thus: "The first part tells that the nymphs, the daughters of the Rhine, for some reason guard gold in the Rhine, and sing: Weia, Waga, Woge du Welle, Walle zur Wiege, Wagala-weia, Wallala, Weiala, Weia, and so forth."[5]

Critics and composers who opposed the Five were hostile to Wagner for different reasons. G. A. Laroche, a leading nonpositivist music critic, considered Wagner essentially a symphonist rather than a com-

poser of operas and maintained that the *Gesamtkunstwerk* was unfeasi-
ble. The composers Peter Ilyich Tchaikovsky (1840–1893) and Sergei
Taneev (1856–1915) considered Wagner and Wagnerism synonyms for
the death of musical art, "something damned and terrible." In 1894
Taneev, succumbing to the growing interest in Wagner, organized a
"seminar against Wagner" for his conservatory students. As he distributed copies of *Tristan* he assured the participants, "We will study
the villain thoroughly."[6]

In this inhospitable climate, performances of Wagner's music were
rare. In 1863 Wagner had visited Russia, at the invitation of the grand
duchess Elena Pavlovna, patroness of the Russian Musical Society, but
his music elicited mixed reviews.[7] Until 1889, when a touring opera
company from Prague performed the *Ring,* only *Lohengrin* and *Tannhäuser,* the latter in Italian translation, had been staged in Russia. Reviews of the 1889 performance praised Wagner's music but tended
either to fault the idea of the music drama itself or to maintain that its
real originator was Dargomyzhsky (or Glinka), whose execution of it
was superior. Aleksandr Benois recalled that such innovations as the
dimming of the house lights and the refusal to seat latecomers until
intermission caused more comment than the performance itself. But
the 1889 production introduced young Russians such as Benois to
Wagner and resulted in a radical change in their musical tastes and
cultural aspirations, especially with regard to the theater.[8]

By 1889 new forces were at work. The grip of the utilitarian aesthetics was weakening. Its carrier, the populist intelligentsia, was deci-
mated by the reaction that followed the assassination of Tsar Alexander II in 1881, while industrialization and urbanization were undermining the agrarian base of the populist ideal. Beset by doubts about
the validity of its own message, the intelligentsia read Schopenhauer,
whose popularity among students in the 1880s testifies to their pessimism and confusion. Populism, moreover, had served as a substitute
religion, a creed by which to live, for the atheistic intelligentsia. When
that creed was challenged, some intellectuals turned to Marxism; others found religion in art.

Wagnerism thus arose at a critical time in the evolution of Russian
culture. The very painters and poets who were undergoing these
changes were also the popularizers of Wagner and Wagnerian ideas.
Proclaiming the supreme importance of art and beauty, they were
enthusiastically receptive to Wagner; campaigning on behalf of their

values, they helped create a new cultural climate that was permeated with Wagnerian and Nietzschean ideas. While Wagner and Nietzsche were not the sole influences on the Silver Age, they must be seen as occupying a central place in this rich cultural era.

THE AESTHETIC-CULTURAL ELEMENT

Russian art was by tradition didactic, and the poets and painters who seceded from the populist intelligentsia developed a complete credo of their own: aesthetic individualism. Formulated in conscious opposition to the ethos of the 1860s, aesthetic individualism held that art is humanity's highest metaphysical activity, the creation of beauty its noblest pursuit, and the artist a superior form of being. Vehemently apolitical, stressing the individual over society and self-expression over duty, its proponents used the philosophy of Nietzsche, especially *The Birth of Tragedy from the Spirit of Music,* to justify their stance. Wagner's influence cannot be separated from Nietzsche's, for Nietzsche's works provided the intellectual ammunition with which Wagner's admirers defended their views against positivists and realists. Russians perceived Nietzsche as a mystic and a prophet, progenitor of a new culture of freedom and beauty; they regarded Wagner as the modern bearer of the "spirit of music" itself.[9]

Russian Wagnerians can be divided roughly into aesthetes and symbolists. Such aesthetes as Aleksandr Benois (1870–1960) and Sergei Diaghilev (1872–1929) expounded an "art for art's sake" philosophy, while symbolists regarded art as a theurgy, a path to religious truth.[10] Both groups esteemed the fantasy and imagination condemned by positivists. They believed that the phenomenal world was but a reflection of a higher and deeper world, a world accessible only to the artist, with his superior intuition and imagination. Focusing on the world within the soul or the psyche, they admired Wagner's aesthetic treatment of internal conflict and moral dilemmas[11] and marveled at his ability to express emotional states, to appeal to all the senses, to transport his audiences to other worlds. Like their French counterparts, Russian symbolists tried to make poetry musical, to use words for effect rather than for meaning, to suggest rather than to describe. Konstantin Balmont, especially, loved the music Wagner made with words. Symbolist writers collaborated with painters or composers; their poems were set to music and their books illustrated in a common attempt to overcome the limitations of their separate arts. Symbolist painters found resonance in line, regarding it as the visual counterpart of rhythm; rejecting realism, they sought ever higher levels of abstraction in painting.

Aesthetes and symbolists yearned to create a new and distinctly Russian culture that would contribute to world culture and not merely ape the West. Not nationalists in the narrow sense, they were familiar with and appreciative of the latest trends in Western art and thought and took an active role in introducing them to Russian audiences. These thinkers accepted the Wagner-Nietzsche apotheosis of Greek tragic drama as the expression of the public conscience. As passionate Grecophiles, they believed that in classical Greece the artist had been an esteemed member of society and that art and beauty had been pursued for their own sakes. They were also influenced by the Wagner-Nietzsche tenet that disintegration of Greek tragedy into its component arts presaged the death of the "whole man" and the rise of the mind-body, flesh-spirit dichotomy. Art that appealed to all the senses, not just the intellect, they believed, could restore the lost psychological and cultural unity of classical Greece. Assuming that Wagner's staging of Germanic myths and legends facilitated German cultural unity after 1870, many of these intellectuals hoped to stimulate a similar process in Russia. These factors inspired the most outstanding single example of Wagner's impact on Russian art and culture—the Ballets russes.

The Ballets russes had their debut in Paris in 1909, but their intellectual origins were in St. Petersburg in the 1890s. Years later, Benois, who had been considered the company's ideologue, wrote:

> The ballet is one of the most consistent and complete expressions of the idea of the *Gesamtkunstwerk, the idea for which our circle was ready to give its soul*. It was no accident that what was afterwards known as the Ballets russes was originally conceived not by professionals of the dance, but by a circle of artists, linked together by the idea of art as an entity. Everything followed from the common desire of several painters and musicians to see the fulfillment of the theatrical dreams that haunted them. . . . Our ideals were not limited to the ballet alone, but concerned the whole world of art. *Mir Iskoustva* [sic], *The World of Art,* is the name we gave to our review; it was our first effort to influence society—before we had any connection with theater or ballet.[12]

Let us turn, then, to the *miriskussniki* (the founders of *The World of Art*) and explore in turn the importance of Wagner to them, their activities on behalf of art, other trends then current in Russia, and how these elements all converged in the Ballets russes.

The *miriskussniki* were primarily painters, music lovers, and ardent Wagnerians. Diaghilev was intent on a musical career until Rimsky-Korsakov convinced him that he lacked talent. The painters Benois and K. A. Somov (1868–1939) were also frustrated musicians. In 1902 V. F. Nouvel (1871–1949) and A. P. Nourok (1863–c. 1945) organized "Evenings of Contemporary Music," that turned out to be as important for Russian music as *Mir iskusstva* was for Russian art. While still students in the early 1890s, the future *miriskussniki* held seminars on art and philosophy. Wagner was their god. Diaghilev, a latecomer to the circle, at first did not share their enthusiasm, but when he heard *Lohengrin* in Vienna, he was enthralled. Glinka's importance, he said, was national and historical, but Wagner and Tchaikovsky "soar above nationality, they are universal."[13] In those years, Benois recalled, "we were all Wagnerians. We demanded from operatic music, neither arias, *fiorituri,* nor virtuosity, but moods, dramatic effect, and a close relationship between music and action."[14] The journal *Mir iskusstva* was formed in 1898 to propagate their views on art and culture.

Diaghilev, the editor, selected writers who shared his interests. Serialized excerpts from Henri Lichtenberger's *Wagner as Poet and Thinker,* translated from the French, explained Wagner's views on the music drama, the *Gesamtkunstwerk,* and myth.[15] The music critic A. M. Koptaiev's translation of Nietzsche's "Wagner in Bayreuth" appeared in 1900.[16] There were articles on the theater of the future,[17] symbolist interpretations of Wagner's myths,[18] and extensive reviews of Wagner productions in Russia and abroad, including a regular "Letter from Munich." Painting was emphasized, but all of the arts were included. Symbolists, finding common ground with the aesthetes in their hostility to positivism and realism, dominated the literary section. Reviews of concerts, plays, and art exhibits in St. Petersburg, Moscow, and Kiev appeared regularly, as did reports on art and artistic trends in Paris, Munich, and Vienna. The diversity of the subject matter—which ranged from Japanese art to church architecture of the Russian far north, from such Russian landscape painters as Isaac Levitan to the music of Richard Strauss, Max Reger, and Vladimir Rebikov—reflected the journal's desire to encompass the entire world of art as well as the multiplicity of influences on the Silver Age.

Mir iskusstva ceased publication in 1904, racked by financial difficulties, disputes between painters and writers, and quarrels between aesthetes and symbolists on the role of religion in art. But the aesthetic and cultural ideas it championed continued to circulate. Successor journals took up its battle for art, beauty, and cultural renovation: *Novyi put'* (New path, 1903–1904), *Vesy* (The balance, 1904–1909), *Zolotoe runo* (Golden fleece, 1906–1909), and *Apollon* (Apollo, 1909–1917). After 1907, moreover, aesthetes and symbolists were able to publish in such newspapers as the Constitutional Democrats' *Rech* (Speech) and in such "thick journals" as *Russkaia mysl'* (Russian thought), thereby gaining an ever-widening audience. Organization of art exhibits and a brief stint at the imperial theaters enabled the *miriskussniki* to promote their views and to refine them between 1897 and 1905.

The art exhibits organized by Diaghilev from 1897 on were designed to acquaint Russians with contemporary artistic trends in Russia and abroad and to convey the unity of impression Wagnerians prized. Paintings were selected and arranged to create a mood, which was then enhanced by appropriate background music and specially designed decor. The exhibit of Russian historical portraits at the Tauride Palace in the winter of 1905 was particularly successful—in Diaghilev's words, a "grandiose summing up of a brilliant, but, alas, dead period of our history."[19] Diaghilev left for Paris in February, but the journal *Zolotoe runo* continued the tradition of artistic synthesis in Russia; from 1907 to 1909 it organized exhibits of painting that attempted to engage all of the senses by music, decor, and scents wafted through the air. Special events were connected with the exhibit as well—literary-musical afternoons that might feature string quartets or Greek dancers.[20]

The German-born empress, Alexandra, also loved Wagner and wanted his operas staged. This encouragement led to the appointment of Prince S. M. Volkonsky, an ardent Wagnerian, as director of the imperial theaters in July 1899. Under his aegis, *Tristan und Isolde* was produced at the Mariinsky Theater in 1899–1900, followed, between 1901 and 1905, by all four parts of the *Ring,* one each year.

Volkonsky, an occasional contributor to *Mir iskusstva,* intended to inaugurate an era of theatrical reform. He appointed Diaghilev his special assistant and editor of the *Annual* of the imperial theaters. Diaghilev, determined to refute the charges of decadence and dilettantism that hounded the *miriskussniki,* created a monumental and luxurious production. Combining illustrations, carefully selected type, elaborate lettering, and attention to layout, he made every page a treat for the eye. Documentary and statistical materials were published in a supplement, reinforcing the impression of seriousness. Several *miriskussniki* worked on the *Annual* and were named to the Repertory Committee. Diaghilev, Benois, Léon Bakst (1866–1924), and others were invited to stage Léo Delibes's *Sylvia* as a ballet. But the production never appeared, for in 1901 Diaghilev was dismissed after a quarrel with Volkonsky over the staging; Diaghilev's open homosexuality was a factor in the background. Bakst, Benois, and Konstantin Korovin (1861–1939) stayed on, despite Diaghilev's cries of betrayal, because they felt a duty to promote their theatrical ideals, a stance supported by other *miriskussniki*. In 1903 they staged *Götterdämmerung*. Benois's staging was influenced by contemporary Finnish landscape painters and by Konstantin Stanislavsky's principle of "truth on the stage." By this precept, the author's intentions were to be carried through in every detail of the production in order to create a psychologically unified impression. Benois depicted a simple northern landscape instead of what he called the "false romantic monumentalism" of most Wagner productions. In fact, his commission to stage the opera stemmed from his critical review of the staging of *Die Walküre* in *Mir iskusstva*. But Diaghilev, still smarting, attacked the pictorial aspects of the production, accusing Benois of "naturalism" (an insult in their circle) and of omitting the "incredible fantasy" that comprised the Wagnerian genius.[21]

Benois and Diaghilev were reconciled, but Vladimir Teliakovsky, the new director of the imperial theaters (Volkonsky resigned later in 1901 after a quarrel with the ballerina Matilda Kchessinskaia, favorite of the grand duke), was not receptive to innovation. Furthermore, Diaghilev's continued attacks on the opera productions of the imperial theaters made renewed collaboration almost impossible. Even though the theatrical ideas of Benois and Diaghilev were not yet fully formed, they had gained experience and a framework for further development. They resolved to have a theater of their own, where they could freely implement their own ideas and present them to new audiences.[22] The Ballets russes were the result.

The Ballets russes represent the confluence of the Wagnerian ideal of the *Gesamtkunstwerk* with trends then current in Russia. These trends included most notably the "Russian style," derived from work done in the Abramtsevo art colony; the vogue of Isadora Duncan; and the search for new theatrical forms that gained impetus after 1905. The fact that ballet was the favorite art of the imperial court helped this movement along.

Abramtsevo was founded by the magnate Savvi I. Mamontov (1841–1918) to promote and develop the folk-artistic heritage. The colony had a powerful influence on music and theater. Regarding the theater as a way to enlighten the people and awaken in them the spirit of service to good and beauty, Mamontov founded his own opera company in 1885, on the termination of the imperial theatrical monopoly. Intended to be a "people's opera," it highlighted Russian composers. Lush colors, sensuous lines, and folk motifs formed the basis of decor and theme, the hallmark of the Russian style. Great painters, rather than craftsmen, did the sets, costumes, and designs; among them were Mikhail Vrubel' (1856–1900); Viktor M. Vasnetsov (1848–1926); Valentin A. Serov (1865–1911), the son of the composer Aleksandr Serov; Sergei Maliutin (1859–1937); Aleksandr Golovin (1863–1937); and Korovin. The latter two strove to create what they called "music for the eyes," a harmonious fusion of painting, music, costumes, and theme. A Mamontov production was a collaboration of several artists, each endeavoring to transcend the limits of his own discipline in order to create an overwhelming aesthetic spectacle. The famous basso Fedor Chaliapin, renowned for his acting as well as his singing, began his career at Abramtsevo. In 1897 Diaghilev saw a production of the Mamontov opera and was deeply impressed. Possibly at his behest, Volkonsky invited Golovin and Korovin to join the imperial theaters. Korovin, Serov, and Maliutin soon became part of the *Mir iskusstva* circle. Mamontov, incidentally, subsidized *Mir iskusstva* before his bankruptcy, as did Princess Tenisheva, founder of the art colony of Talashkino, which also fostered folk art. Continuing interest in the Russian folk heritage is also evidenced by ethnographic investigations and archaeological expeditions and by Aleksandr Afanasiev's (1826–1871) collections of Russian folk tales, published from 1866 on and widely read by successive generations. These various streams flowed into the Russian style of the Ballets russes, a unique art form that used folk themes and motifs and was as much spectacle as ballet.

Isadora Duncan danced in Russia during the 1904–1905 season and again after the Revolution. Barefoot, wearing a semitransparent tunic that suggested nakedness, she enchanted Russian audiences, especially the *miriskussniki,* who shared her Hellenism and her desire to extract new beauty from the forms of the past. Michel Fokine, future choreographer of the Ballets russes, fell in love with her and resolved to apply her principles to his own work.[23] Fedor Sologub hailed Duncan as an incarnation of the "Beautiful Lady" (the eternal feminine celebrated in Blok's poetry).[24] Like Duncan, Sologub believed that dance returns the dancer to pristine freedom. "The rhythm of emancipation," he said, "is the rhythm of the frolic dance. The passion of emancipation is the joy of the beautiful naked body."[25]

Duncan read widely. Rousseau, Walt Whitman, and Nietzsche were her "dance masters," Beethoven and Wagner her musical inspiration. She wanted to bring about a great renaissance of religion through the dance, to celebrate the beauty and holiness of the human body, rather than to "dance for the amusement of the overfed bourgeoisie after dinner."[26] She refused an invitation to dance in *Tannhäuser* at Bayreuth because to her, despite Wagner's theories on the natural dance, the ballet episodes in his operas were conventional; she disliked mere virtuosity.

The Revolution of 1905 imparted a sense of urgency to these dreams of a new theater. Benois repudiated aesthetic individualism as conducive to anarchy and urged artists to contribute to the organic development of the national culture.[27] Believing that the old court ballet was obsolete, he called for fresh forms of the dance, for an infusion of the folk spirit.[28] Vyacheslav Ivanov, a symbolist, urged artists to go forth and meet the folk soul and formulated a mystique of the chorus as the carrier of the Dionysian principle and the embodiment of the ideal society. Turning to folk myths and legends, symbolists became fascinated with religious ritual and the primitive; art thus burst the bound of its separate disciplines. In Ivanov's words, "Painting craves frescoes, architecture craves assemblages of the people, music craves chorus and drama, drama craves music; the theater aspires to unite in a single 'act' the whole crowd gathered for the celebration of a communal [*sobornyi*] joy."[29]

As artists and writers, fleeing revolutionary turmoil, gravitated to Paris, Diaghilev and Benois conceived the idea of bringing Russian culture to the West. In 1906 Diaghilev initiated a series of "Russian seasons," exhibits of Russian painting and concerts of Russian music. In 1908 arrived the triumphant production of Mussorgsky's opera *Boris Godunov,* with Chaliapin as Boris. In 1909 came the debut of the Ballets russes in Paris, before enthusiastic audiences.[30] The *miriskussniki* had reached their goal.

The *miriskussniki*'s focus on dance rather than opera stemmed from the importance of ballet in Russia. As the favorite art of the imperial court, ballet was subsidized lavishly, and a wealth of dance talent was available. Benois was nostalgic for the ballet of his childhood, the special matinees he had attended at Christmas, Carnival, and Easter. Finding the productions of the imperial dance master, Marius Petipa, routine and uninspired, a decline from the ballet he had loved as a child, Benois hoped to revitalize the balletic tradition.

The Ballets russes mark the Russification of the *Gesamtkunstwerk;* the company represented the export and, in a sense, the commercialization of the Russian style. Like the Mamontov opera, and unlike Wagner's operas, its productions were collaborations of artists. Stage decorations, scenery, costumes, and props were designed by great painters: Benois, Bakst, Korovin, Nicholas Roerich (1874–1948), and later Natalia Goncharova and Mikhail Larionov. The scores of Rimsky-Korsakov, Borodin, and others were furnished with choreography. Igor Stravinsky composed *Petrushka* and *The Rite of Spring* specifically for the ballet.[31] Fokine's choreography, influenced by Isadora Duncan's "natural dance" and Emile Jaques-Dalcroze's eurhythmics, emphasizes gesture and mime to express his view of dance as the poetry of motion. Intent on avoiding episodic displays of virtuosity, Fokine integrated the ballet with the music, painting, and plot, and insisted that the dancers act. Vaslav Nijinsky, Anna Pavlova, Tamara Karsavina, and Ida Rubinshtein were the leading dancers.[32]

Russian music and Russian folk themes predominated. Rimsky-Korsakov's *Scheherazade* was staged as a ballet, and the Polovtsian Dances of Borodin's *Prince Igor* were reinterpreted and staged in an entirely new setting. New works were also created. *The Firebird* was a composite of Russian folk tales; *Petrushka* celebrated the street fairs before Lent, its puppet hero recalling Blok's 1906 play, *The Puppet Show.* Choral song and dance in *Prince Igor* and *Petrushka* reflect the tradition of the folk chrous as well as Ivanov's apotheosis of the choral principle. In *Petrushka* the action of the crowd was not strictly planned; each dancer interpreted the music, within limits, in his or her own way. *The Rite of Spring* depicts a ritual sacrifice of the pagan Slavs in which a virgin dances herself to death to propitiate the gods. The concept was Nicholas Roerich's, for he was fascinated by the pagan Slavs. The ballet also indicates contemporary interest in Dionysian rituals and in dance as a major part of primitive life. Stravinsky welcomed the idea; since little was known of the music of the ancient

Slavs, he had full scope for invention. Wagner's refurbishing of old Germanic myths had reinforced and was then subsumed by the Russians' ongoing quest for their own identity.

The Dionysianism and sensuality of the Silver Age found expression in the Polovtsian Dances of *Prince Igor,* in *Carnavale, Scheherazade,* and the bacchanale and love scenes of *Cleopatra.* Fokine's choreography of the Venus' Grotto episode was so spectacularly sensuous that Benois was left wondering why Tannhäuser left the grotto "for the virtuous but rather dull Elisabeth."[33] Nijinsky's *Afternoon of a Faun* (music by Claude Debussy) concluded with a gesture suggesting orgasm that shocked even Paris. The Hellenism of the *miriskussniki* was manifested in such "antique" ballets as *Narcissus.* Several ballets had Oriental settings that reflected the lure of the exotic, as well as the Silver Age's fascination with the East (particularly marked among mystics) and the perennial issue of the relation of Russia to Asia. Symbolist epistemology regarded music as the basis of existence and movement as the essence of music. To Benois, dance was the basis not only of the *Gesamtkunstwerk* but of life itself.

He and Bakst often doubled as librettists, writing the story line as well as designing the scenery. Their settings blended with the music, dance, acting, costumes, and props, thereby creating "music for the eyes." The lush collection of Bakst's settings for *Cleopatra* and *Scheherazade* evoked the sensuality often associated with the Orient and provided a perfect accompaniment for the music and dance.[34] Parisian audiences were as impressed by the decor as by the ballet itself, finding the exotic elements particularly intriguing. Already captivated by Wagner, Paris hailed the Russian spectacles as a triumph of the *Gesamtkunstwerk* ideal.

Russian national pride exulted in the critical reception of the Ballets russes. With Diaghilev's ballet, said the critic Iakov Tugend'kholdt, Russia had assimilated and surpassed the technical achievements of the West. He credited the ballet's success to Russian love of spectacle, the choral principle, and the Russian ideal of overcoming reality with the magic force of beauty; he viewed its reception as a victory for the Russian spirit.[35] Anatoli Lunacharsky (1873–1933) criticized Diaghilev for commercialism and for innovation for innovation's sake; he disapproved of *The Rite of Spring* (noting that it was twice booed off the stage) and blamed the lush (and costly) decorations for pricing the tickets beyond the reach of "young Paris" (students and workers).[36] Nevertheless, his Russian pride was evident. After 1912 the ballet became less Russian and more deliberately modern and cosmopolitan. Benois, the strongest partisan of the creation of a distinctly Russian cultural identity, broke with Diaghilev in 1912 and joined the Moscow Art Theater. World War I isolated Diaghilev from his Russian coworkers and left the Ballets russes even more international afterward.

Meanwhile, Wagner's music and ideas gained ever-wider circulation in Russia. Beginning in 1907, the *Ring* was performed annually at the Mariinsky in a four-day cycle. In 1909 Vsevolod Meyerhold (1874–c. 1942) produced a stylized *Tristan und Isolde* that showed the influence of the Ballets russes and of the symbolist theater. Stressing visual impact, he had the singers use gesture and mime, comparing them to items of sculpture that the director arranges. In defense of his innovations, he insisted that the opera cannot possibly be realistic, because in operas "people sing."[37] He was accused of downplaying the expressiveness of the music. The death scene in particular was criticized as "cold." The 1913–1914 season at the Mariinsky featured eight Wagner operas, all but *Rienzi* (probably because of its revolutionary theme), *Der fliegende Holländer*, and *Parsifal*, the latter restricted by copyright to Bayreuth. Days after the copyright expired, A. D. Sheremetov produced *Parsifal* at the St. Petersburg People's House. The Theater of Musical Drama was founded in 1912 by I. M. Lapitsky to replace the routine presentation of traditional opera with Stanislavsky's dramatic understatement and emphasis on the unity of the ensemble; the following year it staged a particularly successful *Meistersinger*. Lapitsky also produced Tchaikovsky's opera *Eugene Onegin* as a music drama. Wagner's music was regularly performed at concerts as well.

Between 1905 and 1914 translations and popularizations of Wagner's work appeared in rapid succession. *Art and Revolution* was translated in 1906 and a four-volume Russian edition of *My Life*, which included memoirs, diaries, and letters, appeared in 1911.[38] Henri Lichtenberger's *Richard Wagner, poète et penseur*, was translated in 1905, and Edouard Schuré's *Richard Wagner, son oeuvre et son idée*, in 1909.[39] Articles in the "thick journals" included "What Wagner Did for Opera Reform," "Richard Wagner and His Artistic Reformation," and "The Theater of Wagner."[40] There were also articles comparing Wagner with such Russian composers as Rimsky-Korsakov and Dargomyzhsky, not always to Wagner's detriment.[41] The almanac *Trudi i dni* (Works and days) contained a regular feature called "Wagneriana."

By 1913 Wagner was so powerful a presence in Russian culture that a young theater critic, Sergei Durylin, proclaimed (using the either/or formulation typical of the Russian intelligentsia), "With Wagner or against him, but not outside him," and "Not to want to hear Wagner is possible, but not to hear him is impossible."[42]

Wagner's star declined during World War I. Attempts to purge Russia of all German influence—the change of St. Petersburg's name to Petrograd, for example—dictated the removal of Wagner's operas from the imperial repertory. Increasingly he and Nietzsche were viewed as the epitome of the German spirit and its lust for power, and the greed of Wagner's characters for possession of the Ring came to be seen as symbolic of this quest for world dominion.[43] With the revival of revolutionary sentiment in 1916, however, Wagner's star rose again, as we shall see shortly.

THE MYSTICAL-RELIGIOUS ELEMENT

Symbolist poets and writers were particularly receptive to the mystical and religious features of Wagner's work. Russian symbolist poetry was esoteric, deliberately inscrutable, otherworldly, often manifesting its creator's fascination with exotic themes, and preference for the fantastic. Seceding from society, the "first wave" of Russian symbolists—Dmitri S. Merezhkovsky, Valery Briusov, and Konstantin Balmont—focused on the self; their orientation was aesthetic, psychological, nonrational. Around 1900, however, Merezhkovsky "turned to Christ" and began to preach a "new religious consciousness." Convinced that Christianity and paganism (really Hellenism) represented "two truths," each part of a yet unknown greater truth, he tried to reconcile them in a new form of Christianity based on the Second Coming of Christ, which would combine personal immortality with permission to enjoy life in this world. In 1901 he and his wife, Zinaida Hippius, founded the Religious-Philosophical Society of St. Petersburg to propagate their "religious search."[44] Featuring debates between the higher clergy and the intelligentsia, the society attracted a broad spectrum of artists and intellectuals interested in religious questions; it became a focal point of the religious revival.[45] After 1900 a "second wave" of symbolists emerged—Aleksandr Blok, Andrei Bely, and Vyacheslav Ivanov—influenced by the "new religious consciousness" and the philosophy of Vladimir S. Soloviev (1853–1900). A mystic, Soloviev taught that art contains divine powers that can transform the world and advocated ecumenism, union of the Greek and Roman churches, and religious tolerance. Fascinated by the occult, Soloviev learned Hebrew in order to read the cabala. In 1900 he predicted the imminence of Antichrist. Many symbolists perceived the Revolution of 1905 as a confirmation of his and Merezhkovsky's apocalyptic prophesies. They also recognized the impossibility of isolating themselves from social problems. Their mysticism took on a social coloration as they formulated "solutions" to current problems, ideas that were secularizations of Orthodox religious ideals or variants of Christian socialism. Wishing to reach the people, symbolists hoped to shape the popular consciousness through variants of Wagner's theater-temple, which they interpreted as a theater of religion.

As symbolists became prominent in Russian cultural life after 1905, their views began to exert wide influence. Music was the basis of their epistemology. It was seen as the expression of Schopenhauer's world will and of Nietzsche's Dionysian principle, and as the highest metaphysical and mystical activity of humanity.[46] Their writings are studded with references to the feelings of "mystery" that music inspired in them, its ability to conjure up sensations from other worlds.[47] Except for Merezhkovsky, who feared the intoxicating effects of music, symbolists influenced by Nietzsche also loved Wagner. In his music they heard cosmic harmonies, the sounds of nature, the soul's inner depths, the divine in all creation.[48] Whereas their populist predecessors had scrutinized art for its social content, symbolists focused on the spiritual or religious ideals and values a particular work or author embodied. They fostered the perception of Wagner as a religious thinker. Preoccupied with death and the void beyond, symbolists found parallels in their own search for faith in Wagner's progression from Feuerbach to Schopenhauer to Christ. The symbolist writer Ellis (pseudonym of Lev Kobylinsky) wrote that Wagner reached the "abyss" (in *Tristan* death is the only way out; in the *Ring* the gods themselves die), recoiled in horror, and turned to Christ for salvation.[49] The critic Max Hochschüler viewed the *Ring* and *Parsifal* as Wagner's search for ethical norms, as his atonement for the sins of sensuality and egoism. Another critic, N. Suvorovsky, saw messianic longings in Wagner's work and perceived in Wagner a tendency to wait for the superman.[50]

Reviews of Wagner productions, often written by symbolists or those influenced by them, expressed admiration for the way Wagner made philosophy into music (or music into philosophy), depicting aesthetically the struggle between flesh and spirit, Olympus and Golgotha. *Parsifal* was routinely called a "mystery play." The music critic Vyacheslav Karatygin considered the staging of *Parsifal* an "event of high moral significance," viewing the Christian knight as a new prophet of the ascetic ideal.[51] Parallels between Kundry and Mary Magdalene were noted by almost all commentators. Bely more than once proclaimed, "We wait for Parsifal," the symbol of the poet's messianic hopes.[52] Echoing symbolist rhetoric, the writer I. G. Ashkinazi found a "new liberating truth" in Wagner, a "deeply religious understanding of life." Hailing *Parsifal* as a liturgy (unlike Nietzsche, he intended the term as a compliment) and as the "incarnation of all the religious ideas that nourish the contemporary religious renaissance," Ashkinazi called for the further development of Christian art as the "airy bridge from Valhalla to the new religion."[53]

The impact of the mystical and religious features of Wagner's thought was felt in other areas as well: in Ivanov's theories of a new theater, symbolist theatrical experiments, Aleksandr Scriabin's project *Mysterium,* and discussions of "the Jewish question" and of a religious renaissance. In such a manner were Wagner's ideas (in conjunction with other influences of the Silver Age) filtered through the prism of the issues and problems that most concerned his Russian admirers, and in the process they were reinterpreted and transformed.

The most influential of Russian interpreters of Wagner, the symbolist poet and theorist Vyacheslav Ivanov, was trained as a classicist and widely esteemed for his erudition. Weekly meetings held at his home (dubbed "The Tower") were as important to intellectual life in St. Petersburg as Mallarmé's "Tuesdays" were in Paris.

Ivanov regarded Nietzsche as the "prime mover of the contemporary soul" because of the challenge his thought posed to Christians.[54] Dissenting from Nietzsche's interpretation of the Dionysian rites as a purely aesthetic phenomenon, Ivanov maintained that the religion of Dionysus was one of mysticism, of musical ecstasy. Its rites, he said, were based on the inner experiences common to all people, regardless of rank or class. Specifying them as passion and love, sacrifice and suffering, death and the hope of rebirth, he said they created in the participants a feeling of oneness with each other and with all that exists. He called this feeling the "religious-psychological phenomenon of Dionysianism" and considered Dionysus, the eternally resurrected god, a precursor of Christ.[55] His interest in Wagner derived from his interest in Nietzsche. He viewed Wagner as the second pioneer (after Beethoven) and of the new Dionysian creativity and the first precursor of universal myth creation. Although he accepted the Wagner-Nietzsche tenet that the disintegration of the Greek theater presaged the decline of the unified consciousness necessary for personal and social well-being, he found Wagner's attempt at synthesis "inharmonious and incomplete."[56] Wishing to improve on Wagner's concept of the theater-temple, Ivanov focused on the chorus rather than the orchestra, and on the theurgical aspects of myth.

"Over the dark ocean of the symphony," Ivanov stated, "Wagner-sorcerer overlays the transparent gold-brocaded mirage of the Apollonian dream-myth."[57] But the myth, he continued, is theologically unclear, for it lacks the human word, tragic speech. Choral activity, absent in Wagner, must celebrate the mystery and create the myth; the orchestra embodies only potential Dionysianism. Ivanov wanted the theater to return to its religious origins and become a "common festival and service," or a liturgy.[58] "The crowd must dance and sing," he said, "praise the god with words." Alluding to a "struggle for the democratic ideal," Ivanov objected to the passivity Wagner induced in his audiences.[59] "Wagner-hierophant does not give a choral voice to the community. Why not? It has a right to this voice, because it is not supposed to be a crowd of spectators, but a crowd of orgiasts."[60] The Dionysian rites, he maintained, were both an "orgy of action" and an "orgy of purification"; their purpose was to make holy and to become holy, to attract the divine presence and to receive the divine gift.[61] Each participant was both active and passive. Ivanov's use of the word "crowd," however, the emotional equivalent of Nietzsche's "herd," suggested a new hierarchy with the artist as priest.

Departing from Wagner's idealization of chastity, Ivanov implied a close connection between the life-giving force of Eros and the world soul, linking sexual passion to the religious experience of catharsis and highlighting the ecstatic, orgiastic aspects of the Dionysian rites. He claimed that passion causes the participants to lose consciousness of the distance between themselves and others, to feel themselves one with the cosmos, with all existence. The actors in the Dionysian rites, he constantly emphasized, were not performers but participants in a religious rite in which they truly believed, members of a religious commune for which Ivanov coopted the Russian term *obshchina*. No stage separated the actors from the spectators, for each was an actor.

Despite their prophetic formulation, Ivanov's theatrical theories reveal his reaction to the Revolution of 1905 and his desire for a sociocultural resolution of conflict. "The historical task of the theater," he said in 1904, "is to forge the link of union between the poet and the crowd." He urged the poet to express the folk soul (*narodnaia dusha*), to evoke those symbols around which the people can unite and rework them into mythic tales. Reassuming his ancient sacerdotal role, the poet was to become a myth creator, formulator of a new "all-national art," the progenitor of a new culture.[62] At the same time, Ivanov warned that myths cannot be contrived; they are not creations of individual artistic genius but derive from the folk soul.

As revolutionary turmoil increased, "chorus" replaced "crowd" in his writing and took on a metaphysical and social dimension that is best defined as the embodiment of *sobornost'*: originally a religious term connoting the unity of all believers in the mystical body of Christ, it had been secularized to mean a tightly integrated loving community whose members retain their individuality. *Sobornost'* is sometimes translated as "choral principle." Ivanov hoped to extend this choral unity to society at large, transcending the divisions and conflicts of his own time with a new mystical vision.

Between 1905 and 1908 his writings on the theater stressed not only this principle but also collective creativity and myth creation as part of a "new religious synthesis," the emotional core of the "new organic society of the future" he desired. Despite his essentially apolitical stance in these years, Ivanov was associated with Georgi Chulkov, formulator and chief promulgator of a doctrine he called "mystical anarchism." One of the politicized versions of symbolism that developed after 1905, mystical anarchism refused to accept the limitations of reality. Assuming that the apocalypse was imminent, it preached the abolition of all external restraints, including government, law, religious dogma, social customs, and traditional morality, in order to clear the field for a new society based on internal and voluntary bonds of love and sacrifice. Ivanov's theory of a theater-temple was the positive or constructive aspect of mystical anarchism. It was intended to evoke and develop the sense of mystical unity that Ivanov and Chulkov (who was also a Wagnerian) believed existed in all people, thereby making possible their ideal of a society without compulsion.[63]

Ivanov and Chulkov feared the influence of bourgeois liberalism, especially after the October Manifesto of 1905 instituted a parliamentary system and a legal order. To combat it they opposed chorus to parliament, commune to individual, and myth to law and reason. The chorus, not the parliament, Ivanov insisted, expressed the will of the people. "Only when the choral voice of the *obshchina* [commune] becomes the authentic referendum of the people's true will, will real political freedom exist."[64] By *obshchina* Ivanov meant what he called the "prophetic *obshchina*," a holy or religious body, as distinct from the "civil *obshchina*," which is bound together by legal and economic ties. Disdaining rationalism, individualism, and bourgeois civilization in general, Ivanov considered political revolutions superficial and political parties divisive. He believed that the "organization of the choral activity of the future is the organization of the 'all-national art' and this last is the organization of the folk soul."[65] Those who organize political parties and campaign for electoral victories, he charged, ignore the folk soul, deny the creativity of the people's inner life.

Ivanov and Chulkov considered Wagner's theater-temple only the precursor of the new theater they desired, not the finished form. From their sociocultural perspective, Wagner's audiences were too passive and his ideal of a theater-temple was too narrowly aesthetic, lacking real religious impact. Music by itself, they believed, cannot perform the creative synthesis a new culture requires, nor can aesthetic appeal alone provide the emotional force, the conviction and commitment, to build a new society. *Parsifal,* moreover, harked back to the medieval past, while Ivanov and Chulkov wanted new myths that would transcend history. Objecting to *Götterdämmerung* without resurrection, Chulkov felt that Wagner lacked a clear idea of the End, that he tended toward a static or cyclical rather than a forward-looking world view and wavered between the optimism of Feuerbach and the pessimism of Schopenhauer. Rather than look to the past, Chulkov said, "we must find the 'after tomorrow,' and this 'after tomorrow' is the exit from drama to event, from representation to action, from a theater outside religion to a theater cult. The actor will identify with the priest in the moment of mystery, when, by a miracle, he finds himself equivalent to an actual symbol."[66] He and Ivanov looked to common "religious activity" that would carve out the path to the new organic society. Such activity, they believed, would engender the new consciousness— collective, egalitarian, indifferent to material goods and temporal pursuits—that their sociocultural ideals required.

Never clearly defined, "religious activity" implied spontaneous worship, "ecstasy," and, most important, myth creation. The creative evocation of mythic truths, Ivanov and Chulkov believed, was a "choral" process, an essential element of the Dionysian rites that voiced the people's will and embodied its tie to the world soul. Unlike Nietzsche, Ivanov saw a higher truth lying beyond the Dionysian flux that is conveyed by myth. Myths, he said, constitute the link between the "inner experience" of the individual and the timeless suprapersonal "I" of the world soul. (Jung had not yet advanced his theory of the collective unconscious.) He believed that new myths quite naturally resemble old myths, because they reflect the same underlying metaphysical reality. Even though Ivanov credited Wagner with restoring myth as a defining factor in the national consciousness, he was critical of Wagner's refurbishing of old Germanic myths. The "theater of the future," Ivanov maintained, requires contemporary content, new myths that arise from the "collective creativity" of the chorus. "Enough of spectators," he proclaimed, "we don't need circuses. We want to gather together in order to create, 'to act,' communally, and not just to contemplate. . . . Enough of pseudo-action, we want action."[67] He advocated clearing the orchestra pit for the dancers (reviving the choral dithyramb of ancient Greece), giving special costumes to the musicians, and removing the stage to eliminate the distinction between actors and spectators. But mechanical arrangements alone, he cautioned, would not achieve the merger of actor and spectator; the theater must become the "internal affair of the folk *obshchina*."[68]

Ivanov was hazy on exactly how new myths would actually arise. Nor was he very clear on the relationships between the myth-creator poet and the chorus, on what constitutes choral activity, or on what the contemporary content of myths would be. He simply assumed that once the spectators turned into one choral body, a new theater-temple would emerge and would somehow turn into an "instrument of myth creation," an "organ of social self-definition," and a "breeding ground of folk creativity or prophesy." He regarded the people as the new barbarians, the elemental creative forces destined to revitalize the decadent society of his day. He pointed to Walt Whitman and Richard Wagner as examples of barbarian freshness and power.[69]

The idea of turning the theater into a temple was attacked by some symbolists. In "Against Music," Andrei Bely fulminated against the Dionysian amorality of the mystical anarchists, whom he opposed for personal and political reasons.[70] In "Theater and Contemporary Drama" he asked, "Why make the theater into a temple when we already have temples?" Temples are for the worship of God and the celebration of mystery, he continued, but what God will be worshiped? "Christ, Mohammed, Buddha . . . or Satan?" What, he asked, is meant by mystery and how will the dramatic activity of Ibsen be transformed into "holy activity"? Welcoming the separation of theater from religion, he opposed their reintegration as retrogressive. Denying that a new cult could arise from the theater, Bely concluded: "Let the theater remain theater and mystery, mystery."[71] Dmitri Filosofov (1872–1942), who advocated a specifically Christian society, maintained that "a new Bayreuth will save no one" and argued that the advocates of a theater-temple were reversing cause and effect.[72] First the people had to be united by a common faith; only then could a new theater develop.

Yet disagreements among the symbolists concerned means more than ends. All of them aimed to reach a still largely illiterate people, and some kind of new theater was therefore vital to each of the symbolist "solutions" to the social crisis. Bypassing the intellect to appeal directly to the unconscious, symbolist dramaturgy used liturgical forms to build an emotional bridge between themselves and the people and stressed mysticism, mystery, myth, and cult. Symbolists shared a common intellectual heritage: Nietzsche, Wagner, medieval mystery plays,[73] the avant-garde theories of George Fuchs, Max Reinhardt, Adolph Appia, and Gordon Craig. They admired variously the Spanish mystic Pedro Calderón de la Barca, Shakespeare, and Schiller for their successful articulation of national ideals; the Belgian symbolist Maurice Maeterlinck for his lyricism and his ability to cast a spell with words; and Henryk Ibsen, whose characters they considered Nietzsche's superman in action. But Wagner's ideal of the theater-temple was perhaps the single most important influence, the framework within which other ideas were incorporated and interpreted.

Rejecting realism and naturalism, symbolists preferred illusion to mundane reality and considered "inner experience" more important than external events. Stanislavsky's attention to details of the physical environment they found an "unnecessary truth."[74] From 1904 on, symbolists conducted theatrical experiments geared to develop new means of staging abstract concepts and psychological states.[75] The Theater Studio of the Fellowship of the New Drama was the first; its goal was theater as "cult" or "holy communion," the expression of the eternal mysteries and the "voices of the soul."[76] The Revolution of 1905 cut short their plans, but Vsevolod Meyerhold, the director, was invited to join the Theater of Kommissarzhevskaia in St. Petersburg, the most famous of the theatrical experiments. Following the failure of a Theater of Dionysus, which opened in St. Petersburg in 1906, and of Ivanov's and Chulkov's plans for a new theater to be called Fakely (Torches), the symbolists realized they had to be more contemporary. Partly under their influence, the actress Vera Kommissarzhevskaia founded her theater in 1906. Director Meyerhold emphasized illusion and mood. Both he and his successor, Nikolai Evreinov, were influenced by Wagner. They used musical forms, pure rhythm, and abstract harmony to manipulate the emotions of the audience and transcend the limits of the subject. Western dramatists, particularly Maeterlinck and Ibsen, dominated the repertory. Among the Russian plays produced were Leonid Andreev's *Life of Man,* Fedor Sologub's *Victory of Death,* and Blok's *Puppet Show.* In the latter, actors left the stage and moved among the audience, speaking directly to it—an innovation that marked a step toward the symbolist goal of abolishing the stage.

Although Meyerhold achieved his greatest fame under the Soviets, many of his basic ideas on theater derived from symbolist influence, especially Ivanov's idea of collective creativity. Under Meyerhold's direction, Ivanov's chorus was metamorphosed into gymnasts dressed in workers' overalls. Meyerhold's post-1917 slogan, "Put October into the theater," descends directly from his earlier conviction that "the most dangerous thing for the theater is to serve the bourgeois taste of the crowd. It is necessary to struggle with it . . . [to go] forward, forward, always forward."[77]

Other theatrical experiments and theories also reflected the impact of the Nietzsche-Wagner-Ivanov syndrome; they attempted, in various ways, to appeal to the unconscious and to engage all the senses. Nikolai Evreinov's Theater of Antiquity (1907–1908 and 1911–1912) staged medieval mystery plays and the baroque dramas of Lope de Vega and Calderón. Evreinov's theater-café, The Crooked Mirror, featured subjectivist monodramas intended to evoke intimacy and a sense of communion between actors and audience. Fedor Kommissarzhevsky's Theater for Grown-up Children (1908) staged Sologub's *Nocturnal Dances,* directed by Evreinov, choreographed by Fokine, and with sets designed by Léon Bakst. Sologub's essay "Theater of One Will" (his own) envisioned total domination over the audience; his novel *A Created Legend* constituted his own attempt at myth creation. Blok was particularly influenced by Wagner's idea of a theater that served all the people, not just the ruling class. "The theater," he said, "is a powerful educational force [that] can educate the will."[78] His 1912 drama *The Rose and the Cross,* set in medieval Provence and originally conceived as an opera, with music by Aleksandr Glazunov, was yet another attempt to synthesize the arts.

Symbolist theatrical experiments failed to attract popular audiences. Indeed, very few symbolist plays were actually produced, for their abstract, esoteric nature made them difficult to stage. Even so, they led to other theatrical experiments designed to alter consciousness that attracted revolutionaries and influenced early Soviet culture, as we shall see shortly.

The composer Aleksandr Scriabin (1872–1915) offers a particularly spectacular example of the confluence of Nietzsche, Wagner, and Russian mysticism. Nietzsche's influence shaped Scriabin's Prometheanism, his belief in the artist as superman, and, to an extent, justified his unabashed sensuality.[79] His first impression of Wagner's music, at Sergei Taneev's 1894 seminar, was that it was formless. Scriabin was overwhelmed, however, by a performance of *Siegfried* in 1902 and began to write an opera whose hero was a composite of Nietzsche's superman and Wagner's Siegfried. The opera was never finished, but Wagner's influence remained a powerful factor in Scriabin's work; it is evident in the complexities of Scriabin's music, especially his orchestration, and in the grandiose conception of such compositions as *Poem of Ecstasy, Poet of Fire,* and his grand project, *Mysterium.* The latter, specifically inspired by Wagner, was to be, in Malcolm Brown's words, the "ultimate *Gesamtkunstwerk,* an eschatological mystery that would transfigure the universe in a glorious Act of Celebration, freeing man's creative spirits and resolving life's dissonances into perfect harmony."[80] Its creation became his obsession; one has the decided impression that Scriabin was determined to out-Wagner Wagner.

He considered Wagner's idea of unity of the arts superficial, merely representational. The *Mysterium* was planned to achieve "all-unity" (*vse-edinstvo*), unity of the senses (synaesthesia) and unity of man and the cosmos. In the belief that he could bring on the apocalypse by the force of his music, he devised a "mystic chord" toward that end. A "Preliminary Activity" would precede the performance of the *Mysterium* and prepare the audience for reconciliation with God as divine force. The *Mysterium* would take place in India, in an edifice composed of a semicircle of concentric arcs whose reflection in a pool of water would complete a circle. The form of the edifice would not be "monotonously fixed forever, but [would] be forever changing, together with the mood and movement of the Mystery—and all that, of course, with the aid of the incense smoke and the illumination which [would] alter architectural lines and contours." An altar would stand at the center. Those closest to it would assume a more active role than those at the periphery, but there would be movement among ranks. "There will be no spectators," Scriabin emphasized, "all will be participants."[81] Scriabin's visions, which allowed the requirements of the separate arts more scope than Wagner's did, included dances, incense, cavalcades, processions, an orchestra, a large mixed chorus, rhythmic incantation of sacred texts, special attire for the participants, and an instrument for lighting effects—all designed to create the feeling of "all-unity." Scriabin believed that each note of the keyboard corresponded to a particular color, which he saw as he played. The lighting instrument could augment each note by producing its parallel color or could be used to produce visual counterpoint.[82] The *Mysterium* could be performed only once. Special bells, suspended from clouds in the Himalayas, were to summon people to the event, which would last for several days. "Just as people travel to Bayreuth . . . so they will travel to [the site of the *Mysterium*]."[83] A flash of blinding white light would terminate the festivities and inaugurate the end of the material world, the triumph of the spirit.

Although the *Gesamtkunstwerk* inspired the *Mysterium*, Scriabin considered Wagner too theatrical; Scriabin was virtually fixated on abolishing the stage and providing for participatory activity. Most significant, he did not plan stage decor; he was critical of *Parsifal* as too "churchly" and insufficiently spiritual. Scriabin was an optimist and a sensualist; he shared neither Wagner's Schopenhauerian pessimism nor his ascetic ideal. Wagner's concept was only the point of departure for Scriabin's *Mysterium*, a project permeated with the ideas of Russian mysticism, especially Soloviev's "all-unity," symbolist theatrical theory, and apocalypticism. "All-unity," it will be recalled, is a synthesis of religion, art, and science; Soloviev believed that art was a microcosm of "all-unity," latent with theurgic energy, and that the artist was able to harness supernatural forces and transfigure the world. Scriabin became familiar with his ideas through his friendship with Soloviev's admirers: the neo-idealists of the Moscow Religious Philosophical Society and the symbolists Balmont, Yuri Baltrushaitis, and Ivanov.[84] The latter's theories of "collective creativity," abolition of the stage, and art as celebration were particularly influential; after Ivanov moved to Moscow in 1912, he and Scriabin discussed Beethoven, Wagner, and the importance of Christ and Christianity for hours on end. In 1912 Ivanov was not especially apocalyptically oriented, but eschatology, derived from Soloviev, Merezhkovsky, and other sources, had become a major motif of Silver Age art and thought. The choice of India for the site of the *Mysterium* and the inclusion in the liturgy of the sacred texts of all the major religions reflect Scriabin's theosophy. A doctrine developed by Elena Blavatsky, theosophy had interested Soloviev and by 1914 had attracted adherents all over Europe.[85] Among its tenets was the progressive dematerialization of the world (to be achieved in the *Mysterium*) in an eschatological scenario that concluded with the victory of the spirituality of the East, especially India, over the rationalism of the West. Scriabin spoke of a new race, an occult-theosophist race.[86]

Scriabin became a cult figure. His devotees proposed a Scriabin society modeled on the Wagner societies. But in 1915 he was suddenly stricken by a massive streptococcus/staphyloccus infection. Within a week he was dead.

Wagner's ideas resounded as well in symbolist discussions of religion, particularly as they related to the "Jewish question"[87] and to a religious renaissance. Suffering acutely from government-instigated pogroms, Jews were denied even the most elementary civil rights, were limited to 2 to 3 percent of university admissions (their percentage of the population), and were restricted to residence in the towns and villages (not the countryside) of the Pale of Settlement.[88] Russian Wagnerians, not wishing to be linked with the savage Black Hundreds and the pograms they incited, distinguished between equal political and legal rights, which they claimed to favor, and Jewish participation in Russian culture, which they opposed. They denied that Jews could be assimilated.[89]

Vol'fing, for example, maintained that the Jewish question was a cultural question and that to raise doubts about the Jewish contribution to civilization did not imply anti-Semitism. The issue, he insisted, was the relation of Judaism to the cultural-national types of the "Aryan" peoples. It was not that Jews were bad (*durnoi*) but that they were different (*inoi*), alien. Repeating the themes of Wagner's *Judaism in Music,* Vol'fing claimed that Jews were forever alien to the folk spirit of the nations in which they reside. Contrasting alleged Jewish materialism and rationalism with purported German spirituality and idealism, he declared that "musical Germanism" created values, while "musical Judaism" created a bazaar. Accusing the Jews of having a negative effect on the spiritual life of Europe, he charged them with turning music into a business and of "Judaicizing" German music. An opponent of modernism in music, Vol'fing blamed Jewish influence for the abstract rationalism he perceived in Max Reger and Richard Strauss. According to Vol'fing, Jews so dominated the musical life of Berlin that if a "real German type" arose, they would view him as an "exotic" or turn on him in instinctive racial hostility. Comparing Bach to Offenbach, Beethoven to Mendelssohn, and Wagner to Meyerbeer, he called the Jews "musical barbarians" and, like Wagner, denied Jewish musical creativity. Particularly hostile to the Jewish *Wunderkinder,* Vol'fing pointed to "errors" made by Jewish performers of the music of Christian composers to substantiate his contention that musicians should be of the same nationality as the composer. He also called for a new system of musical education to recruit talent from the folk.[90] In subsequent articles he inveighed against the power of critics, many of whom were Jews.

Bely agreed with the general thrust of Vol'fing's article, believing that the distinctive national cultures of the Aryan peoples of Europe were threatened by "stamped-out culture, i.e., an international factory for the delivery of genius . . . by factory production of thought"—a factory, so to speak, owned and operated by Jews. Jews, he claimed, were interested in all cultures because they lacked roots in any one culture. Devoid of a "genuine understanding of the tasks of a given national art," they exhibited a "superficial eclecticism" and developed an "international bazaar of art," an international connection that was remote from the people. Instinctively Jews strove to rework the national cultures of Europe, to " 'nationalize' (Judaicize)" them, in order to enslave the Aryan peoples spiritually.[91] Just as instinctively, Jews first opposed Wagner and the "pure-blooded Aryan Nietzsche" and then attempted to monopolize interpretation of their work. Bely regarded internationalism as a Jewish concept, evidence of an ongoing racial struggle between Jews and Aryans that was cultural rather than political.[92] Applying Vol'fing's ideas on German music to Russian literature, Bely exaggerated Jewish influence on the latter, maintaining that the major Russian publishing firms were owned or directed by Jews. Jewish publishers, he said, threatened the Russian writer with starvation, while Jewish critics, writing in "jargon" (a cliché used by Wagner and the other anti-Semites), blocked every attempt to broaden and deepen the Russian language. Protesting alleged Jewish hegemony in all areas of Russian culture, Bely still favored equal political rights. Indeed, he believed that Jews had a special talent for state service. If they were allowed to enter fields now closed to them, they would abandon journalism and the performing arts and leave the creation of Russian culture to Russians. Unlike Vol'fing, Bely recognized the contribution of such Jews as Heinrich Heine, Isaac Levitan, and Felix Mendelssohn to "Aryan" culture, but considered them rare exceptions.

Whether Scriabin's views on the Jewish question were elicited by the above exchange is unclear. According to Leonid Sabaneev, Scriabin's circle included vehement anti-Semites, including his wife, but Scriabin himself claimed that the Jews had a special mission: to realize the feminine and sensual aspects of culture repressed by Christianity. After that mission was accomplished, they would disappear; he didn't say how. Like Wagner, Scriabin regarded the Jews as a feminine people, hence uncreative. Nevertheless, he attributed to Jews a unique sensitivity that made them particularly good performers, and specified that no fewer than 15 percent of the seats in the string and wind sections of an orchestra should be occupied by Jews.[93]

A different note was sounded in the religious nationalism of Sergei Durylin, a writer then associated with the symbolists. Finding a spiritual affinity between Russians and Germans, he explained Wagner's popularity in Russia by their common "thirst for religious art," their "yearning for a religious sensation of the world," for Christian myth creation. But he wanted myths that expressed the particular religious experience of the Russian people. Whether these myths would be entirely new or old ones reworked is unclear; the point was that Russians must not merely imitate Wagner. Bayreuth, he continued, could have been the locus of a real religious movement, a place for national self-affirmation; there religious values beloved by the entire German people could have been created. Instead, Bayreuth had turned into a "new pagan urbs, with capital letters," and contemporary Germany was "religiously numb." Should a true German religious renaissance develop, it would not originate in Bayreuth. Explaining Bayreuth's failure to fulfill its potential, Durylin contrasted Wagner with Rimsky-Korsakov, emphasizing their common progression from pagan to religious folk myths and their mutual use of Christian legends: the Holy Grail and the lost city of Kitezh, respectively.[94] Wagner, he said, moved from literature to myth to holiness to a holy place, a mere material entity, but Rimsky-Korsakov progressed "from holiness, from a holy place, hitherto rich with religious reality—to the myth of creative, fertilizing, and saving art." Russian artists, he continued, must follow Rimsky-Korsakov's path and make their own pilgrimage to Kitezh, to an "invisible church in an invisible city," for Kitezh expressed the Russian folk conception of faith and truth. Born out of religious enthusiasm (as distinct from Schopenhauerian pessimism), the legend symbolizes the Russian desire for a city ruled by God, an abstract, eternal, and yet realistic ideal, for Russians expected the City of God to be attained on earth. For Russians, Durylin concluded, the meaning of Wagner was the "meaning of a morning prayer on the day of battle—the battle for ultimate religious values . . . for a religious and all-national art—for myth creation." Striking the messianic note of the Russian religious renaissance, Durylin proclaimed: "We believe in [the message of the rainbow], that the promise is not false, and we are saved."[95]

The religious renaissance coincided with, indeed was partly caused by, changes in Russian society that were eroding traditional values and beliefs. Personal confusion and social conflict stimulated a widespread search for mystical or religious solutions to contemporary problems, especially on the part of Russians determined to avoid becoming what they perceived bourgeois Westerners to be—soulless, materialistic, indifferent to art. These considerations led many Russians to emphasize the mystical-religious elements in Wagner's art and thought, and, in some cases, the revolutionary as well.

THE REVOLUTIONARY ELEMENT

In the maelstrom of the Revolution of 1905, artists and intellectuals at all points of the ideological spectrum reevaluated their previous stances. Such symbolists as Blok, newly aware of the suffering of the people, emerged from the revolution with radical visions of apocalypse and the redemption of Russia and the world. At the same time, such Marxists as Lunacharsky came to recognize the powerful hold of myth, religion, and the irrational on the masses. These symbolists and Marxists interpreted the *Ring* as a revolutionary drama: the *Götterdämmerung* of bourgeois society, the end of laws, contracts, treaties, and ancient rules. Emphasizing Wagner's far-left revolutionary stance in 1848–1849 (a type of anarchocommunism), they believed that Wagner's opposition to a constitution and a republic as alien to the German spirit paralleled their own rejection of bourgeois institutions. Finding Wagner's hatred of capitalism, symbolized by the power of gold, equally appealing, they noted that his original Siegfried was modeled after the Russian anarchist Mikhail Bakunin (1814–1876) and that Wagner had fought alongside Bakunin on the barricades at Dresden. Loving Wagner's artistry, they applauded his undermining of traditional musical norms and hailed his music as a revolt of the human soul against any and all external constraints. Aware of the profoundly unsettling effects of Wagner's ability to play on the unconscious fears and fantasies of his audience, radicals were inspired by his vision of a new theater that would appeal to the entire public, not just to the bourgeoisie. Through such a theater they hoped to achieve a spiritual revolution, a transformation of human consciousness, and to forge a new culture that would deepen the social revolution. The theme of Wagner as revolutionary was most prominent from 1905 to 1909 and from 1917 to 1919, but it remained important through the 1920s. *Art and Revolution* (1849) was translated into Russian in 1906 and again in 1918.

The impact of the revolutionary Wagner on the artistic imagination can be clearly seen in the works of Aleksandr Blok, the greatest symbolist poet. Blok, Bely, Evgeni Ivanov, and Ellis (Lev Kobylinsky) were part of a circle of Wagner devotees; performances of his operas inspired them to imagine themselves as Wotan or Siegfreid, and Liubov, Blok's wife, as a Valkyrie. To them, Blok's estate, Shakhmatovo, was "in its own way the future 'Bayreuth' of Blok-Wagner"; Blok himself called his dacha "Valhalla."[96] He owned the fourteen-volume Leipzig edition of Wagner's collected works and shared Wagner's nostalgia for the Franco-Germanic Middle Ages. Also influencing Blok's perception of Wagner were theories of religious revolution formulated by symbolists in response to the events of 1905. Chulkov's and Ivanov's mystical anarchism and their debt to Wagner have already been discussed. Blok frequented Ivanov's "Tower," and Chulkov was a close friend. Blok was also associated with Dmitri Merezhkovsky, who was then extolling Christianity as a revolutionary religion and insisting that Jesus Christ was the greatest revolutionary of all times. Merezhkovsky viewed the Revolution of 1905 as the beginning of the apocalypse, as did Bely, who was then trying to reconcile symbolism with Marxism.[97] Valeri Bryusov's poem "The Coming Huns" and Konstantin Balmont's poem "The Dagger" exemplify the aesthetic attractiveness of revolutionary destruction and violence.

The Revolution of 1905 coincided with a crisis in Blok's personal life. Repudiating his ethereal aestheticism, he denounced "childish mysticism" and spent the nights carousing. Tormented by guilt over his privileged position, he strove to reach the people. Between 1906 and 1908 he wrote four plays, each with a contemporary theme. *The Puppet Show* (1906) cruelly parodied mysticism; the clown-hero "bled" cranberry juice and the heroine turned out to be a cardboard doll—a bitter allusion to the "Beautiful Lady" of Blok's pre-1904 poetry. *The King in the Square* contained so much explicit social content that the theatrical censor forbade its production.

Viewing Russia's problems through the prism of Wagner's social theories, Russian apocalypticism, and his own Dionysianism, Blok began to prophesy social revolution around 1908. Using the Wagnerian categories of culture and civilization, he forecast the destruction of the intelligentsia by the enraged people. Wagner had described culture as organic, spontaneous, noncerebral, and residing in the German folk, as distinct from and opposed to abstract, rational civilization, which, he said, was exemplified by the French. Wagner's view of German culture paralleled the Slavophiles' idealization of pre-Petrine (unwesternized) Rus'; indeed, both views stemmed from the same romanticism. Russian Wagnerians could easily read "Russian" culture and "Western" civilization, or, as Blok did, popular culture and intellectual civilization.

Like Wagner, Blok believed that culture was musical, but his own concept of music entailed a component of cruelty, a call to destruction. He referred to the "musical sounds of our own cruel nature" and hailed Wagner as "a summoner and invoker of ancient chaos."[98] Blok's identification of culture with elementary Dionysian forces repressed by human reason can be seen in his 1908 essay "Nature and Culture," stimulated by a particularly disastrous earthquake in Sicily, which he viewed as nature's revenge for man's technological hubris.[99] He regarded earthquakes as the victory of Dionysus over Apollo (reason to him was an "Apollonian illusion," the "dream of an art" rebuilding its shattered anthill but unable to control the forces that shattered it) and as signaling the return of the repressed in general. Popular revolution is portrayed as the inevitable earthquake in human affairs, the flaming revenge of the elemental folk breaking through the "crusted lava" of bourgeois civilization. Citing the spread of apocalyptic doctrines among the people, he argued that further eruptions were imminent and referred to the "Zion" of the sectarians as their Valhalla. Other essays and poems of the 1908–1909 period convey the same sense of impending disaster.[100]

The confluence of *Götterdämmerung* and apocalypse was recapitulated in 1917–1919 along with Wagnerian images of the artist and Christian prophesies of a new man and a new society. "The task of Russian culture," Blok wrote in 1917, was to burn what must be burned, to turn the storm of the Cossack rebels Stenka Razin and Emilian Pugachev into a "volitional musical wave."[101] Paraphrasing the New Testament, he told his audience, "The spirit is music. With all your heart, with all your mind, with your entire body, listen to [the music] of the revolution."[102] The sounds that he heard were of the old world crashing down. Never a reformer, Blok considered structure and institutions intrinsically repressive; it was the Dionysian aspects of Bolshevism that attracted him. Hating "the devil, the bourgeoisie, and the liberals," in 1909 he had compared the machinery of state (including the parliament established by the October Manifesto) to a "seventy-year-old syphilitic"[103] who infects the healthy young. He did not regret the dissolution of the Constituent Assembly in 1918. "I am an artist," he said, "consequently not a liberal," and added, "The question 'What is to be done?' I can answer only as an artist."[104]

Blok's 1918 essay "Art and Revolution," his tribute to Wagner, was originally intended as a preface to a new translation of Wagner's *Art and Revolution,* but the project never materialized, and the essay was published separately.[105] Seeing Wagner's pamphlet and Karl Marx's *Communist Manifesto* as two emanations of the revolutionary storm that blew over Europe in 1848–1849, Blok stressed Wagner's 1849 revolutionism, his fidelity to his artistic calling, and his indifference to practical politics. He admired Wagner's attempt to reach the thinking proletariat of Europe. But, Blok continued, the proletariat did not hear Wagner's call. The ruling classes reviled him, tried to starve him; when his "star" brought him fame and fortune, the philistines mutilated his work. Bayreuth, conceived as an "all-national theater," attracted "petty tribes" of tourists; the "social tragedy" of the *Ring* played to theaters packed with state officials, right up to the "chief officer," Tsar Nicholas II. Kaiser Wilhelm, he claimed, used Wotan's leitmotiv for his automobile siren during the war.

> Nevertheless, Wagner still lives and is always new. When revolution begins to sound in the air, Wagner's art resounds in response. It makes no difference; sooner or later, his works are heard and assimilated. These works are not meant for entertainment but for the use of the people, because art, so "removed from life" . . . in our day, is leading spontaneously to practice, to the deed; only its task is broader and deeper than the tasks of "realistic politics" and therefore more difficult to embody in life.[106]

Wagner, Blok continued, carried in him the "saving poison of creative contradiction," of loving and hating at the same time. He called Jesus the "unhappy son of a Galilean carpenter" yet proposed to erect an altar to him. According to Blok, this hate-love, unendurable to the average person, accounts for Wagner's survival.[107] Blok shared Wagner's ambivalence about Jesus. "The Twelve," his most famous poem, about a Red Guard detachment on patrol in Petrograd, concludes with an invisible Jesus at its head. But the same poem alludes to "freedom . . . without the cross," and elsewhere Blok expressed hatred for "that feminine specter."[108] The new times, Blok concluded, would be stormy and anxiety-ridden. They demanded a person able to accept ambiguity and contradiction, a person who could rise above "self-satisfied nothingness." He would be the new man, a step toward the artist.[109]

Maintaining that "It is not the world that is ending, but a process," Blok viewed history as an alternation between culture and civilization. His cosmology was based on music.[110] "In the beginning," he wrote in his diary, "was music. Music is the essence of the world. The world grows in resilient rhythms . . . the growth of the world is culture. Culture is musical rhythm." Distinguishing between calendar time (history) and musical time, he equated the latter with the eternal rhythms of life and perceived civilization not as the enrichment of the world but as its "encumbering and overloading (a Tower of Babel)."[111]

In his 1919 essay "The Collapse of Humanism," Blok wrote that all movements are born in music but degenerate into civilization.[112] The people then become the guardians of the "spirit of music," and a new movement is born. Humanism was once musical, but as the "cement" of music that held it together deteriorated, humanism became bourgeois civilization. Again and again he reiterated his conviction that bourgeois civilization was dead, that the rationalism and individualism that had dominated Europe since the Renaissance were doomed. Already, he said, only isolated islands remained of the once great continent of civilization, and they too would be engulfed by the rising flood. The intelligentsia must accept the revolution or perish. Note the metaphor of the flood, connoting on one level natural disaster, on another Noah and the beginning of a new humanity.

Invoking Wagner as the "best example" of the "synthetic forces of the revolution, its elastic rhythms, musical draws, resolute pressures, ebbs and flows," Blok discerned the birth of a new culture. Where others heard a "wild chorus, an unstructured howl, unendurable to the civilized ear,"[113] Blok heard the musical preparation of a new cultural movement, those elemental primordial rhythms that would form the overture to the new era:

> The bell of antihumanism resounds. The world washes itself, sheds its old clothes; man is becoming closer to the elements, and therefore— man is becoming musical. . . . All mankind begins to move, having awakened from the great dream of bourgeois civilization; spirit, soul, body are seized by a whirlwind of movement; in the whirlwind spiritual, political, social revolution have cosmic consequences, producing a new selection [Otbor], a new man is being formed; man—human animal, social animal, moral animal—is being reconstructed as an artist, speaking in the language of Wagner. . . . [Only the artist] will be able avidly to live and act in the epoch of whirlwind and storm that is opening before us.[114]

Opposed to systems on principle, Blok's approach was almost completely intuitive. The poet never developed a coherent ideology, but he did have a definite world view, composed of contradictory elements. Wagner's vision of man-artist blended with Soloviev's doctrine of art as transfiguration and with apocalyptic prophecies of the end of time, the inauguration of "a new heaven and a new earth," a realm of freedom, beauty, and love. In all eschatologies, the coming of the messiah is preceded by unheard-of catastrophes in both the human and the cosmic spheres; the apocalypse itself, moreover, is a terrifying event. Unprecedented suffering accompanies the destruction of the old order; even the physical universe itself is destroyed, by fire, earthquake, and violent storms.

Although Blok condemned religion as unmusical, his own concept of music had a religious dimension: music was the expression of the divine harmony ruling the world. Music is particularly important in the Russian Orthodox liturgy. While Blok probably did not consciously intend to do so, by invoking the "spirit of music" he secularized the religious idiom of the people. Through music, the gulf between the intelligentsia and the people that so troubled him was overcome. Illiteracy thereby posed no barrier to understanding, and a classless society became more feasible.[115] Although these factors shaped Blok's vision of the Russian Revolution, his ultimate goal was a "great world orchestra" where all conflicts would be resolved and discord would become harmony. He accepted the inhuman cruelty of the 1918–1919 period (when civil war, typhus, starvation, and political terror were brutalizing the population) as merely temporary.[116] But before his death, in 1921, disillusioned and heartbroken, he complained, "There are no more sounds."[117] In the Soviet Union and in the West he is regarded as a martyr to poetic idealism.

Andrei Bely's 1917 pamphlet *Revolution and Culture* expresses a similar vision—revolution as *Götterdämmerung,* apocalypse, and resurrection. Like Blok an opponent of Bolshevik materialism and positivism, Bely declared that Nietzsche and Max Stirner, not Marx and Engels, were the true revolutionaries and termed Wagner "an authentic revolutionary in his own sphere."[118] A disciple of Rudolph Steiner's anthroposophy, Bely believed that the entire cosmos was in the process of transition to a higher state.[119] He interpreted the Bolshevik Revolution as the negative apocalypse and expected a positive apocalypse to follow.

Such symbolists as Blok, Bely, Ivanov, Chulkov, and Aleksei Remizov saw the Bolshevik Revolution as part of a greater revolution of the spirit, the destruction of bourgeois ideals and values. Through literary activities and work on TEO, the theatrical section of Narkompros (the Commissariat of Enlightenment, headed by Lunacharsky), they influenced early Soviet attempts to create a new consciousness.

Whereas the Revolution of 1905 politicized some symbolists, it induced some Marxists to take cognizance of the power of myth, religion, and the irrational. Dismayed that the Revolution of 1905 had not inaugurated a socialist republic, they recognized the still powerful hold of tradition and sought new ways to reach the people. They were influenced by the mystique of violence of Georges Sorel (1847–1922) and the attempt of Joseph Dietzgen (1828–1898) to make Marxism into a belief system capable of inspiring mass action. They were also aware of experimental "people's theaters" in Western Europe and of a similar tradition in Russia. Diverging from Lenin's reliance on economic transformation to create, almost automatically, a new proletarian consciousness, the Bolshevik left emphasized the deliberate construction of a new culture that featured distinctly proletarian ideals and values.[120] Lunacharsky's interest in Wagner's idea of a theater-temple reflects the search of the Bolshevik left for means to supplement rational argumentation with forays into the psyche.

Lunacharsky prided himself on being "an intellectual among the Bolsheviks" and "a Bolshevik among the intellectuals." A devotee of theater, music, and art, he had lived many years in Paris and was fascinated by the avant-garde of the Left Bank and St. Petersburg. Lunacharsky had a mystical bent and was interested in religious questions; he attended the St. Petersburg Religious Philosophical Society and Ivanov's "Tower." After 1906, hoping to counter the inroads that symbolist "God seeking" was making among the intelligentsia, Lunacharsky, Gorki, and Bogdanov formulated "God building," a type of socialist religion.[121] A participant in the 1908 symbolist theater symposium, Lunacharsky wrote mystery plays and sympathized with avant-garde dramatists who stressed individual consciousness; he was also aware of the socialist vision of such dramatists as Maeterlinck and Emile Verhaeren. For Lunacharsky, Wagner's ideal of a theater-temple held the special attraction of fusing art and politics, the Bolshevik utopia and the vision of the avant-garde. Art and the social movement, he believed, had the same goal: "the creation of a strong and beautiful man. May the revolution make him strong, and art beautiful."[122]

Rhapsodizing over *Art and Revolution,* he emphasized Wagner's revolutionary stance in 1848 and declared that "the revolutionary movement of 1848 that gave birth to the great *Communist Manifesto* of our brilliant teachers Marx and Engels was also reflected in the small, lively, deep, and revolutionary brochure of the no less brilliant Richard Wagner."[123]

From 1906 until his death in 1933, Lunacharsky insisted that even though Wagner did not fulfill his ideals, even betrayed them later on, his theater-temple remained "an almost classic expression of the theory of the theater as we want to see it," a means for the spiritual emancipation of the proletariat.[124] He recognized the power of Wagnerian theatrics, especially light and music, to manipulate the emotions of the audience, and hoped to use them to make the theater into an agency of social transformation. Discerning an inner tie between musical creativity and revolution, he described revolution as a "grandiose symphony." Bach's music, he said, emerged from the "gigantic storm of the Reformation"; Beethoven's, with its "theme of struggle and victory," derived from the French Revolution.[125] Explaining Wagner's turn to reaction, Lunacharsky stressed the harmful influence of Schopenhauer's pessimism, maintaining that Schopenhauer's concept of will expressed the bourgeois spirit in its decline—always questing, never satisfied, turning to art as a narcotic. Pointing out that Wagner's first Siegfried was a world conqueror, Lunacharsky believed that Wagner killed him in a fit of despair at the failure of the revolutions of 1848–1849. Lunacharsky expected the Russian Revolution to bring forth a new music, permeated with the optimistic vision that inspired and sustained the revolutionaries.

Lunacharsky favored artistic experimentation and held that the proletariat was the rightful heir to the achievements of bourgeois culture, a stance that placed him in opposition to such aesthetic conservatives as V. I. Lenin (indeed, most Bolsheviks) and to avant-garde artists who wanted to scrap the art forms of the past. In "Socialism and Art" (1908), an essay written for the symbolist symposium on the theater, he called for a "barbarian socialist high art," a synthesis of the best of the past for the "Great Lords of the future—the people."[126]

Influenced by Wagner and by contemporary theatrical theories, Lunacharsky sketched the parameters of his own vision of the theater-temple. His vision would duplicate the architectural simplicity and the loftiness of the religious-philosophical thought of the Greeks but without their declamatory monotony, which was "alien to us"; it would capture the external splendor and psychological coloration of Shakespeare but without his "extreme objectivity," since the new theater must play a "positive cultural role." It would express the civic and cultural passion of Schiller but without his sentimentality or flight from reality. If his theater-temple would incorporate the Moscow Art Theater's fidelity to the author's intentions and its emphasis on unity of impression, it would shun the "excessive realism" of that theater, indeed, its failure to convey a vision of the new order. Though he approved of the Theater of Kommissarzhevskaia's "revolt against reality," Lunacharsky admitted that the people were not attracted to it. The new theater, he concluded, "must be a barbarian theater . . . with all the nuances and details," even the noise and the smells that affront the sensitive noses of the cultured public. "The salvation of society is in its barbarians," he concluded, since "they carry real culture, they reveal light and long paths, and so-called cultured society is rotting."[127] In articles written shortly afterward, however, Lunacharsky criticizied symbolist "fog" and mystification and ceased calling the people barbarians.

Marxist critics responded to the new emphasis on the theater with a symposium of their own, *Crisis of the Theater* (1908). Calling for a progressive "people's theater" in tune with contemporary problems, they were also influenced by Wagner. In 1910 Romain Rolland's *Théâtre du peuple* (1903) was translated into Russian and published by Gorki's firm, Znanie. Specifically acknowledging his debt to Wagner, Rolland argued for reviving the mass festivals of the French Revolution and suggested plays on historical and political subjects in which the people could participate and reexperience their own fate.[128] Lunacharsky's introduction criticized Rolland's idea of replacing the traditional theater with mass festivals and disagreed with Rolland's dismissal of the value of the classics for the working class.

Appointed director of Narkompros after the Bolshevik Revolution, Lunacharsky pursued a policy of relative cultural tolerance. Distracted by economic collapse and civil war, the Bolsheviks had not formulated a definite cultural policy. They tolerated, even welcomed, non–Bolshevik artists and intellectuals who were willing to work for them, despite the doctrinal unorthodoxy of such people. TEO, the theatrical section of Narkompros, encompassed not only symbolists, who advocated a new theater of myth creation, collective creativity, and participatory activity but also Futurists, who wanted to bring art out of the theaters and museums into the streets. Present as well were proletkult activists, a highly politicized group whose members wished to purge culture of bourgeois influence.

The Bolsheviks quickly recognized the propaganda potential of theater and cinema. Wagner's *Art and Revolution,* in a new translation (1918), was one of the first books Narkompros published; Lunacharsky himself wrote the introduction. In 1919 Narkompros issued a new translation of Rolland's *Théâtre du peuple,* with an introduction by Ivanov, and published *The Creative Theater,* by the proletkult theorist Platon Kerzhentsev (1881–1940), a book that went through four more printings by 1923 and was translated into German in 1922. The proletkult movement contained various strains, but most advocates desired a new form of theater that would release the creative instincts of the masses and favored mass festivals and participatory activity. Some assumed that the revolution was eliminating the traditional divisions between physical and mental labor, and between the audience and the actors, making a truly participatory theater feasible at last.

Echoes of Wagner, Rolland, Ivanov, and proletkult ideologists were evident during the first Congress of Workers' and Peasants' Theaters in November 1919. The theater was apotheosized as a "force that united people [*liudi*] in common enthusiasm and understanding, rejoicing and grief, decisiveness and hopes . . . a force that organizes the folk [*narodnyi*] soul, forges and expresses folk thought and folk will," and as a means to "popular [*narodnoe*] self-education."[129] Mass festivals became a central feature of public life. Living panoramas depicted the Spactacus revolt, the blockade of Russia, the "mystery of freed labor," and the "world's commune."[130] Conducted on outdoor stages decorated by leading Futurist painters, the events ended with all those present rising and singing the "Internationale." In 1920, Nikolai Altman staged and Nikolai Evreinov directed *The Storming of the Winter Palace,* with a cast of thousands. Agittrains and agitboats brought theater to the countryside to spread the revolutionary message; short films called *agitki* were made to promote the Bolshevik cause.

Vsevolod Meyerhold joined the Bolshevik party in January 1918. Lunacharsky appointed him director of the newly formed TEO in 1918 and director of the TEO of the whole Soviet Union in 1920. Forging an explicitly political theater, Meyerhold expanded Wagner's synthesis by introducing such elements as circus clowns, gymnasts, radio bulletins, propaganda posters, and film clips. The result was a fast-moving kaleidoscope of sensations. In 1918, for the first anniversary of the October Revolution, he staged *Mystery-Bouffe*, by the Futurist poet and playwright Vladimir Mayakovsky (1893–1930). A revolutionary mystery play based on the biblical tale of Noah's ark, it depicts a struggle between the Clean (the ruling classes) and the Unclean (the workers), bitterly mocks Christian concepts of heaven and hell, and celebrates the workers' determination to build a paradise on earth.[131] The stage decor, by the Futurist painter Kasimir Malevich (1878–1935), posed a sharp contrast to the lush color and sensuous lines of Meyerhold's prerevolutionary collaborators. The workers wore identical gray overalls, a huge blue globe represented the earth, and cubic forms depicted the ark, while hell was a Gothic green-and-red hall and heaven a gray cardboard structure with multicolored clouds. Paradise was represented as a mechanized state of socialism where tools and machines served humanity.

After his appointment as head of the all-Union TEO, Meyerhold became increasingly radical. Turning TEO into a military headquarters, he proclaimed a revolution in the theater: all productions would have revolutionary content and revolutionary form.[132] In his capacity as editor of *Vestnik teatra* ('Theatrical herald'), the organ of TEO, he carried on a vehement polemic against the concentration of financial and human resources in the academic theaters, which included the former imperial theaters, the Bolshoi and the Maly (the Bolshoi had specialized in opera and ballet, the Maly in dramatic productions), and the formerly privately owned Moscow Art Theater. He demanded that their resources be redirected to worker, peasant, and Red Army theaters, staffed by nonprofessionals.

As director of RSFSR Theater No. 1 (Theater of the Russian Soviet Federative Socialist Republic, established by decree of Lunacharsky), Meyerhold chose Verhaeren's symbolist drama *The Dawn* (*Les aubes,* given first in 1898) for its first production. Set in a mystical village, *The Dawn* depicted the transformation of a capitalist war into an international proletarian uprising. Assisted by Bryusov, Meyerhold updated it to include recent events. In an attempt to convey the atmosphere of a political meeting, admission was free, the actors spoke directly to the audience, and propaganda posters lined the walls. Stage decor followed the geometric schematization of the Futurists; a harsh white light that dispelled all illusion was the sole illumination.

The Dawn played to packed houses for more than a hundred performances. Lenin's wife, Nadezhda Krupskaia, resented Meyerhold's manipulation of the emotions of the audience. Lunacharsky found the Futurist staging pretentious, but he supported Meyerhold mainly because of the director's revolutionary fervor. Wary of Meyerhold's total repudiation of the art of the past, however, Lunacharsky removed the academic theaters from Meyerhold's control, thereby precipitating the latter's resignation as head of TEO in February 1921. In May 1921, while still director of RSFSR Theater No. 1, Meyerhold staged a particularly successful production of Mayakovsky's *Mystery-Bouffe*, rewritten to conform more explicitly to Marxist doctrine. Lloyd George and Clemenceau were added to the Clean, and a new character, the Conciliator (a Menshevik), was introduced. The characters were crudely drawn propaganda figures and the acting was heavy-handed, but the audience was delighted. Edward Braun described the production as a "hilarious, dynamic, caricaturist rough-and-tumble, a carnival celebration of victory in the Civil War, in total contrast to the still, hieratic solemnity of *The Dawn*."[133]

By the spring of 1921, Russia was starving, and Lenin, to stimulate production with capitalist incentives, instituted the New Economic Policy (NEP). Since limited private enterprise was now permitted, some state theaters were returned to private ownership. In June 1921 the Moscow Soviet closed RSFSR Theater No. 1 on grounds of extravagance, but its discomfort with Meyerhold's artistic extremism and iconoclasm was also a factor.

Theatrical experimentation flourished in the NEP period, partly because of the relative tolerance of the party and partly because no one theatrical "ism" yet dominated. In Bolshevik Russia, disputes on theatrical policy transcended aesthetic and even philosophical issues; they involved conflicting visions of the Soviet culture of the future, with fundamentally different political and economic implications. Because each competing group claimed to be the sole embodiment of the revolutionary spirit, often turning to the party to enforce its claim, disagreements over theory turned into struggles for power. Responding to demands that art serve the social struggle, in 1923 the twelfth Party Congress called for art that reflected episodes of the heroic struggle of the working class but did not specify how this theme should be treated. After Lenin's death, the struggle for power intensified in all areas of Soviet life. The fourteenth Party Congress, remaining neutral on aesthetic issues, directed artists to appeal to a broad worker and peasant audience. Lunacharsky, still committed to preserving the academic theaters and to supporting revolutionary theatrical experiments, was attacked by groups of the Left. Proletkult activists, joined by writers who claimed to represent the proletariat, wanted to abolish the theater altogether, while Left Front, a group of artists that included Vladimir Mayakovsky, wished to radicalize it. For various reasons, including shared suspicion of "bourgeois formalism," and despite their differences on other theatrical issues, these groups supported Meyerhold as he pressed his attack on the academic theaters and experimented with new theatrical forms.

Ironically, both Lunacharsky and Meyerhold were Wagnerians; they advocated synthesis of the arts and supported a politicized people's theater. But Lunacharsky was relatively conservative as a Wagnerian, a believer in cultural continuity, while Meyerhold was a radical who had broken with the Wagnerian model of a theater-temple[134] and was developing a new synthetic art that incorporated elements of the Machine Age. He believed that traditional opera and theater were obsolete. As director, since the autumn of 1921, of the State Theatrical Workshop and, since 1923, of his own theater, TIM (Teatr imeni Meyerkholda), he had considerable talent and financial resources available to him. Among his innovations was "biomechanism," the use of movement to express emotion; special gymnastic exercises were developed to train the actors.

Meyerhold is best known, however, for his interpretation of the theory of constructivism. A movement that encompassed several disciplines, among which architecture was prominent, "constructivism" is difficult to define, but one of its outstanding features was an attempt to convey the spirit of industrialism. In its theatrical form, constructivism connoted extreme functionalism and topicality. Stage designs were stark, angular, geometric, mechanical. Decor for *The Magnificent Cuckold* (1922) featured a huge contraption with moving parts that did not always move on cue. In *Give Us Europe!* (1924) Meyerhold employed moving walls that never stood still. The only props were those required for the action—a telephone, an automobile, a mobile kitchen. Costumes were naturalistic, and the actors usually wore no makeup. The plots were simple, the characters as stereotyped as a political poster, and the villains grotesque archetypes, scarcely human.

Meyerhold also emphasized humor and slapstick, for he assumed that the public demanded spectacle, variety, entertainment. In *The*

Teacher Bubus (1925) he modified his functionalism, returning to his prerevolutionary emphasis on music as the subtext of the plot and rhythm as the basis of dramatic action. (Biomechanism bears traces of the latter emphasis, but its assumptions are quite different.) *Bubus,* based on a comedy by Aleksei Faiko, is about a weak European intellectual who, objecting to the cruelty of revolution, attempts to reconcile the bourgeoisie and the proletariat and ends up serving the interests of the former. Meyerhold produced it as a dramatic symphony, synchronizing every movement with its musical accompaniment (primarily excerpts from Chopin and Liszt). Each performer had his or her own rhythm of speech, almost a leitmotiv. The text was spoken as a kind of recitative; long pauses between dialogues had a musical intent. Lunacharsky attacked *Bubus* as mechanistic and superficial, a desecration of the sanctity of art.

Lunacharsky felt betrayed by Meyerhold, whom he had supported against attacks by party opponents of the avant-garde since the first year of the revolution. In a series of articles, Lunacharsky attributed Meyerhold's militance to his youth and to his "martial temperament," and accused him of destroying rather than creating. He particularly resented Meyerhold's "announcement that the theater should not be psychological or elevated, that its chief task is a glittering diversion, a jolly half circus, half cinematographic 'play' in the most direct meaning of this word."[135] Approving of Meyerhold's emphasis on revolutionary content and revolutionary form, Lunacharsky charged that Meyerhold approached ideological content as if it were a political poster and that his characters were superficial caricatures, hyperbolic exaggerations, "dolls" devoid of inner depth. Meyerhold, he said, was moving from biomechanism to sociomechanism; both theories lacked a sense of the individual and turned the theater into a music hall, the epitome of the bourgeois conception of art as entertainment. Lunacharsky found the concept of the body as a machine especially objectionable and was enraged at the liberties Meyerhold took in his 1926 production of Gogol's *Inspector General.*

The confrontation brought to the fore different elements of Lunacharsky's personality. The thinker in him desired a more serious theater, while the mystic in him yearned for a sense of art as exaltation. In several speeches made between 1921 and 1926, Lunacharsky invoked Wagner to defend his insistence on continuity with the past. Implicitly justifying his retention of control of the academic theaters, Lunacharsky quoted Wagner's statement that the theater should be turned into a state institution like the schools or the university. Defending the importance of the theater as a social institution, he described it as the "artistic educator of humanity, especially of the new generation," and as a "place where the people recognize their greatest ideals and the paths of their sufferings, their struggles, and their victories." He insisted that Wagner's theater-temple continued to be the model for Bolsheviks.[136] Claiming to agree, in principle, with Robespierre's belief that the masses are attracted to spectacles where they are themselves spectacle and spectator, Lunacharsky then contended that Robespierre was unrealistic, for under an open sky acoustics are poor, only the mass is visible, and monumentality is lost.[137] He was alluding, of course, to the mass festivals championed by his rivals. Lunacharsky also opposed the pointedly unaesthetic and mechanical quality of constructivist productions, their lack of transcendence. Arguing that every great movement requires symbols, he cited the "Internationale," Lenin's tomb, and portraits and busts of Lenin as the symbols of the Russian Revolution.

In his judgment, for all that had been done, the revolution had not yet created an opera that was comparable in symbolic significance to *Wilhelm Tell* for the Swiss or Glinka's *Life for the Tsar* for Russian monarchists. Convinced of the psychological importance of music, he called for the creation of a worker-peasant opera as the supreme symbol of the revolution. In melodramatic language he described it as

> the grandiose symbol of our experiences, which will reflect in synthetic forms our past, our now so distant past, a past of passionate struggle, our anxious and glorious present, full of hope, our radiant, militant, and then triumphant future, the struggle of light and darkness, of labor and exploitation . . . the exchange of the all-oppressive winter of reaction for the all-liberating spring of revolution . . . the role of the hero, sacrificing himself . . . saving the mass.[138]

Elaborating on his vision, Lunacharsky alluded to revolutionary ceremony, the simultaneous creation and celebration of some kind of great myth that reflected the people's ideas and hopes. The ceremony would be a festive spectacle that included orchestra and chorus, dancers, costumes, and a special place for ballet. Summer performances would take place in a huge amphitheater that seated thousands. As there was a dearth of good material on worker-peasant themes, Lunacharsky concluded that the Bolshoi would stage the great works of the past in order to demonstrate that Russian opera and ballet forces did "not decay" but would continue to grow in power until "that not distant day when the first great revolutionary oratorio, the first festive spectacle, [would] blaze up on its stage, in its clear and concentrating mirror, able to reflect the rising sun of communism."[139]

Lunacharsky's struggles with the Left continued. The termination of NEP in 1928 and the inauguration of the first five-year plan in 1929 signaled new travails. Lunacharsky was accused of "lack of communist vigilance" and "failure to understand the 'significance of the class war on the cultural front.'"[140] Deposed as head of Narkompros in 1929, he was appointed ambassador to Spain in 1933 but died en route. "The Path of Richard Wagner" (1933), a speech made to commemorate the jubilee of Wagner's death in 1883, reflected the changed situation in Russia and Germany. Using the simpler categories of the Stalin era, he called Wagner a "renegade" (Stalin's term for Trotsky), a "national-ist," a "court musician," and a "man of will" who wanted power most of all and who strove to enslave the masses by "enchanting" them, by hypnotizing them with music and theatrics.[141] Still, Luna-charsky insisted that Wagner raised the theater to new heights of artis-tic and social significance. The model for Russians was not the "magi-cian" of Bayreuth but Wagner as a young man, whose revolutionary passion he urged his listeners to sustain.

During the Stalin era Meyerhold also experienced difficulties. Ac-cused of "formalism," he continued to challenge, not always success-fully, bureaucratic attempts to control his theater. Attacks on "for-malism" and "decadence" intensified in the late 1930s. Meyerhold was arrested in 1939, after a speech in which he excoriated socialist realism. The date and place of his death are not clear; it is generally assumed that he was shot in prison. The mutilated body of his wife, Zinaida Raikh, was discovered several days after his arrest.

The early Soviet period demonstrates the political adaptation of Wagner's ideas by the Left as well as the artistic diversity possible within a Marxist framework. By then Wagner's ideas had so melded with other ideas of a people's theater then current that it is difficult to isolate them. As important elements in the air, however, they influ-enced and inspired Soviet artists both directly and indirectly. Sergei Eisenstein (1898–1948) is one who felt his influence. Originally a pro-tégé of Meyerhold's, Eisenstein was associated with proletkult in the

early 1920s and was one of the first to realize the potential of the
cinema to enable the artist to reach a truly mass audience. His films can
be viewed as attempts at myth creation in the sense in which the term
was used by Vyacheslav Ivanov. The proletariat is the collective hero
of such films as *Strike* and *Potemkin,* which were a means of keeping
revolutionary zeal alive during the prosaic NEP period. Eisenstein
adapted Meyerhold's theatricality to the silent film and developed new
techniques for manipulating the emotions of the audience, such as the
use of music asynchromatically as a counterpoint to the visual image
and the use of color to emphasize dramatic content. His most famous
innovation was the "collision montage," a rapid juxtaposition of
clashing shots that became world famous as "Russian cutting."

An admirer of Wagner's idea of dramatic spectacle, Eisenstein recognized a link between himself and Wagner. In 1932 he said, "I would
like to create one day, on film, a kind of modern *Götterdämmerung,* a
visual history of the deaths of the Titans, of Basil Zaharoff, Löwens-
tein, Kruger, Deterding—a kind of dynamic Pergamon frieze, possibly with Richard Wagner's music post-synchronized."[142] Though he
came under attack during the first five-year plan, Eisenstein later con
tributed to the development of a new national myth in *Alexander Nev-
sky* (1938) and *Ivan the Terrible* (1944), showing the heroic defenders of
Russia battling foreign invasion and domestic treason.

In November 1940 (during the period of the Hitler-Stalin pact)
Eisenstein produced *Die Walküre* at the Bolshoi. He made the production a testing ground for his own ideas on the unity of sound and
image and on the dramatic function of color. In the last act, for example, he interpreted Wagner's orchestration in terms of color, alternat-
ing silver, copper, and blue lighting over the stage background and
using shades of sky blue and flame purple lighting during the "Magic
Fire Music." Eisenstein's decor was on a monumental scale that accorded with his view that "the music's visual embodiment must be
incisively clear cut, impalpable, frequently shifting material," for, as
Yon Barna describes it, "the mountain of scenery was made to oscil-
late in a rising and falling motion in rhythm with the performers'
movements."[143] Another innovation was the integration of panto-
mime choruses with the drama to reflect and accentuate the thoughts
and emotions of the characters.

The visual and musical techniques developed in *Die Walküre* represented a step toward *Ivan the Terrible,* which was really an allegory on

Stalin. Part I (1944), depicting Ivan as a benevolent despot, won Eisenstein the Stalin prize. Part II (1945), however, which treated Ivan as a neurotic despot, was denounced by the party. It was Eisenstein's last work. In Russia, as in Germany, art was coopted to serve the state. All of the media were at the dictator's disposal: the entire nation was his theater. Borrowing techniques pioneered by the "great enchanter," developed by his admirers, supplemented by modern technology and psychology, and supported by a vast apparatus of sheer terror, Hitler and Stalin practiced the art and science of mass manipulation.

CONCLUSION

When one examines the phenomenon of Wagner's enormous influence in Russia, one is struck by certain parallels between mid–nineteenth-century Germany and early twentieth-century Russia. Both societies were just entering the industrial era and experiencing the social and psychological upheavel that modernization often entails: a weakening of traditional social patterns, a resentful aristocracy, a displaced peasantry, a disoriented, semiurbanized proletariat, and an alienated intelligentsia. Similar situations produced similar reactions: socialism, including Christian socialism, as a response to the "cash nexus" (Carlyle's term) of capitalism, religious ferment as a response to the apparent obsolescence of traditional values and beliefs, and indeed the revolutions of 1848 and 1905.[144] Most important, Russian artists and intellectuals desired a new cultural and social synthesis. The world they knew was being torn apart; they wanted to make it whole, to end the confusion and conflict all around them and within them.

Mid-nineteenth-century German thinkers, then, spoke directly to the concerns of early twentieth-century Russians. The influences were diverse: Ludwig Feuerbach's call for "healthy sensuality," Max Stirner's anarchism, and Marx and Engels' "scientific socialism"; Wagner's synthesis of the arts as the path to psychological unity, cultural coherence, and social integration; and Nietzsche's attack on Christian morality and apotheosis of the creators of culture. Striving to define a distinct national identity, Wagner expressed the earlier German revolt against French cultural domination. Similarly, Russians were intent on avoiding mere imitation of the West. Wagner's use of Germanic folk myth reinforced an interest in Russian folk art, music, and legends that had been developing since the 1860s. Just as Wagner had tried to make Bayreuth a symbol of the new politically unified Germany, Russians hoped to develop a new theater that would serve their own social and political goals.

There is always a potential dimension to the reception of a particular artist or thinker, particularly one whose creativity encompasses many areas. Wagner's work was, in a sense, a synthesis of artistic, mystical, and political elements. Russians who came into contact with it perceived the elements most relevant to them, highlighted those elements, and reinterpreted them. Painters and music lovers blended Wagner's ideal of the *Gesamtkunstwerk* with Russian attempts at synthesis to create the Ballets russes. Mystics of the Russian religious renaissance interpreted Wagner's theater as a religious theater, the focal point of a new cult or culture, and viewed Wagner as a religious thinker whose progression from Feuerbach to Schopenhauer to Christ paralleled their own search for faith. Radicals emphasized the revolutionary Wagner of 1848–1849 and developed a political theater designed to create a new revolutionary consciousness.

Wagner's appeal was greatest to Russians who sought synthesis, a "new organic society." By the 1930s, one had developed; socialist realism had become the obligatory style, and new myths prevailed. Although Wagnerian elements were absorbed into the new synthesis, the high tide of his influence had passed.

6. At Wagner's Shrine: British and American Wagnerians

ANNE DZAMBA
SESSA

W hen Richard Wagner's music first became known in Great Britain and America during the 1840s and 1850s, it was regarded as an intrusion upon the polite Mendelssohnian musical culture of the day. Wagner's works were described as sinful, meretricious, unmelodious, and insufferably long; at best, they were, in the words of Longfellow, "strange, original, and somewhat barbaric."[1] While the difficulty of understanding this new music accounted for some of the initial resistance, Wagner's compositions were immediately suspect for nonaesthetic reasons as well; they were denounced as "atheistic, sexually immoral, and tending to further socialism and the throwing of bombs."[2] At mid-century the militant revolutionary in art and in politics seemed to be slated for rejection and dismissal. But by the end of the 1880s, more than any other composer in the age of industrial capitalism, Darwinism, and bourgeois culture, he was thought to provide a way of thinking and feeling that might resolve the contradictions of the times in a new social vision.

Wagner's music dramas unceasingly celebrated spiritual awareness, the themes of redemption and love, and the possibility of improving humanity. Many British and American Wagnerians, faced with the intellectual confusion of nineteenth-century theology and the prestige of positivist science, took Wagner's mythology, which needed no his-

246

torical or scientific verification, as a basis for religious feeling and regarded this mythology either as compatible with Christianity or as essentially Christian. Other Wagnerians interpreted his musical symbols theosophically or were heartened by his vitalism.

Wagner's works also denounced modern industrial society for its pursuit of purely utilitarian ends. British and American Wagnerians realized that they lived in an age of unprecedented prosperity that was, however, unevenly distributed. They shared an apolitical concern for social ethics and valued the music dramas for their moral condemnation of greed, corruption, tyranny, and materialism. Only a few, quite distinguished Wagnerians, chief among them Bernard Shaw and Rutland Boughton, were also attracted to political activism in a socialist vein.

If the mid–nineteenth century signified Darwinism and materialism to some Wagnerians, others questioned its moral prudishness. Whenever commentators argued that good music could only be composed by artists who met Victorian standards of propriety, Wagnerians enjoyed challenging such tenets. In fact, by the century's end the Wagnerian movement included an influential contingent of aesthetes, decadents, and symbolists who celebrated the rediscovery of the nonlogical, the unconscious, and especially the erotic in Wagner's art. These intensely self-preoccupied Wagnerians probed the dimensions of human psychic experience.

Though Wagner's influence was stronger in the more homogenous culture of England than in America, the Wagnerism of the two countries followed essentially the same pattern. Certainly this movement helped stimulate the internationalist view of art that became such an important feature of the fin-de-siècle mentality. Nevertheless a filtering did take place. Wagner's anti-Semitism embarrassed his English and American disciples from the outset, and their Wagner societies never took on the characteristics of a racist political cult, as some Wagner societies elsewhere had done. Nationalism did not affect the movement in either country until the outbreak of World War I, although Wagner's example supported the recovery of the English, Scottish, and Irish folk tradition in art that was already under way. If, as David Large has argued earlier in this book, what was truly great in Wagner's legacy was considerably dwarfed in his Bayreuth disciples, then the Wagnerians in London and New York may provide a richer measure of his influence.

I

The first admirers of Wagner in Britain and the United States included a small number of German-born musicians and businessmen, a few members of the English artistic avant-garde, and a group of American critics determined to raise the level of the nation's musical culture.[3] Although Wagner's reception cannot be chronicled in full here, a brief account of the key episodes will establish the general picture.

Wagner made three visits to England. In 1839 he passed unnoticed through London on his way from Riga to Paris. In 1855 he was again in London to conduct a series of concerts for the Philharmonic Society. These experiences brought him little public acclaim, although his performance won the approbation of Queen Victoria and the Prince of Wales. His third visit, in 1877, was completely different, a stunning success artistically and socially, albeit not financially. Between 1855 and 1877 his way had been prepared by private performances of his works, by study groups, and by the writings of the Pre-Raphaelites and Francis (originally Franz) Hueffer, a German-born scholar who took up residence in London in 1869 and five years later published his book *Richard Wagner and the Music of the Future*. In 1873 the first London Wagner Society was founded, and in 1876 many English traveled to the opening of the Bayreuth Festival. Thus by the time of Wagner's 1877 visit it is no wonder that he and Cosima were the center of gala social evenings attended by artists and writers such as George Eliot, Robert Browning, George Meredith, George Grove, William Morris, Hubert Parry, and Moncure Conway, or that he was wined and dined by the civil engineer William Pole and the industrialist Wilhelm Siemens, or that he was the main attraction at a reception attended by four hundred people at the Grosvenor Gallery.

Fully staged productions of Wagnerian opera in London, which began with *Der fliegende Holländer,* sung in Italian in 1870, reached a peak in 1888 with the initial performances of *Tristan und Isolde, Die Meistersinger von Nürnberg,* and *Der Ring des Nibelungen,* all sung in German. Charles Santley reminisced that in 1876 he sang the title roll of *Lohengrin* not only in the capital but also on a strenuous tour of fifty performances in the provinces.[4] In the critical commentary on these productions, two features of Wagner's English reception stand out. First, London audiences included a "Teutonic element," Germans who by their example instructed astonished aristocratic patrons that singers were secondary to the work they were interpreting and should be applauded only at the end of the performance.[5] Second, critics reported the rise of a more earnest and educated audience from the business classes who enjoyed opera in the original languages and gradually infiltrated the subscription lists.[6]

The introduction of Wagner's music to nineteenth-century America appears to have followed a similar pattern. Both long-settled Americans and recent German immigrants helped establish it on American shores. One of the former was William Mason, a music educator and pianist who belonged to a large family of New Englanders that had contributed much to music in the new nation. Mason had studied in Europe when a young man, and in his memoirs he records that during an interview with Wagner in 1852 he had been captivated by Wagner's exuberance and that he had also been one of a claque of Wagner admirers at a performance in Weimar.[7]

That same year in New York, Karl Bergmann, an enterprising musician from Eisenach, conducted the first known performance of any of Wagner's music in the United States, a selection from the finale of *Tannhäuser*. News of the concert spread, and Bergmann's Germania Orchestra was invited to Boston, where they gave the first all-Wagner concert in America on December 3, 1853. It was on that evening that Henry Wadsworth Longfellow listened to music he described as "strange, original, and somewhat barbaric." Bergmann also conducted the first American performance of *Tannhäuser* at the old Stadt Theatre in New York on April 4, 1859, seventeen years before the first London performance. The audience could not fairly have been called typical of the American public, and only the *Staats-Zeitung* published a review and a full list of the cast.[8] Bergmann was joined by other European-born conductors: Frederic Louis Ritter, Leopold Damrosch, and, most significantly, Theodore Thomas, later the founder of the Chicago Symphony Orchestra. Thomas opened his first concert as director of the Brooklyn Philharmonic in May 1862 with the first American performance of the overture to *Der fliegende Holländer*. He founded the New York Wagner Union in 1872, raised ten thousand dollars for Bayreuth, and conducted Wagner's music frequently.

Wagner himself never visited the United States, but he nonetheless carried on a romance with that country, which he regarded, in contrast to parsimonious England, as a haven from his creditors, a potential gold mine, and a wide-open space waiting to be populated by musicians. American entrepreneurs were sympathetic. In 1855 the Mason Brothers firm offered Wagner a lucrative honorarium to conduct for six months in the United States. Too busy with the *Ring,* Wagner eventually refused. Gustav Kobbé, an American Wagnerian, interpreted this offer as "one of the most remarkable facts in the history of Wagnerism because it could truly be said that Wagner's genius was recognized here far earlier in his career than it was abroad."9 Americans, "unfettered" as they were by musical tradition, wrote Kobbé, were freer to appreciate new musical forms. In 1873, opera patrons in Chicago, perhaps from the local Wagner society, offered to produce the *Ring* there.10 In 1876 the women's centennial committees of Philadelphia, New York, and Cincinnati raised the funds to pay for Wagner's "Grand Inauguration March." Reasonably well received at the time, it was soon recognized for the potboiler it was. As Wagner himself said, "The most beautiful thing about it was the check for five thousand dollars."11

In 1879, Wagner contributed a two-part article to the *North American Review* entitled "The Work and Mission of My Life." In it he expressed the Wagnerian brew of cosmopolitan nationalism, stating that there were really two sets of Germans. The Germans living in the Germany of his day were petty philistines, essentially not German, a condition he attributed to the historical corruption of German culture by foreign elements, especially French and Jewish. The real Germans did not live in Germany but were citizens of other states, either through immigration or because their ancestors had amalgamated in ancient times with other peoples in places where the development of German art and genius might flourish. "The ideal of the German spirit," said Wagner, "shows continually that it is a strength not national but *international;* and it preserves for the great motherstem of the race the esteem and honor of the countries of the world."12 There followed an account of his vision of the historical evolution of German art mingled with the tale of his own hopes and plans, trials and tribulations. He explained that the experience of his long life had taught him to his sorrow that support of such a purely ideal cause as the Bayreuth Festival could not be expected from the Germans. "German art will never be placed in a position of security by the voluntary act of the German nation."13 Wagner concluded his essay by reminding readers that he had given his "Grand Inauguration March" a motto from Goethe's *Faust:* "He only has true liberty—true life— / To whom they are the prize of daily strife." Wagner had tried to express this quality, which he called "ideal energy," in the march, and he was gratified to observe that his purpose had been recognized in the reviews of its performance.

In the conclusion of his article Wagner invoked the name of former President Ulysses S. Grant, reminding American readers that Grant had prophesied that all the world would one day speak a common language. Considering that when Wagner and Grant met in Heidelberg in 1877 they could not communicate with one another in any language, we may think that Wagner had his tongue placed firmly in his cheek here. But be that as it may, he made the suggestion that German music become the unifier of nations and that Americans join with him as "earnest co-workers in the domain of ideal spiritual progress."[14] It was this domain of ideal progress that attracted his American followers.

Between 1884, the year following the opening of the Metropolitan Opera, and 1891, Wagner's American "coworkers" enjoyed the Met's first staged performances, in German, of the *Ring, Tristan und Isolde,* and *Die Meistersinger.* Like London, New York had a German-speaking population, a quarter of a million people, according to contemporary estimates. Irving Kolodin credits this German presence with the success of these productions. Three-quarters of the Metropolitan's public was German; it wanted and it got both German opera—Wagner primarily—and opera in German.[15] Kolodin also suggests that, as in London, a knowledgeable audience was emerging. After the new company's first seasons, tension erupted during performances, between the holders of boxes and the ordinary ticket buyers; the latter wanted to hear opera and hissed the former, who wanted to talk.[16]

In the United States, however, unlike in Britain, Wagner was also championed by a group of critics, including W. F. Apthorp, H. E. Krichbiel, C. D. Warner, and J. R. G. Hassard, whose Emersonian goal was to tame (though not abolish) American materialism with the power of cosmopolitan culture. J. A. Mussulman, who examined the criticism of the period in a study entitled *Music in the Cultured Generation* (1971), challenges the common assumption that American culture at the end of the nineteenth century was governed largely by commercial considerations and bad taste. Analyzing monthly literary magazines, he found that the essayists who appeared in their pages carried on reasoned discourse about progress in the arts, believing that the power of culture should moderate the power of wealth. The preponderance of opinion in these magazines favored Wagner. Between 1870 and 1900, fifty articles on Wagner appeared in the *Atlantic Monthly, Harper's New Monthly Magazine, Century Illustrated Monthly,* and *Scribners Magazine.* These critics welcomed Wagner's contributions to both musical theory and the ideal of cultural progress.

Both in Britain and the United States, many Wagnerians ignored or attempted to explain away portions of what the public considered to be Wagner's eccentricities; that is, his political radicalism, anti-Semitism, and flamboyant life-style. Francis Hueffer was instrumental on both sides of the Atlantic in persuading people to view Wagner's participation in the revolutions of 1848 as an artistic rather than a political enterprise. As we shall see later on, however, one notable exception to this tendency to gloss over Wagner's political activism was the often iconoclastic Bernard Shaw.

Wagner's anti-Semitism was particularly troublesome to his admirers. His *Judaism in Music* first came to the attention of the English-speaking public in February 1855, when Ferdinand Praeger, a German music teacher living in London, mentioned the tract in an article published in the New York *Musical Gazette* and then summarized by English papers. Wagner was about to conduct some of his own music in a series of concerts in London in March. Praeger, a self-appointed defender of Wagner, wrongly anticipated negative reviews of the concerts from London critics, many of whom were known to be Mendelssohn supporters. He therefore heaped insults on the critics. His article merely annoyed them and also underscored Wagner's anti-Semitism. William Ashton Ellis, Wagner's most obsessive English acolyte, said years later that he wished Praeger had acted more prudently and ignored the *Judaism* essay. Ellis told the Royal Music Association in 1892 that the essay was one of Wagner's least important writings and that the only one that he would "honestly like to see suppressed" was "A Capitulation," the Master's diatribe against the French.[17] Meanwhile, the crown princess of Prussia had written to her mother, Queen Victoria, that she had never read anything "so violent, conceited, or unfair" as Wagner's pamphlet on the Jewish influence in music.[18]

In the United States, *Dwight's Journal of Music,* the leading publication in the field between 1852 and 1881, called Wagner's essay "ignoble," "small-minded," and "a disgrace."[19] Edward Burlingame quietly dropped the essay from his 1875 edition of Wagner's writings, along with other pieces he regarded "as of too temporary and merely national interest to survive."[20] In his 1893 two-volume biography of Wagner, Henry T. Finck devoted twenty-five pages to the essay. He did not deny Wagner's anti-Semitism or the prevalence of anti-Semitism generally, but he minimized its virulence, emphasizing Wagner's criticism of Mendelssohn and Meyerbeer as artists. On the other hand, piano teacher Albert Ross Parsons, in the course of defending *Parsifal* as a Christian drama repeated Wagner's harsh view of Old Testament Judaism.

The complaints about Wagner's personal behavior arose from his negligent attitude toward creditors and from the scandal of his love affairs. In England the famous Wagner biographer Ernest Newman did not hesitate to speak of Wagner's "moral shabbiness" in business and love, though this did not lessen his admiration for Wagner as a musician. The matter was also raised in various articles concerning Wagner that appeared between 1881 and 1893 in the *Proceedings of the Royal Music Association*. Americans, on the other hand, tended to admire Wagner's entrepreneurial vigor, which they equated with "yankee push" and praiseworthy determination.[21] While mention was occasionally made of his unconventional mores and more often of offensive relationships in the operas, most Americans could excuse a little eccentricity or even degeneracy in a European.

The Anglo-American experience of Wagnerian opera was continually renewed owing to a procession of British and American tourists—from the aristocratic diplomat Lord Redesdale to the anarchist Emma Goldman—who visited Bayreuth and other European music centers. Londoner Joseph Bennett made the trip to Bayreuth, where he observed "enthusiastic Yankee ladies . . . wild-looking Germans . . . , unbelieving Frenchmen and English pilgrims not a few."[22] Philadelphian Clare Benedict went abroad in 1879 and remained in Europe for fourteen years, often in the company of her aunt, novelist Constance Fenimore Woolson. After making a pilgrimage to Bayreuth, she eulogized Wagner as the recipient of a divine spark.[23] She thought that a godlike power worked through him and that he had an ennobling influence on his disciples. Less fervidly, Charles Dudley Warner, American essayist and editor, commented on the success of the Bayreuth atmosphere: "It is of course possible that the crowds of Bayreuth were victims of a delusion, and of skillful contrivance. I can answer for many of them that they would like to be deluded again in just that way."[24] His friend and one-time collaborator Mark Twain also visited "the shrine of St. Wagner." Twain's observations, as might be expected, were irreverent, but he was by no means immune to Bayreuth's power to enchant. Claiming that he was present merely as an escort, he was nevertheless attentive to all aspects of the Bayreuth experience. As a good American he complained of the hypnotic and antidemocratic effect on the audiences made by the appearance of royalty at Bayreuth performances. He also questioned why so many Americans should turn up in Bayreuth when they could have heard the same operas in New York, but he soon realized that the two experiences were quite different:

> Yesterday the opera was *Tristan and Isolde.* I have seen all sorts of audiences . . . . but none which was twin to the Wagner audience of Bayreuth for fixed, reverential attention. . . . You know they are stirred to their profoundest depths; that there are times when they want to rise and wave handkerchiefs and shout their approbation, and times when tears are running down their faces, and that it would be a relief to free their pent emotions in sobs or screams; yet you hear not one utterance till the curtain swings together. . . . Then the dead rise with one impulse and shake the building with applause. . . . Here the Wagner audiences dress as they please, and sit in the dark and worship in silence. At the Metropolitan in New York they sit in a glare, and wear their showiest harness; they hum airs, they squeak fans, they titter, and they gabble all the time. . . . Can that be an agreeable atmosphere to persons in whom this music produces a sort of divine ecstacy?[25]

Mark Twain loved *Tannhäuser,* describing it as "an opera which has always driven me mad with ignorant delight whenever I have heard it." Though he felt out of place at Bayreuth, sometimes "like a sane person in a community of the mad," he concluded that it was "one of the most extraordinary experiences of my life. . . . I have never seen anything so fine and real as this devotion."[26]

II

By the 1880s, Wagner, having been introduced by the few, now clearly belonged to the many. Germans living abroad, the artistic avant-garde and the idealistic guardians of culture had all played a role in his rise to favor in the English-speaking world. Though Wagner's theories, music, and personality would always remain repugnant to some and subjects for satire to others, by the last decades of the century the public on the whole heard his music frequently and with plea-sure.[27] The acceptance of Wagner's musical style, however, was only the beginning of the story: the popular enthusiasm for Wagner grew into a mania that had little to do with admiration for his musicianship. It is impossible to explain on aesthetic or formal grounds alone why so many nineteenth-century Britons and Americans should have consid-ered Wagner to be worthier than other great composers. Rather, the explanation lies in his role as cultural critic and moralist. His passionate though parochial analysis of the weaknesses of nineteenth-century civ-ilization, buoyed by his art, was the source of his extraordinary appeal.

Debate on this larger significance of Wagnerian opera and thought rose to extraordinary heights in the 1880s and 1890s, leaving its im-print as well on the generation that was born in the Edwardian era and matured after the First World War. The London Wagner society, orga-nized in 1873 to support performances of Wagner's music, had served its purpose. In 1888 English Wagnerians formed a new Wagner society and, inspired by the Parisian *Revue wagnérienne,* began to publish a quarterly journal called *The Meister.* The burden of *The Meister*'s mes-sage was that Wagner's genius was not only musical but also philo-sophical. Its editor, William Ashton Ellis, wrote that through his art Wagner "fought his way to social problems of the deepest interest and to the vital questions of religion and a higher world" and that "had he never composed one bar of music and never conceived one scene of drama, his prose works alone would have ranked him among the foremost thinkers of his day."[28] Though in less extravagant terms than *The Meister,* Theodore Thomas acknowledged that Wagnerian opera appealed to the modern spirit and attracted even the less musical to the opera and concert stage.[29] Clare Benedict also observed that Wagner's following included many "fine, unmusical souls who asked nothing better than to spend their strength and substance serving his ideas."[30] And Sir Thomas Beecham remarked upon the linking of Wagner with "every recent 'ism' in philosophy, politics, and even hygiene."[31]

The Meister's characterization of Wagner's appeal suggests a dichoto-my between two kinds of Wagnerians, some who emphasized the social implications of Wagner's works and others who stressed spir-itual, esoteric, or inner meanings. The former considered themselves practical, secular, and rational. Among the latter could be found the traditionally pious, the occultists, and the connoisseurs of emotion. Unlike the British, few notable American Wagnerians emphasized purely secular interpretations. Most Americans approached his music dramas in search of spiritual uplift. Even so, Wagnerians of both groups thought themselves progressive and modern-minded.

In Britain, the best examples of the first group were David Irvine, Bernard Shaw, Rutland Boughton, and, to a lesser degree, Ernest Newman. The first two concerned themselves with a critique of capitalism and classical liberalism, but in very different ways.

Scotsman David Irvine (1856–1930) wrote six individual volumes on Wagner and his music dramas. As devoted a disciple as anyone at Bayreuth, he turned the Master to a different end. Irvine considered churches and conservative political regimes intellectually, morally, and socially bankrupt. He saw himself as a proponent of liberalism, by which he meant "a compound of radical politics, Protestantism, and Rationalism."[32] The liberalism of his day, however, lacked a firm basis in moral philosophy. It was a creed that relieved mankind of its moral responsibility "in the belief that things will come right of themselves."[33] Excessive individualism was its cardinal weakness. Believing that moral progress required a more secure foundation than that of biological evolution, Irvine devoted his energies to supplying the missing philosophy in two treatises, *Philosophy and Christianity* (1905) and *Metaphysical Rudiments of Liberalism* (1911), and in the six volumes on Wagner.

Irvine considered Schopenhauer and Wagner "the leading geniuses of Liberalism."[34] His remedy for liberalism's defects combined the former's ethical pessimism with the spiritual insights of the latter's music dramas. Like Wagner, Irvine believed that the essence of religion was revealed through art. Wagner's operas, he believed, were the artistic analogue of Schopenhauer's message. According to Irvine, in the *Ring* cycle Wagner portrayed an unconscious struggle between partisans of power for its own sake and believers in life and love. By contrast, in *Parsifal* the struggle took place within the consciousness of the characters. *Parsifal* was the greatest artistic embodiment of Schopenhauer's moral philosophy. As Irvine summarized it: "To combat the egoistic sensual will, there is needed the compassionate and spiritual will. All of this battleground is on earth. Man is both God and

Devil."[35] For Irvine, the true site of Christianity lay not in the churches or in God but in the heart of humanity.

Irvine had no specific political program; he wrote briefly of the need for socialistic government and democracy but spent much of his time criticizing other viewpoints. His "compleat liberal" was not an elected official, or necessarily anyone in power, but an independent philosopher or artist. Nevertheless he argued that the Schopenhaurian-Wagnerian philosophy he articulated "was the only means of giving democracy the moral instruction necessary for its unalloyed welfare."[36]

The service of Bernard Shaw, playwright and Fabian socialist, to music criticism in general and to the understanding of Wagner's music in particular is well known. His plays, novels, and prefaces are replete with Wagnerian allusions. In both *Widowers' Houses* and *Major Barbara,* Shaw offered Wagnerian variations on the themes of capitalism and social justice.[37] His idea of the "drama of impassioned thought" reflected his understanding of Wagner's notion of the theater.[38] *Back to Methusaleh,* in particular, was a tribute to Wagner. This quintet of plays was an optimistic legend of evolution, a sort of moral and spiritual science fiction, beginning with the Garden of Eden and ending with the self-completion of human evolution thirty thousand years later. Shaw regarded both Wagner's *Ring* and his own *Back to Methusaleh* as a reaching forward to a new vitalist art.

Shaw's major contribution to Wagnerism, however, was *The Perfect Wagnerite,* which was first published in 1889 and went through four revised editions by 1923. It argued that blind devotion was "no true Wagnerism"; the Wagnerite must comprehend Wagner's ideas. Shaw saw in Wagner's *Ring* "a poetic vision of unregulated capitalism as it was made known in Germany in the middle of the nineteenth century by Engels' *The Condition of the Working Class in England in 1844.*"[39] The *Ring* was a socialist allegory with "a most urgent and searching philosophical and social significance." Though most other Fabians were unmoved by this interpretation, Shaw insisted that Wagner's gods, dwarfs, and dragons were not medieval but modern symbols.[40] *Das Rheingold,* of course, opens with the theft of the gold by an ugly dwarf who renounced love for power. "Such dwarfs are quite common in London," wrote Shaw; they had enslaved millions of workers.[41]

The *Ring* satisfied Shaw up to the point where Siegfried shatters Wotan's world-governing spear. The rest of the tetralogy, as far as he was concerned, deteriorated into old-fashioned grand opera and romantic utopianism. By the time the third edition (1913) of *The Perfect Wagnerite* appeared, Shaw had come up with a new view of what constituted the *Ring*'s anticlimax.[42] Between 1850 and 1876, he wrote, the Alberichs had transformed themselves into the Carnegies. Capitalism had changed, become more complex, more capable of transforming itself. State socialism and welfare capitalism had been anticipated. Siegfried was outdated. Much shaken by World War I, Shaw in his fourth preface (1922) saw a new prophetic and pessimistic meaning in *Die Götterdämmerung*. The world war had not invalidated the *Ring;* it had only made the Alberichs richer.

Bernard Shaw was already famous when a young man named Rutland Boughton (1878–1960) publicly took him to task because, in Boughton's opinion, Shaw's brand of socialism failed to live up to what Boughton thought were Wagner's communistic ideals.[43] There followed a bantering correspondence between the two men that in later years ripened into friendship. Best known today as the composer of the opera *The Immortal Hour,* Boughton worked for forty years on an Arthurian cycle, his version of a *Ring,* which he completed in 1945.

Boughton's politics and aesthetics were a rich nineteenth-century blend of the social ideals of Tolstoy, William Morris, Ruskin, Whitman, Edward Carpenter, Marx, Carlyle, and Wagner. In 1907 he composed a symphonic setting for "Midnight," a poem from Carpenter's "Toward Democracy." This, according to Boughton's biographer, was the "first unequivocal statement of his socialist beliefs."[44] Poems by Morris and Whitman also received musical settings. Some of Whitman's admirers had felt a strong connection between the works of Wagner and of Whitman and had regarded Wagner's operas as *Leaves of Grass* done into music.[45] Boughton was determined to create a Whitmanesque democratic musical art for the English people.

In 1911, Boughton coauthored a Wagnerian tract, not surprisingly entitled *Music Drama of the Future*. At that time he thought of composing an epic drama in the style of Wagner (and requiring fourteen days to perform) on the subject of the life of Jesus as applied to modern circumstances. After further reading on the theme of music and democracy, however, he decided that the greatest artists acquired their power not by using the "alien" symbols of traditional church dramas but by giving expression to the "oversoul" of their people. "Then I understood why Wagner had chosen those folk subjects which had been produced by that oversoul."[46] Thus Boughton decided to abandon the Holy Scriptures for national scriptures—the Arthurian legends. At this juncture he was offered a set of original poems on that subject by Reginald Buckley (1882–1919), an eager young writer. Buckley explained that it was Wagner's *Tannhäuser* that first revealed to him a new world and had sent him to the study of Wagner's prose essays. He dreamed of using the English legends as "the quarry from which to hew a large music drama on the lines of Wagner's *Ring,* with Merlin as Britain's Isaiah, Galahad her Parsifal, Arthur her type of manhood. Amid all the talk of 'super-men,' in an age of philosophical and artistic healers and quacks, I longed for a dramatic and poetic art, wherein the sane, healthy English might bathe, as in the pure rhythmic seas of Cornwell, loved by all flaming souls, from the Round Table till now."[47] Boughton and Buckley together proposed a scheme for a "temple theater." This was not to be, as some Wagnerians suggested, an English Bayreuth performing Wagner's operas exclusively.[48] Rather it was to be a temple of English art, erected at the center of an agricultural commune. Boughton and Buckley believed that "real art can only grow out of real life."[49] It was their intention to join two honorable types of men: the workman and the artist. The workman would have room to develop his soul through art and the artist to develop his body in contact with the basic facts of existence. In 1914 they created the Glastonbury Festival for opera and drama. Though Glastonbury, which flourished until 1926, was not the utopian community Boughton had envisaged earlier, it did provide him with the opportunity to use local performers and to produce his own English music dramas.

Boughton also proposed reforming existing English music festivals. Again his inspiration was Bayreuth. He complained that the typical triennial provincial festival consisted of "gatherings of folks as are too kind, or too lazy to pot grouse" and offered very tame fare.[50] The newer festivals that stressed musical competition were apt to be boring as well, he thought. Who wanted to hear twenty-five children play the same excerpt from Handel? He proposed that competition be limited. Citing Bayreuth and ancient Greece as examples, he suggested that the festival be a public holiday for all. "Fine art cannot be made or appreciated by toiltorn people."[51] Finally, such festivities should be local. Musicians should not be hired from other places; rather, as in Germany, local performers should be encouraged.

It should not be supposed that Boughton was entirely uncritical of Wagner. As far as he was concerned, Wagner's great flaw was his neglect of the chorus. Wagner, he thought, had used choral singing minimally; Wagner's Greek chorus was really his orchestra. In contrast to such a choral orchestra, Boughton promised an orchestral chorus:

> The outstanding reason for this orchestral chorus is to give expression to that national mass feeling to which I have already alluded. . . . The choral orchestra of Wagner has for its function the sense-expression of the primitive wonder [of Life]; but only our orchestral chorus can link-on the feeling and the action to the minds of the audience, and join them in the feeling that the drama is their own, both individually and as a joyously united body.[52]

Wagner's orchestra might suggest character and mood but could not appeal to the higher centers of the mind or raise the level of consciousness from the personal to the universal, according to Boughton. His view of the chorus is comparable to that of the Russian Wagnerians Vyacheslav Ivanov and Georgi Chulkov, whom Bernice Rosenthal has discussed in chapter 5 of this volume, but it was less politically charged. They substituted the chorus for elective political institutions as the most authentic expression of the popular will. Unlike the Russians, Boughton did not suggest that chorus and parliament were opposites or that the chorus was the only true expression of democracy. His chorus was but one vehicle of community consciousness.

Boughton never repudiated his youthful enthusiasms; indeed he developed them. Undeterred by Shaw's worry that he might produce a second-rate *Ring,* he continued to work on his Arthurian cycle.[53] In the completed work, King Arthur has cemented an alliance between church and state. All are corrupt. The masses rebel and are defeated. Eventually, Christian civilization is saved from the east in a vision of red stars and revolution.[54] It is ironic that the most popular of these music dramas was *The Lily Maid.* Despite the fact that Boughton's Lancelot has a fascist cast of mind, the story of Elain was mainly personal and romantic, not political.

Boughton was a member of the Communist Party in Britain between 1926 and 1929, and again between 1945 and 1956. The General Strike in Britain precipitated his first enrollment in the Party, and the Soviet repression of the Hungarian revolt ended his second try. His communism was hardly the orthodox Marxist-Leninist or Stalinist variety; rather it was more in keeping with the spirit of Marx and Wagner, the revolutionaries of 1848. According to his biographer, Boughton believed that communism was "the natural goal of Christian civilization and that peace and goodwill were only to be secured in a world where people live in conditions of approximate material equality.[55] In 1926 Boughton outlined his position on communism and art. As a musician, he was "continually robbed of the real benefits" of his work and at the same time was the object of charity (sentiments that had been shared by Mozart and Liszt as well as Wagner). Boughton further argued that the capitalist system permitted only a few artists to create "artistic dope" for the consumption of the elite. There would be no room for true appreciation of art "until all human beings [including musicians] are properly fed, clothed, housed, and educated."[56]

Boughton's brand of Wagnerism had no exact analogue in the United States. Poet, playwright, and librettist Percy MacKaye (1875–1956) came close, however. One contemporary described him as "a crusader for the gospel of democracy in drama and for the development of the theater as a force toward the kindling of a higher social consciousness."[57] MacKaye lamented the role of the profit motive in retarding the growth of national art and deplored the American tendency to remain, in aesthetic inspiration, the "suburbanites of Paris, Berlin, Rome, [and] London."[58] He identified two categories of American drama and called for an additional type. The first kind was drama for the few, exemplified by American imitations of the decadent bourgeois theater of Europe. The second was vaudeville, a melange of trifling amusements. His ideal was the drama of democracy, or a fine art for the many. In defending this ideal, MacKaye turned first to the Greeks and ended with the example of Wagner:

> In our own time, in the cognate field of music, we have beheld the analogous birth and growth of a universal fine art, through the vision and will of a single artist. Less than fifty years ago, the Wagnerian opera had neither theatres, audiences, nor interpreters; its technique was scoffed at; its practicality was denied; its possibilities of popular appeal ignored or ridiculed. We know what it is today. But what Wagner accomplished for the drama of song and musical motif may equally be accomplished for the drama of speech and the motif of verse, and with far deeper effect upon the self-development of our whole people, inasmuch as the spoken drama may enter, not as a beautiful thing apart, but as a forming influence, a critical and self-revealing inspiration, into the very sources of our national life.[59]

Comparing Mozart's *Don Giovanni* with Wagner's *Siegfried,* Ibsen with Shakespeare, and Maeterlinck with Sophocles, MacKaye argued that elitist art, isolated and fragmented, depicts only individuals and segments of society; democratic art, images of all humanity. MacKaye was a prolific playwright. Educated at Harvard and in Italy and Germany, he attempted to put his ideals into practice by writing community drama, that is, masques and "pageant-rituals" with state, local, or national themes. One such drama, *St. Louis, A Civic Masque,* MacKaye said, had a cast of seventy-five hundred citizens and attracted half a million spectators. Its characters included hundreds of pioneers and earth spirits engaged in battle with the villain Gold and his wicked followers, an epic that was Wagnerian in theme and scale. Several of MacKaye's dramas became librettos for operas composed by Reginald de Koven and Frederick S. Converse.

Ernest Newman (1868–1959), perhaps the most important English music critic of this century, brought coolness and detachment to English Wagnerism. Born William Roberts, he began his professional life in a Liverpool bank and gradually moved into journalism. In an early work, *Pseudo-Philosophy at the End of the Nineteenth Century,* written under the name Hugh Mortimer Cecil, he argued against "modern forms of unreason."[60] Dedicated to Charles Darwin, the book was an attack on latter-day defenders of religion. Its author accepted no truce or compromise between the rationalist and the irrationalist. After writing this book and changing his name to Ernest Newman, he went on to apply the standards of scientific inquiry to the field of music criticism and to acquire a considerable reputation for meticulous scholarship combined with a distaste for attaching metaphysical or other extraneous meanings to music.[61] For example, in an article on music and race, Newman took Hubert Parry's study of music history to task for its illogical definition of such concepts as "Teutonic," "Gallic," "Celtic," and "Slavic." According to Parry, said Newman, one was forced to conclude that Haydn was a Teuton and Mozart was not, "the upshot of it all being that by 'Teutonic' Dr. Parry simply means earnestness and depth. If a composer has not the spirit, he is not a 'true Teuton.' The formula is utter chaos."[62] Newman agreed with John Stuart Mill that racist explanations of national character were vulgar.

Though Newman's musical interests were very broad, he was best known for his studies of opera, and of Wagner in particular. His four-volume biography of Wagner, written between 1926 and 1947, is still the standard life, despite the availability now of more archival material. Newman argued: "To appreciate a work of art it is not in the least necessary to subscribe to its author's philosophical or religious opinions; a rationalist can be as deeply thrilled by the *Matthew Passion* as any Christian can be. The "Thesis" of a work of art is the one thing in it that does not concern us as artists. Who is to decide between rival philosophies or sociologies? Personally, I believe that one philosophy is about as good as another, and worse, as the Irishman would say."[63] The theme of redemption in the operas did not impress Newman, who remarked that he did not understand redemption theologically but only as a feature of the pawnbroking business.[64] As for *Tristan,* he observed that "really musical people" never saw anything erotic in the music as "half-musical people" generally did. Nor did half-musical people ever appreciate what to the musician was glorious in *Tristan.*[65] Newman also argued that morals, whether Wagner's or his patrons', should have nothing to do with appreciation of his operas. He recalled, for instance, one critic who remarked, "in awestricken tones," that *Parsifal* was the favorite of a set of men who were mixed up in an unwholesome German scandal and "obviously thought that this discredited Wagner's *Parsifal*"; "whereas," Newman says, "it struck me as being very like asking us to give up having breakfast because some horrible murderer or other liked bacon and eggs."[66] Newman's skepticism was partly responsible for what one scholar has called the "critical muddle" he created for himself by denying the conflict between his need to place Wagner within Europe's musical tradition and his desire to recognize the composer's uniqueness in surpassing that tradition.[67] Wagner's art was a hybrid of music, poetry, and drama, often damned and certainly not easily accomodated by traditional music critics. In the end, Newman believed that Wagner would have been better served had he composed symphonic poems.

Thus Newman was no Wagnerian at all in the ideological sense of the term, for he did not see Wagnerian opera as the cultural accompaniment to political or social reform. To his way of thinking, the rational, secular approach precluded partisanship. Thus he battled to focus criticism on Wagner's music, not his ideas, in order to save it from friends and foes alike. On the other hand, he sometimes seemed to protest too much. In Vera Newman's biography of her husband, she noted his emotional response to both the musical form and thematic content of the operas.[68] Like Shaw, Irvine, and Boughton he despised churches, and it is not unlikely that, like them, he was also moved by humanistic concerns. *Parsifal,* he said in a deceptively disarming way, was "simply an artist's dream of an ideally innocent world, purged of the lust, the hatred, the cruelty that deface the world we live and groan in."[69] Moreover, it was in large part Newman's intense devotion and steadfast industriousness that kept Wagner before the British public. But had Newman, as William Blissett suggests, killed Wagner as priest and king?[70] Not so. Let us turn from those who, like Shaw, Boughton, or MacKaye, were interested in how Wagner's ideas were applicable to the "real," everyday world to the many more British-American Wagnerians who milked the music dramas for arcane, esoteric, or psychological knowledge.

III

Nietzsche once described *Parsifal* as Christianity arranged for Wagnerians. The reverse is also true. Many Christian thinkers adopted Wagner, although not without considerable debate. They welcomed his concern with the theme of redemption and interpreted his leitmotives as expressing a set of moral attitudes and religious symbols. They realized that by relying on myth and not history, Wagner avoided knotty issues raised by biblical criticism. In essence, Wagner offered the listener the experience of religious emotion without requiring him or her necessarily to bother about its orthodoxy. Thus Anglicans, Roman Catholics, and Presbyterians, clergy and lay people, on both sides of the Atlantic, found spiritual comfort in Wagner's music dramas.

Two of the more thoughtful Christian commentators were Peter Taylor Forsyth and Washington Gladden. Forsyth (1848–1921) was a Scottish Congregationalist minister who studied at Göttingen, where he became familiar with German theology and culture. He discussed Wagner in a series of lectures entitled *Religion in Recent Art,* which were published in 1911. To Forsyth, Wagner was the most gifted exponent of the semi-Christian atheism associated with Schopenhauer. Schopenhauer had overcome the superficialities of positivism, naturalism, and evolution, and Wagner had even transcended Schopenhauer. "It is doubtful," said Forsyth, "if any artist since the great medieval painters has worked under such a sense of the redemptive idea as Wagner."[71]

Washington Gladden (1836–1918) was a liberal American theologian, one of the founders of the social gospel movement. In 1903 he delivered the William Beldon Noble lectures at Harvard University, the purpose of which was "to extend the influence of Jesus as the way, the truth, and the light, the perfection of spiritual man." Gladden's theme was "witnesses of the light," and he included among them Dante, Michelangelo, Fichte, Hugo, Ruskin, and Wagner.[72] According to Gladden, Wagner's services to art included creating a new definition of melody and a new concept of the fellowship of the arts. A greater service, however, was his elevation of the whole concept of music drama. Gladden told his Harvard audience that Wagner believed the drama "ought to be a source of refinement and moral invigoration; that it ought to suggest great thoughts and high ideals. . . It must spring from the life of the people; and it must reflect and criticize and idealize the life of the people; its function was therefore an exalted and even a sacred one."[73] Even more important, Gladden said, was that Wagner's dramas grappled with the great themes of spiritual life. In all his operas "deep ethical laws are found working themselves out; sin and its consequences—the retributions of violated law, and redemption through suffering and sacrifice—these great religious ideas are presented over and over, with tremendous power."[74]

For religious Wagnerians the *Ring* justifiably inspired many interpretations. Freda Winworth, in *The Epic of Sounds,* set forth an "ethical exegesis" of the cycle.[75] The American Mary B. Lewis, in *The Ethics of Wagner's "Ring of the Nibelung"* (1906), explained that the characters of the *Ring* represented steps or degrees in the ethical progress of mankind. Oliver Hückel, a Congregationalist clergyman from Greenwich, Connecticut, pointed out the "great spiritual and eternal truths" in the music dramas.[76] Octavia Hensel (Mary Alice Ives Seymour), American author of novels, music history, and Episcopalian tracts, wrote *The Rheingold Trilogy,* a study of the *Ring*'s ideals in the spirit of Wagner discipleship. Forsyth acknowledged that the last lines of *Die Götterdämmerung* sounded to him "like Scripture, and one reads them over and over again with new delight and cheer."[77]

Parsifal was the most compelling opera to Wagnerian Christians. Gladden recorded his heartfelt impressions of its performance at Bayreuth, as did Hugh Reginald Haweis, a well-traveled Anglican cler-

gyman. Essayist Charles Dudley Warner did not feel that he had merely attended an opera but that he had witnessed "some sacred drama,
perhaps a modern miracle play."[78] He objected only to the Flower
Maidens scene, which he thought could have been more subtle. Sabine
Baring-Gould, English clergyman and scholar, confessed that he did
not care much for the music but said that *Parsifal* was a true "poem of
the Sacramental Presence."[79] He characterized Kundry as a Catholic,
saved by faith and good works, and Amfortas as a Protestant, relying
on faith alone and unwilling to lift a finger on his own behalf. Many
commentaries of this kind were published. A complete study of them
would shed light on what Wagnerian Christians thought to be the
problems of religious faith in their day, issues not only of dogma but
also of the conduct of the church as a social institution.

In 1878, Sidney Lanier, the Georgia-born poet, wrote, "O Wagner,
Westward bring thy heavenly art."[80] On December 24, 1903, *Parsifal*
was brought, contrary to the wishes of the Bayreuth establishment,
westward to the Metropolitan Opera. Cosima insisted that *Parsifal* be
performed only in Bayreuth; the Metropolitan's manager, Heinrich
Conried, disagreed. A civil suit was instituted in New York, and the
courts ruled that because no copyright agreement existed between the
United States and Germany, no violation of the law had taken place,
and no injunction to stop performances could be granted. The litiga-
tion aroused much public excitement about the production, and so did
the quarrels between Wagnerian and anti-Wagnerian clergymen as to
the propriety of the drama. The Rev. George L. Shearer, of the American Tract Society, charged that the Lord's Supper was prostituted by
being depicted in a stage play. Frederick Burgess, Episcopal bishop of
Long Island, voiced the same concern. Others thought, mistakenly,
that the Parsifal character was to appear as Christ. Clergymen of many
denominations were reported to be organizing a committee to discourage the public from attending. Pro-Wagner clergy and other pros-
elytizers quickly arranged a series of educational lectures and publications. Howard Duffield, minister of New York's Old First Presbyter-
ian Church, was one defender. In *Parsifal, the Guileless Fool,* he described the opera as a reinterpretation of the medieval miracle play.
Richard Heber Newton (1840–1914), an Episcopal clergyman in New
York, was another advocate. Considered a liberal theologian, he had
commented in the past on such diverse subjects as biblical criticism,
evolutionary biology, civic and labor questions, psychic research, and

womanhood. His *"Parsifal"*: *An Ethical and Spiritual Interpretation* was originally given as a lecture in a private home "with a view to helping some genuine music-lovers and devout Christians, who were troubled by the denunciations of *Parsifal* on the part of eminent clergymen"[81] and was subsequently repeated at least twice more publicly. Newton traced Wagner's growth from pagan to Christian and in the process recommended other writings on Wagner by Gladden, Oliver Hückel, and especially Albert Ross Parsons. Parsons, the dean of New York piano teachers, had received his education in Germany and had translated Wagner's study of Beethoven. In 1889, Newton invited him to deliver a lecture at All Souls Church in New York, which Parsons entitled *"Parsifal,* The Finding of Christ through Art; or Richard Wagner as Theologian." Parsons subsequently published an expanded version heavily larded with quotations from Schopenhauer and from Wagner's later prose essays.[82]

Despite, or perhaps because of the controversy, the Metropolitan Opera's first *Parsifal* was a success. According to the newspaper accounts, which considerably exaggerated the seating capacity of the Met, seven thousand people attended, and ten thousand tried and failed to get in. Much of New York society was present, as was a large contingent from Chicago and four hundred Philadelphians who had chartered a special train. Most of the protests subsided immediately after the performance, descriptions of which were recorded far and wide. In the April issue of *Pacific Monthly,* sandwiched between articles on the labor problem in San Francisco and beautiful Pacific coast homes, was an account of the famous evening.[83] Was *Parsifal* sacrilegious, the article asked? Was Wagner a Christian or a malicious atheist? The correspondent judiciously concluded that regardless of ethics, finance, or aesthetics, manager Conried had achieved a brilliant triumph.

If Wagner was enlisted as a supporter of Christianity, he was also hailed by many as a prophet of occultism. For example, an international group of distinguished artists, including Vasily Kandinsky, Aleksandr Scriabin, and William Butler Yeats, who were Wagnerians, were also students of theosophy, and they viewed Wagner as an unusually gifted seer. According to James Webb, in his detailed study of "the occult establishment," the hallmarks of occultist theosophy are: belief in new kinds of consciousness, spiritual journeys, and other worlds; belief that astrology, the cabala, herbal medicine and the like

are forms of knowledge that should never have been rejected by mainstream scholars; and a devotion to discovering esoteric symbolic
meanings in art as well as history. Hierophants awaited the coming of
the great new age of Aquarius. Webb describes Wagner's *Religion and
Art* as in many ways "the synthesis of all the goals of the Progressive
Underground in the period before the First World War."[84] In particular, he found that occultists regarded Wagner's treatment of myth as
confirmation of their own esoteric interpretations.

The case of William Ashton Ellis (1853–1919) demonstrates the
close relationship between Wagnerians and occultism in England. Ellis
was a physician and a member of the Theosophical Society; he attended its founder, Mme. Blavatsky, during her final illness. He was
also the most dedicated of Wagnerians, serving as editor of *The Meister*
(1888–1895), translating all of Wagner's prose, researching a biography of Wagner, and writing several articles and pamphlets about him.
Although evidence of Ellis's occultist views appears frequently in his
Meister articles, it is most apparent in an article written for *La société
nouvelle,* published in 1888, in which Ellis explained the meaning of
Wagner's operas in theosophical terms. The end of the nineteenth
century represented the culmination of a great historical cycle; it constituted both the apogee of materialism and the dawn of spiritual
wisdom.[85] Wagner was the herald of the new dawn. Each of his music
dramas made use of both exoteric and esoteric symbols, the former
easily comprehended and specific, the latter hidden and pointing to
universal religious truths. Ellis found examples of astral vision, reincarnation, and purification rites in the operas. The *Ring,* in his view,
described the progress of history toward a more spiritual plane. *Parsifal*
was pure theosophy, its symbolism an almost perfect union of the
Christian and the Buddhist.[86] Wagner stressed compassion, broth-
erhood, and renunciation of self. The Grail fraternity was clearly a
body of occultists similar to *mahatmas* and *chelas* (masters and novices).
Klingsor was a black magician, Parsifal a Buddha.

The occult Wagnerian undercurrent in England flowed into the
twentieth century. Cyril Scott (1879–1970), an English composer, pianist, and writer, believed that Wagner was used, albeit intermittently,
by "the Masters Who recognized in him the finest musical medium
They were likely to have for the next fifty years or so."[87] In several of
his operas, Wagner portrayed Divine Love; that is, he reached the
"Buddhic" plane. Scott warned, however, that Wagner's music also

contained a strong element of nationalism: "Had Wagner's music been less 'German,' had the Buddhic element in it preponderated, had the bulk of the German people been sufficiently evolved to respond to its lofty vibrations," World War I might not have taken place.[88] Moreover, Wagner was used extensively by higher beings known as Devas; hence, his single-mindedness, egoism, and lack of a sense of proportion.

In the United States as late as 1948, Corrine Heline (1882–1953), a prolific writer on occult subjects, continued to claim that Wagner was "the New Age Messenger of music," an emmissary sent to earth from "the great inner-plane Temple of Music" where initiates learn to hear the music of the spheres.[89] According to Heline (whose work was reprinted in 1953), Wagner himself was working on a curriculum for esoteric musical training at the time of his passing. *Der fliegende Holländer* was a study of black and white magic; *Tannhäuser,* of purification; *Tristan und Isolde,* of the rite of mystic marriage; *Parsifal,* of temple initiation and consciousness; and the *Ring* a picture of the past, present, and future development of the human race. Applause was not allowed at Bayreuth, Heline wrote, because it disturbed "the beautiful astral patterns."[90]

More important in Anglo-American thought than occultism per se, in the twentieth century, was the confluence of occultism and Jungian psychology with Wagnerism. Jung's concept of archtypes functioning in the collective unconscious of humankind, which derived partly from his own studies in spiritualism, fit in well with the occultists' craving for universal religious symbols and distrust of positivist science. Robert Donington's *Wagner's "Ring" and Its Symbols* (1963) is a well-known Jungian interpretation of the operas, couched in terms of persona, anima, and shadow. Less well known is Franz Winkler's book *For Freedom Destined: Mysteries of Man's Evolution in the Mythology of Wagner's "Ring" Operas and "Parsifal,"* based on lectures given between 1964 and 1967 and published posthumously. This work combines criticism of modern materialism and technology, search for lost intuition, and an interest in Jungian archetypes, folklore, Wagner, and anthroposophy. Winkler (1907–1972) was an Austrian who emigrated to the United States in 1939. He specialized in internal and psychosomatic medicine, advised the Rudolf Steiner schools in the greater New York City area on health issues, and lectured extensively on drug abuse. Popular misconceptions of Darwin and Freud, he thought, which led to concentration on the satisfaction of merely biological drives and material ambitions, could only produce confusion and apathy, particularly in the young. In the lectures from which the book is derived, he argued that the "barren intellectual materialism of our age will drive our youth in ever-growing numbers into the pseudo-intuitive dream world of psychedelic drugs." What was needed was to revive the spiritual and intuitive faculties of happiness, love, and compassion that had grown weak through centuries of neglect and misunderstanding. Wagner understood that "a purely intellectual approach to cognition leads to disaster." Human beings must make use of both their intuitive and their intellectual faculties. Through Wagner flowed a wealth of long-forgotten truth and a kind of music that could "reopen the gateways of spiritual perception."[91] Winkler drew on Jung, the Bible, alchemy, and folklore to analyze the evolution of the psyche and the history of consciousness as given in the *Ring*. He found *Parsifal* the most profound of Wagner's works. Winkler's interpretive style is visible in his concluding remarks on *Parsifal:*

> The alchemists, for instance, knew about the possibility of transforming one metal into another, and they also knew that beneath solid matter . . . lay a cauldron of disintegration. Since the discovery of nuclear fission, this concept has been partly accepted today. What modern science is not yet willing to concede is that at the pole opposite to the mysterious realm of disintegration must exist an equally mysterious force of creation. . . . If modern terms are permissible, one might speak of a chain reaction of transsubstantiation, as contrasted with the chain reaction of nuclear disintegration.[92]

Like the philosopher's stone, the Grail, as Jung pointed out, represented matter on earth as permeated by the power of the Creator. Winkler viewed Parsifal and Kundry as the Adam and Eve of the future, partaking of wholesome, creative change. In Winkler's hands Wagnerism had become a prescription for individual balance and cultural good. The concern of Wagnerians for metaphysics had been channeled into mental health.

Many Wagnerians have described the remarkable psychological effects experienced by listeners to the music dramas. German emigré novelist Thomas Mann told a New York audience that he had experienced "hours of deep and single bliss, . . . nervous and intellectual transport and rapture."[93] Shaw said that he was "helpless under the spell of the *Ring*" and went "raving about the theatre between the acts in ecstacies of deluded admiration."[94] *Tannhäuser,* as we have seen, made Twain drunk with pleasure. The English music critic John Runciman reported that after listening to *Tristan,* he found all other operas reduced to babble. Who can stay even to listen to the most wonderful works of Mozart or Bach, he asked, "when Wagner calls us to listen concerning the innermost workings of our own being and speaks to us in a tongue every word of which enters the brain like a thing of life?"[95] William Wallace, a Scottish composer, found his mind released "in a flood of sound, careless about what [Wagner] meant, more solicitous about and concerned with the magician who captures and enthralls us by the spell of his music."[96] The music of Wagner also flooded the soul of the Rev. Hugh Haweis with "over-powering thoughts of the divine sacrifice and the mystery of unfathomable love. . . . Praise and criticism seemed dumb."[97] The narcosis described by clergymen attending Bayreuth seems little different in emotional substance from that experienced by aesthetes at performances of *Tannhäuser* or *Tristan.*

What accounts for these altered states of consciousness other than the beauty of Wagner's sound and his theatricality? Bryan Magee has suggested a Freudian solution: that Wagner's music acts in a way similar to the dream. It allows for the fulfillment of forbidden, often sexual wishes at once desired but also censored by the listener. The repressed contents of the psyche find an opportunity for indirect expression in some mysterious fashion through the listener's experience of the music.[98] Elliott Zuckerman, in his excellent *First Hundred Years of "Tristan,"* has distinguished between Wagnerism and Tristanism. Wagnerism is in part the result of doctrines and movements derived selectively from Wagner's ambiguous prose and often requiring little direct experience of the music. Tristanism, on the other hand begins with a direct response to the music and is private rather than public, the result of personal emotion rather than political commitment. "The Wagnerite must learn theories and cultivate habits. The Tristanite has only to be overwhelmed."[99] Scholar Donald Branam has proposed an explanation of what it meant to be overwhelmed by Wagner's opera. In an unpublished study of the Wagnerism of a Scottish physician, Agnes Savill, he argues that her touchstone was "a functional psychological one." Savill was the author of *Music, Health, and Character* (1923). Branam believes that her conversion to a love of music (*Par-*

sifal, in particular) after years of steadfast indifference cannot be attributed to religious anxiety, hypnosis, or release of the sexual unconscious but may be explained by the power of Wagner's music to lift people out of their daily mental and emotional preoccupations and to free their imaginations for contemplation of the immaterial and the infinite. Although some Wagnerians might have been addicted or obsessive, the majority of them were probably attracted to his music because it liberated rather than enslaved them.[100]

Wagner inspired not only clergymen and healers but also poets and novelists. Writers who rejected Victorian cultural conventions or literary traditions regarded Wagner as their mentor. Maurice Baring spoke for many of his generation in his autobiographical novel *C* when his youthful protagonist proclaimed that he would like a "crashing thundering Venusberg song to be sung before all his aunts, which would cause their conventions, creeds, prejudices, morals, and ideals to come crashing to the ground."[101] For William Butler Yeats, the Anglo-Irish poet, Wagner was a symbolist and mythmaker, contributing to "the new sacred book that all the arts were seeking to create."[102]

Often creative artists as well as critics responded to the operas because of the psychological insight into sex. Wagner, American critic James Huneker claimed, was "the greatest poet of passion the world has yet encountered."[103] English decadents, such as Aubrey Beardsley, Oscar Wilde, and Arthur Symons, agreed, although they derived their pleasure from the conflict of worldliness and renunciation within the music dramas and not from the passion alone.[104] The decadents' inversion of aesceticism had no appeal for Rutland Boughton. Having learned from Wagner's early writings analyzing the failure of Christian art and medieval civilization, Boughton argued that "because of the unnatural religious opposition to sex which had permeated Christian civilization, musical expressions of sex were comparatively unreal until the reaction from capitalism produced a music of revolt." Sex had been a subject for contempt, for fun, or for sickness. Only the most rebellious composers linked individual sexuality with the deeper mysteries of life, and only in the works of Wagner did sex become "a completed conscious force of the greatest importance." According to Boughton, Wagner tried but did not succeed in overcoming the Christian dichotomizing of sex and love in *Tannhäuser*. *Tristan* was more successful, but Boughton regretted that Tristan and Isolde had to die merely because of the ridiculous outlook of Wagner's own age, not yet fully freed from "the sexual absurdities of Christian teaching."[105] Wagnerian and theologian Peter Taylor Forsyth suggested in a study of religion in art that the greatness of these operas derived from Wagner's awareness "that the passion of sex is the deepest passion of the race, except for the passion to be delivered in God from the abuse of passion."[106]

There are many and varying references to Wagner and Wagnerian themes scattered throughout British literature of this period. Both major and minor writers found Wagner useful; inevitably his love music became a cliché. An author need only to seat hero and heroine at the parlor piano and have them run through passages of a Wagnerian score, and the rest was a foregone conclusion. One example is George Moore's novel *Evelyn Innes*. The heroine is a Wagnerian singer who regards each of the Wagnerian roles she studies—Elisabeth, Isolde, Brünnhilde, and Kundry—as central to her life both on and off the stage. The young Evelyn leaves her father and a quiet country village and goes to Paris with a lover whom she regards as a kind of Tristan. She travels through various stages of life and lovers and ends up— voiceless—in a nunnery.[107] D. H. Lawrence's early novel *The Trespasser* concerns a love affair, adulterous in spirit though unconsummated, between a violinist and her teacher. Originally entitled *The Saga of Siegmund*, it contains many obvious allusions to Wagnerian operas. Lawrence also figures in a recent study of Wagner and the modern British novel by John DiGaetani, who traces Wagnerian patterns in Conrad, Forster, Woolf, and Joyce as well.[108] In *Women in Love* Lawrence created an antihero with the beauty of Siegfried and the character of Alberich, meant to suggest the pillaging of England by modern industrialists. Virginia Woolf made allusions to Wagner in order to establish character or social scene or to create "mythic situations." James Joyce, although relatively unaffected by Wagner's music, was interested in the operas as mythic dramas and as material for parody and punning wordplay. William Blissett has researched English literary references to Wagnerism, and Herbert Knust has traced the influence of Wagnerian aesthetics and symbols on T. S. Eliot's *The Wasteland*. Knust regards Eliot's ambivalence toward Wagner as comparable to Nietzsche's.[109]

Wagner's impact on literature was also apparent in the United States. Gertrude Atherton, who wrote over twenty novels, most of them set in her native California, was also charmed by Munich and

used the town and the Bavarian castle of Neuschwanstein as the setting
for what she described as her favorite among her books, *Tower of
Ivory*. The story concerns the love affair of an idle young English
aristocrat and an American singer of very humble background. As in
Moore's novel, the heroine not only sings Wagner's music but also
lives it.

Willa Cather also treated Wagnerian themes. In her short story "A
Wagner Matinee," the narrator is visited in Boston by his aunt Geor-
gine from Nebraska. The aunt was a music teacher in her youth but
eloped with a man who took her to live on a barren and remote
homestead. The narrator escorts her to a concert of Wagner's music,
where she is overcome by the contrast between the richness of life it
evokes and the hardship of her thirty years on the prairie.[110] More
subtle and more original is Cather's *Song of the Lark*, whose heroine,
the daughter of a Swedish clergyman from Colorado, becomes a great
opera singer. One of the influences of the protagonist's childhood was
what she calls "a strange little book" entitled *My Musical Memories*, by
H. R. Haweis—the Wagnerian clergyman. What distinguishes Cather's novel from most other Wagnerian romances is the lesser importance of love affairs and the absence of immolation scenes. The story is
that of the emergence of an artist who is consumed not by love but by
her work. Cather loved Wagnerian opera and most probably used
soprano Olive Fremsted as the model for her lark.[111]

IV

World War I caused a decline in the performance of Wagner's music
in Britain and put a complete stop to it in New York. William Ashton
Ellis, staunch to the last, protested the British reaction. In an article
entitled "Richard Wagner contra Militarism," he quoted statements
Wagner had made criticizing Prussia and argued that it should be clear
as day that modern Germany was "flying dead in the face of every
principle of life and genuine culture that Wagner held dear."[112] Conductor Sir Thomas Beecham continued to carry *Tannhäuser* and *Die
Walküre* in his repertoire, despite criticism, and observed that Wagner
was the favorite composer of the British in uniform.[113] The Covent
Garden Opera, closed from 1915 to 1918, resumed performances of
Wagner in the 1919–1920 winter season and continued them until it
closed again in 1939. In 1923, after the fall of the German mark, a
benefit performance of *Tristan* was given for the Wagner family.

The news that the United States had declared war reached the Metropolitan Opera audience on April 6, 1917, Good Friday, midway in a performance of *Parsifal*. The Metropolitan Opera board decided to abandon German repertory, despite some objections in the press. Tentative plans to bring back German music were made for the 1919 season but were halted owing to public pressure. In November 1920, however, an English version of *Tristan* was performed. In 1921, Benjamin Steigman published a small book entitled *The Pertinent Wagnerite* in which he protested the absence of Wagner's operas during the war and defended the *Ring* as "a prophetic account of the world war and international politics today."[114] In the same year Isadora Duncan, acclaimed innovator of dance, also lamented the exclusion of Wagner's music during the war, "for the work of Wagner flows through every drop of blood in every artist of the world, and his mighty rhythm has become part of every heart-beat of each one of us."[115] In 1923, Siegfried Wagner, Wagner's son, came to the United States on a money-raising expedition, and Wagnerian opera sung in German was again accepted.

In the subsequent decade, performances of Wagner's works became more common, and by 1935, largely because of Kirsten Flagstad's singing, they were the mainstay of the Met. In 1937 another Wagner Society was founded in New York and published a quarterly during the next two years. A Boston branch was established, and almost at once the society claimed to be supported by numerous performers and by members from all walks of life. It bragged that "there were Wagnerites on the farms of Wisconsin, the oil fields of Texas and Oklahoma, the fruit groves of California and Florida, and the cotton fields of Georgia and South Carolina." While, according to the quarterly, the organization's purpose was "wholly artistic, and not social, racial, or political," and its aim was to encourage the production of German opera in English, the organizers also sought to promote serious study of the music dramas' dramatic and philosophical content.[116] At the outset of World War II, the Metropolitan Opera board considered but rejected a proposal to boycott Wagner and Strauss.

In a strange coincidence, during the fascist period the English-speaking world lost one famous daughter with Wagner connections to Germany, and gained another. Unity Valkrie Mitford, sister-in-law of Oswald Moseley,[117] leader of the British Fascist Union, was also the granddaughter of the Lord Redesdale whose memoirs had ended with a paeon of praise for the cosmopolitan atmosphere of Bayreuth in

1912.[118] Mitford was attracted by Nazism and became devoted to Hitler. When Hitler attended the Bayreuth opera in 1938, Mitford followed. She occasionally received an invitation to sit at his table during the intermissions. After Hitler left, Mitford remained in Bayreuth with a case of bronchitis for which she refused medication from the local doctor. She was taken to a clinic and there brought back to health by Hitler's physician. At the outset of the war, she shot herself in Munich. The bullet was never removed, and she died several years later in England while under the care of her family.

Friedelind Wagner was the daughter of Richard Wagner's son Siegfried. In 1940, at the age of twenty-two, she deserted the Nazi Germany she believed to be a travesty of her grandfather's hopes[119] and sought asylum in England. Establishing residence with a Jewish refugee settled in London, Friedelind wrote for English newspapers until she was interned with other enemy aliens on the Isle of Man. Arturo Toscanni effected her release and enabled her to make her way to New York.[120] There she again stayed with refugees, and took out citizenship. Upon reading her autobiography, published in 1945, Ernest Newman was pleased to report that Friedelind and her grandfather resembled each other in many ways, particularly "in an unbreakable toughness of fibre."[121]

Though he acknowledged that Hitler had made Bayreuth a nationalist and racist circus rather than an international festival, Newman attempted to dissassociate the music of Wagner and other German composers from politics. It was not until the close of World War II, when the full horrors of Nazism became widely known, that Wagner in particular was linked with Nazi crimes in the public mind. Even so, in *Musical Opinion* in June 1945, R. W. S. Mendl deplored the absence of Wagner from the London theater: "Either we have allowed ourselves to be persuaded by the Nazis that Wagner was their prophet, or we have deceived ourselves into thinking that there was really something 'Nazi' in the music."[122] In 1950 Londoners heard a new production of the *Ring,* and a new era had begun.

v

On both sides of the Atlantic, Wagnerians received Wagner as an explorer of cultural values concerned with expressing no less than the truth about life. British and American Wagnerians, alarmed by the materialism and scientism of their thriving and bustling age, sought in him a way to reconnect science and the spirit, society and the self. Wagnerism served as the context for an eclectic, spiritualistic humanism. Although Anglo-American Wagnerians yearned to make their world whole and good, they did not rally around a single political style but were content and perhaps fortunate to savor their redemption through art alone.

Listeners of many kinds bonded together in the experience of Wagnerian performances. Though critics such as Nietzsche warned that Wagner was the consummate illusionist and that his will to power expressed itself in the need to bend the world to his art come what may, Wagnerians willingly placed themselves in his hands. Their Wagnerism did not look back. For, as Sidney Lanier wrote, Wagner had the power "to say the Time in terms of tone" and to compose "big ballads of the modern heart."[123]

Conclusion

Our tour through the leading centers of Wagnerism may have left readers dizzied by the variety of ideas, styles, and attitudes that were thought of as part of Wagnerism but were clearly inspired by many other influences as well. One would have to conclude that the movement behaved very much like a chameleon, and a particularly crafty one at that, in its ability to insinuate itself into so many different cultural and political scenes. Was Wagnerism therefore only a means for other intellectual ends? If so, was it only so much cultural hokum? In these concluding remarks, we will explore these questions first in general terms and then in regard to the individual countries. Finally we will examine the process by which support for Wagner ceased to be a movement and shrank into a purely personal and primarily aesthetic enthusiasm.

General Characteristics

However the substantiality of Wagnerism may ultimately be evaluated, the variety of its political directions suggests a very important point: that Wagnerism was not by nature "proto-fascist." If Wagner's name has been increasingly associated with Nazism and the Third Reich, our survey shows some quite different tendencies. Among the national movements we have seen, a tendency toward the Left was if anything more common than one toward the Right. In Germany during the 1850s the early clan of Wagnerians around Franz Liszt borrowed the progressive political vocabulary of German liberalism and as well a militancy that sprang from the Revolution of 1848–1849. Even though the movement that grew up around the Festspielhaus in Bayreuth quickly took on a rightist cast, that was not always shared by the musically oriented Wagnerians in other German cities. In France, in the late 1850s, the leading Wagnerians, including the eminent statesman Emile Ollivier, were primarily liberal or republican. Although in Italy the movement was ranged against the "liberal" (but in practice increasingly authoritarian) founders of the unified state, it attacked the new establishment from principles of Mazzinian republicanism. In England George Bernard Shaw's socialist interpretation of the *Ring* reflected a widespread tendency to employ Wagner's work in the cause of social reform. And who would accuse the genteel American Wagnerians of any proto-fascist ambitions? Perhaps most interesting of all, the Russian movement influenced figures representing many strands of revolutionary thought, Bolsheviks included, right up to the 1920s. Even though Wagner had condemned the 1849 Dresden uprising soon after its failure, his conception of the theater as a popular force for social change came to life again as a revolutionary ideal in twentieth-century Russia.

Let us not, however, exaggerate the leftist inclinations of these Wagnerians. The movement had a diffuse political personality and did not belong to any one political faction. That was true not only because of the ambiguous, indeed contradictory, character of Wagner's political statements but also because his followers were rethinking their political directions and found his ideas especially helpful. During the second half of the century, of course, all of the major schools of political thought and affiliation—liberalism, republicanism, socialism, for example—were undergoing fundamental transformations, though as yet without very clear results. Wagnerism provided a setting within which intellectuals could try to sort out their ideas. Wagner's call for social regeneration through the theater—the utopian element in his thought—offered both an intellectual vision and a related social experience, and thus a varied set of tools through which thinkers could shape their own perspectives on state and society. The absence of any party label on Wagnerism made the movement appropriate for that task, and the artistic focus of the movement made it politically safe in most places.

One factor that enhanced the impact of Wagnerism was the fading of liberalism as a force for change after the 1850s. We have seen a number of figures associated with liberalism who turned to Wagnerian thinking. The case of Emile Ollivier is particularly instructive, for however much he avowed liberalism, he clearly did not find it entirely sufficient to his political needs, as his shift toward Napoleon III suggests, and he rallied to Wagner at the very moment when that shift began. In England, David Irvine similarly turned toward Wagner, evidently in search of broader intellectual horizons and a more vivid sense of social revival than the liberal ethos afforded him. Other Wagnerians were bitter critics of liberal thinking. In Germany, Hans von Wolzogen and other Bayreuth luminaries inveighed against parliamentary government as a corrupt, isolated institution and called for a more deeply rooted politics based on the strengths and needs of the *Volk*. In Italy the *scapigliati* used Wagnerism to attack the liberal leadership of the new Italian state and to redefine their sense of national identity. In their confusing array of popular and elitist political notions, we can see especially well how Wagnerians were moving beyond liberalism and republicanism and searching for new political perspectives.

But did this search lead anywhere? For most of those attracted to its political content, Wagnerism was a starting point rather than an end point. More a heuristic device than a system of thought, it failed to leave a permanent mark in political or social thought. In the case of Russia and Italy, it displayed a certain vitality in its period of efflorescence, but little remained thereafter. Only in Germany did traces of the movement as a political force hang on, as Bayreuth became incorporated into nationalist mythology and then found its place in the Third Reich. But even there the persistence of Wagnerism was at least partly a matter of gullible Wagnerians such as Wolzogen being coopted into the new German order.

Wagnerism was a means to a great many artistic as well as political ends. Among the movements influenced by Wagnerism we have seen most prominently the composers around Franz Liszt; the French Impressionist painters in their early years; the French symbolists at their peak; the Italian *scapigliati* and the aesthetic movements that succeeded them; the British decadents and the late American transcendentalists; and an extraordinary array of Russian innovators in poetry, theater, and dance. While in this volume we have not tried to reach any final assessment of Wagnerian artistic influence, we have shown that for a certain period a remarkably wide range of artists and aestheticians across Europe and America spoke a common Wagnerian language. Wagnerian ideas proved easily exportable after the excited controversy caused by the Master's essays of 1849–1851. It was as if commentators in any field could don the Wagnerian mask, thereby all the better to play their roles in the ongoing drama of artistic controversy.

Yet despite all this diversity, the movements held in common an aggressive sense of being in the artistic avant-garde. Even if they differed enormously in the nature of their ideas or their artistic tendencies, they conceived of themselves as progressive and forward-looking and as being opposed to the philistine tastes of some cultural establishment. Admittedly, one would not want to say that Wagnerians such as Baudelaire or Shaw identified themselves as part of an avant-garde, for their aesthetic interests were too individual for that. But the movements that surrounded them nonetheless showed such a character. The most common Wagnerian persuasion was a kind of artistic idealism, an assertion that the arts must return to a set of high principles and thereby regenerate society. We can see this sort of idealism not only in the demand throughout Europe for reform of the musical theater but also in the Italian Wagnerians' critique of the nation's cultural leadership, in the British trend toward Wagnerian social criticism, and in the Russian conceptions of popular theater. Most important of all, this kind of idealism is evident in the otherworldliness and insistence on social purification voiced by Wolzogen and other rightward-leaning members of the Bayreuth circle.

Wagnerism was thus a central force in the evolution of artistic avant-gardes. If the notion of the avant-garde first appeared prominently in the bohemian culture of Paris in the 1830s, it underwent its principal development in the period between 1871 and 1914. Wagnerism was extremely useful to artists who considered themselves part of the avant-garde, because it provided a way of acting this intellectual role, it furnished a posture, a way of doing aesthetic battle, a style of decrying the old and advancing the new. The antimodernism of Henry Thode and others of the Bayreuth Circle appears quite the exception within the Wagnerian movement.

Another characteristic of Wagnerism in all its national manifestations was the urge to use Wagner to embellish one's own creative or critical talents. Whether in claiming to produce "Wagnerian" poetry or painting, or in adapting Wagnerian aesthetic theories to the structure of the novel, or in employing Wagnerian social philosophy in the dissection of some cultural malaise or finally in proposing to awaken the national consciousness by creating new and more ambitious theater temples or *Gesamtkunst* extravaganzas, the practitioners of Wagnerism generally did not content themselves with (in Mark Twain's phrase) "worshipping at the shrine of St. Wagner."[1] In fact, it was precisely their "creative" confrontation with the Wagnerian legacy—or what they took to be the Wagnerian legacy—that most irritated the chief keeper of the shrine, Cosima Wagner, as well as those "ordinary" Wagnerians like Agénor Boissier, the financial backer of the *Revue wagnérienne*, who quickly withdrew his support from the journal when it began publishing symbolist poetry more commonly than appreciations of Wagner.[2]

One can legitimately display a certain skepticism regarding the "creative" accomplishments of much Wagnerian thinking. Too often it seems to have represented attempts by aspiring writers or artists to promote their own creations; some of them pressed their cause with such onslaughts of sloganeering and applied the Master's name in such farfetched ways that it amounted to little more than puffery. This tendency derived in part from the competitive atmosphere brought about by the turbulent expansion of the European cultural public and the institutions that served it—periodicals, organizations, movements—during the late nineteenth century.

Different perspectives upon this problem can be seen in the previous chapters. At some points the contributors have stressed the idealism and the sincere determination of Wagnerians, seeing a common spirit in their activities that deserves to be taken seriously. At other points, however, we have cast considerable doubt upon the substantiality, or at least the fruitfulness, of much of Wagnerian thinking. If we disagree on these questions to some degree, the differing points of view derive in part from the heterogenity of the movement itself, which attracted followers of widely divergent purpose, commitment, talents, and sophistication.

But what about the music? Wagner advertised himself as more than just a musician, and so it is perhaps only appropriate that the absolutist claim he sometimes made for his art and for his self-appointed role as reforming genius often preceded a thorough knowledge of his music in the inflation of what J. Rowbotham called the "Wagner Bubble."[3] Nor is it surprising that once aloft, this dazzling construction was kept moving more by literary-philosophical hot air than by the much cooler currents of musical analysis. Téodor de Wyzewa nicely summed up a central tenet of *wagnérisme* when he observed in his introduction to a series of essays on Wagner that "great works, to transform a race, do not need to be known."[4]

Nevertheless, in some places the music meant a great deal to the Wagnerian movement. That certainly was true of the first episodes of Wagnerism, which occurred in Weimar and Leipzig in the 1850s, and as well of the Viennese movement in which Gustav Mahler and Hugo Wolf played central roles. Then, too, we should not give short shrift to the operagoing habits of many English Wagnerians; there is every reason to believe that Shaw and many of his fellow Wagnerians cared deeply about the music. It is indeed difficult to imagine how so powerful a mythology could have grown up around Wagner if many of his disciples had not been "converted" by the overpowering experience of the music dramas. The preoccupation with elemental emotions—the subconscious—in Wagnerian thought was sparked at least originally by the unique nature of this musical and dramatic experience. Even the young poets associated with the *Revue wagneriénne* who picked up these ideas without themselves going through this aesthetic experience were influenced by it at second hand; they did not simply postulate their beliefs in a complete vacuum.

THE NATIONAL CENTERS

The ultimate direction of German Wagnerism cannot be understood without reference to Bayreuth, which served as a kind of Vatican to which the faithful looked for guidance. The "truest of the true" who clustered around the Villa Wahnfried believed themselves to be in possession of the last word in matters of Wagnerian doctrine, and they certainly spoke with an air of infallibility. When challenged or questioned by some errant fellow acolyte, they could and did reply with threats of excommunication. Of course, there were internecine quarrels even among the "inner circle," for the Bayreuth discipleship was never so homogeneous as it may have seemed to outsiders, and it was certainly not without its rebellious spirits.

Nor was it entirely without its value as a source of information and elucidation regarding the artistic legacy it strove to perpetuate. Even the least critically gifted of the Bayreuth disciples, such as Wolzogen and Glasenapp, performed a useful service through their pious preservation of often arcane Wagneriana, and more talented interpreters like Stein and Chamberlain produced some quite impressive work. And yet the overall impression here is hardly one of intellectual distinction. Indeed, when viewed within the broader perspective of imperial and Weimar intellectual history, Bayreuth stands out not for its brilliance but for its mediocrity. We are referring here less to the festivals themselves (though they certainly had artistic deficiencies) than to the intellectual output of the Bayreuth Circle, especially as displayed in the house journal, the *Bayreuther Blätter*. That corpus of work, taken as a whole, is distinguished largely for its cranky obscurantism, its parochialism, and its monumental tediousness. Moreover, despite Wagner's own rich appreciation for exotic *Sinnlichkeit* (sensuality), Bayreuth Wagnerism was fundamentally prudish, dour, and ascetic. Its true guiding spirit after Wagner died was Cosima, and Cosima as moral arbiter of Bayreuth proved once again that no one is more pious than a repentant sinner. The atmosphere under her dispensation was not only pious—it was rigidly conservative, steadfastly opposed to modernist trends in politics and culture. Although cosmopolitan in the sense that it catered to an international audience, Bayreuth was essentially inward-looking and Germanocentric: it meant to be a monument to the superiority of German *Kultur*. Yet one of the ironies of the Bayreuth enterprise as a whole involved its inability (or, more accurately, its unwillingness) to embrace the most powerful talents in German intellectual and cultural life. We can see this particularly in the *Bayreuther Blätter*. Germany's best-known intellectuals and writers rarely if ever appeared in its pages. To peruse this journal and to find but one contribution by a German writer of the first rank (an essay by Fontane[5]) is to encounter at least one of the limits of Bayreuth Wagnerism. To remember that Germany's best-known commentators on Wagner, Friedrich Nietzsche and Thomas Mann, stood well outside the Bayreuth orbit, is to encounter another.[6]

If Bayreuth *Wagnerismus* seems rather a dull affair when compared to the Wagner criticism of Nietzsche and Mann (or to the later commentaries by Theodore Adorno and Hans Mayer[7]), it is even duller when placed against the imaginative quality of French *wagnérisme*. Unlike their counterparts in Bayreuth, the men who launched *wagnérisme* in France were among the most prominent, albeit highly controversial, artist-intellectuals of their time. From Baudelaire and Nerval through Mallarmé and Mendès, the French literary avant-garde regarded Richard Wagner as an inspiration for their own creations. They established a journal, the *Revue wagnérienne,* designed to serve as a forum for their creative confrontation with the Master. In the course of this intellectual confrontation, they produced a sizable corpus of aesthetic theory and symbolist verse, highly experimental in technique and meant somehow to employ the Wagnerian legacy in an ongoing war of "idealism against materialism, of poetry against science."[8]

The problem with this entire venture, as we suggested before, is that it was often based on very little direct familiarity with Wagner's work, for most of these *wagnéristes* had not had the chance to attend many of the operas, and few knew enough German to wade through his prose writings in the original. This is why the young Houston Stewart Chamberlain was so invaluable to the fledgling *Revue wagnérienne;* he was virtually the only person in France who could report authoritatively on the full spectrum of Wagner's work.[9] This is also why so many of the Wagner-inspired efforts of the *wagnéristes,* while stylistically intriguing, were rather problematical both artistically and intellectually. In their attempt to adapt aesthetic theories that they only partly understood or to comment on music dramas that they had rarely if ever seen, the *Revue wagnérienne* circle managed, in the verdict of one observer, to produce "neither good art nor competent criticism."[10]

While this last judgment may be too harsh, it is certainly true that the literary-intellectual Wagnerians associated with the *Revue wagnérienne* inspired little confidence among that growing segment of the French musical public that wanted primarily to learn more about Wagner's music. This journal, then, is hardly an adequate guide to the reception of Wagner's works in France, and it certainly did not, as Jacques Barzun boldly declares, leave "Paris almost more Wagnerian than the home of the Master."[11] If Wagner's music indeed gained steadily in popularity in France during the last third of the century, this was due less to the contributions of Dujardin and his journal than to the efforts of French opera directors, who mounted Wagner's music dramas regularly in these years (though less regularly, we might add, than in London, not to mention Munich), and to the French pilgrims to Bayreuth, who were more loyal visitors in the lean period of the 1880s than were the Germans themselves.[12]

If there was more to the French Wagner vogue than the *Revue*

wagnérienne, there was also more to *wagnérisme* than avant-garde aestheticism. The French intelligentsia's attraction to Wagner was based
not only on its perception of him as a stylistic innovator but also on its
sense of him as a political radical. As Gerald Turbow has shown,
Wagner became the darling of the liberal-republican salons of the late
1850s and early 1860s, which was one of the chief reasons why
Napoleon III, suddenly anxious to court liberal opinion, was so willing
to sponsor Paris' ill-fated *Tannhäuser* premiere in 1861. His popularity
among "progressive" circles in France survived the patronage of
Napoleon III as well as the political tensions of the 1870s and 1880s.
Indeed, though Paris was not "more Wagnerian than the home of the
Master," France's liberal intelligentsia and artistic avant-garde were
certainly more caught up in Wagner than were their counterparts in
Germany, where *Wagnerismus* was rapidly falling under the domination of Bayreuth conservatism.

French intellectuals were not only the first to name the movement
we have been discussing (the term *wagnérisme* preceded *Wagnerismus*
and *Wagnerism*); they were also instrumental in spreading the Wagner
cult through much of the rest of Europe. Indeed, one might well make
the case that French *wagnérisme,* being essentially more "exportable"
than the increasingly Germanocentric Bayreuth *Wagnerismus* of the late
nineteenth century, was the chief model for the European artistic-
intellectual confrontation with Wagner in this period. In Russia and
England we find that many important Wagner intellectuals made their
first acquaintance with the Master's work through the writings of such
French interpreters as Baudelaire, Schuré, and Lichtenberger.

In Italy, Wagner had become a name to be reckoned with well
before most of those who bandied it about knew anything of the
Master's music. His name alone, which already in the 1860s connoted
an iconoclastic assault on all that was conventional and proper, carried
such strong overtones that it was employed both as a label of distinction and an epithet of opprobrium, with almost equal imprecision.
Wagner's art was perceived by some Italians as a threat to their own
operatic traditions and even to their sense of national identity. And yet
the prominent nationalist poet-soldier Gabriele D'Annunzio could take
up the Wagnerian cause in Italy and adapt some of the composer's
social-political ideals to the needs of a newer, "integral" nationalism.
Like Wagner, D'Annunzio saw artistic revolution as the necessary
precursor to social and political rejuvenation, and like Wagner he be-

lieved that the artist-cum-warrior (not the hack politician) must take the lead in restoring his country's greatness. Of course, D'Annunzio's speculations, not to mention his flamboyant actions, were by no means slavish imitations of the Master's example. His "Wagnerian" novels made reference to themes from the music dramas and featured characters of a distinctly Wagnerian cast, but their essential raison d'être was a lively critique of contemporary Italian society, a society that D'Annunzio saw as flabby and devoid of heroic will. Similarly, his quixotic Fiume enterprise had something of Bayreuth in its grandiose amalgamation of poetry, music, and "heroic" politics, yet in its mass choreography of "sacro egoismo" it pointed more to the coming spectacles of Rome and Nuremberg than back to the festivals of Bayreuth.

In Italy, the Wagner wave crested in the 1890s with the formation of a Bologna chapter of the Associazione Riccardo Wagner and the publication of yet another short-lived Wagnerian journal, the *Cronaca wagneriana*. This last enterprise differed from its French predecessor, the *Revue wagnérienne*, in that it neither attracted prominent literary lights nor served as a vehicle for ambitious artistic adventures. Aiming to steer clear of all the controversy and polemics surrounding the Master, it succeeded only in becoming what its name suggested: a *chronicle* of Wagnerian performances and pilgrimages to Bayreuth. In recording the growing number of these events, however, it showed that Wagner's music was becoming a fixture in the national culture, despite continuing—albeit gradually diminishing—opposition to such "alien" art. By the First World War the Italian Wagnerian mania had certainly ebbed, but Wagner's works were well established in that country's operatic repertoires.

In Russia, Wagnerism, like industrialization, arrived late on the scene: it did not really "take off"—as some economists like to say of industrial revolutions—until the 1890s. Indeed, there was a connection between the two phenomena, since the Wagnerian movement in Russia was at least partly fueled by a reaction against the moral, cultural, and political values that seemed implicit in the industrial modernization of the country. As in Italy, then, the Russian reception of Wagner's works and the adaptation of his ideas had a great deal to do with fundamental questions of national identity and purpose. Wagner's earliest Russian followers (who were also, more often than not, followers of Nietzsche) believed that these "Western" masters might lead them to a truer perception of their own native culture, even though the essence of that culture might lie outside the Western tradition. This is why Russian Wagnerism was interwoven so tightly with such key threads in the national tapestry as religious mysticism and primitive anarcho-communism. The adherents of these movements, as well as the symbolist aesthetes who also looked to Wagner for inspiration, differed significantly in what they found essential or usable in the Master's legacy. They were united, however, in their willingness to impose on that legacy a distinctly Russian flavor. This was obviously the case with the mystics and the revolutionaries, but it was also true of the seemingly more westernized aesthetes. The Ballets russes, as Bernice Rosenthal points out, amounted to a "Russification of the *Gesamtkunstwerk.*" The symbolists' journal, *Mir iskusstva,* was ambitiously cosmopolitan in scope, dutifully translating French and German interpretations of Wagner's works and keeping its readers abreast of the latest trends in European art, but its focus was on the uses to which all these extraneous influences could be put in the cultural renovation of Russia.

As if making up for lost time, Russian Wagnerians engaged in a flurry of activity on behalf of their cause in the first years of the new century. Productions of the music dramas followed each other in rapid succession, as did translations of the Master's major prose works and of the important French interpretive studies by Schuré and Lichtenberger. Here as elsewhere, avant-garde intellectuals played a key role in the dissemination of Wagnerism, though members of the imperial court, in particular the German-born Empress Alexandra and her theater director Prince Volkonsky, were instrumental in promoting performances of the Master's works in St. Petersburg. In this respect, Russia was hardly unique: in Germany, France, and England the Wagnerian cause enjoyed the blessing and support of monarchical backers at key moments in its evolution.

The unusual feature of the Russian experience was that its Wagnerians employed the Master's ideas in a successful political and social revolution. The revolutionary idealism inherent in Wagner's early career found practical application not in Germany but in distant Russia, where such radical Wagnerians as Ivanov, Chulkov, Blok, and Lunacharsky mixed Wagnerian aesthetics into their distinctly Russian blend of mysticism, neopopulism, and revolutionary activism. In returning primarily to the young Wagner for inspiration, they were mirroring their countryman Lenin's revival of the early Marx.[13] In both cases, ironically enough, an initial voluntarist activism, frustrated in the country of its birth, found eventual realization in the nation that had epitomized political and cultural reaction. Wagnerism played a role in the Russian revolutionary movement between 1905 and the early Soviet period, but it could no more survive the transition to "socialist realism" than early Marxist humanism could survive the imposition of political dictatorship. Wagnerism had its revolutionary moment in Russia, but it did not have lasting influences on the society that ultimately emerged from the "Dionysian chaos" of those heady years.

Unlike Russia's shaky autocracy, England's political institutions in the late nineteenth and early twentieth centuries were flexible enough to undergo substantial reform without falling victim to full-scale revolution. This is not to say, however, that the political, social, and above all cultural changes that affected England in the Victorian and Edwardian periods were insignificant or painless. Of course the industrialization of the country had long been a source of great social and cultural dislocation—so much so that by the mid-nineteenth century, when this process had reached its symbolic zenith in the Crystal Palace Exhibition, it had generated the beginnings of a countermovement dedicated to resisting the effects of industrial modernization on English culture and society. In fact, the counter-revolution was present right in the Crystal Palace itself, which housed not just the latest engineering and technological marvels but also Augustus Pugin's Medieval Court, whose Neo-Gothic ethos challenged the prevailing notion that to be English was to be a devotee of steam engines, satanic mills, and Manchester liberalism. As Martin Wiener has recently argued, this anti-industrial challenge, motivated by nostalgia for an older, rural England of farms and cottages, intensified as the century wore on; eventually it was so successful in reorienting the Englishman's sense of self that it contributed to that country's modern decline as an industrial nation.[14] Wiener does not mention Wagner's English interpreters in connection with this process, but he might legitimately have done so. For as Anne Sessa has shown, Wagnerism took hold in England as part of that nation's ongoing reassessment of utilitarian values, technological "progress," and conventional religious practices. The English Wagnerian William Ashton Ellis summed up this impulse and Wagner's importance to it when he asserted that the Master's music and ideas would help to liberate mankind "from the tightening grip of crushing scientific materialism," because "at no time [had] there been such a widespread desire to search all things, and to wring forth some of the hidden secrets of that which is above and beyond matter."[15]

This particular interpretation of Wagner's meaning and significance was not uniquely English; similar perspectives cropped up in all the European (as well as in the American) Wagnerian movements. Nor was England's "decadent" Wagnerism of the Yellow Nineties truly sui generis: Wilde, Beardsley, and Moore all came to Wagner through the back door of French aestheticism, and the uses to which they put his legacy had much in common with the experimentalism of the *Revue wagnérienne* group. As for that other main direction in English Wagnerism identified by Sessa—the social meliorist camp—here too we encounter a certain derivative quality: even Shaw's rather more idiosyncratic approach to the Master's work owed much to Nietzsche's pioneering interpretations, as well as perhaps to Marx, whom Shaw was reading at the same time he was working on his famous analysis of the *Ring*. Indeed, one of the more intriguing aspects of English Wagnerism is the extent to which it reflected—first in the passion for Wagner's works in general, and second in the way those works were interpreted and adapted—a growing receptiveness to cultural stimuli from the Continent. Here again, as in the related reassessment of classical liberalism and industrial progress, the local Wagner movement played a small but significant role in the gradual reorientation of English culture at the end of the nineteenth century.

While noting the parallels between English and continental Wagnerism, however, we should also take care to see where the English experience might have diverged from European models. One instance of this seems to have involved that curious need to make Wagner fit for Christianity (and Christianity fit for Wagner) that preoccupied so many English and American Wagnerians. Of course one finds instances of this in Europe as well, especially in Russia, but the accent on reconciling Wagner with Christianity was particularly strong in the Anglo-Saxon countries. If we ask why this might have been so, the answer could well lie in the connection between Wagnerism and those cultural/moral doubts regarding industrialization that we discussed above: Christian Wagnerians like Peter Forsyth and Washington Gladden apparently hoped that a Christianity rejuvenated through Wagnerian spirituality might more effectively soften the sharp edges of capitalist–industrial society.

This attempt to reconcile Christianity with an influence that more conventional believers often saw as morally corrupting, if not satanic, reminds us a little of similar efforts to Christianize Darwinism in the nineteenth century. Here too, liberal-minded Christians felt the attraction of an idea that if not somehow intellectually domesticated, could lead to ever more adventurous heresies. But if Darwin made things somewhat difficult for the Christians, Wagner (except for his scandalous life-style) generally did not. Indeed, the vague spiritualism of his later works harmonized well with a rejuvenated Christianity precisely because it was so heterodox, so independent of hidebound orthodoxies. The reconciliation process was not without its complexities and absurdities. Sometimes it failed entirely, the attempt to make Wagner a Christian yielding to ever more bizarre impulses to make him a theosophist, cabalist, Buddhist guru, or finally (in Los Angeles, of course) "the New Age Messenger of Music."

The Germanic origins of many English and American immigrant groups also affected the character of Wagnerism in the Anglo-Saxon countries. In both England and America the local German emigré communities played an unusually decisive role in spreading Wagner's influence among the citizenry of their adopted lands. These transplanted Germans were often professional musicians themselves, and they were prominent carriers of that "musical idealism" (as William Weber terms it) that was transforming musical taste in the late nineteenth century. They were also dedicated enough in their reverence for Wagner to familiarize themselves with the Master's prose works and to translate these works for the edification (and often mystification) of their English-speaking audiences. As they gradually won over more of the natives, the Wagnerian movements in England and America succeeded in shedding the exclusively Germanic image that had featured prominently in the polemics of the local anti-Wagnerians. But a certain Germanic, or to be more precise, Bayreuth-like influence persisted. This can be seen above all in England's short-lived Wagner journal *The Meister,* which was apparently inspired by the *Revue wagnérienne* but was in fact much closer in spirit and style to the *Bayreuther Blätter.* Like that journal, it presumed that Wagner's prose works were virtually as important as his music, and it sought to document this notion by publishing long excerpts from his writings. Also like the *Blätter, The Meister* did not succeed in attracting prominent writers (even prominent Wagnerian writers) to its pages. England's most famous Wagnerian, George Bernard Shaw, would have nothing to do with the journal because he found its blandness un-Wagnerian. *The Meister's* "evident indisposition to provoke hostility," he observed, "was not an indisposition to which the Meister himself was at all subject."[16]

We have spoken here of an "Anglo-Saxon" Wagnerism because the English and American Wagnerian movements had a great deal in common. But the American Wagnerians did not simply emulate their English counterparts, or those in France, Italy, or Russia. Neither the power of these European examples nor the Germanic roots of many of the first New World disciples prevented the translation of Wagner's legacy into a uniquely American idiom. The uniqueness of the American experience is understandable. The United States was the one country we have been discussing in this volume that the Master never visited. Perhaps because of this, it was also the country about which he harbored his most romantic fantasies. Like his countryman Karl May, who also never set foot on American shores, he chose to see the New World as the last refuge of true nobility but also as a promised land of infinite financial opportunity. He often threatened to pack up and go there—to that place where he might be properly appreciated, and properly paid. We have seen that towards the end of his life he fantasized that he might raise enough money through subscription in order to set up a new festival and artistic school in Minnesota.[17] The Americans, for their part, returned the compliment. As early as 1855, notes Anne Sessa, two promoters from Chicago offered Wagner large sums—in the hope, of course, of earning larger ones—to lure this latest European culture-star to the United States. What was the attraction, beyond the hope of financial gain? Of course there was the music, but there was also the man: in American eyes, it would seem, Wagner was a great entrepreneur as well as great artist; he knew how to make things—*big* things—happen. (With this perception, we might say, these promoters completed the circle of Romantic fantasy: if Wagner could make the Americans into wealthy yet uncorrupted idealists, they in turn could make Wagner into an artistic "go-getter" with plenty of "Yankee push.")

Musical promoters were not the only Americans interested in what Wagner might do for the New World. If there were not a few Americans who looked askance on the Master's morals, there was also an important group of highbrow cultural arbiters associated with the "serious" magazines who hoped his work might exert a civilizing influence on the American sensibility. Critics like W. F. Apthorp valued Wagner for his moral idealism, which they believed was essentially in harmony with the ideals of New England transcendentalism. His influence, carefully filtered through these critics' own fine-meshed censor screens, would help Americans smooth out the rough edges of their evolving culture. From this perspective, Wagner's message was hardly revolutionary: it would certainly not undermine any of the three central certainties—faith in the eternal moral verities, belief that human nature was improvable and improving, conviction that culture could ennoble—that were the mainstays of nineteenth-century American culture and the source of its soon to be shattered "innocence."[18] Wagnerism did not play an important role in the loss of that innocence during the years immediately preceding America's entry into World War I. The United States never generated a "decadent" Wagnerian avant-garde that might have shown its countrymen a quite different side of the Master's legacy and thereby compromised his usefulness to the forces of moral uplift. Even the remnants of American Wagnerism that resurfaced after the First World War, only to be set back again in the Second, avoided any serious confrontation with what Thomas Mann called the "subtle perversity" and "devil's artistry" of Richard Wagner.[19]

THE DECLINE OF WAGNERISM

"No matter where one goes," wrote Karl Marx in 1876, "one is plagued with the question 'What do you think of Richard Wagner?'" Marx himself knew what to think—Wagner was a preposterous charlatan—and Marx was clearly alarmed by all the fuss surrounding what he called "the Bayreuth fools' festival of *Staatsmusikant* Wagner."[20]

Marx had reason to be concerned. The radical principles inherent in Wagner's *Ring* poem may have been inspired by the Master's early encounters with Hegel and Feuerbach, but the final production that premiered in Bayreuth in 1876 hardly impressed people as an exercise in "scientific" socialism. Rather, it offered its largely bourgeois audiences a release or a haven from a world that had become all too "demystified" (to use Max Weber's term) through the pressures of industrial modernization. What Wagner achieved, in the end, was a kind of remystification or remythification of quite "real" social questions through his compelling use of myth, though of course he brought these myths to life by employing the latest stage machinery and the most "realistic" (at least by traditional operatic standards) dramaturgical techniques. His immense appeal lay in his unmatched ability both to "make the world of the dream and myth credible"[21] and, conversely, to dissolve the world of quotidian reality into all-powerful myth.

We have countless testimonials of Wagner's power to "transport" his admirers from their pallid ordinary existences into a realm of power, vitality, mystery, and love, a journey that at once reawakened the magic intuition of the inner life and promised the reconciliation of man and nature. Romain Rolland, describing his generation's obsession with Wagner, asserts that

> if we had need of that music, it was not because it was death to us, but life. Cramped by the artificiality of a town, far from action, or nature, or any strong or real life, we expanded under the influence of this noble music—music which flowed from a heart filled with understanding of the word and the breath of nature. In *Die Meistersinger*, in *Tristan*, and in *Siegfried*, we went to find the joy, the love, and the vigor that we so lacked.[22]

In Wagner's music, wrote the English novelist George Moore, "art and nature abandone[d] their accustomed strife."[23] He and his fellow pilgrims to the "rural idyl" of Bayreuth could therefore listen to those "exalted melodies" and be released from the isolation imposed by the demands of conquering nature through artifice.

It is probably safe to say that Rolland and Moore articulated the feelings that animated thousands of others who during the heyday of the Wagner infatuation trooped to witness the Master's art at Bayreuth or at opera houses and concert halls throughout Europe and America. Perhaps it is also safe to say that these or very similar feelings continue to animate some of the Wagner enthusiasts of our own day—animate those, at least, who can still be *transporté*, despite all the benumbing effects of our electronic civilization.

But if Wagner's art still has the power to inspire selected audiences everywhere, Wagnerism in the sense described by the essays in this volume—that is, as an ideological crusade and as a proclivity (again in the words of Romain Rolland) "to see and judge the whole world in the light of Bayreuth"[24]—has long been all but dead. Of course it did not die in a single instant but rather in the fashion of a dramatic hero who manages to utter a few dozen final lines after having been mortally wounded. But what interests us here is not the duration of the final contortions but the fact of death itself: what brought it about? What trends in European culture and politics in our own century have combined to do in this most curious of cultural/political isms?

To the degree that the international Wagnerian movement was dependent on the support of certain avant-garde cultural factions, it was bound to weaken as those groups gave way to intellectual movements with quite different styles and interests. As is well known, the early twentieth century was an era of rapid cultural and intellectual change; the passions of one "circle," clique, or school were rarely the passions of another. To be more specific: Wagner may have featured prominently (even if only as a "gigantic red herring"[25]) on the intellectual menu of the French symbolists, but he was not even an hors d'oeuvre for the proto-dadaists of the "Banquet Years."[26] The cultural style evolved by artist-intellectuals like Henri Rousseau, Erik Satie, Alfred Jarry, and Guillaume Apollinaire, with its childlike irreverence and absurdist fantasies, was far removed from the programmatic didacticism of Wagner's music, not to mention his prose. This style, observes Roger Shattuck, was sui generis and quite un-Teutonic: "Satie," he points out, "could never have happened in Germany."[27]

Across the Channel in England, Wagner had been the darling of the decadent aesthetes of the fin-de-siècle, and he continued to be an important influence in Edwardian culture. As John DiGaetani notes, "Anybody [in this period] who considered himself at all intellectual had to know something about Wagner."[28] Certainly the members of the influential Bloomsbury Group considered themselves intellectuals, and they did know something about Wagner. Their response to his art, however, was by no means uniformly enthusiastic, and we can perhaps find in the Bloomsbury perspective a certain cooling of the Wagnerian fever. At one extreme, Saxon Sydney Turner was clearly a fervent Wagnerian, attending over three hundred performances.[29] Leonard Woolf represents the opposite side of the spectrum; though recognizing the *Ring* as a "masterpiece," he found it and other Wagner works "intolerably monotonous and boring."[30] His wife Virginia's relationship to Wagner was more ambiguous and more interesting. According to Leonard, she went to Bayreuth "ritualistically" in the first years of the century.[31] Our only detailed account of her reaction to Wagner's festival, however, comes in the form of a long piece she wrote for the *Times* in 1909.[32] It is evident from this report that she was deeply moved by the *Parsifal* she saw that season. At the same time, however, she confessed to being bewildered by the "unfamiliarity of the ideas" and by a music that resisted translation into "our old tools" of language and rational analysis.[33] Ultimately the Bayreuth scene began to oppress her—"The grossness of the Germans is astonishing," she wrote to her sister[34]—and she could never be persuaded to return.[35]

Of course neither Bloomsbury nor the Rousseau-Satie group had the final word on cultural taste in England and France, and their influence could not make or break Wagner's popularity. As we have noted above, Wagner's music remained very much in vogue in England and on the Continent at least until the war, and frequent allusions to his work in period novels suggest that his name continued to carry a certain *frisson*.[36] Nevertheless, with the notable exception of the Russian example, one has the sense that by the eve of the war (not to mention during the 1920s) Wagner's legacy was no longer quite so important to the European avant-garde as it had been in the late nineteenth century.

If Wagnerism began to tremble slightly in the fickle winds of cultural fashion, it had yet more difficulty weathering the stormy gusts of political change. We have seen that in much of Europe, Wagnerism was associated with reformist-liberal or radical politics during the mid- to late nineteenth century. Moreover, despite occasional chauvinistic outbursts by Wagner himself, and despite his abortive attempt to make his theater the artistic sister of German unification, the Wagnerian heritage was cosmopolitan enough to allow adaptation in a variety of national idioms. But the world's image of Wagner began gradually to change after the turn of the century, and this change had at least partly to do with an increasing tendency to identify Wagner with the new Germany of Wilhelm II, whose *arriviste* imperialism was rapidly isolating the Empire behind its vaunted new fleet and its equally vaunted *Kultur*. Samuel Hynes has noted that when Edwardian Englishmen "discovered" the culture of the European Continent, "The continent they discovered included their new allies, France and Russia, but it did not include Germany."[37] A decade before World War I, he suggests, German culture was becoming suspect in England as the culture of a bitter rival and potential military enemy. Although this did not lead to an actual boycott of German music—certainly not of Wagner's music—until World War I, it encouraged commentators on the Master's work to see that work as intimately linked with the strident brashness of the German Empire and its unbalanced Kaiser. Thus the English journalist Wickham Steed could emphasize the "Wagnerian" dimension of the imperial style and of the Kaiser himself, that would-be warrior strutting about in his "Lohengrin uniform—white tunic, dazzling breast-plate, and silver helmet surmounted by the Prussian eagle."[38] One finds similar tendencies in France. Romain Rolland, an old admirer of Wagner, was prompted to observe in 1908 that the end of *Die Meistersinger* "reflected the spirit of this military nation of shopkeepers [Germany], bursting with rude health and complacent pride."[39] Somewhat later the German statesman Walter Rathenau would blame many of the Kaiser's troubles on his "Wagnerian disposition"[40]—which suggests that the Germans themselves were not oblivious to this connection.

Indeed, German writers and intellectuals were among the first to develop this parallel between Wagnerian art and Wilhelmian politics, a pairing also encouraged by the Master's rightist disciples in Bayreuth and by the fact that Wagner was the favorite composer of the Kaiser's entourage.[41] We might recall in this connection that Heinrich Mann's philistine superpatriot in *Der Untertan* finds *Lohengrin* to be the perfect opera for the new Germany: "Shields and swords, lots of rattling iron, good imperial sentiment, manly greetings, banners held high, and the solid German oak."[42] In another satiric novel, Lion Feuchtwanger's *Erfolg*, Wagner is again identified with German nationalism but this time with the "romantic nationalism" of postwar Munich, whose middle-class citizens (their ancestors having run him out of town) now celebrate Wagner as one of their own. Why are they so high on the Master? "Wagner's operas required a lot of elaborate scenery, and the *Münchener* liked his theater fat and thick, with all the trappings of a revue."[43] Richard Wagner as musician laureate of German nationalism, militarism, and philistinism: it would seem that this image of the composer had gained considerable currency in Germany even before Hitler came along to give it an added dimension.

In the 1920s and 1930s, German critics associated with the Frankfurt Institute for Social Research subjected Wagner's art to more systematic scrutiny. They were less concerned with tying Wagner to a specific national malaise than with showing how his work reflected the deficiencies of the European bourgeoisie in its dotage. Walter Benjamin identified Wagner with that "bourgeois false-consciousness" that attempted to "abstract [art] from the social existence of man."[44] Benjamin's friend Theodore Adorno wrote a complex critique of Wagner[45] in which he exposed the Master's "radicalism" as a posturing, pseudorevolutionary penchant *épater la bourgeoisie;* Wagner, he said, indulged in "gesture" and "illusion"—in "Phantasmorgie"—which had the effect of masking the class basis of his work: "The disguising of production through the appearance of the product is the formal law of Richard Wagner." For Adorno, even the *Ring* was not genuinely revolutionary, for the essentially utopian visions of the earliest sketches had given way in dialectical fashion to the Schopenhauerian nihilism of the *Götterdämmerung*. What was characteristically Wagnerian (and characteristically "late bourgeois") in all this was the "glorification of death as intoxication."[46]

It was not too far from the Frankfurt School's image of Wagner as prophet of late-bourgeois decadence to the portrait of him put forth by the Frankfort School's favorite dramatist, Bertold Brecht. Brecht equated Wagner's work with the middle classes' self-destruction through fascism. For him both Wagnerism and fascism represented the triumph of the irrational and the antithesis of that cool, distancing effect he hoped to achieve in his Epic Theater.[47] No wonder he connected the Hitler figures in his dramas—especially Schweyk in *Schweyk im Zweiten Weltkrieg*—with the figure of Richard Wagner.

Brecht's perception was hardly unique: in general, the tragedy of the Third Reich awakened a new era in the demonization of Wagner. To put the matter bluntly: Hitler's favorite composer was identified as one of those nineteenth-century Germans most responsible for Hitler. Leonard Woolf summed up this perspective when he wrote: "The Germans in the nineteenth century developed a tradition, a philosophy of life and art, barbarous, grandiose, phoney. Wagner was both cause and effect of this repulsive process which ended in the apogee and apotheosis of human bestiality and degradation, Hitler and the Nazis."[48] A more elaborate statement of this same theme came from the pen of the American scholar and poet Peter Viereck. In a 1939 essay entitled "Hitler and Richard Wagner," he argued that "this warped genius" [Wagner] was "perhaps the most important single fountainhead of Nazi ideology."[49] By "psychoanalyzing" the Nazis' "emotional and intellectual roots in one man"—Wagner—Viereck believed that one could "better combat" the National Socialist menace. There followed a dissection of Wagnerian "metapolitics" as articulated essentially in Wagner's writings, as well as an attempt to portray those writings as the chief inspiration behind Hitler's criminal policies.

Viereck had begun this tirade by mentioning Thomas Mann, then in exile in America, as one of those anti-Hitler Germans who tried to maintain their love for Wagner by overlooking the fundamentally evil nature of the Master's legacy. Mann's response to this accusation is interesting, for it shows how a highly sophisticated interpreter of Wagner's art could get caught up (if only temporarily[50]) in the demonization of the Master. In essence Mann defended himself against Viereck's charge by agreeing with the substance of Viereck's anti-Wagnerian attack. He declared that Viereck was correct in exposing, for the first time in America, "the intricate and painful interrelationships which undeniably exist between the Wagnerian sphere and the National Socialist evil." Mann then proceeded to out-Viereck Viereck by claiming that connections to the Nazi ethos could be found not just in Wagner's prose but also in his music. This intensely German music, this art that could spring only from the "German spirit," was deeply problematical in its "Wagalweia and its illiteration, its mixture of roots-in-the-soil and eyes-toward-the future, its appeal for a classless society, its mythical-reactionary revolutionism," all of which was "the exact spiritual forerunner of the 'metapolitical' movement today terrorizing the world."[51]

The tendency to treat Wagner as a spiritual precursor of Hitler continued through the war and even beyond. Scholarly investigations into the "roots" of National Socialism, as well as more popular accounts of Hitler's rise to power, rarely failed to make Wagner one of the leading villains of the piece. Rohan d'O. Butler's influential *The Roots of National Socialism* (1941) featured Wagner prominently among a kind of antipantheon of German racists, militarists and totalitarian philosophers who allegedly made Hitler possible.[52] Edmond Vermeil suggested that the Nazis acted "with the germanic innocence and guilelessness that Richard Wagner . . . glorified in the persons of Siegfried and Parsifal."[53] And William Shirer's monumental best-seller *The Rise and Fall of the Third Reich* treated Wagner's *Ring* as the guiding inspiration behind Germany's *Götterdämmerung:* "It is not at all surprising," he wrote, "that Hitler tried to emulate Wotan when in 1945 he willed the destruction of Germany so that it might go down in flames with him."[54]

More recent scholarly studies have generally gotten away from this simple linkage, but the habit unfortunately persists in some quarters, especially in artistic attempts to get at the essence of Hitlerism. A few years ago the American artist Edward Kienholz exhibited a series of images and artifacts from Nazi Germany that were to be viewed while listening to Wagner's music.[55] Hans-Jürgen Syberberg's recent epic film *Hitler: Ein Film aus Deutschland* has the Führer rising from the grave of Richard Wagner to wreak his havoc on the world.[56] It is apparent that Wagner, now one hundred years in that grave, continues to be haunted by his most famous admirer.

The readiness with which many people have accepted Hitler's famous claim that one could not understand the Third Reich without understanding Wagner[57] has clearly dimmed the popularity of his music in some quarters,[58] but in general we can safely say of Wagner's art (as someone once said of Christianity) that it has managed to survive the best efforts of its more fanatical adherents. But we can also safely say that although Nazi-German Wagnerism did not kill Wagnerism in the rest of Europe—it was already more or less moribund—the Führer's curse has made it highly unlikely that any movement dedicated to interpreting "the whole world in the light of Bayreuth" will ever again sweep across the land, as Eduard Hanslick said, "like an intellectual plague."[59]

Notes

Introduction

1. Edouard Dujardin, "*La revue wagnérienne,*" *La revue musicale,* 4 (1923), 248. See also Erwin Koppen, *Dekadenter Wagnerismus* (Berlin, 1973), p. 76.
2. Oscar Wilde, *The Picture of Dorian Gray* (New York, 1930), p. 185.
3. Kurt Jäckel, *Richard Wagner in der französischen Literatur,* 2 vols. (Breslau, 1931), 2:289.
4. J. F. Rowbotham, "The Wagner Bubble," *Nineteenth Century,* 24 (Oct. 1888), 511.
5. On this subject, see H. Stuart Hughes, *Consciousness and Society* (New York, 1958), pp. 3–66.
6. Gertrud Lenzer, ed., *Auguste Comte and Positivism* (New York, 1975), pp. xxi, xxvii.
7. Jane Fulcher, "Wagner, Comte, and Proudhon: Aesthetics of Positivism in France," *Symposium* (Syracuse University), 33 (1979), 142–52.
8. For a well-edited selection of Comte's writings, containing excerpts from all his "systems," see Lenzer, *Auguste Comte and Positivism.* Frank E. Manuel's *The Prophets of Paris* (New York, 1962) provides a short and cogent analysis of Comte's intellectual evolution. See pp. 249–96.
9. Hughes, *Consciousness and Society,* p. 39.
10. For a discussion of Marxism's relationship to positivism and the intellectual opposition it inspired, see ibid., pp. 67–104. The best discussion of Marxism's historical evolution from a philosophy of revolutionary activism into a deterministic "science" is George Lichtheim's *Marxism: An Historical and Critical Study* (London, 1961).
11. For a particularly well-developed discussion of these tendencies, see William J. McGrath, *Dionysian Art and Populist Politics in Austria* (New Haven, 1974).
12. Carl E. Schorske, "The Politics of the New Key: An Austrian Trio," *Fin-de-siècle Vienna* (New York, 1980), pp. 116–80.
13. Peter Gay, *The Bourgeois Experience: Victoria to Freud,* vol. 1, *The Education of the Senses* (New York, 1984), p. 60.
14. Ibid., p. 59.
15. Peter Gay's brilliant new study, *The Bourgeois Experience,* provides a fascinating tour through the nineteenth-century bourgeoisie's rich and complex sexual world.
16. A classic case of "low" cultural sublimation of sexual needs can be seen in the entertainments acted out by Kaiser Wilhelm II's entourage during the Kaiser's interminable sea journeys. These affairs often featured trans-

vestism, and one sketch proposed that one of Wilhelm's friends be paraded before the Kaiser dressed as a poodle, with "a noticeable rectal opening" under "a real poodle's tail." Such playacting was one way the Kaiser and some of his entourage could give vent to their repressed homoerotic inclinations. See Isabel V. Hull, *The Entourage of Kaiser Wilhelm II, 1888–1918* (Cambridge, England, 1982), pp. 68–9.

17. Thomas Mann, "Erinnerungen ans lübecker Stadttheater" (1930), in *Gesammelte Werke*, 13 vols. (Frankfurt, 1960–74), 11:418.

18. H. S. Chamberlain, *Lebenswege meines Denkens* (Munich, 1917), p. 241.

19. Romain Rolland, *Musicians of Today*, Mary Blaiklock, tr. (London, 1915), p. 65.

20. Leo Tolstoy, *What Is Art?* Aylmer Maude, tr. (Oxford, 1930), pp. 203–17.

21. Quoted in E. T. Cook, *The Life of John Ruskin*, 2 vols. (London, 1911), 1:457.

22. *Neue Zeitschrift für Musik*, 19 (Jan. 1, 1852), 37.

23. Quoted in Max Moser, *Richard Wagner in der englischen Literatur des XIX. Jahrhunderts* (Berlin, 1938), p. 18.

24. Ibid.

25. Katia Mann, *Meine ungeschriebene Memoiren* (Berlin, 1974), p. 12.

26. G. B. Shaw, *London Music in 1888–1890 as Heard by Corno di Bassetto* (London, 1937), p. 30.

27. See Jack M. Stein, *Richard Wagner and the Synthesis of the Arts* (Detroit, 1960); and Lucy Beckett, "Wagner and His Critics," in *The Wagner Companion*, Peter Burbidge and Richard Sutton, eds. (New York, 1979), pp. 365–88.

28. See chap. 3, nn. 87–93; Anne Dzamba Sessa, *Richard Wagner and the English* (Rutherford, N.J., 1979), pp. 88, 99–105; Aleksandr Benois, *Reminiscences of the Russian Ballet* (London, 1941).

29. See Sessa, *Richard Wagner and the English;* J. L. DiGaetani, *Richard Wagner and the Modern British Novel* (Cranbury, N.J., 1978); the contributions of Michael Black, Ronald Gray, Michael Tanner, and Lucy Beckett to Burbidge and Sutton, *Wagner Companion;* Léon Guichard, *La musique et les lettres au temps du wagnérisme* (Paris, 1963); James Northcote-Bade, *Die Mythen im Frühwerke Thomas Manns* (Bonn, 1975); and Raymond Furness, *Wagner and Literature* (Manchester, England, 1982).

30. See below, chap. 4, pp. 203–212, and especially Isadora Duncan's discussion of Wagner in *My Life* (New York, 1927), pp. 145–57.

31. Anna Jacobsen, *Nachklänge Richard Wagners im Roman* (Heidelberg, 1932), p. 15.

32. See below, pp. 298–300.

33. *The Ultimate Bourgeois: Artists and Politics in France, 1848–1851* (Greenwich, Conn., 1973); *Image of the People: Gustave Courbet and the Second French Republic* (Greenwich, Conn., 1973).

34. For a discussion of his exile, see Waldemar Lippert, *Wagner in Exile, 1849–1862*, Paul England, tr. (London, 1930).

35. A popular novelist of pan-German persuasion, however, was later to depict Wagner's relationship to Ludwig as a threat to German unification, describing Wagner as a money-hungry freeloader who had acted as a "slave of the

French Emperor and an obedient servant of Jesuitism." See Carl Werder, *Der Fürst vom Hochland* (Nuremberg, 1872), p. 90.

36. George C. Windell, "Hegel, Feuerbach, and Wagner's *Ring*," *Central European History*, 9 (1976), 27–57.

37. Carl E. Schorske, "The Quest for the Grail: Wagner and Morris," in *The Critical Spirit: Essays in Honor of Herbert Marcuse*, Kurt H. Wolff and Barrington Moore, Jr., eds. (Boston, 1967), pp. 216–32.

38. Elliott Zuckerman, *The First Hundred Years of "Tristan"* (New York, 1964).

39. André Coeuroy, *Richard Wagner et l'esprit romantique* (Paris, 1965), p. 7. Among the observers who take Wagnerian thinking particularly seriously might be mentioned as well J. L. Rather, whose *Dream of Self-Destruction: Wagner's "Ring" and the Modern World* (Baton Rouge, 1979) portrays that idea as pervasive in the literature surrounding Wagner. Jacques Barzun, however, had a more skeptical point of view in "Perfect Wagnerites," in *Darwin, Marx, Wagner: Critique of a Heritage*, 2d ed. (New York, 1958).

1. Wagner, Wagnerism, and Musical Idealism

1. Laudon, *Sources of the Wagnerian Synthesis: A Study of the Franco-German Tradition in Nineteenth-century Opera* (Munich, 1979).

2. John Warrack, "The Musical Background," in *The Wagner Companion*, Peter Burbidge and Richard Sutton, eds. (New York, 1979); Hans Redlich, "Wagnerian Elements in Pre-Wagnerian Opera," in *Essays Presented to Egon Wellesz*, Jack Westrup, ed. (London, 1966).

3. Little has been written on the reasons why musical taste was by tradition contemporary or on the rise in the classical repertoire. It is particularly remarkable that examinations of this question for the nineteenth century have hardly gone beyond the cult of Beethoven. See most profitably Walter Wiora, ed., *Die Ausbreitung des Historismus über die Musik* (Regensburg, 1969); Jacques Chailley, *40,000 Years of Music: Man in Search of Music*, Rollo Myers, tr. (London, 1964). My contribution to the subject includes "Learned and General Musical Taste in Eighteenth-century France," *Past and Present*, 89 (1980), pp. 58–85; "Intellectual Bases of the Handelian Tradition, 1759–1800," *Proceedings of the Royal Musical Association* (London), 108 (1981–1982), 100–14; and "The Contemporaneity of Eighteenth-century Musical Taste," *Musical Quarterly*, 70 (1984), 175–94.

4. "Obsérvations concernant la recette," [1781–1782], Archives Nationales, Paris, doc. o-624. See W. Weber, "*La musique ancienne* in the Waning of the Ancien Régime," *Journal of Modern History*, 56 (1984), 58–88.

5. For further discussion, see Weber, "Learned and General Musical Taste in Eighteenth-century France."

6. [M.-F.-P. de Mairobert], "Les prophéties du grand prophète Monet," (Paris, 1753), in *Querelle des bouffons*, 3 vols., Denise Launay, ed. (Geneva, 1973), 1:304.

7. Mozart to his father, Dec. 28, 1782, in Emily Anderson, tr. and ed., *Letters of Mozart and His Family* (New York, 1966), 3:1242.

8. See Arthur Loesser, *Men, Women and Pianos: A Social History of the Piano* (New York, 1954).

9. *Euterpe: Or Remarks on the Use and Abuse of Music as Part of Modern Education* (London, 1778). For nineteenth-century instances of such comments, see W. Weber, *Music and the Middle Class: Social Structure of Concert Life in London, Paris and Vienna, 1830–48* (London, 1975), p. 59n.

10. Nicholas Temperley, "Domestic Music in England," *Proceedings of the Royal Musical Association*, 85 (1958–1959), 31–47.

11. W. Weber, "The Muddle of the Middle Classes," *19th Century Music*, 3 (1979), 175–85.

12. See Klaus Hortschansky, "The Musician as Music Dealer in the Second Half of the Eighteenth Century," in *The Social Status of the Professional Musician from the Middle Ages to the Nineteenth Century*, Walter Salem, ed., Herbert Kaufman and Barbara Reisner, trs. (New York, 1983); and W. Weber, "Mass Culture and the Reshaping of Musical Taste," *International Review of the Aesthetics and Sociology of Music*, 8 (1977), 5–21.

13. Wagner to Liszt, Nov. 16, 1853, in *Correspondence of Wagner and Liszt*, 2 vols., Francis Hueffer, ed. and tr. (London, 1897), 1:341–42. I have employed English editions such as this, but the translations of passages cited in German in the notes are my own.

14. See Weber, *Music and the Middle Class*, pp. 18, 21, 42–44, 52, 165.

15. Leo Schrade, *Beethoven in France* (New Haven, 1942), is the most valuable work of this kind. See as well two important studies: Leon B. Plantinga, "Schumann's View of 'Romantic,'" *Musical Quarterly*, 52 (1966), 221–32, and Bellamy Hosler, *Changing Aesthetic Views of Instrumental Music in Eighteenth-century Germany* (Ann Arbor, 1981).

16. "Ueber reisende Virtuosen," *Allgemeine musikalische Zeitung*, 4 (Aug. 18, 1802), 753.

17. "Kritische Paraphrasen," ibid., 49 (Nov. 3, 1847), 754.

18. "Miscellen," ibid., 48 (Sept. 9, 1846), 603.

19. Franz Brendel, "Der Beifall des Publikums und der Werth desselben," *Neue Zeitschrift für Müsik*, Apr. 26, 1849, 189.

20. Ibid., p. 190.

21. "Dialogen über Zeitgegenstände in der Musik," *Allgemeine musikalische Zeitung*, 25 (Feb. 5, 1823), 87.

22. *Allgemeine Musikzeitung* (Vienna), May 26, 1819, pp. 337–38.

23. *Allgemeine musikalische Anzeiger* (Vienna), Mar. 9, 1848, p. 47.

24. *Harmonicon*, June 1829, p. 145; Sept. 1833, p. 187.

25. Hawkins, *An Account of the Institution and Progress of the Academy of Ancient Music* (London, 1770), p. 13. See as well the "Preliminary Discourse" and conclusion of his *General History of the Science and Practice of Music*, 2 vols., Charles Cudworth, ed. (New York, 1963).

26. "Ueber das jetzt gewöhnliche Aufführungen einzelner Opernscenen in Konzerte," *Allgemeine musikalische Zeitung* (May 1, 1799), p. 481.

27. "Vorschläge zu Betrachtungen über die neueste Geschichte der Musik," ibid., July 3, 1799, 628.

28. Source of data is Alfred Dörffel, *Geschichte des Gewandhausconcerts zu Leipzig*, 2 vols. (Leipzig, 1881–1884), vol. 2, app. I have computed these

seasonal percentages from Dörffel's list of works performed by the orchestra, which is organized by composers and works.

29. The series is more significant in the early history of the classical repertoire than that of the oft-cited Society of the Friends of Music of Vienna, which offered programs of a much more conventional (contemporary) sort. See "Miscellaneous Programs, 1813–48," archive of the Gesellschaft der Musikfreunde, Vienna.

30. M. B. Foster, *History of the Philharmonic Society of London*, (London, 1912). During the early 1820s, the percentage of works by dead composers was about 30 percent; in the 1850s, 50 percent; and by the 1870s, 80 percent.

31. Dörffel, *Geschichte*, 1:40–41, 80.

32. *Album de Sainte-Cécile*, Jan. 20, 1846, p. 3.

33. "Kritische Paraphrasen," *Allgemeine musikalische Zeitung*, Nov. 3, 1847, p. 755.

34. Wagner, "German Music," in *Wagner Writes from Paris: . . . Stories, Essays and Articles by the Young Composer*, Robert L. Jacobs and Geoffrey Skelton, eds. and trs. (London, 1973), p. 40.

35. Wagner, "The Virtuoso and the Artist," in ibid., pp. 53–54.

36. Ibid., p. 57.

37. Wagner, *Rossini's "Stabat Mater,"* in *Richard Wagner's Prose Works* (hereafter *RWPW*), 8 vols., William Ashton Ellis, tr. (London, 1892–1899), 7:143.

38. Wagner, "Death in Paris," in Jacobs and Skelton, *Wagner Writes from Paris*, p. 88.

39. Wagner, "A Pilgrimage to Beethoven," in ibid., p 79.

40. Wagner, "Death in Paris," in ibid., pp. 86–87.

41. Wagner, review originally in the Dresden *Abendzeitung*, May 5, 1841, reprinted in ibid., p. 129.

42. Wagner, "A Happy Evening," in ibid., p. 178.

43. See M. J. E. Brown, *Schubert: A Critical Biography* (London, 1958); O. E. Deutsch, *Schubert: Die Erinnerungen seiner Freunden* (Leipzig, 1957). On Schubert's income, see a fine debunking piece by Otto Biba, "Schubert's Position in Viennese Musical Life," *19th Century Music*, 3 (1979), 106–13.

44. Wagner, "Farewell Performances," in Jacobs and Skelton, *Wagner Writes from Paris*, p. 126.

45. See Schindler's *Beethoven as I Knew Him*, D. W. McArdle, tr. (London, 1966). All of his writings on Beethoven are riddled with errors, many of them self-serving.

46. Wagner, "Farewell Performances," in Jacobs and Skelton, *Wagner Writes from Paris*, pp. 126–27.

47. Wagner, "Death in Paris," in ibid., p. 101.

48. *Evenings with the Orchestra*, Jacques Barzun, tr. and ed. (Chicago, 1956), p. 180.

49. Ibid., p. 164.

50. Ibid., pp. 283, 265.

51. See Carl E. Schorske, "The Quest for the Grail: Wagner and Morris," in *The Critical Spirit: Essays in Honor of Herbert Marcuse*, Kurt H. Wolff and Barrington Moore, Jr., eds. (Boston, 1967); and George C. Windell,

"Hegel, Feuerbach, and Wagner's *Ring,*" *Central European History,* 9 (1976), 27–57.

52. For Wagner's activities during the Dresden uprising, see especially Frank B. Josserand, *Richard Wagner: Patriot and Politician* (Washington, 1981), pp. 63–108; and Woldemar Lippert, *Richard Wagners Verbannung und Rückkehr, 1849–1862* (Dresden, 1927).

53. Wagner to Liszt, Jun. 5, 1849, in Hueffer, *Correspondence of Wagner and Liszt,* 1:25.

54. Wagner, *Art-Work of the Future,* in RWPW, 1:85.

55. Wagner, *Art and Revolution,* in *RWPW,* 1:64.

56. Wagner, *Plan of Organization,* in *RWPW,* 7:335.

57. Wagner, *A Theater in Zürich,* in *RWPW,* 3:36.

58. Wagner, *Music of the Future,* in *RWPW,* 3:306.

59. Wagner, *Art and Revolution,* in *RWPW,* 1:42.

60. Wagner, *Plan of Organization,* in *RWPW,* 7:355.

61. *Musical World,* Jan. 16, 1845, p. 16.

62. On the rise of a classical repertoire among the virtuosos, see Loesser, *Men, Women and Pianos,* pp. 417–30; and Pamela Susskind Pettler, "Clara Schumann's Recitals, 1832–50," *19th Century Music,* 4 (1980), 70–76. My conclusions are based on a study of programs in collections maintained chiefly in the following libraries: the Bibliothèque de l'Opéra and the Musée de l'Histoire de Paris, in Paris; the Royal College of Music and the British Library, in London; the Archive of the Gesellschaft der Musikfreunde, in Vienna; and the Stadtbibliothek in Leipzig.

63. See James H. Davison, *From Mendelssohn to Wagner: Memoirs of J. H. Davison* (London, 1912), and Eduard Hanslick, *Aus meinem Leben* (Berlin, 1894).

64. For the programs, see Antoine Elwart, *Histoire de la Société des Concerts* (Paris, 1860), app. For the 1863 decision, see "Rapport à l'assemblée générale du comité: Compte-rendu de l'exercise 1863/4," Fonds Conservatoire, Bibliothèque Nationale. Most of the major orchestras adopted the practice of holding "trial" performances, private sessions where new works would be played for possible inclusion in repertoire. Despite the museumlike role of the orchestras, they kept up their influence over new music by this practice and by the occasional selection of works for public performance. Aside from those presented by the orchestra of the Conservatoire, most symphonic programs included about 20 to 30 percent works by living composers. Though a far cry from the situation at the start of the century, these numbers put to shame the roughly 5 percent of new works presented yearly by present-day American orchestras (which is often done only because foundations demand it).

65. By the late 1860s, over half of the performances of the Théâtre Italien in Paris included works by dead composers; see Albert Soubiès, *Le Théâtre-Italien de 1801 à 1913* (Paris, 1913).

66. *Allgemeine musikalische Zeitung,* May 16, 1847, p. 354. See also Dec. 22, 1847, pp. 873–75.

67. Barzun, *Evenings with the Orchestra,* p. 321.

68. Wagner, *Pergolesi's "Stabat Mater,"* in *RWPW,* 7:103.

69. Wagner, *Art-Work of the Future*, in *RWPW*, 1:182.
70. Quoted in Ernest Newman, *The Life of Richard Wagner*, 4 vols. (Cambridge, England, 1933–1946), 2:369.
71. See Jack M. Stein, *Richard Wagner and the Synthesis of the Arts* (Detroit, 1960), p. 6 and passim.
72. See Michael Ewans, *Wagner and Aeschylus: "The Ring" and "The Oresteia"* (New York, 1983).
73. Lorenz, *Das Geheimnis der Form bei Richard Wagner*, 4 vols. (Berlin, 1924).
74. Bailey, "The Structure of the *Ring* and Its Evolution," *19th Century Music*, 1 (1977), 48–61; "Wagner's Sketches for Siegfrieds Tod," in *Studies in Music History: Essays for Oliver Strunk*, Harold Powers, ed. (Princeton, 1968); "The Genesis of *Tristan und Isolde* and a Study of Wagner's Sketches and Drafts for the First Act," Ph.D. dissertation, Princeton University, 1969. I am grateful to Malcolm Cole for his teaching on this subject.
75. See Laudon, *Sources of the Wagnerian Synthesis*, pp. 43–55, 90–110.
76. Ibid., pp. 13–60; Robert Gutman, "*Leitmotif* and Wagner's Musical Architecture," in *Richard Wagner: The Man, His Mind, and His Music* (New York, 1968), chap. 14; Deryck Cooke, "Wagner's Musical Language," in Burbidge and Sutton, *Wagner Companion*, pp. 225–68.
77. See the recorded and printed notes by Deryck Cooke, "An Introduction to *The Ring of Nibelungen*," included in the recording of the *Ring* by the Vienna Philharmonic Orchestra conducted by Georg Solti, London Records no. RDNS-1 (London, 1961).
78. Hausegger, "Richard Wagner and Modism," in *Bayreuther Festblätter in Bild und Wort* (Munich, 1884), p. 23.
79. Wolzogen, "Zur Einführung," in ibid., p. 4.
80. Sessa, *Richard Wagner and the English* (Rutherford, N.J., 1979).
81. On the Querelle des bouffons, see Louisette Reichenburg, *Contribution à l'histoire de la Querelle des bouffons* (Philadelphia, 1937). Cage's work comprised 4' 3" of silence, the performer David Tudor seated motionless at the keyboard. See Paul Griffiths, *John Cage* (London, 1981), p. 28.
82. Pohl, "Aus den ersten Zeiten des Wagnerismus," in *Bayreuther Festblätter*, pp. 10–14.
83. See Leon B. Plantinga, *Schumann as Critic* (New Haven, 1967), pp. 3–51. On Brendel, see James Deaville's perceptive "Franz Brendel: Ein Neudeutscher aus der Sicht Wagners und Liszts," forthcoming in *Liszt-Studien III*.
84. Brendel, "Ein Ausflug nach Weimar," *Neue Zeitschrift für Musik*, 19 (Jan. 1, 1852), 37.
85. "Ein Verteidiger Richard Wagners," *Die fliegende Blätter*, 1, no. 1 (1853), 55.
86. See *Anregungen für Kunst, Leben, und Wissenschaft* (Leipzig), especially vols. 1–3 (1856–1858). Richard Pohl was coeditor from 1857 on. I am grateful to James Deaville for pointing out the political tendencies in this journal.
87. See John L. Snell, *The Democratic Movement in Germany, 1789–1914*, Hans A. Schmitt, ed. and contributor (Chapel Hill, N.C., 1976), pp. 101–29. On the vigorous revival of liberalism during the 1850s, see ibid., pp. 130–61; James J. Sheehan, *German Liberalism in the Nineteenth Century* (Chicago,

1978), pp. 79–121. In *The Social Foundations of German Unification, 1858–1871* (Princeton, 1969), Theodore S. Hamerow points out a pattern of radicalism in the smaller German states among shopkeepers, merchants, professional men, and small independent landowners who opposed "autocracy, clericalism, jingoism, centralizing bureaucracy, and restrictive economic regulation." Hamerow finds this tendency chiefly south of the Main, but this small-town radicalism, with its "charmingly ingenuous flavor," has distinct similarities to the Wagnerian movement in Saxony (p. 150).

88. See "Johann Uhlig," *New Grove Dictionary of Music and Musicians* (London, 1980), 19:322.

89. Wagner to Uhlig, Aug. or Sept. 1850, in *Richard Wagner's Letters to His Dresden Friends,* J. S. Shedlock, tr. and ed. (London, 1890), pp. 52–54. See as well his letters to Uhlig, in ibid., Oct. 20, 1851, p. 130; Oct. 30, 1851, p. 135; Nov. 18, 1851, p. 146; Dec. 3, 1851, pp. 150–51; Dec. 18, 1851, p. 160.

90. Wagner to Uhlig, in ibid., Jan. 1, 1852, p. 167.

91. Wagner complained to Liszt, "*Pereant* all Brendels and Köhlers, so long as they can think of nothing better than this eternal confused speculation about—art!" Quoted in Newman, *Life of Wagner*, 2:368.

92. Discussion of this aspect of Liszt's career is still limited. Though old, Julius Kapp's *Liszt: Eine Biographie* (Berlin, 1916) confronts the problem to an unusual degree; see as well W. Felix, "Die Reformideen Franz Liszts," in *Festschrift Richard Münnick,* Hans Pischner, et al., eds. (Leipzig, 1957).

93. Liszt to Wagner, July 1850, in Hueffer, *Correspondence of Wagner and Liszt,* 1:70.

94. Liszt to Wagner, Apr. 8, 1853, in ibid., p. 275.

95. "Ein Verteidiger Richard Wagners," *Fliegende Blätter,* 1, no. 1 (1853), 54–55. The editor of *Fliegende Blätter,* J. C. Lobe, bore a grudge against the *Neue Zeitschrift,* since he had been editor of the competing *Allgemeine musikalische Zeitung* in its last three years before it ceased publication in 1848. *Fliegende Blätter* contains articles of great interest regarding the evolution of musical taste, written from the idealist perspective; see, for example, "Salonmusik," vol. 1, no. 3 (1853), 154–55.

96. Brendel, "Fragen zur Zeit," *Neue Zeitschrift für Musik,* 15 (Sept. 2, 1848), 103.

97. Liszt to Wagner, Dec. 13, 1853, in Hueffer, *Correspondence of Wagner and Liszt,* 1:345.

98. "Woher ist das Reden von der musikalischen Zukunft entstanden und welche Folgen hat es?" *Fliegende Blätter,* 2, no. 5 (1854), 299.

99. "Ein Verteidiger Richard Wagners," *Fliegende Blätter,* 1, no. 1 (1853), 55n.

100. See Richard Pohl, *Die Tonkünstler-Versammlung zu Leipzig am 1. bis 4. Juni 1859* (Leipzig, 1859), pp. 172–81. On the revival of liberalism—both political and cultural—at the end of the 1850s, see Sheehan, *German Liberalism in the Nineteenth Century,* pp. 95–107.

101. Pohl, *Tonkünstler-Versammlung,* pp. 48–49.

102. Brendel, "Der Allgemeine Deutsche Musikverein," in *Almanach des Allgemeinen Deutschen Musikvereins* (Leipzig, 1868), p. 99. I am indebted to Dr.

Reich of the Niedersächisches Landesarchiv, Dresden, for acquainting me with this volume. For discussion of the problems composers faced over royalties, see *Die Signale für die musikalische Welt* (Leipzig), 24 (1867), 967–70; 25 (1868), 225–26.

103. Brendel noted that during August the Musikverein held "farewell festivities for the departing master"; see his article on the organization in the *Almanach des Allgemeinen Deutschen Musikvereins*, p. 103.

104. Pohl, *Tonkünstler-Versammlung*, p. 46.

105. "Chronik der Ereignisse des Jahres 1864," in *Almanach des Allgemeinen Deutschen Musikvereins*, p. 157.

106. Ibid., p. 162.

107. "Novitäten Fragen," *Neue Zeitschrift für Musik*, 37 (Nov. 21, 1872), 475–7; "Künstler und Publikum," ibid., 37 (Sept. 13, 1872), 379.

108. In the late 1880s, for example, the Wiesbaden Tonkünstler-Sammlung identified itself as a chapter of the Allgemeiner Deutscher Musikverein; see Arthur Seidl, *Wagneriana*, 3 vols. (Berlin, 1901), 2:328.

109. *Musik-Politik: Beiträge zur Reform unseres Musiklebens* (Stuttgart, 1911), p. 121. Wagnerian rhetoric carries on in Storck's writing, especially in polemics against the *Unvolkstümlichkeit* he saw in musical life and the materialism he saw in recent styles.

110. Hermann Kretschmar, *Musikalische Zeitfragen* (Leipzig, 1903), pp. 2–3. See also pp. 128–30.

111. See, for example, Storck's *Musik-Politik*, Paul Stefan, *Neue Musik und Wien* (Vienna, 1921), and Friedrich Wedl, *Krise der wiener Konzert-Orchester* (Vienna, 1919).

112. For further discussion, see chapter 2, "Wagner's Bayreuth Disciples."

113. McGrath, *Dionysian Art and Populist Politics in Austria* (New Haven, 1974).

114. See W. Weber, "A Myth of Musical Vienna," in *Report of the 12th Congress of the International Musicological Society, Berkeley, 1977*, Bonnie Wade and Daniel Heartz, eds. (Regensburg, 1981), pp. 314–18; Robert Hirschfeld, "Konzerte in Wien," *Zeitschrift der internationalen Musik-Gesellschaft*, 1 (1900), 226–34. The Philharmonic was so intensely disliked for its social exclusiveness that in 1885 the Vienna City Council voted fifty to four against a motion commending it upon its twenty-fifth anniversary; see the *Vorstadt-Zeitung*, Apr. 2, 1885.

115. Albert Gutmann, *Volksconcerte in Wien: Vorschläge zur Bildung eines Concert-orchesters* (Vienna, n.d.). See also Theobald Kretschmann, *Tempi passati: Aus den Erinnerungen eines Musikanten*, 2 vols. (Vienna, 1913), 2:55–59.

116. Wedl, *Krise der wiener Konzert-Orchester*, passim.

117. See Frank Walker, *Hugo Wolf: A Biography*, 2d ed. (London, 1968); Heinrich Werner, ed., *Hugo Wolf und der wiener akademische Wagner-Verein* (Regensburg, 1926); Richard Batka and Heinrich Werner, *Hugo Wolfs musicalische Kritiken im Auftrage des wiener akademischen Wagner-Vereins* (Leipzig, 1911).

118. Walker, *Hugo Wolf*, pp. 432–33.

119. Batka and Werner, *Hugo Wolfs musikalische Kritiken*, pp. 160–61.

120. Stefan, *Neue Musik und Wien*, p. 21.

121. Graf, *Vienna: Legend of a Musical City* (New York, 1945), p. 136.

122. Batka and Werner, *Hugo Wolfs musikalische Kritiken,* pp. 164, 243. I have hardly begun to describe the intensity of the conflict, which on some occasions even involved disturbances at concerts. Brahms did not answer Wolf's attacks in print. As the *Prag Rundschau* said, his followers tried to make him "play the antagonist [*Gegenkönig*] to modern music against Wagner, Liszt, and Bruckner," but "he did not engage in such factional squabbling" (Apr. 15, 1897, pp. 251–52). On the decline of the dispute after the turn of the century, see Stefan, *Neue Musik und Wien,* pp. 46–49.

123. Gay, "Aimez-vous Brahms? Reflections on Modernism," in *Freud, Jews and Other Germans: Masters and Victims in Modernist Culture* (New York, 1978), pp. 231–56.

124. Schoenberg, in *Style and Idea,* 2d ed., Dika Newlin, tr., Leonard Stein, ed. (New York, 1975). The essay, originally given as a lecture in 1933, was first published in the original edition of *Style and Idea* in 1947. On Schoenberg, see Carl E. Schorske, *Fin-de-siècle Vienna: Politics and Culture* (New York, 1980), pp. 344–66, and Charles Rosen, *Arnold Schoenberg* (New York, 1975).

125. On the deep involvement of modernists with music of the classical tradition, see J. Peter Burkholder's penetrating discussion in "Museum Pieces: The Historicist Mainstream in Music of the Last Hundred Years," *Journal of Musicology,* 2 (1983), 115–34.

126. Byran R. Simms, "The Society for Private Performances: Resources and Documents in Schoenberg's Legacy," *Journal of the Arnold Schoenberg Institute,* 3 (1979), 3–15. I am indebted to Dr. Paul Pisk and the late Dr. Felix Greissle, secretaries to Schoenberg during that period, for the valuable information they provided me during interviews on the history of the organization.

2. Wagner's Bayreuth Disciples

Note: All translations are my own, unless otherwise indicated. Although an English edition of Cosima Wagner's diary is available, I have used the original German text in this chapter.

1. Austria as well as Germany was an important center of *Wagnerismus.* A major locus of Austrian Wagnerism was the so-called Pernerstorfer Circle, which included—in addition to Engelbert Pernerstorfer—such diverse figures as Victor Adler, Gustav Mahler, Siegfried Lipiner, Richard von Kralik, Heinrich Friedjung, and Georg von Schönerer. On Wagnerism and the Pernerstorfer Circle, see William McGrath, *Dionysian Art and Populist Politics in Austria* (New Haven, 1974), pp. 89–99. Austria's most influential music critic, Eduard Hanslick, however, had no use whatsoever for *Wagnerismus.* In his autobiography he predicted that the writings of the Wagnerites would soon "be looked on in amazement as the relics of an intellectual plague" (quoted in Robert W. Gutman, *Richard Wagner: The Man, His Mind and His Music* [Harmondsworth, England, 1971], p. 16).

2. The academic Wagner societies at the universities of Berlin, Leipzig, and Marburg joined together in the Verband akademischer Richard Wagner-

Vereine in August 1894. For its bylaws, see *Bayreuther Blätter* [henceforth *BB*], 18 (1895), 81–82. The University of Vienna, too, had an important academic Wagner society, which published the *Jahresberichte des wiener akademischen Wagner-Vereins.*

3. There is one book-length study of this group: Winfried Schüler, *Der bay-reuther Kreis von seiner Entstehung bis zum Ausgang der wilhelminischen Ära* (Münster, 1971) [henceforth *BK*]. As will be evident from my notes, I found it a highly useful source for this essay, though I do not agree with all its conclusions. Geoffrey Field's recent biography of Houston Stewart Chamberlain is also a good source for the Bayreuth Circle as a whole: *The Evangelist of Race: The Germanic Vision of Houston Stewart Chamberlain* (New York, 1981).

4. This reference was especially uncharitable because in addition to recalling the infamous Lola Montez, it coyly hinted that Ludwig's relationship with Wagner was homosexual. Although Ludwig undoubtedly felt a kind of love for Wagner, he eventually learned to love Wagner the artist and not Wagner the man.

5. Gutman, *Richard Wagner*, p. 382.

6. For a more detailed discussion of Wagner's abortive imperial suit, see David C. Large, "The Political Background of the Foundation of the Bayreuth Festival, 1876," *Central European History,* 11 (1978), 162–72.

7. Wrote Wagner: "From its condition of civilized barbarism true art can lift itself to its proper rank only on the shoulders of our great social movement. The two have a common goal, and both can reach it only if they realize it in common. This goal is the strong and the beautiful human being: revolution gives him strength, art gives him beauty" (*Die Kunst und die Revolution,* in *Gesammelte Schriften und Dichtungen,* 8 vols. [Leipzig, n.d.], 3:32).

8. Ibid., pp. 11–18.

9. *Das Kunstwerk der Zukunft,* in *Gesammelte Schriften,* 3:42–44.

10. Ibid., p. 44.

11. George C. Windell, "Hegel, Feuerbach and Wagner's *Ring,*" *Central European History,* 9 (1976), 27–57.

12. For a discussion of Schopenhauerian motifs in the *Ring,* see Ronald Gray, "The German Intellectual Background," in Peter Burbidge and Richard Sutton, eds., *The Wagner Companion* (New York, 1979), p. 42.

13. The Nietzsche-Wagner relationship has been the subject of considerable scholarly attention. Good discussions can be found in Gutman, *Richard Wagner;* F. R. Love, *Young Nietzsche and the Wagnerian Experience,* University of North Carolina Studies in German Language and Literature, no. 39 (Chapel Hill, N.C., 1963); Ronald Hayman, *Nietzsche: A Critical Life* (New York, 1980); Martin Gregor-Dellin, *Richard Wagner* (Munich, 1983). For a very readable popular study, see Dietrich Fischer-Dieskau, *Wagner and Nietzsche* (New York, 1976).

14. Quoted in George R. Marek, *Cosima Wagner* (New York, 1981), p. 117.

15. The best short study on Lagarde is Fritz Stern, *The Politics of Cultural Despair* (Berkeley, 1961), pp. 25–128.

16. Cosima Wagner, *Tagebücher*, 2 vols., Martin Gregor-Dellin and Dietrich Mack, eds. (Munich, 1976–1977), 1:966.
17. Paul de Lagarde, "Über die gegenwärtige Lage des deutschen Reiches," in *Deutsche Schriften*, 3d ed. (Munich, 1937), p. 184. See also Stern, *Politics of Cultural Despair*, p. 3.
18. Quoted in Stern, *Politics of Cultural Despair*, p. 89n.
19. On Gobineau see Ludwig Schemann, *Gobineau: Eine Biographie*, 2 vols. (Strassburg, 1913–1916); and, more recently, M. D. Bildiss, *Father of Racist Ideology: The Social and Political Thought of Count Gobineau* (London, 1970).
20. Gutman, *Richard Wagner*, p. 586. Gutman also makes much of the homosexual motif in *Parsifal*, suggesting that the chaste hero was modeled on King Ludwig II of Bavaria, the *Weibjüngling* whom Wagner had hoped "would redeem a debauched kingdom by means of a thorough racial cleansing and thus achieve his destiny as a dragon fighter" (p. 610). An earlier critic of *Parsifal*, Oskar Panizza, had also noted (and lamented) the homosexual tendencies in Wagner's last work, which he attributed mainly to the sexual inversion that (allegedly) often afflicts elderly artists. But Panizza, interestingly enough, did not see anything racially ennobling in Parsifal's *Männerliebe*; rather, he connected homosexuality with the enfeebled "non-Germanic races" like the Latins, Orientals, and Jews and warned that *Parsifal* was hardly wholesome fare for healthy Nordic males. See Oskar Panizza, "Bayreuth und die Homosexualität," *Die Gesellschaft* (Munich), 11 (1895), 88–92. For an intelligent critique of Gutman's *Parsifal* interpretation, see Lucy Beckett, *Richard Wagner: "Parsifal"* (Cambridge Opera Handbooks, Cambridge, England, 1981).
21. The most recent Wagner biographer to take this line is Robert Gutman. He argues that Wagner believed himself to be the illegitimate offspring of his stepfather, Ludwig Geyer, whom he also thought (albeit incorrectly) to be Jewish. His anti-Semitism, then, was rooted in Jewish self-hatred (pp. 28–29). Martin Gregor-Dellin's yet more recent biography convincingly disposes of the "self-hatred" argument by pointing out that while Wagner may indeed have agonized over his parental origins, and thus made the problem of the unknown father a recurring theme in his art, he never saw the possibility that Geyer was his father as a cause for shame. On the contrary, he loved his stepfather deeply. See Gregor-Dellin, *Richard Wagner*, pp. 34–49.
22. *BK*, p. 233.
23. On Wagner's behavior toward Hermann Levi, see Peter Gay, "Hermann Levi: A Study in Service and Self-Hatred," in *Freud, Jews and Other Germans* (New York, 1978), pp. 189–230. Gay points out (p. 223) that Wagner could both "heartily commiserate with Levi about the cruel destiny that doomed him to be born a Jew, and congratulate him for retaining his obviously Jewish name." He could also urge Levi to accept baptism.
24. R. Wagner, "Ueber das Judentum in der Musik," in *Gesammelte Schriften und Dichtungen*, 3:67.
25. Wagner proposed the "solution of Ahasver—destruction" as the only recourse open to Jews wishing to escape their "curse." Ibid., p. 85. (Ahasver

was the "Wandering Jew" of medieval legend who carried a double curse: his Jewishness and his inability to find a place to rest. Wagner's proposed "solution" to this "Jewish problem" sounds very much like Hitler's.)

26. Ibid.
27. On this strange episode in Herzl's career, see Carl E. Schorske, *Fin-de-siècle Vienna* (New York, 1980), p. 161.
28. R. Wagner, "Heldentum und Christentum," *BB*, 4 (1881), 249–58. See also Field, *Evangelist of Race*, p. 153.
29. George Bernard Shaw, *The Perfect Wagnerite: A Commentary on the Niblung's Ring* (New York, 1909), p. 118.
30. *BK*, p. 12.
31. Ibid., p. 18.
32. R. Wagner, "Erkenne dich selbst," *BB*, 4 (1881), 40; *BK*, p. 19.
33. Gutman, *Richard Wagner*, p. 440.
34. *BK*, p. 18.
35. On Wolzogen, see *BK*, pp. 86–93; Erik Böhm, *Hans von Wolzogen als Herausgeber der "Bayreuther Blätter"* (Munich, 1943). Wolzogen wrote a short memoir entitled *Lebensbilder* (Regensburg, 1923).
36. R. Wagner to Ludwig II, Feb. 9, 1879, in *König Ludwig II Richard Wagner Briefwechsel*, 5 vols. (Karlsruhe, 1936–1939), 3:146.
37. Wolzogen to Wolfgang Korber, Dec. 15, 1867. Quoted in *BK*, p. 89.
38. C. Wagner, *Tagebücher*, 1:1092.
39. Ibid., 2:233, marginal note.
40. Ibid., p. 189.
41. Wolzogen, "Unsere Lage," *BB*, 1 (1878), 9–10.
42. Ibid., p. 10.
43. Wolzogen, *Lebensbilder*, p. 15.
44. Wolzogen, "Zur sozialen Frage," *BB*, 3 (1880), 162.
45. Ibid., p. 160.
46. Wolzogen's ideas on the stock market are contained in another essay on the "social question." See *BB*, 3 (1880), 181–92.
47. Wolzogen, "Aus unserer Zeit," *BB*, 3 (1880), 311.
48. Ibid., pp. 312–13.
49. Wolzogen to L. Schemann, Aug. 17, 1877, quoted in *BK*, p. 91, n. 32.
50. Wolzogen, "Unter Uns: Ein Brief über Kunst und Kirche," *BB*, 18 (1895), 204.
51. *BK*, p. 91.
52. Wolzogen attributed his religious perspective to "Frau Cosima's consoling ideas about Protestantism" (quoted in *BK*, p. 91).
53. C. Wagner, *Tagebücher*, 1:1097. Wagner was also annoyed by Wolzogen's suggestion that Parsifal represented Christ and Kundry the Magdalen. See Beckett, *"Parsifal,"* p. 11.
54. Wolzogen, "Die Ungleichheit der menschlichen Racen," *BB*, 5 (1882), 263–92.
55. Ibid., p. 266.
56. At one point Wagner wished Wolzogen and Ludwig Schemann would "go to the devil" for constantly bothering him about the Wagner societies. See C. Wagner, *Tagebücher*, 2:610.

57. *BK,* p. 59.
58. Wolzogen to L. Schemann, Mar. 7, 1905, quoted in *BK,* p. 141.
59. Gerhard Masur, *Imperial Berlin* (New York, 1970), p. 237.
60. Richard Linnemann, "Fünfzig Jahre Allgemeiner Richard Wagner-Verein," *BB,* 50 (1927), 221.
61. Wolzogen, "Wagnervereine nach dem Kriege," *BB,* 42 (1919), 133.
62. Ibid., p. 131.
63. Ibid., p. 132.
64. Ibid., p. 133.
65. See Fritz Stern's masterful essay, "The Political Consequences of the Unpolitical German," *The Failure of Illiberalism* (New York, 1972), pp. 3–24.
66. *BK,* p. 92.
67. Erik Valentin, "Der getreue Eckart: Dankgruss an Hans von Wolzogen," *Völkischer Beobachter,* June 4, 1938.
68. Hermann Rauschnigg, *Gespräche mit Hitler* (Vienna, 1940), p. 216. See also *BK,* p. 92.
69. *BK,* p. 92.
70. Adolf Rapp, "Die Erscheinung Richard Wagners im Geistesleben," *Architektur für Kulturgeschichte,* 11 (1913), 97, quoted in *BK,* p. 87.
71. There are many biographies of Cosima Wagner, but none is entirely satisfying. The pioneering hagiography by Count Richard Du Moulin-Eckhart (*Cosima Wagner: Ein Lebens- und Charakterbild,* 2 vols., [Munich, 1929–1931] was followed by several works written in a similar spirit but lacking as much detail. For more modern and readable studies, see Alice Sokoloff, *Cosima Wagner: Extraordinary Daughter of Franz Liszt* (New York, 1969) and (better yet) George Marek, *Cosima Wagner* (New York, 1981).
72. C. Wagner, *Tagebücher,* 1:1025.
73. Marek, *Cosima Wagner,* p. 48.
74. C. Wagner, *Tagebücher,* 1:476.
75. R. Wagner to Angelo Neumann, Sept. 29, 1882, quoted in *Bayreuther Festspielführer* (Bayreuth, 1937), p. 61.
76. Michael Karbaum, *Studien zur Geschichte der bayreuther Festspiele, 1876–1976* (Regensburg, 1976), p. 41.
77. Quoted in ibid., p. 36.
78. Ibid., p. 33. Siegfried was Cosima's fifth child, her only son and the only child she had while married to Wagner. She had two daughters (Daniele and Blandine) by Hans von Bülow. Her next two children, Isolde and Eva, were both fathered by Wagner while Cosima was still married to von Bülow. In 1914, Isolde sought in court to have Wagner declared her legal father so that she might share in the family inheritance. She was unsuccessful in her suit but managed in the process to humiliate her estranged mother, who was forced to testify in the trial about the details of her premarital relations with Wagner.
79. George Marek argues convincingly that Cosima's marriage to von Bülow was never really a love match (*Cosima Wagner,* pp. 26, 64).
80. C. Wagner, *Tagebücher,* 1:1041.
81. C. Wagner to H. S. Chamberlain, Apr. 20, 1891, in *Cosima Wagner und H. S. Chamberlain im Briefwechsel,* Paul Pretzsch, ed. (Stuttgart, 1933), p. 222.

82. C. Wagner, *Tagebücher*, 1:377–78.
83. On Cosima's interpretation of Richard's works, see, *inter alia*, *BK*, p. 81; Karbaum, *Studien*, p. 32; and Hans Mayer, *Richard Wagner in Bayreuth* (New York, 1976), p. 72.
84. R. Wagner to Friedrich von Schön, June 28, 1880, quoted in Karl Heckel, *Die Bühnenfestspiele in Bayreuth* (Leipzig, n.d.), p. 35.
85. C. Wagner, *Tagebücher*, 1:1080.
86. Geoffrey Skelton, *Wagner at Bayreuth* (New York, 1965), p. 71.
87. Albert Schweitzer, *Out of My Life and Thoughts* (New York, 1949), p. 30.
88. Marek, *Cosima Wagner*, p. 225.
89. Egon Gartenberg, *Vienna: Its Cultural Heritage* (University Park, Pa., 1968), p. 195.
90. Mayer, *Wagner in Bayreuth*, p. 81.
91. Quoted in ibid., p. 75.
92. Ibid., pp. 74–75.
93. Quoted in ibid., p. 75.
94. Wolzogen to Schemann, Dec 12, 1897. Quoted in *BK*, p. 82.
95. Quoted in *BK*, pp. 81–82.
96. Quoted in *BK*, p. 82.
97. C. Wagner, *Tagebücher*, 1:351, 354.
98. Ibid., p. 512.
99. Cosima and Richard agreed that the whole continent of America was "nothing, compared to our tiny spaces." See ibid., p. 537. Of course, neither had ever been there, and Richard was soon to fantasize about emigrating there, culture or no.
100. Gutman argues that Cosima's racism was—like her husband's—in part inspired by anxieties about ancestry. Noting that her mother's father, the Viscount de Flavigny, married the daughter of Simon Moritz Bethmann, a wealthy Jewish banker, he concludes: "Ashamed of her descent from the patriarchal Schimsche Naphtali Bethmann, Cosima spent a lifetime seeking to deny it through anti-Semitic abuse" (p. 303). Gutman may be correct in this conclusion, but he offers little concrete evidence to support it.
101. Wagner not only enjoyed the artistic cooperation of Jews like Hermann Levi, Josef Rubinstein, Karl Tausig, and Angelo Neumann; he also garnered considerable financial support from Jewish members of the Wagner societies, especially in Berlin. Indeed, Germany's assimilationist Jews were so enamored of Wagner that it became fashionable in the late nineteenth century for them to give Wagnerian names like Siegmund and Siegfried to their children. See Frederic V. Grunfeld, *Prophets Without Honor* (New York, 1980), p. 3.
102. C. Wagner to K. F. Glasenapp, Jan. 1885, quoted in Karbaum, *Studien*, p. 45.
103. On Cosima's revolting behavior toward Levi, see Gay, "Hermann Levi," pp. 219–23.
104. Ibid., pp. 219–20.
105. C. Wagner to Richard Strauss, June 7, 1890, in *Cosima Wagner–Richard Strauss: Ein Briefwechsel*, Franz Trenner, ed. (Tutzing, Germany, 1978), p. 9.
106. Mayer, *Wagner in Bayreuth*, p. 72.

107. Cosima destroyed Peter Cornelius's letters to Wagner, as well as some of Nietzsche's. See Marek, *Cosima Wagner*, p. 68.
108. Karbaum, *Studien*, p. 34.
109. Elizabeth Förster-Nietzsche was a great friend of Cosima's and admired the way she administered her husband's legacy. See Skelton, *Wagner at Bayreuth*, p. 71. For a biography of Elizabeth, see Heinz Frederick Peters, *Zarathustra's Sister* (New York, 1976).
110. Karbaum, *Studien*, p. 47.
111. C. Wagner to R. Strauss, Oct. 12, 1889, *Briefwechsel*, p. 4.
112. Karbaum, *Studien*, pp. 47–49.
113. Wahnfried, one might say, never forgave the Prinzregententheater for poaching on its territory. The only Wagner to set foot in the rival Munich house was Wagner's granddaughter Friedelind, herself a renegade from Wahnfried. See her memoir, *Heritage of Fire* (New York, 1945), p. 21.
114. Gutman, *Richard Wagner*, pp. 573–574n. According to Wagner's contract with the Court Opera, Munich was to have the right to perform the work in the capital in return for lending Bayreuth musicians and singers. Wagner later reneged on this agreement, then considered the arrangement with Neumann.
115. Karbaum, *Studien*, pp. 51–52.
116. Gutman, *Richard Wagner*, p. 573; Skelton, *Wagner at Bayreuth*, p. 96.
117. Siegfried, however, later relented, allowing Burgstaller to return to Bayreuth and sing Siegfried in 1908 and Siegmund in 1909. See Skelton, *Wagner at Bayreuth*, p. 97.
118. Quoted in Max Moser, *Richard Wagner in der englischen Literatur des XIX. Jahrhunderts* (Berlin, 1938), p. 18.
119. The *Tannhäuser* performances of 1891 played to full houses, but the production was so expensive it lost money.
120. Thomas Mann wrote of the "unsavory influence of *the woman* . . . over *the man* in his most corruptible manifestation, namely in his art, and in the way that art is administered." Quoted in *BK*, p. 78.
121. Quoted in Marek, *Cosima Wagner*, p. 226. For more of Shaw's perceptions of Cosima's Bayreuth, see the excerpts from his reviews published in *Bayreuth: The Early Years*, Robert Hartford, ed. (Cambridge, England, 1980), pp. 223–38.
122. On this see Karbaum, *Studien*, pp. 44–45.
123. Skelton, *Wagner at Bayreuth*, p. 97.
124. On Stein see *BK*, pp. 94–95; Gunther Wahnes, *Heinrich von Stein und sein Verhältnis zu Richard Wagner und Friedrich Nietzsche* (Jena, 1926); Herman Glockner, *Heinrich von Stein: Schicksal einer deutschen Jugend* (Tübingen, 1934); Gunther Ralf, ed., *Heinrich von Stein: Idee und Welt* (Stuttgart, 1940); Roderick Stackelberg, *Idealism Debased: From "Völkisch" Ideology to National Socialism* (Kent, Ohio, 1981), pp. 17–59.
125. Malwida von Meysenbug was a close friend of Wagner's (though never his mistress) who was also a pioneer in nineteenth-century feminism. She initially admired Wagner as a fellow radical, although later, like Nietzsche, she became disenchanted with his growing conservatism. There is as yet no biography of Meysenbug, although she is often mentioned in cultural

histories of the period. For information on her relationship with Wagner I have made use of the late George C. Windell's unpublished essay "Wagner and Malwida von Meysenbug."

126. Wahnes, *Heinrich von Stein*, p. 32.
127. C. Wagner, *Tagebücher*, 2:418, 428, 427–428, 779.
128. *BK*, p. 95.
129. Cosima called Stein her "darling" and her "golden son" and delighted in his "sensitivity." See Wahnes, *Heinrich von Stein*, p. 37.
130. Heinrich von Stein, "Scènes historiques par le comte de Gobineau," *BB*, 4 (1881), 13–20.; "Shakespeare als Richter der Renaissance," ibid., 185–98; "Über Werke und Wirkungen Rousseaus," ibid., 345–56; "Über Goethes Wanderjahre," ibid., 217–33; "Schopenhauer Scholien," ibid., 8 (1885), 133–40, 165–71, 228–36.
131. C. Wagner, *Tagebücher*, 2:631.
132. Ibid., p. 849.
133. Wahnes, *Heinrich von Stein*, p. 75.
134. Karl Friedrich Glasenapp and Heinrich von Stein, eds., *Wagner-Lexikon. Hauptbegriffe der Kunst- und Weltanschauung Richard Wagners in wörtlichen Anführungen aus seinen Schriften zusammengestellt* (Stuttgart, 1883).
135. Wahnes, *Heinrich von Stein*, pp. 146–47.
136. Heinrich von Stein, "Die Darstellung der Natur in den Werken Richard Wagners," in *Zur Kultur der Seele: Gesammelte Aufsätze*, F. Poske, ed. (Stuttgart, 1906), pp. 90–96.
137. *BK*, pp. 96–97.
138. C. Wagner to L. Schemann, June 8, 1888, in *Cosima Wagners Briefe an Ludwig Schemann*, Bertha von Schemann, ed., (Regensburg, 1937), p. 43, quoted in *BK*, p. 97.
139. H. S. Chamberlain to Daniele Thode, Sept. 13, 1898, quoted in *BK*, p. 97.
140. Quoted in *BK*, p. 95.
141. On Stein's relationship to Nietzsche, see Stackelberg, *Idealism Debased*, pp. 50–59, and Hayman, *Nietzsche*, pp. 276, 283.
142. Nietzsche to Overbeck, Sept. 14, 1884, quoted in Stackelberg, *Idealism Debased*, p. 53.
143. Quoted in ibid., p. 56.
144. This term of Fritz Stern's refers to "a particular stance of bourgeois denial of bourgeois realities . . . a metaphysic of snobbery which could idealize their material interests—to the still greater injury of those below them" (*Failure of Illiberalism*, p. xxxvii).
145. Stackelberg, *Idealism Debased*, pp. 57–59.
146. Little has been written about Glasenapp aside from a few obituaries. See Hans von Wolzogen's in *BB*, 38 (1915), 148; L. Karpath's in *Merker*, 6 (Vienna, 1915):420. See also *BK*, pp. 99–101.
147. K. F. Glasenapp, *Das Leben Richard Wagners*, 6 vols. (Leipzig, 1894–1911).
148. Glasenapp, *Wagner-Enzyklopädie*, 2 vols. (Leipzig, 1891).
149. When Cosima told Richard that she was sending Glasenapp a recently stuffed pheasant, he laughingly replied that as soon as anything came to grief in Wahnfried one must stuff it and send it to poor Glasenapp. C. Wagner, *Tagebücher*, 2:254.

150. So, at least, suggests Gutman in *Richard Wagner,* p. 10.
151. Du Moulin-Eckart, *Cosima Wagner.*
152. H. S. Chamberlain, *Richard Wagner* (Munich, 1896).
153. C. Wagner, *Tagebücher,* 2:108.
154. Ibid., p. 138.
155. L. Schemann, *Lebensfahrten eines Deutschen* (Leipzig, 1925), p. 176; *BK,* p. 100.
156. *BK,* p. 100n.
157. See *BK,* p. 101.
158. On Schemann, see Bertha von Schemann, "Ein Gedenkblatt für meinen Vater," *Zeitschrift für Musik* (Regensburg), 113 (1952), 568; and *BK,* pp. 101–6.
159. See the personal epilogue attached to his biography of Paul de Lagarde: *Paul de Lagarde* (Leipzig, 1919), pp. 342–58.
160. Ibid., p. 344.
161. *BK,* p. 102.
162. C. Wagner, *Tagebücher,* 2:369.
163. Ibid., p. 749.
164. Quoted in *BK,* p. 103.
165. Fritz Stern, *The Politics of Cultural Despair* (New York, 1965).
166. L. Schemann, *Gobineau: Eine Biographie,* 2 vols. (Strasburg, 1913–1916).
167. Ibid., 2:551, 563, 521.
168. *BK,* pp. 104–5.
169. Quoted in *BK,* p. 104n.
170. Schemann, "Lagarde," *BB,* 15 (1892), 208.
171. Ibid.
172. "Lagarde," wrote Schemann, "is not as appreciated in his own country as he deserves to be, or as his people need him to be." Ibid., p. 202.
173. *BK,* p. 105.
174. Quoted in Stern, *Politics of Cultural Despair,* p. 254n.
175. Bernard Förster, "Ein Deutschland der Zukunft," *BB,* 6 (1883), 44–56.
176. Paul Förster, "Die Bewegung wider die Vivisektion," *BB,* 9 (1886), 125–34.
177. See Wagner's "Offenes Schreiben an Herrn Ernst von Weber," *Gesammelte Schriften,* 14 vols., J. Kapp, ed. (Leipzig, 1914), 13:298–300; *BK,* p. 145.
178. Schemann to Wolzogen, Nov. 10–12, 1935, quoted in *BK,* p. 106n.
179. *BK,* p. 106.
180. Schemann to Wolzogen, Nov. 10–12, 1935, quoted in *BK,* p. 106.
181. Walter Frank, "Ludwig Schiemann—Ein Nachruf," *Historische Zeitschrift,* 158 (1938), 218.
182. Ibid.
183. On Thode, see *Deutsche Biographie: Überleitungsband II: 1917–1920* (Stuttgart, 1928), p. 762; R. Bruck, "Henry Thode," *BB,* 43 (1920), 5; *BK,* pp. 107–12.
184. For Thode's interpretation of Renaissance culture, see his *Franz von Assisi und die Anfänge der Kunst der Renaissance in Italien* (Vienna, 1934); and *Michelangelo und das Ende der Renaissance* (Berlin, 1908–1913). See also *BK,* p. 110.

185. Henry Thode, *Schauen und Glauben* (Heidelberg, 1903), p. 10.
186. One important exception was the great art historian Aby Warburg, who studied with Thode in Bonn and was greatly influenced by his views. See Peter Gay, "Encounter with Modernism: German Jews in Wilhelminian Culture," in *Freud, Jews and Other Germans,* p. 128.
187. See Henry Thode, "Richard Wagners Bedeutung für die akademische Jugend," *Die Volksbühne* (Berlin), 2 (1901), 351; *Wie ist Richard Wagner vom deutschen Volk zu feiern?* (Heidelberg, 1903); and *Schauen und Glauben.*
188. Thode, "Richard Wagners Bedeutung."
189. *BK,* p. 109.
190. Thode to Max Lehrs, July 20, 1882, quoted in *BK,* p. 108.
191. Thode to Lehrs, Sept. 23, 1885, quoted in ibid.
192. Thode to Lehrs, July 20, 1882, quoted in ibid.
193. *BK,* p. 109.
194. Thode made this claim in one of his Wagner lectures. See ibid., p. 111, n. 66.
195. Thode, *Böcklin und Thoma: Acht Vorträge über neudeutsche Malerei* (Heidelberg, 1905), pp. 3, 7.
196. Ibid., pp. 7, 93, 101, 103.
197. On this, see Peter Paret, *The Berlin Secession* (Cambridge, Mass., 1979).
198. Wilhelm II to Cosima Wagner, May 10, 1887, quoted in *BK,* p. 130. Despite his enthusiasm for Wagner's music (he had his car horn tuned to the Donner motif in *Rheingold*), Wilhelm ultimately proved to be something of a disappointment as a Bayreuth patron. He did not—as his grand father did not—support the festival with state funds.
199. The Baroness Spitzemberg could record in her diary that "half the world" had turned out to witness Wagner's *Tristan und Isolde* in the Berlin opera. Most returned from the experience "wornout but appropriately moved" (*Das Tagebuch der Baronin Spitzemberg* [Göttingen, 1964], p. 156).
200. Quoted in Erwin Koppen, *Dekadenter Wagnerismus* (Berlin, 1973, p. 69).
201. Chamberlain is the subject of Geoffrey Field's recent *Evangelist of Race,* an excellent biography that supercedes all previous work.
202. Chamberlain can be considered part of Bayreuth's inner circle from the early 1890s, although he did not actually settle in Bayreuth until 1908, when, after divorcing his first wife (Anna), he married Eva Wagner, the composer's youngest daughter. Before moving to Bayreuth he had lived in Vienna for some twenty years, and it was there that he wrote his most important books.
203. Chamberlain, *Lebenswege meines Denkens* (Munich, 1917).
204. Ibid., p. 180.
205. Actually, Blumenfeld was one of two Jews (the other was named Lowenthal) who instructed the young Chamberlain on things Wagnerian. Unfortunately this never led him to any reassessment of prevailing racial stereotypes; rather, he claimed to pity those "nobly educated" Jews who "obviously suffered" because of their racial heritage. See Field, *Evangelist of Race,* p. 52.
206. Chamberlain, *Lebenswege,* p. 193. Page numbers for the quotations in the next paragraphs, also from this book, are given in parentheses in the text.

207. *BK*, p. 115.
208. On Chamberlain's relationship with Cosima, see Pretzsch, *Cosima Wagner und H. S. Chamberlain im Briefwechsel;* see also Field, *Evangelist of Race,* passim.
209. See especially "La revue de Bayreuth: Analyse du numéro de février 1885," *Revue wagnérienne,* March 1885; "Notes sur *Tristan und Isolde,*" ibid., February 1887; "Notes sur *Parsifal,*" ibid., August 1886.
210. Field, *Evangelist of Race,* p. 68.
211. Chamberlain, *Richard Wagner,* p. 17. He also praised Nietzsche's *Richard Wagner in Bayreuth* as a book that stood out in a "sea of mediocrity."
212. Chamberlain, *Lebenswege,* p. 163.
213. Chamberlain, *Die Grundlagen des 19. Jahrhunderts* (Munich, 1899).
214. The *Grundlagen* is thoroughly analyzed in Field, *Evangelist of Race,* pp. 169–224, and Stackelberg, *Idealism Debased,* pp. 120–31.
215. Henry Thode, *Literarisches Zentralblatt für Deutschland* (Leipzig), 51 (1900), 438.
216. Chamberlain, *Grundlagen,* 3d ed. (Munich, 1901), p. xiv.
217. *BK*, pp. 117–18.
218. Chamberlain to Thode, May 2, 1901, quoted in *BK*, p. 119.
219. Stackelberg, *Idealism Debased,* p. 127.
220. *Grundlagen,* p. xi. See also Field, *Evangelist of Race,* p. 345.
221. For the text of the speech, see *Münchener allgemeine Zeitung,* Feb. 25–28, 1899. See also Field, *Evangelist of Race,* p. 341.
222. C. Wagner to Chamberlain, Mar. 26, 1899, quoted in Field, *Evangelist of Race,* p. 342.
223. Chamberlain, "Richard Wagner und die Politik," *BB,* 16 (1893), 137–58. See also Field, *Evangelist of Race,* pp. 134–36.
224. Chamberlain, "Richard Wagner und die Politik," p. 146.
225. Wagner claimed to have been influenced by Proudhon and also to have picked up some ideas from Bakunin. But he never evolved a systematic socialist philosophy, nor was he consistent in his attitude toward the act of revolution. He unquestionably was active in the Dresden uprising of 1849, but its failure left him disillusioned about the efficacy of radical political upheaval. In the 1870s, by which time Schopenhauer had long replaced Feuerbach as his most important philosophical mentor, Wagner could even urge the authorities to ruthlessly crush a workers' revolt in Vienna. See C. Wagner, *Tagebücher,* 1:540. On Wagner's "socialism," see Gutman, *Richard Wagner,* p. 181; *BK,* pp. 15–16; Gregor-Dellin, *Richard Wagner,* pp. 286–91.
226. Field, *Evangelist of Race,* p. 226. On the impact of the *Grundlagen* in Britain and America, see ibid., pp. 459–67.
227. Ibid., p. 340.
228. Chamberlain, *Lebenswege,* p. 161.
229. Chamberlain, *Richard Wagner,* p. 372.
230. Chamberlain, "The Personal Side of Richard Wagner" and "How Richard Wagner Wrote His Operas," *Ladies' Home Journal,* 15 (Oct. 1898), 11–12; 15 (Nov. 1898), 11–12.
231. On Chamberlain's relations with Wilhelm II, see *Briefe 1882–1924 und*

Briefwechsel mit Kaiser Wilhelm II, Paul Pretzsch, ed., 2 vols. (Munich, 1928). See also Field, *Evangelist of Race,* pp. 240–41, 252–61, 400–401.

232. On Chamberlain's propagandistic activities during the war, see Stackelberg, *Idealism Debased,* pp. 145–55; Field, *Evangelist of Race,* pp. 352–95.

233. Chamberlain, *Kriegsaufsätze* (Munich, 1915).

234. Ibid., p. 60.

235. See Wagner's letter to Otto Wesendonck on his visit to London in 1855 in *Letters of Richard Wagner,* William Altman, ed. (London, 1927).

236. He was awarded the Iron Cross, First Class, for his propagandistic efforts.

237. On the fate of Wagner's music in England during the war, see Anne Dzamba Sessa, *Richard Wagner and the English* (Rutherford, N.J., 1979), pp. 140–49.

238. The best work on Germany's "New Right" in the Weimar period is still Klemens von Klemperer, *Germany's New Conservatism: Its History and Dilemma in the Twentieth Century* (Princeton, 1957).

239. Chamberlain to Hitler, 7 Oct. 1923, in *Deutschlands Erneuerung. Monatschrift für das deutsche Volk* (Munich), 8 (1924), pp. 2–3. The letter is also quoted in Field, *Evangelist of Race,* pp. 436–37.

240. Winfried Schüler suggests that Chamberlain might well have "distanced himself intellectually" from Hitler's persecution of the Jews" (p. 126). Field, too, points out that Chamberlain's racism, while virulent, was "more gentle and refined" and "less crudely deterministic" than that of many other later racists (p. 119).

241. Field, *Evangelist of Race,* p. 438.

242. Karl Marx, *The Eighteenth Brumaire of Louis Bonaparte* (New York, 1963), p. 15.

243. On Siegfried Wagner, see K. F. Glasenapp, *Siegfried Wagner* (Berlin, 1906); Paul Pretzsch, *Die Kunst Siegfried Wagners* (Leipzig, 1919); Zdenko von Kraft, *Der Sohn: Siegfried Wagners Leben und Umwelt* (Graz, 1969); as well as Mayer, *Richard Wagner;* Skelton, *Wagner at Bayreuth;* Karbaum, *Studien;* and *BK.*

244. Skelton, *Wagner at Bayreuth,* p. 105.

245. Von Kraft, *Der Sohn,* pp. 18–19.

246. Ibid., pp. 45–71.

247. Ibid., p. 149; Skelton, *Wagner at Bayreuth,* p. 107.

248. On Siegfried's Bayreuth, see especially von Kraft, Karbaum, Mayer, and Skelton. Skelton and von Kraft are more sympathetic toward Siegfried and his artistic accomplishments.

249. Quoted in Mayer, *Wagner at Bayreuth,* p. 90.

250. These innovations, such as they were, are discussed in Skelton, *Wagner at Bayreuth,* pp. 108–9.

251. Quoted in Mayer, *Wagner at Bayreuth,* p. 89.

252. Ibid.

253. On Siegfried's operas, see, *inter alia,* Paul Pretzsch, *Die Kunst Siegfried Wagners,* and Otto Daube, *Siegfried Wagner und die Märchenoper* (Leipzig, 1936).

254. Von Kraft, *Der Sohn,* p. 270.

255. Richard Wagner often expressed his loathing for Berlin, which he saw as dominated by an unholy alliance of Jews and Prussian aristocrats. For samples of his hostility, see C. Wagner, *Tagebücher*, 1:486, 525.
256. Von Kraft, *Der Sohn*, p. 231.
257. Ibid., p. 240.
258. Ibid., p. 245.
259. Quoted in ibid., p. 247.
260. Karbaum, *Studien*, p. 62.
261. Mayer, *Wagner at Bayreuth*, p. 90.
262. Von Kraft, *Der Sohn*, p. 222.
263. The reference is to Peter Gay's provocative little book, *Weimar Culture* (New York, 1968).
264. Mayer, *Wagner at Bayreuth*, p. 104; Karbaum, *Studien*, p. 70.
265. On this see especially Karbaum, *Studien*, pp. 61–80.
266. H. Heiber, ed., *Das Tagebuch von Josef Goebbels, 1925–26* (Stuttgart, 1961), p. 77.
267. *BB*, 47 (1924), 10.
268. Wolzogen, "Deutsche Sprüchen," in ibid., pp. 16–20.
269. Hermann Seelinger, "Die Rassenkunde des deutschen Volkes von Hans K. F. Günther," in ibid., pp. 54–57.
270. Quoted in Karbaum, *Studien*, p. 69. See also Otto Daube, "Der bayreuther Bund der deutschen Jugend: Vorgeschichte, Gründung und Ziele, Aufbaupläne, *BB*, 48 (1925), 133–35.
271. Karbaum, *Studien*, p. 67.
272. An account of this meeting can be found in Friedelind Wagner, *Heritage of Fire*, pp. 7–8. Winifred Wagner, née Williams, was an Englishwoman who had been adopted by the German-born musician Karl Klindworth, who brought her to Germany and introduced her to the Wagner family. Like her countryman Houston Stewart Chamberlain, she became a fanatical German patriot.
273. The city of Bayreuth and Wahnfried (though, miraculously, not the Festspielhaus) were heavily damaged by bombs in World War II. For a full account of the bombing of Bayreuth, see Werner Meyer, *Götterdämmerung: April 1945 in Bayreuth* (Percha am Starnberger See, 1975).
274. On Hitler's relations with Germany's wealthy Wagnerians, see the forthcoming study by Henry A. Turner, *German Big Business and the Rise of Hitler*.
275. So Siegfried reportedly said to his friend Alexander Spring. See A. Spring, "Siegfried Wagner: Zum 70. Wiederkehr seines Geburtstages," *Bayreuther Festspielführer* 1939, p. 22. Quoted also in Karbaum, *Studien*, p. 65, doc. 1.
276. Siegfried Wagner to Rosa Eidam, Christmas 1923. Quoted in ibid., p. 65, document 2.
277. Wrote Winifred: "For a few years we [Siegfried and Winifred] have been following with the greatest sympathy the constructive work of Adolf Hitler—this German man so filled with patriotism, so prepared to sacrifice himself for his ideal of an enlightened, unified Greater Germany; this man who has set himself the difficult task of awakening the workers to the dangers of Marxism and the inner enemy. . . . [The power of the Nazi movement] is based on the moral strength and purity of this man, who

tirelessly pursues the goals he knows are best, indeed, which he humbly recognizes as his *God-given calling.* . . . . I readily admit that *we too* march under the banner of this man, whom we support in good times and bad." Letter quoted in Karbaum, *Studien,* p. 68.

278. Winifred's continuing loyalty to "Wolf," her pet name for Hitler, is documented in a film by Marcel Ophuls. The film, *Winifred Wagner,* was reviewed by Robert Craft in the *New York Review of Books,* Nov. 11, 1976.

279. Karbaum, *Studien,* p. 68.

280. Hitler to Siegfried Wagner, May 5, 1924. Full text of the letter is published in ibid., pp. 65–66, doc. 3.

281. See Winifred Wagner's "Denkschrift für die Spruchkammer," quoted in ibid., pp. 113–16.

282. In her *Spruchkammer* testimony, Winifred insisted she was not in the party until 1926, at which point she joined at Hitler's request. Her daughter Friedelind, however, maintains that Winifred first joined in 1920 or 1921 and then joined again in the mid-twenties after the Party was reorganized. See her *Heritage of Fire,* p. 30.

283. Ibid., p. 17.

284. See Karbaum, *Studien,* pp. 81–93.

285. In 1933 Hitler spent some 50,000 reichsmarks from a special fund for the purchase of tickets for that summer's festival; these tickets were then given away with much fanfare "to German youth." The Führer continued this philanthropy in following years, though on a slightly more modest scale: in 1936, for example, he spent 9,399 reichsmarks on tickets; in 1937, 11,820; 1938, 22,680; 1939, 20,490. He also donated 50,000 reichsmarks to help defray the cost of every new production presented in Bayreuth. After the outbreak of the war he set aside another 500,000 reichsmarks to keep the festival running. See Fred K. Prieburg, *Musik im NS-Staat* (Frankfurt, 1982), pp. 129, 307.

286. With respect to the alleged connections between Wagner's art and National Socialism, we should remember that while Hitler himself was certainly a fervent Wagnerian, most of his top lieutenants in the Party were not. In one of the few amusing moments in his memoirs, Albert Speer describes how an angry Führer had to send out special patrols to pull the Party bosses out of brothels and beerhalls and then escort them to the ritual performances of *Die Meistersinger,* which opened the Party rallies in Nuremberg. See Albert Speer, *Inside the Third Reich* (New York, 1970), p. 60.

287. The onset of Bayreuth's artistic provincialism was painfully evident in the first festival after Hitler's seizure of power. Arturo Toscanini was scheduled to conduct *Parsifal* and *Die Meistersinger* at the 1933 festival, but he canceled to protest the new regime's discrimination against Jewish musicians. See Prieberg, *Musik in NS-Staat,* p. 75.

288. George C. Windell, "Hitler, National Socialism and Richard Wagner," *Journal of Central European Affairs,* 1962–1963, pp. 483–85.

3. Art and Politics: Wagnerism in France

1. See Robert M. Isherwood, *Music in the Service of the King: France in the Seventeenth Century* (Ithaca, 1975); William Weber, "*La musique ancienne* in

the Waning of the Ancien Régime," *Journal of Modern History,* 56 (1984), 58–88.

2. *Revue et gazette musicale de Paris* (henceforth *RGM*), 7 (Mar. 22, 1840), 194.

3. Adolphe Jullien, *Richard Wagner: Sa vie et ses oeuvres* (Paris, 1886), p. 28; Richard Wagner, *Mein Leben* (Munich, 1963), p. 185.

4. See Robert L. Jacobs and Geoffrey Skelton, eds. and trs., *Wagner Writes from Paris: Stories, Essays and Articles by the Young Composer* (London, 1973), pp. 196–97.

5. *RGM*, Feb. 7, 1841, quoted in Jullien, *Richard Wagner*, p. 32.

6. See Jullien, p. 30. Cf. Wagner, *Mein Leben*, p. 201.

7. George Sand, "Mouny Robin," *Revue des deux mondes*, ser. 4, 26 (June 15, 1841), 887–905. See also Wagner, *Mein Leben*, p. 207.

8. *RGM*, 9 (Oct. 30, 1842), 431; (Dec. 4, 1832), 482–83; (Dec. 18, 1842), 510.

9. *Journal des débats*, Sept. 12, 1843, in Hector Berlioz, *Mémoires*, 2 vols., Pierre Citron, ed. (Paris, 1969), 2:100.

10. *Journal des débats*, May 18, 1849, quoted in Marcel Herwegh, *Au banquet des dieux: Franz Liszt, Richard Wagner, et leurs amis* (Paris, 1931), p. 95. (Unless otherwise noted, translations are all by the author.)

11. *La presse*, Sept. 18, 1850, reprinted in Gérard de Nerval, *Lorely: Souvenirs d'Allemagne* (Paris, 1852), p. 89.

12. *RGM*, 17 (Dec. 1, 1850), 398. See Maxime Leroy, *Les premiers amis français de Wagner* (Paris, 1925), p. 44.

13. Gautier, *La Presse*, Dec. 2, 1850, reprinted in part in Georges Servières, "Les relations d'Ernest Reyer et de Théophile Gautier," *Revue d'histoire littéraire de la France*, 24 (Jan.-Mar., 1917), 72.

14. Nerval to Liszt, Oct. 8, 1850, in *Lettres françaises de Richard Wagner*, Julien Tiersot, ed. (Paris, 1935), p. 129.

15. *Oper und Drama*, in *Gesammelte Schriften und Dichtungen von Richard Wagner*, 10 vols. (Leipzig, 1907), 3:222–320, 4:1–229. See also Wagner, "Eine Mitteilung an meine Freunde," in ibid., 4:230–344.

16. Charles Baudelaire, *Richard Wagner et "Tannhäuser" à Paris*, in *Oeuvres complètes de Charles Baudelaire*, 15 vols., Jacques Crépet, ed. (Paris, 1923–1948), vol. 2: *L'art romantique* (1925), p. 200.

17. Pietro Scudo, "Littérature musicale, publications récentes en France, en Russie, et en Allemagne," *Revue des deux mondes*, ser. 6 (*nouv. pér.*), 15 (Aug. 15, 1852), 818–22.

18. Fétis, "Wagner, sa vie, son système de rénovation de l'opéra, ses oeuvres comme poète et comme musicien, son parti en Allemagne, appréciation de la valeur de ses idées," *RGM*, 19 (June 6, 1852), 202.

19. Quoted by Maurice Kufferath in "Notes bruxellois," in *Bayreuther Festblätter in Wort und Bild*, Karl Frhr. von Ostini et al., eds. (Munich, 1884), p. 47. The phrase "positive arts" reflects Fétis's attack on Wagner for associating himself with positivism. See the perceptive article by Jane Fulcher, "Wagner, Comte and Proudhon: Aesthetics of Positivism in France," *Symposium* (Syracuse University), 33 (1979), 142–52. See as well her "Wagner as Democrat and Realist in France," *Stanford French Review*, 5 (1981), 97–106.

20. Scudo, "Littérature musicale," p. 281; Champfleury, "Richard Wagner,"

in Champfleury, *Grandes figures d'hier et d'aujourd'hui: Balzac, Gérard de Nerval, Wagner, Courbet* (Paris, 1861), p. 112.

21. See Gerstel Mack, *Gustave Courbet* (New York, 1951), p. 80. See also T. J. Clark, *Image of the People: Gustave Courbet and the Second French Republic, 1848–1851* (Greenwhich, Conn., 1973), pp. 132–46.

22. The dangers to society implicit in the "subversive" philosophy of realism were spelled out in the *réquisitoires* (requisitories) of the imperial prosecutor, Ernest Pinard, at the obscenity trials of Flaubert and Baudelaire in 1857. See especially the parts of his speech quoted in Baudelaire, *Les fleurs du mal*, Georges Blin and Claude Pichois, eds. (Paris, 1968), pp. 444, 446, and in Gustave Flaubert, *Madame Bovary*, Edouard Maynial, ed. (Paris, 1936), p. 392.

23. Fétis, "Wagner, sa vie," in *RGM*, 19 (June 20, 1852), 202. See also George Woodcock, *Pierre-Joseph Proudhon* (London, 1956), pp. 127–80.

24. See Edouard Maynial, *L'époque réaliste* (Paris, 1931), p. 48.

25. *RGM*, 22 (Mar. 18, 1855), 84.

26. Champfleury, *Richard Wagner*, p 129.

27. *RGM*, 22 (July 15, 1855), 223.

28. *L'illustration*, 29 (June 27, 1857), 415, reprinted in *Bayreuther Festblätter*, pp. 48–49.

29. Gasperini, *La nouvelle allemagne musicale; Richard Wagner* (Paris, 1866), p. 50.

30. Prosper Sainton, quoted in Ernest Newman, *The Life of Richard Wagner*, 4 vols. (New York, 1933–1946), vol. 2: *1848–1860*, p 118.

31. On the amnesty, see Pierre de la Gorce, *Histoire du Second Empire*, 7 vols. (Paris, 1894–1905), 3:122.

32. The program: (1) overture to *Der fliegende Holländer*; (2) *Tannhäuser*: march with chorus, introduction to Act III, chorus with pilgrims, and overture; (3) prelude to *Tristan und Isolde*; (4) *Lohengrin*: prelude, betrothal march with chorus from Act II, nuptial fête (introduction to Act III), and the wedding march. Also included on the second and third evenings was the "Song to the Evening Star" from *Tannhäuser*.

33. Paul Bernard, quoted in Gasperini, *La nouvelle Allemagne*, p. 56.

34. Report by Gustave Héquet, *L'illustration*, 35 (Feb. 4, 1860), 75.

35. Wagner, *Mein Leben*, pp. 570, 629, 627, 619.

36. Juliette Lamber Adam, *Mes premières armes littéraires et politiques* (Paris, 1904), p. 217.

37. Ibid., pp. 217–18.

38. See Jacques Vier, *La comtesse d'Agoult et son temps*, 6 vols. (Paris, 1955–1963), vol. 3: *La Révolution de 1848: La République sous l'Empire (1852–1870)*, p. 295.

39. Stuart L. Campbell, *The Second Empire Revisited* (New Brunswick, N.J., 1978), pp. 73–74.

40. Leroy, *Les premiers amis français*, pp. 43–45.

41. Adam, *Mes premières armes littéraires*, p. 237.

42. Theodore Zeldin, *Emile Ollivier and the Liberal Empire of Napoleon III* (Oxford, 1963), p. 49.

43. Campbell, *Second Empire Revisited*, p. 72.

44. Zeldin, *Emile Ollivier,* p. 49.
45. Adam, *Mes premières armes littéraires,* pp. 237–38.
46. Pier Angelo Fiorentino, *Comédies et comédiens: Feuilletons,* 2 vols. (Paris, 1866), 2:83.
47. Edmond Duranty, *Caractéristique des oeuvres de M. Champfleury* (1859), quoted in Jacques Crépet, "Baudelaire et Duranty," in *Propos sur Baudelaire,* Claude Pichois, ed. (Paris, 1957), p. 58.
48. Baudelaire to Wagner, Feb. 17, 1860, in Tiersot, *Lettres françaises,* p. 198.
49. Baudelaire to Poulet-Malassis, Feb. 16, 1860, in Baudelaire, *Correspondance générale,* 4 vols., Jacques Crépet, ed. (Paris, 1947–1948), 3:29–30.
50. Baudelaire to Wagner, Feb. 17, 1860, in Tiersot, *Lettres françaises,* pp. 198–200.
51. Wagner, *Mein Leben,* p. 620. See also Wagner to Mathilde Wesendonck, Mar. 3, 1860, in Julius Kapp, ed. *Richard Wagner an Mathilde und Otto Wesendonck: Tagebuchblätter und Briefe* (Leipzig, [1915?]), p. 268.
52. Champfleury, *Richard Wagner,* pp. 111–12.
53. Wagner, *Mein Leben,* p. 620.
54. Pierre Larousse, *Grand dictionnaire universel du XIX siècle,* 15 vols. (Paris, 1866–1876), 3:898. The eminent position that Champfleury once held has not been remembered, and this has led to innaccurate descriptions (e.g. Newman, *Life of Richard Wagner,* vol 3: *1859–1866,* p. 8, who calls Champfleury a "painter and sculptor") and a failure to comprehend the singular importance of his book on Wagner to contemporaries.
55. Wagner, *Mein Leben,* p. 691.
56. Ibid., p. 703. Mme. Lillie de Hegermann-Lindencrone, *In the Courts of Memory, 1858–1875* (New York, 1912), p. 68; Louis Héritte de la Tour, *Mémoires de Louise Héritte-Viardot* (Paris, 1922), pp. 92–93; Francis Toye, *Rossini: A Study in Tragi-Comedy* (London, 1934), pp. 214–15; Alain Decaux, *Offenbach: Roi du Second Empire* (Paris, 1958), p. 23.
57. Blanche Roosevelt Tucker Macchetta, *Life and Reminiscences of Gustave Doré: Compiled from Material Supplied by Doré's Relations and Friends and from Personal Recollection* (New York, 1885), pp. 185, 286.
58. See Gasperini to Leroy, Sept. 21, 1859, in Tiersot, *Lettres françaises,* p. 175.
59. Wagner, *Mein Leben,* pp. 716–17.
60. See Gustave Claudin, *Mes souvenirs: Les boulevards de 1840–1870* (Paris, 1884), p. 34.
61. Wagner to Mathilde Wesendonck, Mar. 3, 1860, in Kapp, *Wagner an Mathilde Wesendonck,* p. 216.
62. Edouard Drumont, quoted by Georges Servières, *Richard Wagner jugé en France* (Paris, 1887), p. 71. See also A. Carette, *Recollections of the Court of the Tuileries,* Elizabeth Phipps Train, tr. (New York, 1899), pp. 114–18.
63. Gasperini, *La nouvelle Allemagne,* p. 59.
64. Pauline de Metternich-Winneburg, *Souvenirs de la Princesse Pauline de Metternich, 1859–1871* (Paris, 1922), pp. 103–4.
65. Wagner, *Bericht über die Aufführung des "Tannhäuser" in Paris,* in *Gesammelte Schriften,* 7:141.
66. Gasperini, *La nouvelle Allemagne,* p. 76. See Léon Guichard, *La musique et les lettres en France au temps du wagnérisme* (Paris, 1963), pp. 8–16, for a good summary of the letter.

67. Alphonse Royer, *Histoire de l'opéra* (Paris, 1875), p. 202.
68. Ibid., p. 193.
69. Adam, *Mes premières armes littéraires*, p. 296.
70. Quoted in ibid., p. 297.
71. Wagner to Liszt, Mar. 29, 1860, in *Briefwechsel zwischen Wagner und Liszt*, 2 vols., ed. Erich Kloss, ed. (Leipzig, 1910), 2:279.
72. Joseph Antoine Roy, *Histoire du Jockey Club de Paris* (Paris, 1958), p. 55.
73. Ibid., pp. 60–61.
74. H. Rewbel, "Wagneriana," *Revue musicale S.I.M.*, 10 (May 15, 1913), 35; Wagner, *Mein Leben*, p. 738.
75. Adam, *Mes premières ames littéraires*, pp. 302–3; see also p. 304. In his *Richard Wagner et "Tannhäuser" à Paris* (p. 249) Baudelaire also connected the two theatrical failures.
76. Wagner, *Mein Leben*, p. 742.
77. Scudo, "Le *Tannhäuser*, de M. Richard Wagner," *Revue des deux mondes*, ser. 8 (2me pér.), 32 (Apr. 1, 1861), 768.
78. See Edith Saunders, *Age of Worth: Couturier to the Empress Eugénie* (London, 1954), p. 87.
79. Baudelaire, *Richard Wagner et "Tannhäuser" à Paris*, pp. 251–52.
80. Ibid., p. 240.
81. Cf. Grange Woolley, *Richard Wagner et le symbolisme français: Les rapports principaux entre le wagnérisme et l'évolution de l'idée symboliste* (Paris, 1931), p. 77.
82. Villiers de l'Isle-Adam to Jean Marras, July 1869, *Correspondance générale de Villiers de l'Isle-Adam et documents inédits*, 2 vols., Joseph Bollery, ed. (Paris, 1962), 1.134.
83. Catulle Mendès, *La légende du Parnasse contemporain* (Brussels, 1884), p. 96.
84. On the Café Guerbois group, see John Rewald, *The History of Impressionism* (New York, 1961), pp. 197–216.
85. *L'oeuvre* (Paris, F. Bernouard, 1928), p. 87. When Zola describes conversations at the "Café Baudequin," he is actually recalling the Café Guerbois.
86. See François Daulte, *Frédérick Bazille et son temps* (Geneva, 1952), pp. 47, 78, 94–95; Rewald, *History of Impressionism*, p. 116. In 1882, Renoir painted a famous picture of Wagner (see Rewald, p. 461). Later still he reminisced with his son about the Wagner concerts he had attended; see Jean Renoir, *Renoir: My Father*, Rudolph and Dorothy Weaver, trs. (London, 1962), pp. 169–70.
87. Henri Perruchot, *Manet*, Humphrey Hare, tr., Jean Ellsmoor, ed. (New York, 1962), p. 131; Adolphe Jullien, *Fantin-Latour, sa vie et ses amitiés* (Paris, 1909), p. 100.
88. Jullien, *Fantin-Latour*, pp. 93–94. Jullien reproduces the lithograph (1862) that formed the basis for the oil painting (facing p. 88).
89. On Cézanne and music, see Gerstle Mack, *Paul Cézanne* (New York, 1935), pp. 21–23; Alfred H. Barr, Jr., "Cézanne: In the Letters of Marion to Morstatt, 1865–1868: Chapter III, Cézanne and Wagner," Margaret Scolari, tr., *Magazine of Art*, 31 (1938), 188–91.
90. Baudelaire, *Richard Wagner et "Tannhäuser" à Paris*, pp. 217, 211. Baudelaire also praised Wagner's idea that "the myth is the primitive and anonymous poem of the people" (ibid., p. 217), admired Wagner's "painting of

the most *popular* feeling" (italics in the original, p. 224), and spoke of the "divine stamp on all popular fables" (p. 229).

91. See Maxime Leroy, *Les premiers amis français*, p. 146.
92. *Le national*, April 12, 1869, reprinted in Theodore de Banville, *Critiques,* Victor Barrucand, ed. (Paris, 1917), p. 179.
93. Ibid.
94. Maxime Leroy, *Les premiers amis français*, pp. 135–36.
95. Ibid., p. 136.
96. Ibid., pp. 140–43.
97. Ibid., p. 139.
98. Gasperini, review of Gounod's *Roméo et Juliette, La liberté,* Apr. 30, 1867, quoted in Maxime Leroy, *Les premiers amis français*, p. 118.
99. Zola, *L'oeuvre,* p. 218.
100. Antoine Elwart, *Histoire des concerts populaires de musique classique* (Paris, 1864), p. 11; Carl de Vinck, "Hector Berlioz et Richard Wagner au cirque Napoléon," in Institut de France, Académie des Beaux-Arts, Bulletin semestriel, no. 10, 1929, pp. 186–202. See also Adolphe Jullien, "L'ouverture de *Tannhäuser* aux concerts populaires (1865)," *La revue musicale,* 4 (Oct. 1, 1923), 257–61.
101. See *Oeuvres complètes de Paul Verlaine*, 2 vols., Jacques Borel and H. de Bouillane de Lacoste, eds. (Paris, 1959), 2:1052–53.
102. Report by Paul Smith, *RGM,* 34 (Mar. 31, 1867), 99.
103. See, for example, a report by Charles Bannelier, *RGM,* 36 (Apr. 11, 1869), 330.
104. Frédéric Bazille to his father, 1869, quoted in Daulte, *Bazille et son temps,* p. 94.
105. See the thorough discussion of popular and press reaction to *Rienzi* by Servières, *Wagner jugé en France,* pp. 141–52.
106. *RGM,* 34 (Dec. 1, 1867), 387.
107. *RGM,* 36 (Mar. 28, 1869), 111.
108. Ibid., 35 (June 28, 1868), 205; italics in the original.
109. See, e.g., Baudelaire, *Wagner et "Tannhäuser" à Paris,* p. 251; Ernest Reyer, "Souvenirs d'Allemagne," in *Notes de musique* (Paris, 1875), pp. 35, 37; see as well the *Revue germanique* (1859–1868).
110. Edouard Schuré, "Le drame musical et l'oeuvre de M. Richard Wagner," *Revue des deux mondes,* ser. 8 (2me pér.), 45 (Apr. 15, 1869), 990.
111. On Mar. 11, 1868, one month before his death on Apr. 20, 1868, Gasperini became feuilletonist for *Le Figaro*. Gasperini's book on Wagner, *La nouvelle allemagne musicale: Richard Wagner*, published in 1866, added to Gasperini's growing reputation as an "erudite musician" (see "Richard Wagner," *Larousse XIXe,* 15:1245) and "writer of talent" (*RGM,* 34 [Jan. 13, 1867], 15).
112. Juliette Adam, *Mes sentiments et nos idées avant 1870* (Paris, 1905), pp. 105, 341.
113. Aurélien Scholl in *Le Figaro*, quoted in Maxime Leroy, *Les premiers Amis français*, pp. 64–65.
114. Bizet to Edmond Galabert, 1869, quoted in Mina Curtiss, *Bizet and His World* (New York, 1958), p. 233; originally in Edmond Galabert, *Georges Bizet: Souvenirs et correspondance* (Paris, 1877).

115. Edouard Dujardin, "Chronique: Richard Wagner et les parisiens," *Revue wagnérienne* [henceforth *RW*], 1 (1885), 226.

116. Quoted by Edouard Dujardin, "*La revue wagnérienne*," *La revue musicale*, 4 (Oct. 1, 1923), 145.

117. Guichard, *La musique et les lettres . . . au temps du wagnérisme*, p. 56.

118. Ibid., p. 57.

119. Servières, *Wagner jugé en France*, pp. 210–11. Later Pasdeloup wrote a letter to the press in which he invoked his war record to answer accusations of lack of patriotism.

120. See, e.g., Adrien Dansette, *Le Boulangisme, 1886–1890* (Paris, 1938), pp. 66–70.

121. "La question *Lohengrin*," *RW*, 2 (1886), 64.

122. Ibid., p. 52.

123. Alfred Ernst, review of Servières's *Richard Wagner jugé en France*, *RW*, 3 (1887), 24.

124. Schuré, *Le drame musical*, 2 vols. (Paris, 1886), 2:186, 338–42.

125. See, for example, Téodor de Wyzewa, "Villiers de l'Isle-Adam," *Revue indépendante*, 2 (1886), 260–91.

126. Huysmans, quoted in Robert Baldick, introduction to J.-K. Huysmans, *Against Nature: A New Translation of "A Rebours"* (Baltimore, 1959), p. 10.

127. Ibid., pp. 204–5.

128. Chamberlain left Paris in 1886 but continued to contribute to the journal from Germany; he provided a direct link with Bayreuth. See Geoffrey G. Field, *Evangelist of Race: The Germanic Vision of Houston Stewart Chamberlain* (New York, 1981), pp. 64–68.

129. See, as an example of its coverage of the Wagnerian movement, *RW*, 1 (1885), 2.

130. "A nos lecteurs," ibid., 1 (1886), 364. The editors here spell out their goals in undertaking a compaign of "Wagnerian propaganda" (*propagande wagnérienne*).

131. Dujardin, "*La revue wagnérienne*" p. 144.

132. Elga Duval, *Téodor de Wyzewa: Critic without a Country* (Geneva, 1961), p. 22; Dujardin, "Considérations sur l'art wagnérien," *RW*, 3 (1887), 174–75.

133. Philippe Gille, letter to *RW*, 2 (1886), 33–34.

134. "A nos lecteurs," *RW*, 2 (1887), 390.

135. Quoted in Isabelle Wyzewska, "*La revue wagnérienne*": *Essai sur l'interprétation esthétique de Wagner en France* (Paris, 1934), p. 30.

136. Dujardin, "*La revue wagnérienne*," p. 149.

137. Téodor de Wyzewa, "Notes sur la littérature wagnérienne et les livres en 1885–1886," *RW*, 2 (1886), 150–71.

138. Mallarmé, "Richard Wagner, rêverie d'un poète français," *RW*, 1 (1885), 195–200. Dujardin, "*La revue wagnérienne*," p. 152.

139. Mallarmé, "Richard Wagner," 199.

140. Mallarmé, "Homage," *RW*, 1 (1886), 335.

141. Beckett, "Wagner and His Critics," in *The Wagner Companion*, Peter Burbidge and Richard Sutton, eds. (New York, 1979), p. 369.

142. Arthur Symons, *The Symbolist Movement in Literature* (New York, 1958), p. 76. Huysmans, "L'ouverture de *Tannhäuser*," *RW*, 1 (1885), 59–62;

Dujardin, "Amfortas, paraphrase moderne," *RW*, 1 (1885), 310–13; Dujardin and Chamberlain, "*L'or du Rhein*, traduction française littérale de la première scène," *RW*, 1 (1885), 257–68.

143. Wyzewa, "Le pessimisme de Richard Wagner," *RW*, 1 (1885), 167–70; Hennequin, "L'esthétique de Wagner et la doctrine spencérienne," *RW*, 1 (1885), 282–86.

144. Servières, *Wagner jugé en France*, p. 282.

145. Dujardin, "Question wagnérienne et question personnelle," *RW*, 3 (1887), 131, 133.

146. Dujardin, "*La revue wagnérienne*," p. 157.

147. Ernst, "Le wagnérisme en 1888," *RW*, 3 (1888), 294.

148. Marcel Proust, *A la recherche du temps perdu* (Paris, Edition Pléiade, 1954), 3 vols., 1:300–301; 2:491; 3:158–62.

149. See the lists of French people who attended Bayreuth between 1876 and 1899 in Albert Lavignac, *Voyage artistique à Bayreuth*, 4th ed. (Paris, 1900), pp. 549–602.

150. See Beckett, "Wagner and His Critics," pp. 365–74. For a different evaluation, see Michael Black, "The Literary Background," in Burbidge and Sutton, *Wagner Companion*, pp. 80–84.

4. Wagnerism, Wagnerians, and Italian Identity

1. Mazzini's *Filosofia della musica*, originally published in 1836 in the Parisian journal *L'Italiano*, has been included in numerous editions and translations of his writings since then. Regarding the musical ideas of Mazzini in the pre-1914 period, see S. Farina, "Idee musicali di G. Mazzini," *Gazzetta musicale di Milano*, 28, no. 7 (April 1872) 28; A. Gnaga, "Mazzini e la sua filosofia della musica," *La scena illustrata*, Apr. 15, 1890, as cited in Ute Jung, *Die Rezeption der Kunst Richard Wagners in Italien* (Regensburg, 1974), pp. 321–33; Camille Bellaigue, "Les idées musicales d'un révolutionnaire italien," *Revue des deux mondes*, 151, 4th ser. (Feb. 15, 1899), 918–34.

2. Giuseppe Mazzini, *Filosofia della musica*, 2d ed., Adriano Lualdi, ed. (Milan, 1954), p. 138. Lauldi, in his introduction to this edition, states his intention of demonstrating that Mazzini preceded Wagner in the expression of these ideas.

3. Ibid., pp. 154–86.

4. See, for example, the claim for Verdi by Guglielmo Barblan, "La musica a Milano nell'età moderna," in *Storia di Milano*, 17 vols., ed. Giovanni Treccani degli Alfieri, ed. (Milan, 1962), 16:681. Jung cites an article published by the *Allgemeine musikalische Zeitung* (Leipzig) in 1872 (reprinted from the *Neue freie Presse* of Vienna) that cites Enrico Panzacchi, a Florentine professor of aesthetics and a Wagnerian, as making the claim for Wagner (Jung, *Rezeption der Kunst Richard Wagners*, p. 321).

5. Gnaga, in his 1890 article (cited in n. 1), concludes that Wagner took "little notice of Mazzini" (pp. 322–23). Tancredi Mantovani perceives Mazzini as a "precursor" ("I precursori della riforma Wagneriana," *Nuova antologia*, 254, ser. 5, [Apr. 1, 1914], pp. 416–28). On the other hand, Alessandro

Luzio claims that Wagner may well have seen the essay in Switzerland while there following the 1848 revolution. At that time he says a Lugano edition existed ("Le lettere di Arrigo Boito al Bellaigue," *Atti della R. Accademia della scienze di Torino,* 68 [1932–1933], 13–14). Equally forceful is the argument of Giuseppe Pupino-Carbonelli in speeches given in Naples, Taranto, and Genoa. He mentions the influence of Mazzini's Young Italy movement in Europe and the coincidence of Mazzini's and Wagner's sojourns in Switzerland as political exiles (pp. 31–32).

6. Marcello De Angelis, *La musica del Granduca: Vita musicale e correnti critiche a Firenze, 1880–1855* (Florence, 1978), pp. vi–vii, 77, 197–98; Adelmo Damerini, *I. R. Conservatorio di musica "Luigi Cherubini" di Firenze* (Florence, 1941), pp. 14–15.

7. Benedetto Croce, "Riccardo Wagner e Francesco de Sanctis," *La critica,* 28 (1930), 394–95. De Sanctis called both Wagner and Schopenhauer "charlatans" in a letter to a friend, Feb. 26, 1858, "Il de Sanctis in esilio," *La critica,* 12 [1914], 243).

8. Pier Carlo Masini sees these bohemian *scapigliati* as belonging to a number of different circles—literary, political, aristocratic, and democratic (*La scapigliatura democratica: Carteggi di Arcangelo Ghisleri, 1875–1890* [Milan, 1961], pp. 26–27). See also Gaetano Mariani, *Storia della scapigliatura* (Rome, 1967), pp. 90–100.

9. In an 1864 article in the Italian journal *Figaro,* Boito asserted that for opera to reach the destiny he foresaw for it, it needed the following: 1) the complete obliteration of the formula; 2) the creation of form; 3) the realization of the vastest tonal and rhythmic development possible today; and 4) the supreme incarnation of drama" (Arrigo Boito, *Tutti gli scritti,* Piero Nardi, ed. [Milan, 1942], p. 1107). Verdi had reacted to an earlier attempt by Franco Faccio in 1863 at producing *I profughi fiamminghi* at La Scala when he wrote to Clarissa Maffei in December to confess his lack of understanding in the articles "Art, Aesthetics, Revolutions, Past, Future." He is concerned how to react to Faccio's work (*I copialettere di Giuseppe Verdi,* A. Luzio and G. Cesari, eds. [Milan, 1913], p. 506). In 1870 Verdi solicited from Camille Du Locle a French translation of Wagner's writings, only to be informed by Du Locle that such a translation did not exist (William Weaver, *Verdi: A Documentary Study* [London, 1977], p. 223). A more colorful source describing the changes in the musical scene of the 1860s brought about by the *scapigliati* is the letter written by Gioacchino Rossini to Filippo Filippi, the music critic, on 26 Aug. 1868. Rossini complained that the talk of "progress, decadence, future, past, present, and convention" gave him stomach trouble, adding that the imposition of new and foreign things was antidiluvian (*Lettere di G. A. Rossini,* G. Mazzatinti and F. E. G. Manis, eds. [Florence, 1902], p. 330). Wagner had visited Rossini in Paris in 1860 at the time when Wagner was preparing *Tannhäuser* (Edmond Michotte, *Richard Wagner's Visit to Rossini (Paris 1860) and An Evening at Rossini's in Beau-Séjour (Passy 1858)* [Chicago, 1968]).

10. A fellow *scapigliato,* Antonio Ghislanzoni, gave *Mefistofele* a scathing review ("Arrigo Boito," *Gazzetta musicale di Milano,* vol. 23 [Mar. 8, 1868], 77–78).

11. Giulio Ricordi, "Analisi musicale del *Mefistofele* di Arrigo Boito," ibid., Mar. 15, 1868, pp. 81–84.
12. Arrigo Boito, "Mendelssohn in Italia," *Tutti gli scritti,* p. 1257.
13. After Ricordi acquired the Lucca rights to Wagner's operas in 1894, Boito asked Ricordi to remove his name from the translation of *Tristan,* because scores, he said, would be bought by ten people but libretti by two thousand (Renzo de Rensis, *Arrigo Boito: Capitoli biografici* [Florence, 1942], p. 132). See also the letter of Boito to G. Lucca, June 2, 1880, regarding his translations of three songs by Wagner (Biblioteca Livia Simoni, La Scala, Milan [hereafter cited as *BLS*], no. C.A. 751/1–7). Casa Lucca also published Wagner's biblical cantata on the Last Supper, which Boito translated as "La cena degli apostoli" (Piero Nardi, *Vita di Arrigo Boito* [Milan, 1944], p. 343).
14. By 1914 there had been 193 stagings of *Lohengrin* in Italy, Data from G. Gualerzi and C. Marinelli Roscioni, *Wagner in Italia, 1871–1971* (Venice, 1972), passim.
15. Enrico Bottrigari, *Cronaca di Bologna,* Aldo Berselli, ed., vol. 4, 1861–71, (Bologna, 1962), p. 207. The chronicler took occasion to complain that the Teatro Comunale conductor, Angelo Mariani, "leaves much to be desired" because he chose to conduct Meyerbeer rather than Rossini, Bellini, or Donizetti (p. 206).
16. "Pensieri di un parziale," *Gazzetta dell'Emilia,* Oct. 30, 1871. This article was an *appendice.* An article two days before on "the music of the future" claimed that the subject held the same "scarecrows" as Romanticism had in 1820 (ibid., Oct. 28, 1871).
17. "Rivista teatrale," *L'arpa,* Aug. 28, Sept. 5–11, 1871, p. 1.
18. Quoted by Claudio Santini and Lamberto Trezzini, "La questione wagneriana," in *Due secoli di vita musicale: Storia del Teatro Comunale di Bologna,* 2 vols. (Bologna, 1966), 1:118–19. According to Bottrigari, Ludwig of Bavaria had promised Casarini to be present for the occasion. If such a promise was made, it was not kept (Bottrigari, *Cronaca di Bologna,* 4:208).
19. "Cronaca e fatti vari," *Gazzetta dell'Emilia,* Nov. 3, 1871. Throughout November, the *Gazzetta* printed letters on the subject that offer the assessments of the Bolognese cultural elite. One in particular, Carlo Gemelli's, questioned whether Wagner's music was the ultimate form that music of the future would take (ibid., Nov. 20, 1871). The Bolognese company was less well received in Florence in December, even though columns in *La nazione* by G. A. Biaggi tried to prepare Florentines for the new operas. See, for example, "Rassegna musicale," *La nazione,* Dec. 10, 1871.
20. Sangiorgi, "Il *Lohengrin* di Wagner," *L'arpa,* Nov. 11, 1871.
21. *Gazzetta dell'Emilia,* Nov. 20, 1871. See Weaver, *Verdi,* pp. 226–27, for an account of the annotations Verdi made on his score during the performance.
22. The *Gazzetta dell'Emilia* published Wagner's reply (dated Nov. 7) on Nov. 18, 1871.
23. The original of the letter is in the Civico Museo, Liceo Musicale G. B. Martini, Bologna. The discussion of the award of honorary citizenship that took place in the city council meeting and is recorded in the session of May 31, 1872 (*Atti del Consiglio Comunale di Bologna 11 aprile–13 luglio 1872,* Archivio Comunale, Bologna).

24. "Rivista teatrale," *L'arpa,* Nov. 20, 1872; "Rivista teatrale," *Corriere di Milano,* Nov. 11, 1872. Casarini's efforts to get the communal government to finance *Lohengrin* again in 1873 (or any Wagner opera) were not successful (Enrico to Casarini, Apr. 23, 1873, Museo del Risorgimento, Bologna, Carteggi Casarini, II, 1862–1870, casetta 9, no. 15).

25. Licurgo, "Il *Lohengrin* a Bologna," *Gazzetta musicale di Milano,* 26 (Nov. 5, 1871), 377.

26. See "appendice" in *La perseveranza,* Mar. 22, 1873. Filippi republished them in his *Musica e musicisti* (Milan, 1876).

27. "In memoria del suo direttore Giulio Ricordi," *Ars et labor,* 67 (1912), 16.

28. G. Morazzoni, "Il *Lohengrin* e la stampa milanese nel 1873," *Nel cinquantenario della morte di Riccardo Wagner: Teatro alla Scala 13 febbraio 1933,* ed. Francesco Guerrini (Milan, 1933), pp. 29–64. Ricordi denied the charge that he paid hecklers (ibid., p. 42).

29. *Gazzettino rosa,* Mar. 21, 1873, p. 1. In its "last definitive article on *Lohengrin,*" the *Gazzettino* suggested that after midnight "throughout Milan one could still hear the melancholy note of a whistle which seemed to salute the poor swan batting his wings slowly, slowly toward his native Germany" (ibid., Mar. 31, 1873, p. 1.). Giovannina Lucca made a gesture of reconciliation to the orchestra that had had to adjust to nightly disruptions by a donation to the orchestra's charitable organization (Morazzoni, "Il *Lohengrin* e la stampa milanese," ibid., p. 64). Wagner expressed thanks to the singers (by way of Signor Lucca) who had the courage to sing amidst the "tempests." Wagner tried to console her in a letter of Apr. 11, 1873; he advised her not to lose courage and compared his bad fortunes to those of Lucca's compatriot, Machiavelli (Giuseppe Depanis, *I concerti popolari ed il Teatro Regio di Torino* [Turin, 1914], 1:151–52).

30. Morazzoni, "Il *Lohengrin* e la stampa milanese," pp. 47–48. Wagner's offer to Signora Lucca to come to Milan for the final rehearsal, made in a letter of Oct. 9, 1872, was never accomplished (Barblan, *Storia di Milano,* 16:687).

31. S. Farina, "Il *Lohengrin* alla Scala," *Gazzetta musicale di Milano,* 28 (Mar. 23, 1873), 91–94.

32. Francesco d'Arcais, "*Lohengrin,*" *Nuova antologia,* 98 (Mar. 16, 1888), 345. A review of the first production of *Lohengrin* in Naples in 1881 was extremely enthusiastic. The opera was described by one critic as "Dantesque" (Mario Baccaro, "L'opera di Wagner a Napoli," *Cento anni di vita del Teatro di San Carlo, 1848–1948* [Naples, 1948], pp. 89–90). Rome was often described as very tolerant of Wagnerian music. In reviewing *Tannhäuser* at the Teatro Apollo in 1886, D'Arcais remarked, "In Rome, Wagner's music has never met with serious resistance" ("Il *Tannhäuser* di Wagner at Teatro Apollo di Roma," *Nuova antologia,* 87 [June 1, 1886], 553).

33. "La Walkyria," *La nazione,* Mar. 22–23, 1913.

34. Francesco d'Arcais, "Riccardo Wagner, poeta, uomo politico," *Nuova antologia,* 68, (Mar. 1, 1883), 23–24.

35. Filippi's "Secondo viaggio nelle regione dell'avvenire" is included in Joaquin Marsillach Lleonardt, *Riccardo Wagner* (Milan, 1881), pp. 161–304. For an account of the Torinese visit to Bayreuth in 1876, see Depanis, *Concerti popolari,* 1:233–35. The letters of Cosima Wagner to De Gubernatis on July

13 and 23, 1876 are in the Biblioteca Nazionale, Florence, De Gubernatis, cass. 133, no. 3.

36. Alberto Basso, *Il Teatro della città dal 1788 al 1936: Storia del Teatro Regio di Torino*, 2 vols. (Turin, 1976), 2:505–7, 533–39. In 1913, the centennial year of both Wagner's and Verdi's birth, Bologna still showed favoritism for Wagner by producing in honor of Verdi one of Verdi's lesser-known works, *I lombardi*. This decision was not made without controversy (*Il resto del Carlino* [Bolognese newspaper], Sept. 30, 1913).

37. *Cronaca wagneriana, 1 giugno 1893 al aprile 1895*, Biblioteca Archiginnasio, Bologna. See also Luigi Federzoni, "Carducci Wagneriano," *Bologna Carducciana* (Rocca San Casciano, 1961), pp. 108–10. For statistics on productions in Italy between 1871 and 1971, see Gualerzi and Roscioni, *Wagner in Italia*. Between 1871 and 1915 there were 407 productions.

38. Sienna's Duomo inspired the temple of the Holy Grail, which Wagner's friend Paul von Joukowsky reproduced for him; the garden at the Villa Rufolo in Ravello became the model for Klingsor's garden. (See G. Cogni, "Gli scritti senesi di Riccardo Wagner," *Chigiana*, 20 [1963], 116–23; Guido Pannain, "Wagner e l'Italia," in *Da Monteverdi a Wagner* [Milan, 1955], pp. 171–76).

39. Santini and Trezzini, "La questione wagneriana," pp. 150–51. The theme of decadence was suggested by Balbino Giuliano in "L'opera wagneriana: Giudizi e pregiudizi sull'opera di Riccardo Wagner," *Rivista d'Italia*, 17 (1914), 88–119.

40. Enrico Thovez, *Diario e lettere inedite, 1887–1901* (Milan, 1939), p. 343. Nevertheless, in another essay Thovez describes the attempts of teachers and others to counter Wagnerian influence ("La leggenda del Wagner," in *L'arco di Ulisse* [Naples, 1921], p. 161).

41. Francesco d'Arcais, "Riccardo Wagner, poeta," p. 23.

42. Giovanni Papini, "I 'martiri' di Wagner," *Autoritratti e ritratti*, in his *Opere*, 10 vols. (Milan, 1958), 9:803–4.

43. See Santini and Trezzini, "La questione wagneriana," pp. 135–37. Enrico Panzacchi wrote the libretto (Gino Monaldi, *I miei ricordi musicali* [Rome, 1921], p. 70). In 1866 the records of the Royal Conservatory of Music of Florence acknowledged receipt of a gift of the score of *Tannhäuser* from the estate of a Florentine noble, Marchese Leonardo Martellini, accompanied by a wish that the score should be used to instruct the young "what not to do" (*Atti dell'Accademia del R. Istituto Musicale di Firenze*, 4 [1866], 13).

44. *Atti parlamentari, Camera dei Deputati, discussioni, XI legislature V dal 13 gennaio al 18 febbraio 1873* (Rome, 1873), pp. 4512–16, 4594–95.

45. Verdi to Faccio, July 14, 1889, *Copialettere di Giuseppe Verdi*, p. 702; Giulio Ricordi, "Lohengrin," *Gazzetta musicale di Milano*, 44 (Mar. 10, 1889), 159; ibid., Jan. 5, 1890, pp. 6–9. Letters in the La Scala archives demonstrate that many Italian singers had reason for concern. In 1899 Eugenio Giraldoni protested the Wagnerian *tessitura*, and in 1906 Giuseppe Anselmi, a leading tenor, defined Wagner as the "prime assassin of voices." Giuseppe De Luca stated in an unsigned letter that he was studying the role of Beckmesser reluctantly because it was the type of part that "ruins" the voice (Giraldoni to Carlo D'Ormeville, Nov. 10, 1889, *BLS*, Coll. Casati 605; Anselmi to

anon., Feb. 9, 1906, Coll. Casati 28; De Luca to Carlo D'Ormeville, n.d., Coll. Casati, 357).

46. Verdi, though eighty-six years old, said he was still young enough to continue to penetrate the "sublime world of Wagnerian thoughts" (Mario Ferraguti, "Verdi e Wagner," *Vita musicale,* vol. 2 [1914], no. 14, pp. 34–35). Verdi's last two operas, *Otello* especially, were reviewed with reference to Wagner's music dramas (see, for example, *L'arpa,* Oct. 28, 1888).

47. *Gazzetta di Venezia,* Feb. 16, 1883, and Apr. 13, 16, 18–19, 1883.

48. Francesco d'Arcais, "La tetrologia del Wagner in Italia," *Nuova antologia,* 69 (June 1, 1883), 542–43. In Bologna, "A.B.," in the *Gazzetta dell'Emilia,* defended the Wagnerian principles upon which the *Ring* was based while questioning its survival. Many recognized the inadequacies of Italian theaters to produce it. Giovannina Lucca suggested a "pastiche" of the four *Ring* operas tailored to one evening's performance (Depanis, *I concerti popolari,* 1:159).

49. Francesco de Sanctis, *Storia della letteratura italiana,* 2 vols. (Milan, 1941), 2:364–65.

50. De Sanctis made this observation on Wagner in an 1883 appendix to his work on Petrarch (Francesco de Sanctis, *Saggio critico sul Petrarco* [Naples, 1913], p. 309).

51. Benedetto Croce, "Tra i giovani poeti, 'veristi,' e 'ribelli,'" *La letteratura della nuova Italia,* 3d ed. (Bari, 1929), 5:9.

52. Francesco d'Arcais, "La musica italiana e la 'Cavalleria Rusticana' di Pietro Mascagni," *Nuova antologia,* 111 (June 1, 1890), 518–30. D'Arcais also complimented the Sonzogno Commission, which had chosen the opera from seventy-three entries for a prize that the Sonzogno publishing house had offered.

53. Claudio Casini, *Giacomo Puccini* (Turin, 1978), pp. 49, 221, 312. Puccini helped Ricordi with cuts for *Die Meistersinger* after Ricordi took over the Lucca rights to Wagner in 1894. That trip to Bayreuth in 1912 evoked an enthusiastic response from Puccini as "three days of absolute enchantment" and "music lofty, sublime, divine." He also commented upon the "religiouslike" atmosphere there (letter to Luigi Pieri, Aug. 11, 1912, *Carteggi Pucciani,* Eugenio Gara, ed. [Milan, 1958], p. 401).

54. Mario Rinaldi, *Musica e verismo* (Rome, 1932), p. 274. Rinaldi commented that "if each of us had to have his Wagnerian period, it is necessary to guard (especially in youth) against this period changing into a mania" (ibid., p. 275).

55. Giordano, "Ruggiero Leoncavallo," *Cronaca dei teatri,* 2 (June 8, 1892); Mario Morini, *Umberto Giordano* (Milan, 1968), p. 280.

56. Mascagni to V. Gianfranceschi, Apr. 8, 1887, BLS, Aut. Fald. 35/5.

57. Mascagni, "Il melodramma dell'avvenire," quoted in Mario Morini, *Pietro Mascagni,* 2 vols. (Milan, 1964), 2:148–49.

58. Thovez, "L'incorreggibile," in *L'arco d'Ulisse,* pp. 169–70.

59. Filippi, *Musica e musicisti,* p. 222; Alberto De Angelis, "Il critico Filippo Filippi e il wagnerismo," in *Musica d'oggi* (1933), pp. 65–66. Filippi became defensive about criticism of his Wagnerian stance: "They accuse me of Germanism and of making war on Italian music." He proceeded to express

his esteem and support for Verdi, even though he was one of those who had professed to see Wagnerian influences in Verdi's work (ibid., p. 65).

60. Antonio Tari, *Saggi di estetica e metafisica* (Bari, 1911), p. 119.
61. Gino Monaldi, *Verdi e Wagner* (Rome, 1887), pp. 3–20.
62. Luigi Ronga, "Storia della musica," in Carlo Antoni and Raffaele Mattioli, eds., *Cinquant'anni di vita intellettuale italiana, 1896–1946: Scritti in onore di Benedetto Croce,* 2 vols. (Naples, 1950), 2:228.
63. Romauldo Giani, "Per l'arte aristocratica," *Rivista musicale italiana,* 3 (1896), 92–127, 756–69; replies of Torchi, ibid., 4 (1897), 148–50, 304–8.
64. Vincenzo Tommasini, "L'opera di Riccardo Wagner e la sua importanza nella storia dell'arte e della cultura," *Rivista musicale italiana,* 9 (1902), 710–16.
65. Luigi Torchi, *Riccardo Wagner: Studio critica* (Bologna, 1890), pp. 26–28. Torchi's Italian translations of Wagner included *Opera e dramma* (1894), *Musica dell'avvenire* (1893), and *Giudaismo in musica* (1895), all published by Bocca in Turin. When in 1910 a two-volume study on Wagner by Carlo Giulozzi appeared, Torchi reviewed it and claimed priority in placing Wagner against the background of German Romanticism. There was much in Giulozzi's two volumes that displayed a reading of Torchi, but the intent was to discredit Wagner. Arguing that Wagner's music was not popular because of its restricted audience, Giulozzi claimed that the universalism to which Wagner aspired was unachieved, since the ethical content of his works ran contrary to the modern Italian liberal spirit (Carlo Giulozzi, *Riccardo Wagner: La sua opera e la sua utopia* [Milan, 1910], pp. 345–46). For Torchi's review, see "Un libro contro Wagner," *Rivista musicale italiana,* 17 (1910), 677. For appraisals of Torchi's works, see Piero Rattalino, "Gli inizi della critica Wagneriana in Italia," *Musica d'oggi,* 5 (1962), 11–12; Luigi Ronga, "Per la critica wagneriana," *Arte e gusto nella musica* (Naples, 1956), pp. 355–59; Agostino Ziino, *Antologia della critica wagneriana in Italia* (Messina, 1970), pp. 58–74.
66. Quoted by Franco Vatielli, "Luigi Torchi," *Rivista musicale italiana,* 27 (1920), 686.
67. Quoted in ibid., p. 687.
68. Carlo Arner, "L'arte lirica e gli scioperi (Soliloquio di un pessimista)," *Gazzetta musicale di Milano,* 57, Aug. 14, 1902, 450–53.
69. As a Bolognese, Carducci could not help but be aware of the Wagnerian ambience of the musical scene. His enthusiasm for Wagner appeared in several letters, especially in one written following a memorial concert for Wagner in March 1883, a few months after Wagner's death. Moved by the final act of *Tristan* and by Isolde's death, Carducci wrote, "I understand no other music but that of Wagner" (letter to Dafore Gargiolli, Mar. 14, 1883, in *Edizione nazionale delle opere di Giosuè Carducci, Lettere,* 30 vols. [Bologna, 1952], 14:125). His poem of December 1884, "On the Urn of Percy Bysshe Shelley," has Tristan and Isolde and Wagnerian imagery, though its final plea is for a poet liberator of a great Rome. For a study of the *bizantini,* see the excellent study by Richard Drake, *Byzantium for Rome: The Politics of Nostalgia in Umbertian Italy, 1878–1900* (Chapel Hill, N.C., 1980).
70. Gabriele D'Annunzio, *La musica di Wagner e la genesi del "Parsifal"* (Florence, 1914), pp. 22, 25–27. This is another reprint of the articles that had appeared

earlier in *Pagine disperse,* ed. A. Castello (Rome, 1913), pp. 572–88. D'Annunzio tended to waver on the question of whether music served drama or dominated absolutely; his position depended on whether he was the librettist or not. In the decade before 1914, many of his plays and stories became libretti for opera (such as *La figlia di Jorio,* composed by Alberto Franchetti), and he was the librettist for Pietro Mascagni's *Parisina.* In an interview in 1928, he claimed not to "love" Wagner any more because of the "diminution by excessive theme development that diminished the potential of the music" (Arturo Calza, "Wagner e d'Annunzio," *Harmonia,* 2 [1914], 12–23; see also the interview with Enrico Prunières, *Corriere della sera,* Apr. 17, 1928).

71. Barblan, *Storia di Milano,* 16:692.

72. See, for example, Robert Adams, "The Operatic Novel: Joyce and D'Annunzio," in *New Looks at Italian Opera: Essays in Honor of Donald J. Grout* (New York, 1968), pp. 260–73; Elliott Zuckerman, *First Hundred Years of Wagner's "Tristan"* (New York, 1964), p. 131.

73. Alessandra Briganti, *Il parlamento nel romanzo italiano del secondo ottocento* (Florence, 1972), pp. 91–92.

74. Whether D'Annunzio actually was one of the six pallbearers, a legend he never denied, is discussed by his secretary, Tom Antongini, in *Un D'Annunzio ignorato* (Milan, 1963), pp. 129–30.

75. Gabriele D'Annunzio, *Il fuoco* (Milan, 1918), p. 181.

76. Ibid., p. 28.

77. The classical element was very strong in D'Annunzio's writings. See, for example, Alfredo Galletti, "Wagner e D'Annunzio," *Rivista d'Italia,* 27 (Aug. 15, 1924), 401–26; ibid., 27 (Sept. 15, 1924), 3–27.

78. *Il fuoco,* pp. 157–58.

79. Ibid., p. 49.

80. Ibid., pp. 180–81.

81. Ibid., pp. 45–46.

82. See Alfredo Oriani, *Fuori di bivacco* (Bari, 1913), pp. 57–68; Antonio Fogazzaro, *Lettere scelte, 1860–1911* (Milan, 1940), p. 213.

83. Gian Falco, "Chi sono i socialisti," in *La cultura italiana dell'900 attraverso le riviste,* vol. 2, *"Leonardo," "Hermes," "Il Regno,"* Delia Frigessi, ed. (Turin, 1960), p. 125.

84. Giovanni Papini, *Un uomo finito* (Florence, 1968), p. 185.

85. Giovanni Papini, "Un programma nazionalista," *Vecchio e nuovo nazionalismo* (Milan, 1914), pp. 21–22.

86. "S.S.," "Il futurismo," in *La cultura italiana dell'900 attraverso le riviste,* vol. 3, *"La voce" (1908–1914),* Angelo Romano, ed. (Turin, 1960), p. 203.

87. Giovanni Papini, *Scritti postumi,* 10 vols. (Milan, 1966), 10:1175–76.

88. "La grande Milano tradizionale e futurista," in *Opere di F. T. Marinetti* (Verona, 1969), pp. 20–38. See also Alfredo Casella, *Music of My Time* (Norman, Okla., 1955), pp. 123–24.

89. Casella, *Music of My Time,* p. 138; see also Giannotto Bastianelli, "Bologna," *La critica musicale,* 4 (1921), 3–6.

90. *La carta del Carnaro nei testi di Alceste De Ambris e di Gabriele D'Annunzio,* ed. Renzo De Felice (Bologna, 1973), p. 73.

91. Giannotto Bastianelli, *La musica pura: Commentari musicali e altri scritti* (Florence, 1974), p. 109.
92. Quoted in Ziino, *Antologia della critica wagneriana,* p. 88.
93. Galletti, "Wagner e D'Annunzio," p. 424.
94. Enrico Thovez, "Il tesoro mediterraneo," in *Il filo d'Arianna* (Milan, 1924), pp. 103–11; "L'eredità di Bayreuth," in ibid., pp. 97–102.

5. Wagner and Wagnerian Ideas in Russia

1. Richard Taruskin, "Opera and Drama in Russia: The Preachment and Practice of Operatic Aesthetics," Ph.D. dissertation, Columbia University, 1976, p. 535. Wagner may have influenced the Five's use of folk myth and legend as well as the harmonics and orchestral color of their compositions. There is general agreement that Wagner influenced the late operas of Rimsky-Korsakov. Borodin's *Prince Igor,* based on a text that is sometimes considered the Slavic counterpart to the Nibelungen myth (and to the *Chanson de Roland*), may also have been influenced by Wagner. Mussorgsky's *Boris Godunov* was composed during the years when Wagner was composing the *Ring;* Mussorgsky's uncompleted opera *Khovanshchina* was intended to be a trilogy on a Wagnerian scale. The issue of the Five's overall debt to Wagner is so complex and controversial that it calls for a separate musicological analysis. Their hostility to Wagner, however, was definitely a factor in their attack on Serov's music drama *Judith.*
2. Quoted in Taruskin, "Opera and Drama in Russia," p. 467.
3. Quoted in ibid., p. 468.
4. Leo Tolstoy, *What Is Art?* (Indianapolis, 1960), p. 127. See also pp. 118–31, 209–13.
5. Ibid., pp. 122, 209.
6. Leonid Sabaneev, *Vospomananiia o Skriabine* (Moscow, 1925), pp. 11–12; Faubion Bowers, *Scriabin,* 2 vols. (Palo Alto, 1969), 1:163. For an example of growing interest in Wagner, see S. Rzhevsky, "Pobeda Rikharda Vagnera" (The victory of Wagner), *Severnyi vestnik,* no. 3 (1896), pp. 98–106.
7. Nikolai Findeizn, "Vagner v rossii," *Russkaia muzykal'naia gazeta,* no. 35 (Aug. 30, 1903), pp. 755–69.
8. Alexandr Benois, *Memoirs,* 2 vols. (London, 1964), 2:56.
9. On Nietzsche's reception, see N. Berdiaev, *Russkaia ideia* (Paris, 1946), pp. 224–25, 230; Ann Lane, "Nietzsche in Russian Thought," Ph.D. dissertation, University of Wisconsin, 1976, and B. G. Rosenthal, "Nietzsche in Russia: The Case of Merezhkovsky," *Slavic Review* 33 (1974), 429–52. Also important to the aesthetic individualist credo were Baudelaire, the French symbolists, and Schopenhauer.
10. Symbolism was an artistic movement that included writers, painters, and musicians. Its leading figures in Russia were Valeri Bryusov (1873–1924), Konstantine Balmont (1867–1942), Dmitri S. Merezhkovsky (1865–1941), Zinaida Hippius (1869–1945), Nikolai M. Minsky (Vilenkin) (1855–1937), Aleksandr Blok (1880–1921), Andrei Bely (Boris Bugaev) (1880–1934), Vyacheslav Ivanov (1866–1949), Vasili Rozanov (1856–1919), and Fedor

Sologub (Teternikov) (1863–1927). Strictly speaking, the last two were not symbolists, but they were closely associated with them.

11. Like Baudelaire, aesthetes and symbolists interpreted Wagner as depicting the struggle between two principles, flesh and spirit, Satan and God, earth and heaven; they heard in his music the ardors of mysticism, the striving of the spirit toward an ineffable God. Since Christian attitudes toward sex and other worldly pleasures were among the burning questions then being discussed by Russian intellectuals, Wagner seemed especially relevant.

12. Alexsandr Benois, *Reminiscences of the Russian Ballet* (London, 1941), pp. 370–71. The italics are my own.

13. Quoted in Serge Lifar, *Serge Diaghilev* (New York, 1940), p. 366.

14. Benois, *Memoirs,* 2:78.

15. G. Likhtenberger, "Vzgliady Vagnera na iskusstve," *Mir iskusstva,* nos. 7–8 (1899), pp. 107–28, and nos. 11–12 (1899), pp. 195–206. For details on *Mir iskusstva* see Janet Kennedy, "The *Mir iskusstva* Group and Russian Art," Ph.D. dissertation, Columbia University, 1976.

16. Previously Aleksandr Koptaiev had translated excerpts from Wagner's "Artwork of the Future" in *Russkaia muzykal'naia gazeta* (1897–1899) and, in the same journal, excerpts from Wagner's biography (1896). Educated Russians, however, generally read French or German.

17. P. Gnedich, "Teatr budushchego," *Mir iskusstva,* nos. 3–4 (1900), pp. 52–58 (2d pagination).

18. Evgeni Ivanov, "Loge i Zigfrid," *Mir iskusstva,* no. 6 (1904), pp. 128–45.

19. Quoted in Richard Buckle, *Diaghilev* (New York, 1979), p. 87.

20. William Richardson, "*Zolotoe runo* and Russian Modernism," Ph.D. dissertation, University of California, Berkeley, 1976, pp. 180, 204.

21. N. Lapshina, *Mir iskusstva* (Moscow, 1977), pp. 121–25; M. V. Davidova, "'Teatral'no dekoratsionnoe iskusstvo," in *Russkaia khudozhestvennaia kul'tura kontsa xix nachala xx veka* (henceforth *RKK*), 4 vols. (Moscow, 1968–1981), 2:237.

22. Benois, *Reminiscences,* p. 374.

23. Kennedy, "*Mir iskusstva* Group," pp. 350–54.

24. Fedor Sologub, "Mechta Don Kikhota," in *Sobranie sochinenii* (St. Petersburg, n.d.), 10:159.

25. Fedor Sologub, "Teatr odnoi voli," in ibid., p. 158.

26. Gordon McVay, *Isadora and Esenin* (Ann Arbor, 1980), pp. 6, 141–42. For the symbolists' reaction, see Lidia Vil'kina, "Aisedora Dunkan v peterburge," *Vesy,* 1 (1905), pp. 40–42, and Anastasia Chebotarevskaia, "Aisedora Dunkan v prozreniiakh Nitsshe," in *Zolotoe runo,* no. 4 (1909), pp. 81–82.

27. Aleksandr Benois, "Khudozhestvennyi eresi" (Artistic heresy), *Zolotoe runo,* no. 2 (1906), pp. 80–88.

28. Aleksandr Benois, "Beseda o baleta," in *Teatr: Kniga o novom teatre,* ed. Georgi Chulkov (St. Petersburg, 1908), pp. 95–122.

29. Vyacheslav Ivanov, *Po zvezdam* (St. Petersburg, 1909), p. 244.

30. For details see Buckle, *Diaghilev,* pp. 119–57.

31. Again the issue of Wagner's influence is too complex to be treated here. Let us note, however, that Stravinsky (1882–1971) reacted against Wagner,

was antipathetic to the idea of music drama, considered "endless melody" a contradiction in terms, and rejected opera itself as a dead form. Prokofiev (1891–1953) was also against Wagner. The character Farfarello in *Love for Three Oranges* (1919) is often considered to be a caricature of Fafner. Of the seven operas Prokofiev wrote, *The Fiery Angel*, based on a novel by Bryusov, is possibly the most influenced by Wagner. Set in medieval Germany, it is complicated symphonically, and the orchestra is very important. Prokofiev later turned it into the Third Symphony. (I am indebted to Harlow Robinson for this information.) There was a reaction against Wagner in the Ballets russes after the war, but that subject is outside the scope of this study.

32. Nijinsky and his wife Romula were both Wagnerians. In 1916 Nijinsky expressed a desire to create dances to the music of Wagner and to perform them in Bayreuth after the war. See Richard Buckle, *Nijinsky* (New York, 1971), pp. 37, 381, 352–53.

33. Benois, *Reminiscences*, p. 322. As a young man, however, he viewed *Tannhäuser* as a symbol of the struggle between romanticism and classicism, "the striving of Tannhäuser to leave the despotic embrace of Venus for the world created by art" (Kennedy, "*Mir iskusstva* Group," p. 195). For Benois's belief that Dionysian frenzy must be subsumed in Apollonian form, see "V ozhidanii gimna apollonu," *Apollon*, no. 1 (Oct. 1909), pp. 5–11.

34. For details, see Charles S. Mayer, "The Theatrical Designs of Leon Bakst," Ph.D. dissertation, Columbia University, 1977.

35. Iakov Tugend'kholdt, "Russkii sezon v Parizhe," *Apollon*, no. 10 (1910), pp. 5–23.

36. Anatoli Lunacharsky, "Russkie spektakli v Parizhe," reprinted in *Teatr i revoliutsiia* (Moscow, 1924), pp. 328–35 (1913), 431–36 (1914).

37. Vsevolod Meierkhol'd, "K postanovke *Tristana i Izol'dy* na Mariinskom teatre," in *V. E. Meierkhol'd: Stat'i, pis'ma, rechi, besedy*, 2 vols. (Moscow, 1968), 1:143–61. See also Iu. Keldysh, "Opernyi teatr," in *RKK*, 3:332–36.

38. The translator was A. M. Volynski (Flexner), an early advocate of philosophical idealism and literary consultant to V. Kommissarzhevskaia's experimental theater.

39. G. Likhtenberger, *Rikhard Vagner kak poet i mislitel'* (Moscow, 1905); E. Shuré, *Wagner i ego muzykal'naia drama* (St. Petersburg, 1909).

40. Viktor Valter, "Chto sdelal Vagner dlia reformy opera," *Sovremennyi mir*, no. 12 (1908), pp. 134–49; K. Eiges, "Rikhard Vagner i ego khudozhestvennoe reformatorstvo," in *Russkaia mysl'*, no. 6 (1913), pp. 56–68; I. G. Ashkinazi, "Teatr Vagnera," *Obrazovanie*, no. 3 (1909), pp. 101–16 (2d pagination).

41. V. Karatygin, "Vagner i Dargomyzhsky," *Apollon*, no. 8 (1913), pp. 36–50; Iuri Engel, "*Gibel bogov* Vagner i *Snegurochka* Rimskago-Korsakova," *Ezhegodnik imperatorskikh teatrov*, no. 1 (1912), pp. 87–114.

42. S. Durylin, *Vagner i Rossiia: O Vagner i budushchikh putiakh iskusstva* (Moscow, 1913), pp. 3–5. Durylin (1877–1954), then associated with the

religious symbolists of Moscow, wrote and lectured on the history of the theater, music, archaeology, and philology under the Soviets.

43. Evgeni Trubetskoi, "Voina i mirovaia zadacha Rossii," *Russkaia mysl'*, no. 12 (1914), pp. 92–93.

44. For details, see B. G. Rosenthal, *D. S. Merezhkovsky and the Silver Age* (The Hague, 1975); Temira Pachmuss, *Zinaida Gippius: An Intellectual Profile* (Carbondale, Ill., 1971); C. H. Bedford, *The Seeker: D. S. Merezhkovskij* (Lawrence, Kans., 1975).

45. The society was suppressed in 1903, partly because too many heretical views were being expressed. Revived after the Revolution of 1905 (but without the participation of the clergy), the St. Petersburg Society held its last meeting in 1916. Branches were founded in Moscow and Kiev. One major source of the religious revival was the Moscow Psychological Society, founded in 1884, which published the journal *Questions of Philosophy and Psychology* (1889–1917) to disseminate philosophical idealism. Another source was the neo-Kantians: Nikolai Berdiaev, Peter Struve, and Sergei Bulgakov, former Marxists who returned, via Kant, to the Orthodox church after the Revolution of 1905.

46. See, for example, K. Eiges, "Muzyka i estetika," *Zolotoe runo*, no. 5 (1906), pp. 60–62, and "Muzyka kak odno iz vysshikh misticheskikh perezhivanii," ibid., nos. 6–7 (1907), pp. 54–57.

47. See, for example, Vl. Orlov, ed. *A. Belyi, A. Blok Perepiska* (Moscow, 1940), esp. pp. 4, 10; Andrei Bely, "Formy iskusstva," *Mir iskusstva*, no. 12 (1902), pp. 343–61, reprinted in *Simvolizm* (Moscow, 1910), pp. 149–74.

48. See, for example, Evgeni Braudo, "Muzyka posle Vagnera," *Apollon*, no. 1 (1909), pp. 54–57, and "Liubov i smert'," ibid., no. 4 (1910), pp. 35–36.

49. Ellis (Lev Kobylinsky), "Mionkhenskiia pis'ma," *Trudi i dni*, no. 6 (1912), pp. 56–59, and "*Parsifal* Rikhard Vagnera," ibid., no. 7 (1914), pp. 48–53. Ellis translated Wagner's librettos into Russian.

50. Max Hochschüler, "Pis'mo iz Baireuta," *Vesy*, no. 9 (1904), pp. 39–46, and no. 10 (1904), pp. 49–58. See also N. Suvorovsky, "Chaikovskii i muzyka budushchago," *Vesy*, no. 8 (1904), pp. 10–20, esp. p. 18, for his association of Wagner with the "principle of the superhuman in music" and with current messianic expectations.

51. V. Karatygin, "*Parsifal* v S' Peterburge," *Russkaia mysl'*, no. 4 (1914), pp. 20–25.

52. Andrei Bely, *Na perevale*, 4 vols. (Petrograd, 1918–1920; reprinted Ann Arbor, 1974), 1.108, 2:116, 118–21.

53. I. G. Ashkinazi, "Teatr Vagnera," pp. 110–13, 116.

54. Vyacheslav Ivanov, *Po zvezdam*, p. 224; see also Ivanov, "Nitsshe i dionis," *Vesy*, no. 5 (1904), pp. 21–29.

55. Ivanov, "Estetika i ispovedanie," *Vesy*, no. 11 (1908), p. 48. His "Ellinskaia religiia stradaiushchego boga" (Religion of the suffering god) was serialized in *Novyi put'* in 1904 and continued as "Religiia Dionisa" (Religion of Dionysus) in *Voprosy zhizni* in 1905.

56. Ivanov, "Vagner i Dionisogo deistvo," *Vesy*, no. 2 (1905), pp. 13–16.

57. Ibid.
58. Ivanov, *Po zvezdam,* pp. 54–55.
59. Ivanov, "Vagner i dionisogo," pp. 14, 16.
60. Ivanov, *Po zvezdam,* pp. 210–11.
61. Ibid., p. 206.
62. Ibid., pp. 54–55, 40–42.
63. For details see B. G. Rosenthal, "The Transmutation of Russian Symbolism: Mystical Anarchism and the Revolution of 1905," *Slavic Review* 36 (1977), 608–27, and "Theater as Church: The Vision of the Mystical Anarchists," *Russian History* 4 (1977), 122–41. Revolutionary turmoil forced the closing of the theaters for much of 1905, stimulating hopes of an entirely new kind of theater when they reopened.
64. Ivanov, *Po zvezdam,* p. 286; see also p. 219.
65. Ibid., p. 218.
66. Georgi Chulkov, "Printsipy teatra budushchago," in *Teatr,* p. 212; see also pp. 208–11. The essays were delivered as talks at a symposium on the theater organized by Ivanov and Chulnov.
67. Ivanov, *Po zvezdam,* pp. 205–6. This excerpt is from his essay "Novaia organicheskaia epokha i teatr buduschchago" (The new organic society and the theater of the future), reprinted in ibid., pp. 189–219. The essay reflects the influence of George Fuchs's concept of the theater of the future, which was being discussed in Germany and Russia at that time.
68. Ivanov, *Po zvezdam,* pp. 213–14, 218.
69. Ibid., pp. 233–35, 240.
70. Boris Bugaev (Andrei Bely), "Protiv muzyka," *Vesy,* no. 3 (1907), pp. 57–60. Bely published under both names. The article must be understood in the context of his quarrel with the mystical anarchists.
71. Andrei Bely, "Teatr i sovremennaia drama," in *Teatr,* pp. 261–89, esp. 270–76 and 287–89.
72. Dmitri Filosofov, "Dekadentstvo, obshchestvennost', i misticheskim anarkhizm," *Zolotoe runo,* no. 10 (1906), pp. 63–64.
73. Merezhkovsky, Minski, and Remizov themselves wrote mystery plays modeled on those of medieval Europe. For the prominence of mystery plays in early Russian symbolist dramaturgy, see George Kalbouss, "The Birth of Modern Russian Drama," in *Selected Papers in the Humanities from the Banff 1977 International Conference,* ed. R. Freeborn, R. R. Milner-Gulland, and Charles A. Ward (Cambridge, Mass., 1976), pp. 175–89. For early symbolist conceptions of their relation to the people, see B. G. Rosenthal, *D. S. Merezhkovsky,* pp. 43–54.
74. Valeri Bryusov, "Nenuzhnaia pravda," *Mir iskusstva,* no. 7 (1902), pp. 62–74 (3d pagination).
75. For details of some symbolist theatrical experiments, see George Kalbouss, "From Mystery to Fantasy: An Attempt to Categorize Some of the Plays of the Russian Symbolists," *Canadian-American Slavic Studies,* no. 8 (1974), pp. 488–500, and *The Plays of the Russian Symbolists,* (East Lansing, Mich., 1983). See also Harold B. Segel, *Twentieth Century Russian Drama* (New York, 1979), chap. 3, "Revolt against Naturalism," pp. 50–146.

76. A. Remizov, "Tovarishchestvo novoi dramy," *Vesy*, no. 4 (1904), pp. 36–39. Remizov was the literary manager of the fellowship.

77. V. V. Rostotsky, "Modernizm v teatre," in *RKK*, 1:177. For Meyerhold's concept of "collective creativity," see his essay "Teatr: K istorii i tekhnik," in *Teatr*, pp. 123–76; for his association with the symbolists, see Marjorie Hoover, *Meyerhold and the Art of Conscious Theater* (Amherst, Mass., 1974), pp. 29–40, 61.

78. Aleksandr Blok, *Sobranie sochinenii*, 8 vols. (Moscow, 1960–1963), 6:273. See also 6:274, 348–49, for his discussion of theater as the "great school of noble will, of musical will."

79. For Nietzsche's influence on Scriabin, see Lane, "Nietzsche in Russian Thought," pp. 103–24.

80. Malcolm H. Brown, "Skriabin and Russian 'Mystic' Symbolism," *19th Century Music*, 3 (1979), 43.

81. Quoted in Malcolm H. Brown, "Skriabin and the Young Prokofiev, 1909–1915," typescript, p. 4.

82. For Scriabin's color theory, see Ralph E. Matlaw, "Scriabin and Russian Symbolism," *Comparative Literature*, 31 (1979), 10.

83. Quoted in Brown, "Skriabin and the Young Prokofiev," p. 4.

84. Prince Sergei Trubetskoi (1862–1905) introduced Scriabin to the meetings and to the ideas of Soloviev. Scriabin was also influenced by the ideas of the "neo-Christians" Berdiaev and Bulgakov.

85. Elena Blavatsky (1831–1891) attempted to reconcile the doctrines of the major religions of the world. Encompassing occult elements, theosophy assumes there are various planes of life, material and spiritual, including "ethereal" and "astral" planes, and that after death the astral body lives on. Among those interested in theosophy were Bely, the painters Kasimir Malevich and Vasili Kandinsky, and, in the West, Piet Mondrian and the poet William Butler Yeats.

86. Sabaneev, *Vospominaniia o Skriabine*, p. 59.

87. The Jewish question pertained mainly, though not exclusively, to the legal limitations and restrictions on Jews. Liberals and radicals tended to favor the elimination of special disabilities; conservatives and reactionaries, their perpetuation or even intensification. After 1905, bills for Jewish emancipation were introduced in the Duma but did not become law until March 1917 under the Provisional Government. Jews who converted, incidentally, escaped these disabilities.

88. Jews who wished to reside in St. Petersburg or Moscow required special permission. Even the well-connected Leo Bakst (né Rozenberg) was forced to leave St. Petersburg in 1912 because he could not obtain a permit.

89. In contrast, Peter Struve (1870–1944), a right-wing liberal (and not a Wagnerian), believed that Jews should "dissolve" into Russian culture, like one of his favorite painters, I. Levitan. Even Struve, however, considered culture to be "that sphere in which national attraction and repulsion rightly operate." See his "Intelligentsiia i natsional'noe litso," *Slovo* 10, March 1909, reprinted in *Patriotica* (St. Petersburg, 1911), pp. 370–74.

90. Vol'fing, "Estrada" [The stage], *Zolotoe runo*, nos. 2–3 (1909), pp. 100–

108, and no. 5 (1909), pp. 44–52. Vol'fing is the pseudonym of Emil Medtner (1872–1936), brother of the composer N. Medtner. A devotee of German musical culture, Vol'fing wrote several articles for *Zolotoe runo* on the Wagner Festival in Munich and on modernism in music generally, signing them "Notes of a Non-Wagnerian." He was referring, however, to Wagner's successors, who, Medtner claimed, used such Wagnerian techniques as chromaticism and diacriticism mechanically. He advocated a "back to Beethoven" movement to complement the "back to Kant" movement in Russian thought. Bely admired Medtner greatly. "In the raised dust of civilization," said Bely, Medtner "saw the smoke of the burning of Valhalla; his slogan was 'Cut off the head of Fafner'" (Andrei Bely, *Nachala veka* [Moscow, 1933], p. 54).

91. Boris Bugaev (Andrei Bely), "Stempelevannaia kul'tura," *Vesy*, no. 9 (1909), pp. 74, 76–77.

92. Ibid., p. 73; see p. 75 for the "Aryan Nietzsche."

93. Sabaneev, *Vospominaniia o Skriabine*, p. 242.

94. Durylin, *Vagner i Rossiia*, pp. 16, 15, 54–60. Kitezh is a mythical Slavic city that was supposed to have descended uncorrupted to the bottom of a lake at the time of the first Mongol invasion. Rimsky-Korsakov finished the opera during the stormy period 1905–1906; it was produced early in 1907.

95. Ibid., pp. 55, 68. Note the influence of Ivanov. The rainbow sign alludes to Noah and the Great Flood and expresses the sense of imminent world destruction and resurrection common to the age.

96. S. Volkov and R. Red'ko, "A. Blok i nekotorye muzykal'noe esteticheskie problemy ego vremeni," in *Blok i muzyka*, M. Elik, ed. (Moscow, 1972), pp. 95–96.

97. For details see B. G. Rosenthal, "Eschatology and the Appeal of Revolution: Merezhkovsky, Bely, Blok," in *California Slavic Studies* 11 (1980), 105–38.

98. Blok, *Sobranie sochinenii*, 6:115, 109.

99. "Stikhiia i kul'tura," in ibid., pp. 350–59.

100. See, for example, his 1908 essay "Narod i intelligentsia" [The people and the intelligentsia] in *Sobranie sochinenii* 5:318–28, and his poem of the same year "Na pole Kulikovom" (On the field of Kulikovo), in ibid., 3:249–53. Kulikovo is the site of a major battle (1380) between the Russians and the Mongols. The Russians won the battle, but the Mongols ruled over Russia for another hundred years.

101. *Sobranie sochinenii*, 7:297 (diary entry, August 7, 1917). Fire, aside from its general apocalyptic meaning, has a special significance in Russia, where the Old Believers, with whom radicals sometimes identified, burned themselves alive in their struggle against the state, which they regarded as the Antichrist.

102. Ibid., 6:20.

103. Ibid., 8:277; 6:14–15.

104. Vl. Orlov, "Iz neizdannykh tekstov Aleksandra Bloka," in *Literaturnoe nasledstvo* (Moscow, 1938), 27–28:675. The question refers to N. Chernyshevsky's famous novel, *What Is to Be Done?* (1864). It inspired countless revolutionaries, including Lenin, whose first major theoretical treatise was also titled *What Is to Be Done?* (1902).

105. Blok, "Iskusstvo i revoliutsiia," in *Sobranie sochinenii* 6:21–25. See also Blok's *Zapisnye knizhki* (Notebooks) (Moscow, 1965), p. 389 (Feb. 22, 1918) for his statement "One must write about the Russian delirium" and his subsequent resolution to translate Wagner's *Art and Revolution*. He wrote the article in March 1918.

106. Blok, *Sobranie sochinenii*, 6:24.

107. Ibid., pp. 24–25.

108. Ibid., 7:330.

109. Ibid., 6:25. Blok also maintained that Jesus was an artist. See Rolf Kluge, *Westeuropa und Russland im Weltbild Aleksandr Bloks* (Munich, 1967), p. 256.

110. *Sobranie sochinenii*, 7:358 (diary entry, Mar. 27, 1919).

111. Ibid., 7:360, 362 (diary entry, Mar. 31, 1919). See also ibid., 6:101–2.

112. "Krushenie gumanizma," in ibid., 6:93–115.

113. Ibid., p. 112.

114. Ibid., pp. 114–15.

115. For an interpretation of the religious and social dimensions of the symbolists' conception of the "spirit of music," see B. G. Rosenthal, "The Spirit of Music in Russian Symbolism," forthcoming in *Russian History*.

116. *Sobranie sochinenii*, 6:114.

117. Quoted in Marc Slonim, *From Chekhov to the Revolution* (New York, 1953), p. 206.

118. Andrei Bely, *Revoliutsiia i kul'tura* (Moscow, 1917; reprinted Letchworth, England, 1971), p. 12. The same perception of Wagner caused Bulgakov to call him a "German *khlyst'*." The word *khlyst'* refers to a Russian sect that included orgies in its religious rituals; Rasputin was allegedly a member.

119. Originally a theosophist, Steiner broke with the movement when Annie Besant proclaimed a young Hindu boy a reincarnation of Christ. Steiner taught that the cosmos was evolving, that the birth of Christ was the central event in cosmic evolution, and that the sacrifice at Golgotha introduced a new spiritual mystery into the universe. The Second Coming, Steiner predicted, would be a resurrection not of Christ's physical body but of the "divine I" within man. Once humanity attained higher levels of consciousness through spiritual evolution (including extrasensory perception), the etheric Christ (his living spirit) would be visible to all. Steiner expected this event to occur in the early twentieth century. For details, see B. G. Rosenthal, "Revolution as Apocalypse: The Case of Bely," in *Andrey Bely: A Critical Review*, ed. Gerald Janecek (Lexington, Ky., 1978), pp. 182–86, and "Eschatology and the Appeal of Revolution," pp. 116–21.

120. The most prominent figures on the Bolshevik Left were Lunacharsky, Maksim Gorki (1868–1936), and Aleksandr Bogdanov (1873–1928).

121. Similar to Auguste Comte's "Religion of Humanity," "God building" preached immortality through reputation and worship of the greatness in man.

122. Anatoli Lunacharsky, "Ob iskusstve i revoliutsii" (c. 1906), reprinted in *Teatr i revoliutsiia* (Moscow, 1924), pp. 167–68. The essay also attacked "narrow-minded fanatics" concerned solely with economic and political issues.

123. Anatoli Lunacharsky, *O teatre i dramaturgii,* 2 vols. (Moscow, 1958), 1:784.
124. Ibid., p. 356. This excerpt is from the essay "Dlia chego my sokhraniaem bol'shoi teatr?" (For what are we saving the Bolshoi Theater?). See also "Sotsializm i iskusstvo" (Socialism and art), in *Teatr,* pp. 7, 28, 30, 40.
125. Anatoli Lunacharsky, *V mire muzyki: Stati i rechi* (Moscow, 1958), p. 126.
126. Lunacharsky, "Sotsializm i iskusstvo," p. 40.
127. Ibid., pp. 35–38, 40.
128. Lars Kleberg, "'People's Theater' and the Revolution," in *Art, Society, Revolution: Russia, 1917–21,* Nils Ake Nilsson, ed. (Stockholm, 1979), pp. 184–85.
129. Ibid., p. 193. Note that "folk" (*narodnyi*), not "proletariat," was still the term used.
130. Marc Slonim, *Russian Theater* (New York, 1962), p. 252.
131. The plot is simple. Seven Clean and Unclean couples board the ark after the flood. The Clean try to rule the Unclean, but the latter revolt, throw the Clean overboard, and sail off by themselves. They find that hell holds no terror for them, for they have already lived in hell on earth, and that heaven is a delusion. Meanwhile, after the floodwaters recede, the armies of Chaos take over the earth. The Unclean defeat Chaos (idlers, speculators, egoists) and proceed to create paradise.
132. Edward Braun, *Meyerhold on Theater* (New York, 1969), p. 161.
133. Ibid., p. 167.
134. Vsevolod Meierkhol'd, "*Uchitel' Bubus* i problema spektakli na muzyke," in *Stat'i,* 2:67–69, 71.
135. Lunacharsky, *O teatre i dramaturgii,* 1:374. This excerpt is from his essay "Puti Meierkhol'da" (The path of Meyerhold), pp. 373–76. See also in the same volume "Teatr Meierkhol'da," pp. 377–85, and "Eshche o teatre Meierkhold'a" (More on the theater of Meyerhold), pp. 386–90; see pp. 391–407 for his views on Meyerhold's production of *The Inspector General.*
136. Lunacharsky, *Teatr i revoliutsiia,* pp. 12, 127; *O teatre i dramaturgii,* 1:360. The latter statement is from "Rol' Bolshoi teatr" (The role of the Bolshoi Theater) and was made in connection with the centenary of the Bolshoi, 1925.
137. Ibid., p. 357. This excerpt is from "For what are we saving the Bolshoi Theater?," pp. 351–59.
138. Ibid., pp. 357–58. See also "K stoletiiu Bol'shago teatra" (On the centenary of the Bolshoi Theater), pp. 361–72.
139. Ibid., pp. 358–59.
140. Sheila Fitzpatrick, "The 'Soft' Line on Culture and Its Enemies: Soviet Cultural Policy, 1922–27," *Slavic Review,* 33 (1974), 267.
141. Lunacharsky, "Rikhard Vagner," in *O teatre i dramaturgii,* 2:497, 502, 503 (originally published as "The Path of Wagner").
142. Yon Barna, *Eisenstein* (Bloomington, Ind., 1973), p. 141.
143. Ibid., p. 228.
144. This is not to imply, of course, that the revolutions were the same in every respect. There was no real Russian equivalent, for example, to the role played by artisans displaced by industrialization, as was found in the German revolution of 1848–1849.

6. At Wagner's Shrine: British and American Wagnerians

1. James Taft Hatfield, *New Light on Longfellow, with Special Reference to His Relations to Germany* (Boston, 1933), p. 128.
2. Ford Madox Ford, *Memories and Impressions* (New York, 1911), p. 92.
3. The German group in England is discussed in Anne Dzamba Sessa, *Richard Wagner and the English* (London, 1979), chap. 1.
4. Charles Santley, *Reminiscences of My Life* (London, 1909), p. 125.
5. Percy Scholes, *The Mirror of Music*, 2 vols. (London, 1947), 1:253.
6. Harold Rosenthal, *Two Centuries of Opera at Covent Garden* (London, 1958), p. 247. See also Ronald Pearsall, *Victorian Popular Music* (Detroit, 1973), p. 154.
7. William Mason, *Memories of a Musical Life* (New York, 1901), pp. 45–55, 159–60. The art historian Charles C. Perkins, who accompanied him, was less enchanted; see *Dwight's Journal of Music* 4 (Jan. 21, 1854), 125–26.
8. W. J. Henderson, "Who Discovered Wagner?", *Munsey's Magazine* 32 (1905), 673.
9. Gustav Kobbé, "Wagner in America," *Review of Reviews*, 20 (1899), 689. Kobbé also cites another offer made four years later but gives no details (ibid.)
10. Ibid., p. 694.
11. J. S. Cleve, "Wagner in America," *New Music Review and Church Music Review*, 12 (1913), 214
12. Richard Wagner, "The Work and Mission of My Life," *North American Review*, 129 (1879), 111.
13. Ibid., pp. 256–57.
14. Ibid., p. 258.
15. Irving Kolodin, *The Story of the Metropolitan Opera, 1883–1950* (New York, 1953), p. 114. See also pp. 95, 100.
16. Ibid., p. 109.
17. William Ashton Ellis, "Richard Wagner's Prose," *Proceedings of the Royal Music Association* 19 (1892–1893), 232.
18. Roger Fulford, ed., *Your Dear Letter: Private Correspondence of Queen Victoria and the Crown Princess of Prussia* (New York, 1971), p. 232.
19. *Dwight's Journal of Music*, 29 (May 22, 1869), 33–35.
20. Edward Burlingame, *Art, Life, and Theories of Richard Wagner* (New York, 1875), p. xii.
21. Joseph A. Mussulman, *Music in the Cultured Generation: A Social History of Music in America, 1870–1900* (Evanston, Ill., 1971), p. 158.
22. Joseph Bennett, *Letters from Bayreuth* (London, 1877), pp. 146–47.
23. Clare Benedict, *The Divine Spark* (Philadelphia, 1913), p. 8.
24. Charles Dudley Warner, *A Roundabout Journey* (Hartford, Conn., 1904), p. 313.
25. Mark Twain, *What Is Man? and Other Essays* (Ann Arbor, Mich., 1972), pp. 224–25.
26. Ibid., pp. 216, 222, 226–27.
27. For satire see Gustav Holst's score, *The Perfect Fool* (London, 1923); Kate Douglas Wiggin, *Bluebeard: A Musical Fantasy* (New York, 1914), pp. vi-

vii; R. C. Trevelyan, *The New Parsifal* (London, 1914); Rupert Brooke, "Wagner," in *The New Oxford Book of Light Verse,* Kingsley Amis, ed. (Oxford, 1978), p. 215. Anti-Wagnerian commentators included H. W. L. Hime, *Wagnerism: A Protest* (London, 1882); J. F. Rowbotham, "The Wagner Bubble," *Nineteenth Century,* 24 (1888), 501–12; H. Badger, "Wagner and His Work," *Music* (Chicago), 3 (1893), 651–65; Daniel Gregory Mason, *Music in My Time* (New York, 1938); R. W. S. Mendl, "Confessions of an Anti-Wagnerian," *From a Music-Lover's Armchair* (London, 1926), pp. 120–27.

28. *The Meister,* 1 (1888), 3.
29. Mussulman, *Music in the Cultured Generation,* p. 147.
30. Benedict, *Divine Spark,* p. 8.
31. Thomas Beecham, *A Mingled Chime* (1943; repr., Westport, Conn., 1976), p. 54.
32. David Irvine, *Metaphysical Rudiments of Liberalism* (London, 1911), p. xiii. Irvine is mentioned in *Cosima Wagner's Diaries, 1869–1883,* 2 vols. (New York, 1978–1980), 2:560, 616, 1100, as David "Irwine," a monied Scot who made contributions to the Society of Patrons.
33. Irvine, *Metaphysical Rudiments of Liberalism,* p. xxiv.
34. Ibid., p. 254.
35. David Irvine, *"Parsifal" and Wagner's Christianity* (London, 1899), p. 351.
36. David Irvine, *Philosophy and Christianity* (London, 1905), p. 6.
37. See Sessa, *Richard Wagner and the English,* p. 59, and J. L. Wisenthal, "The Underside of Underschaft: A Wagnerian Motif in *Major Barbara*," *Shaw Review,* 15 (1972), 56–64.
38. Martin Meisel, *Shaw and Nineteenth Century Theatre* (Princeton, 1963), p. 61.
39. Bernard Shaw, *The Perfect Wagnerite: A Commentary on the "Niblung's Ring"* (New York, 1967), p. xvii.
40. According to Shaw, "the Fabians were inveterate Philistines," and the society would not publish Wagner's *Art and Revolution.* G. B. Shaw, "Memoranda," in Edward R. Pease, *The History of the Fabian Society* (London, 1963), app. 1, pp. 278–79.
41. Shaw, *Perfect Wagnerite,* p. 9.
42. See L. J. Rather, *The Dream of Self-destruction: Wagner's "Ring" and the Modern World* (Baton Rouge, 1979), chap. 4, esp. pp. 159–61, for a discussion of this point.
43. Michael Hurd, *The Immortal Hour* (London, 1962), p. 28.
44. Ibid., p. 25.
45. Robert D. Faner, *Walt Whitman and Opera* (Carbondale, Ill., 1972), p. 116.
46. Rutland Boughton and Reginald Buckley, *Music Drama of the Future* (London, 1911), pp. 25–26.
47. Ibid., p. 45.
48. In 1910 yet another London Wagner society was founded. One of its objectives (never fulfilled) was to persuade Cosima to allow *Parsifal* to be performed in a London theater devoted exclusively to Wagner. See Louis N. Perker, ed., *Wagner Association, Report of the Second Annual Meeting and*

Address of the President (London, 1912). Parker was the association's president.

49. Boughton and Buckley, *Music Drama of the Future,* p. 39.
50. Rutland Boughton, *The Death and Resurrection of the Music Festival* (London, 1913), p. 2.
51. Ibid., p. 24.
52. Boughton and Buckley, *Music Drama of the Future,* pp. 31–32.
53. Bernard Shaw, *Collected Letters,* vol. 2, Dan Laurence, ed. (New York, 1972), p. 788.
54. Hurd, *Immortal Hour,* p. 161.
55. Ibid., p. 127.
56. Ibid., p. 92.
57. Arthur Hobson Quinn, *A History of American Drama,* 2 vols. (New York, 1927), 2:43.
58. Percy MacKaye, *The Playhouse and the Play* (1909; repr. Westport, Conn., 1968), p. 97.
59. Ibid., p. 112.
60. Hugh Mortimer Cecil [Ernest Newman], *Pseudo-Philosophy at the End of the Nineteenth Century* (London, 1897), p. ?.
61. See Ernest Newman, *A Music Critic's Holiday* (New York, 1925).
62. Ernest Newman, "Music and Race," in *Studies in Music,* Robin Grey, ed. (New York, 1901), p. 307.
63. Ernest Newman, *Wagner as Man and Artist* (New York, 1960), p. 377.
64. Ibid.
65. Ernest Newman, *Testament of Music,* Herbert Van Thal, ed. (New York, 1963), p. 274.
66. Ernest Newman, *Wagner as Man and Artist,* p. 377.
67. Lucy Beckett, "Wagner and His Critics," in *The Wagner Companion,* Peter Burbidge and Richard Sutton, eds. (New York, 1979), p. 379.
68. Vera Newman, *Ernest Newman: A Memoir* (New York, 1964), pp. 7, 268–69.
69. Ernest Newman, *Wagner as Man and Artist,* p. 379.
70. William Blissett, "Ernest Newman and English Wagnerism," *Music and Letters,* 40 (1959), 322.
71. Peter Taylor Forsyth, *Religion in Recent Art* (London, 1911), p. 236.
72. Boughton, Forsyth, and Gladden each picked out a pantheon of five or six great artistic figures; only Wagner was common to all three.
73. Washington Gladden, *Witnesses of the Light* (Boston, 1903), p. 222.
74. Ibid., p. 227.
75. Freda Winworth, *The Epic of Sounds* (Philadelphia, 1897), pp. xviii–xxx.
76. Oliver Hückel, *Richard Wagner, the Man and His Work* (New York, 1914), p. 102.
77. Forsyth, *Religion in Recent Art,* p. 240.
78. Warner, *A Roundabout Journey,* p. 354.
79. Sabine Baring-Gould, *Wagner's "Parsifal" at Bayreuth* (London, 1882), p. 26.
80. Aubrey Harrison Starke, *Sidney Lanier* (New York, 1964), pp. 287–88.

81. Richard Heber Newton, *"Parsifal"*: *An Ethical and Spiritual Interpretation* (Oscawanna-on-Hudson, New York, 1905), prefatory note.
82. Albert Ross Parsons, *"Parsifal"*: *The Finding of Christ through Art* (New York, 1893).
83. A. Gifford, *"Parsifal,"* *Pacific Monthly* (April 1904), pp. 258–63.
84. James Webb, *The Occult Establishment* (LaSalle, Ill., 1976), p. 44.
85. William Ashton Ellis, "La théosophie dans les ouvrages de Richard Wagner," *La société nouvelle*, 5 (1888), 258.
86. Ibid., p. 444.
87. Cyril Scott, *Music: Its Secret Influence throughout the Ages* (Philadelphia, n.d.), p. 108.
88. Ibid., p. 107.
89. Corinne Heline, *Esoteric Music: Based on the Musical Seership of Richard Wagner*, 2d ed. rev. (Los Angeles, 1953), p. 11.
90. Ibid., p. 16.
91. Franz Winkler, *For Freedom Destined* (Garden City, N.Y., 1974), pp. 96, 2, 21.
92. Ibid., pp. 98–99.
93. Thomas Mann, *Freud, Goethe, Wagner* (New York, 1937), p. 118.
94. Quoted in Bryan Magee, *Aspects of Wagner* (New York, 1969), p. 60.
95. John Runciman, *Old Scores and New Readings* (London, 1899), p. 181.
96. William Wallace, *Richard Wagner as He Lived* (New York, 1925), p. 263.
97. Hugh Reginald Haweis, *My Musical Memories* (New·York, 1884), p. 182.
98. See Magee, *Aspects of Wagner*, p. 71.
99. Elliott Zuckerman, *The First Hundred Years of Wagner's "Tristan"* (New York, 1964), p. 30.
100. Donald Branam, Chico State University, Calif., untitled manuscript. See also Jerome R. Sehulster, who discusses the theatrical reforms of Wagner as the means by which Wagner induced altered states of consciousness in his audiences, in Sehulster, "The Role of Altered States of Consciousness in the Life, Theater, and Theories of Richard Wagner," *Journal of Altered States of Consciousness*, 5 (1979–1980), 235–58.
101. Maurice Baring, *C*, 2 vols. (Garden City, N.Y., 1924), 1:141.
102. William Butler Yeats, *Ideas of Good and Evil* (London, 1903), p. 294.
103. James Gibbons Huneker, *Mezzotints in Modern Music* (New York, 1905), p. 294.
104. See Sessa, *Richard Wagner and the English*, pp. 98–106.
105. Rutland Boughton, *The Reality of Music* (New York, 1905), pp. 180, 186, 191.
106. Forsyth, *Religion in Recent Art*, p. 316.
107. For Moore's Wagnerism, see William Blissett, "George Moore and Literary Wagnerism," in *The Man of Wax: Critical Essays on George Moore*, Douglas A. Hughes, ed. (New York, 1971), pp. 185–215 and Sessa, *Richard Wagner and the English*, pp. 107–112.
108. John DiGaetani, *Richard Wagner and the Modern British Novel* (London, 1978). Stoddard Martin's *Wagner to "The Wasteland": A Study of the Relationship of Wagner to English Literature* (Totowa, N.J., 1982) appeared too late to be consulted for this essay.

109. Herbert Knust, *Wagner, the King, and "The Wasteland"* (University Park, Pa., 1967), pp. 62–73.

110. The bleak life of Cather's heroine is reminiscent of the experience of the heroine in Agnes Smedley's autobiographical novel *Daughter of Earth* (Old Westbury, N.Y., 1973), p. 198, in which there is also an allusion to Wagner.

111. Mary Watkins Cushing, *The Rainbow Bridge* (1954; repr. N.Y., 1977), pp. 242–25.

112. Ellis, "Richard Wagner contra Militarism," *Musical Times*, 56 (1915), 397.

113. Beecham, *A Mingled Chime*, p. 270.

114. Steigman, *The Pertinent Wagnerite* (New York, 1921), p. 11.

115. Isadora Duncan, *The Art of the Dance*, Sheldon Cheny, ed. (New York, 1928), p. 105.

116. Richard Wagner Society, *Richard Wagner Quarterly*, 1 (1937), 2.

117. Unity's sister Diana married Sir Oswald Moseley, leader of the British Fascist Union. In 1956, Moseley published *Wagner and Shaw: A Synthesis*, in which he argued that Parsifal was Siegfried transcended. See also Robert Skidelsky, *Oswald Moseley* (New York, 1975), p. 478.

118. Lord Redesdale, *Memories*, 2 vols. (New York, n.d.), 2:242.

119. Friedelind Wagner and Page Cooper, *Heritage of Fire* (New York, 1945), p. xii. See also E. M. Forster, *Two Cheers for Democracy* (New York, 1938), pp. 70–71, in which he views the *Ring*, as did Friedelind, as a parable of Hitler's doom.

120. Vera Newman, *Ernest Newman*, p. 194.

121. Ibid., p. 218.

122. R. W. S. Mendl, "Music and Politics," *Musical Opinion*, 68 (1945), 262.

123. Mary Day Lanier, ed., *Poems of Sidney Lanier* (Athens, Ga., 1981), p. 96.

Conclusion

1. See Twain's witty report from Bayreuth, "At the Shrine of St. Wagner," dated Aug. 2, 1891, and reprinted in Robert Hartford, *Bayreuth: The Early Years* (Cambridge, England, 1980), pp. 149–55.

2. Geoffrey Field, *Evangelist of Race: The Germanic Vision of Houston Stewart Chamberlain* (New York, 1981), p. 67.

3. J. F. Rowbotham, "The Wagner Bubble," *Nineteenth Century*, 24 (Oct. 1888), 501–12.

4. Quoted in Lucy Beckett, "Wagner and His Critics," in Peter Burbidge and Richard Sutton, eds., *The Wagner Companion* (New York, 1979), p. 368.

5. The essay, on Willibald Alexis, appeared in the 1882 *Bayreuther Blätter*.

6. Erwin Koppen, *Dekadenter Wagnerismus* (Berlin, 1973), p. 83.

7. See especially Theodor Adorno, *Versuch über Wagner* (Frankfurt, 1952), and Hans Mayer, *Anmerkungen zu Richard Wagner* (Frankfurt, 1966).

8. Houston Stewart Chamberlain quoted in Field, *Evangelist of Race*, p. 65.

9. Ibid., pp. 64–70.

10. Beckett, "Wagner and His Critics," p. 369.

11. Jacques Barzun, *Darwin, Marx, Wagner: Critique of a Heritage*, 2d ed. (New York, 1958), p. 289.

12. Hartford, *Bayreuth: The Early Years*, p. 188.

13. On Lenin's use of Marx see George Lichtheim, *Marxism: An Historical and Critical Study*.

14. Martin Wiener, *English Culture and the Decline of the Industrial Spirit, 1850–1980* (Cambridge, England, 1981).

15. W. A. Ellis, "Richard Wagner as Poet, Musician and Mystic," (a paper read at the Society for the Encouragement of the Fine Arts, Feb. 3, 1887), p. 26. (Available in the British Museum.)

16. G. B. Shaw, *London Music in 1888–1890 as Heard by Corno di Bassetto* (London, 1937), p. 50.

17. Robert Gutman, *Richard Wagner* (Harmondsworth, England, 1971), p. 568.

18. Henry May, *The End of American Innocence* (Chicago, 1964).

19. Thomas Mann, *Wagner und unsere Zeit* (Berlin, 1963), p. 60.

20. Quoted in Gordon Craig, *The Germans* (New York, 1982), p. 198.

21. Ibid.

22. Romain Rolland, *Musicians of Today*, Mary Blaiklock, tr. (London, 1915), p. 67.

23. George Moore, *Ave* (London, 1911), p. 209.

24. Rolland, *Musicians of Today*, pp. 253–54.

25. Beckett, "Wagner and His Critics," p. 369.

26. Roger Shattuck, *The Banquet Years* (New York, 1968).

27. Ibid., p. 115.

28. John DiGaetani, *Richard Wagner and the Modern British Novel* (Cranbury, N.J., 1978), p. 110.

29. Quentin Bell, *Virginia Woolf*, 2 vols. (London, 1972), 1:149.

30. Leonard Woolf, *Beginning Again* (New York, 1964), p. 50.

31. Ibid., p. 49.

32. The piece is reprinted in Hartford, *Bayreuth: The Early Years*, pp. 247–50.

33. Ibid., p. 250. As John DiGaetani shows in his study on Wagner and the modern British novel, however, Woolf did try to adapt Wagnerian themes to her fiction. He traces the Wagnerian influences in *The Voyage Out, Jacob's Room, The Waves*, and *The Years*. See DiGaetani, *Richard Wagner and the Modern British Novel*, pp. 109–29.

34. Quoted in Bell, *Virginia Woolf*, 1:150.

35. Ibid., 1:151.

36. For a good discussion of Wagnerian themes in English and American literature of the early twentieth century, see Anna Jacobsen, *Nachklänge Richard Wagners im Roman* (Heidelberg, 1932), pp. 110–26.

37. Samuel Hynes, *The Edwardian Turn of Mind* (Princeton, 1968), p. 335.

38. Henry Wickham Steed, *Through Thirty Years, 1892–1922*, 2 vols. (London, 1924), 1:19.

39. Rolland, *Musicians of Today*, p. 217.

40. Walther Rathenau, *Der Kaiser: Eine Betrachtung* (Berlin, 1919).

41. Wagner was much favored by the so-called "Liebenberg Circle," the members of which were very close to Kaiser Wilhelm II. Closest of all was Philipp Prince zu Eulenburg-Hertefeld, whose exposure as a homosexual by

the journalist Maximillian Harden was one of the great scandals of the Kaiser's reign. As we noted above, at least one commentator in this period, Oskar Panizza, explicitly linked Wagnerism and homosexuality, and there can be no doubt that Wagner's cult of idealized *Männerliebe* in *Parsifal* had particular appeal to the Liebenberg group. On the Liebenberg Circle, see Isabel Hull, *The Entourage of Kaiser Wilhelm II, 1888–1918* (Cambridge, England, 1982), pp. 45–75.

42. Heinrich Mann, *Der Untertan* (Berlin, n.d.), p. 307.

43. Lion Feuchtwanger, *Erfolg*, 2 vols. (Berlin, 1930), 2:132.

44. Walter Benjamin, *Reflections* (New York, 1978), p. 158.

45. Theodore Adorno, *Versuch über Wagner* (Berlin, 1952).

46. Ibid., pp. 107, 182–98, 187.

47. See Keith Dickson, *Towards Utopia: A Study of Brecht* (Oxford, 1978), p. 163.

48. L. Woolf, *Beginning Again*, p. 50.

49. Peter Viereck, "Hitler and Richard Wagner," in *Common Sense*, 8 (1939), 3.

50. For a discussion of Mann's evolving interpretation of Wagner, see Beckett, "Wagner and His Critics," pp. 383–88.

51. Thomas Mann, "To the Editor of *Common Sense*" (Jan. 1940), reprinted in *Wagner und unsere Zeit*, pp. 153–60, 159.

52. Rohan d'O. Butler, *The Roots of National Socialism* (London, 1941).

53. Edmond Vermeil, *Germany's Three Reichs* (London, 1945), p. 387.

54. William Shirer, *The Rise and Fall of the Third Reich* (New York, 1960), p. 102.

55. The exhibition was held in 1976 in the Villa Lehnbach in Munich.

56. Syberberg's film was reviewed by Susan Sontag in the *New York Review of Books* (Feb. 21, 1980), 36–43.

57. For Hitler's thoughts on the meaning of Wagner's legacy and its importance to Germany, see Hermann Rauschning, *Hitler Speaks* (London, 1939), pp. 226–30; Adolf Hitler, *Hitler's Table Talk, 1941–1944*, Norman Cameron and R. H. Stevens, trs. (London, 1953), passim.

58. Wagner's music has only very recently been performable in the Soviet Union, and when Zubin Mehta attempted in 1981 to end the forty-three-year-old boycott against Wagner's music by the Israel Philharmonic Orchestra, violence broke out in Tel Aviv, forcing an end to the concert.

59. Quoted in Gutman, *Richard Wagner*, p. 16.

Index

Library of Congress Cataloging in Publication Data
Main entry under title:
Wagnerism in European culture and politics.
Bibliography: p.
Includes index.
1. Wagner, Richard, 1813–1883—Influence.
2. Music and society. I. Large, David Clay.
II. Weber, William, 1940– . III. Sessa, Anne
Dzamba.
ML410.W19W18 1984   782.1'092'4   83-45936
ISBN 0-8014-9283-1